The Portuguese Expedition to Abyssinia in 1541-1543 As Narrated by Castanhoso: With Some Contemporary Letters, the Short Account of Bermudez, and Certain Extracts from Corr##a

Miguel De Castanhoso

Nabu Public Domain Reprints:

You are holding a reproduction of an original work published before 1923 that is in the public domain in the United States of America, and possibly other countries. You may freely copy and distribute this work as no entity (individual or corporate) has a copyright on the body of the work. This book may contain prior copyright references, and library stamps (as most of these works were scanned from library copies). These have been scanned and retained as part of the historical artifact.

This book may have occasional imperfections such as missing or blurred pages, poor pictures, errant marks, etc. that were either part of the original artifact, or were introduced by the scanning process. We believe this work is culturally important, and despite the imperfections, have elected to bring it back into print as part of our continuing commitment to the preservation of printed works worldwide. We appreciate your understanding of the imperfections in the preservation process, and hope you enjoy this valuable book.

WORKS ISSUED BY

The Hakluyt Society.

---o---

THE PORTUGUESE EXPEDITION

TO

ABYSSINIA.

SECOND SERIES.
No. X.

AFFORD LIBY

THE "CASINHA" AT THE CHURCH OF ST. ROMANOS (p. 26.)

THE
PORTUGUESE EXPEDITION
TO
ABYSSINIA
IN 1541-1543,

AS NARRATED BY CASTANHOSO,

WITH SOME

CONTEMPORARY LETTERS, THE SHORT ACCOUNT OF BERMUDEZ, AND CERTAIN EXTRACTS FROM CORREA.

Translated and Edited
BY
R. S. WHITEWAY,
BENGAL CIVIL SERVICE (RETIRED).

ÆTHIOPIA was saved by four hundred and fifty Portuguese, who displayed in the field the native valour of Europeans, and the artificial powers of the musket and cannon.—GIBBON, chap. 47.

LONDON:
PRINTED FOR THE HAKLUYT SOCIETY.

M.DCCCCII.

137163

LONDON:
PRINTED AT THE BEDFORD PRESS, 20 AND 21, BEDFORDBURY, W.C.

COUNCIL

OF

THE HAKLUYT SOCIETY.

Sir Clements Markham, K.C.B., F.R.S., *Pres. R.G.S.*, *President*.
The Right Hon. The Lord Stanley of Alderley, *Vice-President*.
Rear-Admiral Sir William Wharton, K.C.B., F.R.S., *Vice-President*.
Charles Raymond Beazley, M.A.
Commr. B. M. Chambers, R.N.
Colonel George Earl Church.
Sir William Martin Conway.
William Foster, B.A.
F. H. H. Guillemard, M.A., M.D.
Edward Heawood, M.A.
John Scott Keltie, LL.D.
Frederick William Lucas.
Alfred Percival Maudslay.
Mowbray Morris.
Edward John Payne, M.A.
Ernest George Ravenstein.
Howard Saunders.
Henry William Trinder.
Charles Welch, F.S.A.
Richard Stephen Whiteway.

Basil H. Soulsby, B.A., *Honorary Secretary*.

CONTENTS.

	PAGE
PREFACE	xvii
INTRODUCTION	xxi
BIBLIOGRAPHY	civ

CASTANHOSO.

Introduction 3

CHAPTER I.
Of how Dom Christovão began his march, and of his reception in the country of the Barnaguais . . . 5

CHAPTER II.
Of the counsel taken by Dom Christovão with the Barnaguais and the people of the country, as to what should be done . 8

CHAPTER III.
Of how Dom Christovão mustered his people, and divided them as seemed best to him 11

CHAPTER IV.
Of how Dom Christovão sent for the Queen, and of her reception of the Portuguese who went to fetch her . . 12

CHAPTER V.
Of how the Queen arrived at Dom Christovão's camp, and of her reception there 14

CHAPTER VI.
Of how Dom Christovão visited the Queen, and of how the winter was spent till the beginning of marching . . 20

CHAPTER VII.
Of how Dom Christovão began to march, and of the order of his march 23

CONTENTS.

CHAPTER VIII.
Of how Dom Christovão examined the top of this mountain, and of what he found there 26

CHAPTER IX.
Of how Dom Christovão on his march found a very strong hill, and made arrangements to attack it . . . 30

CHAPTER X.
Of how Dom Christovão pitched his camp on the skirts of the hill, and of how he took order to attack it . . 33

CHAPTER XI.
Of how the Portuguese attacked this hill and captured it, with the death of some 34

CHAPTER XII.
Of how Dom Christovão, in nearing the plains of Jarte, met an ambassador from the Preste, and of the warning received that the King of Zeila was near . . . 39

CHAPTER XIII.
Of the Embassy the King of Zeila sent to Dom Christovão . 42

CHAPTER XIV.
Of how Dom Christovão fought the first battle with the King of Zeila, in which the Moor was defeated, and wounded by a matchlock bullet 45

CHAPTER XV.
Of the second battle which Dom Christovão fought with the King of Zeila, in which the King was defeated . . 49

CHAPTER XVI.
Of how, on the arrival of the Barnaguais and of the Portuguese, Dom Christovão followed in pursuit of the King of Zeila . 52

CHAPTER XVII.
Of what Dom Christovão did that winter, and of how he captured a very strong hill which had belonged to a Jew captain 56

CONTENTS.

CHAPTER XVIII.
Of how there was a battle between Dom Christovão and the King of Zeila, in which Dom Christovão was defeated . 60

CHAPTER XIX.
Of how the Moors, following Dom Christovão, found him, and seized him, and of how he died . . . 65

CHAPTER XX.
Of how some one hundred and twenty Portuguese collected with the Queen, and of how the Preste arrived at the hill of the Jews, where the Queen, his mother, and the Portuguese were awaiting him 70

CHAPTER XXI.
Of the reception the Portuguese gave the Preste, and of how after the meeting we determined to all go and revenge the death of Dom Christovão 74

CHAPTER XXII.
Of how the Preste began to march with the Portuguese, and found the King of Zeila encamped on the lake of the Nile; and of the method the King of Zeila adopted to kill the captain of the Preste's camp 75

CHAPTER XXIII.
Of how the Preste and the King of Zeila fought a battle, in which the Moors were defeated and the King slain . 79

CHAPTER XXIV.
Of how the father of the Barnaguais who had rebelled, returned to the Preste, and brought with him the Prince of Zeila . 84

CHAPTER XXV.
Of the lake whence the Nile flows, on the shores of which the Preste passed Easter, and of the customs of the Abyssinians in Holy Week 87

CHAPTER XXVI.
Of the great mourning made, and of the obsequies celebrated by the Preste for the soul of Dom Christovão and for the Portuguese who died in the battle 91

CHAPTER XXVII.

Of how the Preste on his march reached the plains of Jartafaa, and of what he found there; and of how certain Portuguese, with the permission of the Preste, went to Massowa to seek shipping for India 94

CHAPTER XXVIII.

Of how the Portuguese took leave of the Preste for Massowa . 101

LETTERS OF AND TO THE KING OF ABYSSINIA.

I.
Letter from Lebna Dengel, King of Abyssinia, to D. João Bermudez, undated, written in 1540 . . . 107

II.
Letter from Galâwdêwos to the King of Portugal, undated, on the services of Miguel de Castanhoso; probably written late in 1543, possibly early in 1544 109

III.
Letter from D. João III, King of Portugal, to the King of Abyssinia, dated March 13th, 1546, on the pretensions of Bermudez. With this are also given the Letter of the King of Portugal to D. João de Castro, of March 13th, 1546, and of the King of Portugal to the Portuguese in Abyssinia, dated March 15th, 1546 110

IV.
Letter from Galâwdêwos to the King of Portugal, dated Christmas 1550, relating the events of D. Christovão's Expedition 115

V.
Letter from Galâwdêwos to the Governor of India, dated Christmas 1551, relating the events of D. Christovão's Expedition 119

BERMUDEZ.

LETTER OF D. JOÃO BERMUDEZ TO THE KING OUR LORD . 127

CHAPTER I.
Of how D. João Bermudez was elected Patriarch of the Preste, and sent to Rome to proffer obedience to the Holy Father 129

CHAPTER II.
Of how the Patriarch left Rome and came to Portugal, where he was well received by the King, D. João III . . 130

CHAPTER III.
Of how the King sped the Patriarch quickly, and ordered his return 132

CHAPTER IV.
Of how the Patriarch started with those the King gave him, and arrived in India 133

CHAPTER V.
Of how the Viceroy sent to the Preste to learn if the Embassy of the Patriarch were genuine 134

CHAPTER VI.
Of how the Governor, D. Garcia, died, and D. Estevão succeeded, who took the Patriarch to the Red Sea; and of the death of the Emperor of the Preste, Onadinguel . . 136

CHAPTER VII.
Of how D. Estevão left for Suez; and of how there arrived messages from the Preste John, desiring him to send the Patriarch 138

CHAPTER VIII.
Of how sixty men fled from the Fleet, who were killed up the country, and of what else happened consequent on their death 139

CHAPTER IX.
Of how the death of the sixty men was avenged, and of how they slew a Captain of the King of Zeila . . . 142

CHAPTER X.

Of the arrival of the Governor, D. Estevão, and of how he selected his brother, D. Christovão, as Captain for the Preste 144

CHAPTER XI.

Of how the two armies separated, one for India and the other for the Preste John; and of the murmurs that arose against the Patriarch 146

CHAPTER XII.

Of how the Queen of the Preste came to Debarua to visit the Patriarch and D. Christovão, and of the reception they gave her, and of what else passed there 148

CHAPTER XIII.

Of how the army of the Christians started from Debarua to seek the King of Zeila 149

CHAPTER XIV.

Of how the war between the Christians and the Moors began with the victory of the Christians 150

CHAPTER XV.

Of how an Abyssinian Captain, who had joined the Moors, came over to the Christians 153

CHAPTER XVI.

Of how the King of Zeila sent to tell D. Christovão that he desired to see him again; and of the second battle, in which he was again defeated 155

CHAPTER XVII.

Of how the Christians went in pursuit of the Moors, and captured their Camp 159

CHAPTER XVIII.

Of how the King of Zeila recruited his army, and of what the Christians did meanwhile 161

CHAPTER XIX.

Of how the King of Zeila came on with his reinforced army, and of how we prepared to give battle 162

CHAPTER XX.

Of the disastrous battle in which the Christians were defeated 165

CHAPTER XXI.
Of how D. Christovão hid in a thicket . . . 168

CHAPTER XXII.
Of how the Patriarch selected another Captain for the Portuguese 170

CHAPTER XXIII.
In which is related the confinement and death of D. Christovão 171

CHAPTER XXIV.
Of how the King of Zeila went to the kingdom of Dembia, and the Preste's vassals submitted to the Queen, and of how King Gradeus came to the Camp . . . 175

CHAPTER XXV.
Of a speech the Patriarch made to the Portuguese . . 178

CHAPTER XXVI.
Of the speech the Patriarch made to the King Gradeus, asking him to obey the Pope as his father did, and of the King's reply 180

CHAPTER XXVII.
Of how the Patriarch told the Portuguese what passed with King Gradeus 181

CHAPTER XXVIII.
Of how the King Gradeus sent a present to the Portuguese, who would not accept it 182

CHAPTER XXIX.
Of the counsel the King Gradeus followed, and of how he submitted to the Pope 183

CHAPTER XXX.
Of the death of the captain Affonso Caldeira, and of how Ayres Diz was made captain 184

CHAPTER XXXI.
Of how the Patriarch with the Portuguese and some Abyssinians separated from the King, and of how afterwards he sent the Portuguese to the King, and he and the Abyssinians went to where the Goranha was; and of how he again sent for Ayres Diz 185

CHAPTER XXXII.
Of how the Christians climbed the hill of St. Paul . . 188

CHAPTER XXXIII.
Of how the Christians on the hill stood on their guard, of the death of the Captain General of the Abyssinians, and of the passion of the King Gradeus on his behalf, and of other things that happened at that time . . . 189

CHAPTER XXXIV.
Of the death of the King of Zeila, and of the defeat of the Moors, and of certain other things which followed . 191

CHAPTER XXXV.
Of a quarrel among the Portuguese as to who should be captain 194

CHAPTER XXXVI.
Of how the Queen arrived at the camp, and of her reception there 197

CHAPTER XXXVII.
Of how King Gradeus recovered the monastery of Syão, with the territory belonging to it 198

CHAPTER XXXVIII.
Of how the King of Adem made war on King Gradeus, and was killed, and his camp despoiled . . . 199

CHAPTER XXXIX.
Of how King Gradeus and the Captain Ayres Diz began to show their malice, and the treason they meditated . . 203

CHAPTER XL.
Of how the King and the Portuguese sent each other certain messages, until they resolved to have recourse to arms , . 208

CHAPTER XLI.
Of the battles between the Abyssinians and the Portuguese, and of the victory of the Portuguese . . . 211

CHAPTER XLII.
Of how the King made peace with the Portuguese, promising to do what was right, with the intention of banishing them as he did 212

CHAPTER XLIII.

Of how some of the chief Portuguese were banished to certain distant countries 215

CHAPTER XLIV.

Of how the Patriarch was taken to the country of the Gafates, and of how he returned thence . . . 217

CHAPTER XLV.

Of what the King did on the arrival of the Patriarch; of how he received him, and of how he left there . . . 220

CHAPTER XLVI.

Of how the arrival of the Patriarch from Alexandria, called Abuna Joseph, was discovered; and of how it was arranged that he should be Patriarch of the Abyssinians and D. João Bermudez of the Portuguese 221

CHAPTER XLVII.

Of how King Gradeus settled the Patriarch and the Portuguese in the province of Doaro, and of how Calide, Captain of the said province, attacked them to kill them, and was himself slain by them 225

CHAPTER XLVIII.

Of how the Gallas attacked the Portuguese, and drove them from the country of Doaro, where they were . . 228

CHAPTER XLIX.

Of the kingdom of Oggy, and of Gorague its province . 231

CHAPTER L.

Of the kingdom of the Gafates 232

CHAPTER LI.

Of the kingdom of Damute, and of its provinces, and of the great riches there are in it, and of certain marvellous things . 234

CHAPTER LII.

Of the kingdoms of Gojame, and Dembia, and Amar, and of other lands adjoining these, and of the River Nile, in whose neighbourhood they all are 241

CHAPTER LIII.
Of how King Gradeus returned to Simen, and settled the Portuguese in Bethmariam 245

CHAPTER LIV.
Of how the Patriarch went to Debarua, and stayed there two years 247

CHAPTER LV.
Of what happened while the Patriarch was in Debarua, and of how Master Gonçallo came to him and went on to the King's Court 250

CHAPTER LVI.
Of how the Patriarch returned to India with Master Gonçallo . 251

CHAPTER LVII.
Of how the Patriarch embarked for Portugal, remained a year on St. Helena, and returned the year following . . 253

CHAPTER LVIII.
Of the conclusion of the work 254

CORREA 259

INDEX 283

ILLUSTRATIONS.

The "Casinha" at the Church of St. Romanos	*Frontispiece*
Bermudez' Monument	124
Map of Abyssinia	*In Pocket*

PREFACE.

TRANSLATORS without special local knowledge have ever laid themselves open to the scoffer. The eighteenth-century translator of certain French Travels in Egypt, who made his writer say that on a particular day he saw many camels, though none came near enough for a shot, wrote in good faith; for in a note he says that in the original the word is "chameau d'eau," but that he does not know if the water-camel be a particular species or not. His author digged a pit for him by translating the Arabic for a pelican, *Jimmel el bahr*, into "chameau d'eau," and, having no local knowledge, he fell in. The translator of the accounts here printed has had his predecessor's fate before his eyes; still, there is no work in English giving the original narratives of the Portuguese Expedition of 1541-43; and although finality can only be attained by the editor who studies these narratives on the spot, still it will be long before the political conditions of Abyssinia allow orderly work of this kind. Meanwhile, it will be some gain to set out the problems requiring solution, and to bring together the statements of the different authorities.

The main reliance must always be on the Portuguese author Castanhoso; but there are also the Ethiopian writers now accessible in French, German, Italian, and

Portuguese translations, and the Arabic chronicles now rendered into French. As yet English scholars have done little, and, although there is a wealth of manuscripts in this country, Bruce remains, as he has been for over a century, our sole original worker in this field. The contemporary narratives of the Portuguese Expedition into Abyssinia, commanded by D. Christovão da Gama, fourth son of D. Vasco da Gama, which have been brought together here, consist of the books of Castanhoso and Bermudez, some letters to and from the King of Abyssinia, and some extracts from the contemporary chronicler Correa. These have been as far as possible illustrated from the sources above mentioned, as well as from the works of travellers in the country.

The Portuguese Expedition was decisive in that Abyssinia has since remained Christian; it is seldom that results so momentous have been attained by means so disproportionate. To us it has this special interest, that the English campaign of 1867, with its twelve thousand men, started from a point only a few miles distant from Massowa, and joined the route of their predecessors near Senafé; if the Portuguese furthest point south was, as suggested here, the mountain of Amba Sel, it lies but a few miles from the mountain fortress of Magdala stormed by the English.

Conceding that there is interest in the mere coincidence of the lines of advance, there is certainly interest more intense in the disproportion of the means employed, and in the divergence of the aims cherished. In a spirit that had survived from the age of the Crusades, Portugal cast on shore and abandoned her expedition, led by a descendant of one of her most illustrious sons; their lives were nothing provided the desired result were attained. That result was partly religious and partly political. On the other hand, the English Expedition had no religious aim: Muhamedans and Hindus marched with Christians against a Christian ruler. The direct aim was the release of the English and other European prisoners, the indirect was to enforce respect for the English name. Little Portugal then flung aside as of no importance the lives of four hundred of her subjects; more populous England poured out vast treasure to save the liberty of half a dozen of hers. The distinction is one of national importance, and who shall say that England has lost by her jealousy for the honour of her flag?

The Editor has to thank many for their kind assistance, without which this book could never have been completed. In particular he would thank Sir Frederick Pollock, Sir Clements Markham, Mr. Donald Ferguson, Mr. E. Heawood, Mr. W. Bliss, Dr. E. A. Wallis Budge, of the British Museum, Mr. William Foster, and, above all, Mr. Basil H. Soulsby, who, in addition to assisting in the correction of the proofs, has added to his other onerous duties the labour of compiling the Index. To Captain A. S. Thomson, C.B., Elder Brother of the Trinity House, the volume is indebted for the excellent map of Abyssinia, which so greatly adds to any value it may possess.

INTRODUCTION.

INLAND from the western coast of the southern end of the Red Sea lies the knot of mountains and rivers called Abyssinia. These highlands, surrounded by hot and unhealthy tracts, which are inhabited by followers of alien creeds, are by their physical conformation and by their situation fitted to be the refuge of an isolated faith; they have, in fact, become the refuge of two faiths: the earlier is that of the Falashas, or Jews; the later, which has been superimposed on the former, is a primitive, and perhaps debased, form of Christianity. Up to comparatively recent times the Falashas had their own Kings and Queens, the former always called Gideon and the latter Judith; but although there have been sanguinary struggles in that interval, for nearly one thousand years Christianity has been the dominant religion, and the Jews have been branded as wizards and sorcerers. The Christians, however, both in their religious and social customs, bear signs of the influence of Judaism.

The usual derivation of Habash (whence our Abyssinia) is from a root signifying "mixed," the mixture referred to being that of the various Arabian tribes who, prior to the era of Muhamed, emigrated from the east to the west coast of the Red Sea. The Arab of this immigration has, in the course of centuries, become considerably modified by crossing with African races, both negro and other, and to some extent by crossing with European stocks, such as the Greeks and Portuguese: speaking generally, southern Abyssinia is more negroid than northern; the script indeed, runs from left to right, but the languages belong to the Semitic family. Although surrounded by hostile nations, both Muhamedan and pagan, and although the normal condition of the country itself has been civil war, and only at rare intervals has some strong ruler been able to impose respect on his neighbours, the Abyssinians have successfully withstood the advance of Muhamedanism. For some centuries, including the period to which this work refers, the headship of all Abyssinia continued in one family, and the chances of internecine strife were lessened by imprisoning the cadet members of the royal house in a mountain fortress, only giving the selected heir his liberty; but already by the time of Bruce the supremacy of the monarch had been successfully challenged by powerful ministers, and seventy years later the titular King had to earn his living by making parasols.[1] This royal race has now merged in the people, and with marriage customs so lax that there is hardly any family, as we understand it, and with no rule of succession to the kingship at all, the later history of the country is one continual record of civil wars, waged on no principle; wars in which too often thousands have been killed merely to determine which, of equally worthless adventurers, shall obtain the chief power. In times of anarchy every province has its contending

---

[1] Mansfield Parkyns, *Life in Abyssinia* (vol. ii, p. 107), John Murray, London, 1853. Gerhard Rohlfs, *Meine Mission nach Abessinien . . . im Winter*, 1880-81 (p. 258), F. A. Brockhaus, Leipzig, 1883, found descendants of the old family in Gondar in 1881.

claimants for the headship; and gradually from these, after a longer or shorter period of strife, the strongest emerges as the Negus Nagasti, or King of Kings.

That under conditions so unfavourable the Abyssinian people should have been able to maintain their independance, and repel their inveterate foe the Muhamedan, is due to the conformation of their country; not only is the whole of Abyssinia a natural fortress of mountains, intersected by deep and precipitous river valleys, but the mountains themselves are of a formation so peculiar that many of them become isolated forts. Each of these mountain forts is called an "amba." The top is usually flat, with a surface that is sometimes contracted in area, and sometimes extends to several square miles; there is usually an ample water supply, with space to grow the food of the garrison, and give pasture to their flocks and herds. The sides of these mountains are scarped and precipitous; to some access can only be obtained by a single difficult path, while to others there is not even that convenience, and a visitor must await the pleasure of the garrison, which lets down a basket to which he must commit himself, and in which he must be pulled up to the summit.[1]

The climatic conditions also are uncongenial to the low-country Muhamedan, who, if he can at times overrun the land of the Christians, cannot colonise it.[2] The Imam Ahmad, nicknamed Grañ, or the left-handed, came nearer to success between the years 1528 and 1543 than any of

---

[1] A good account of the conformation of these "ambas" in northern Abyssinia will be found in Gen. H. St. C. Wilkins, *Reconnoitring in Abyssinia*, Smith Elder and Co., London, 1870, p. 290. The scarps were, he noticed, composed of a light grey sandstone. Further south the rocks are volcanic.

[2] As to the unwillingness of the Somali to colonise Abyssinia, see Basset, *Histoire*, p. 146. In this Introduction I have used the word Somali as a convenient term for the Muhamedan tribes south and south-east of Abyssinia; it is not used in any tribal sense.

his predecessors or successors. For some five years his advance was gradual; but after that he had possession of practically all Abyssinia save a few hill forts; but the Somalis whom he led were incapable of occupying where they raided, and the only permanent result of his invasion was the incursion of the pagan Gallas who, commencing about 1537, took advantage of the general disorganisation to settle in the more level country and colonise it. Since then these Gallas have become Muhamedan, and Christian Abyssinia has been bisected for all time: Shoa lying isolated to the south, while the remaining provinces lie north of the intruding horde. The object of this volume is to bring together the records of the history of the gallant band of four hundred Portuguese under Dom Christovão da Gama, who, after their leader's death, slew the Imam Ahmad and drove the invading Somalis out of Abyssinia.

During many centuries, news of the existence of the Christian kingdom percolated but vaguely to Europe through the hostile belt that enveloped Abyssinia.[1] There appears to have been an embassy from Abyssinia to the Vatican in the reign of Zara Yakub (1434-68); this embassy was sent on account of a discussion in religious matters between an Abyssinian, Abba Giorgis, and a Frank (probably a Venetian).[2] Some Venetian painters certainly penetrated into Abyssinia soon after this time, as Alvarez met there one Branca Leone, who had reached the country as early as 1485, and whom he describes as "a

---

[1] "Encompassed on all sides by the enemies of their religion, the Æthiopians slept near a thousand years, forgetful of the world by whom they were forgotten" (Gibbon, chap. xlvii).

[2] Basset (*Études*, p. 102). Bruce (vol. iii. p. 97), says the Pope granted the Abyssinians at this time a convent in Rome, St. Stefano in Rotondis. The theological work composed by Giorgis on this occasion still exists. Bruce (vol. iii, p. 119) throws some doubt on his own statement on a previous page.

great gentleman although a painter."[1] None of these adventurers returned, as far as is known, to Europe; and, when the Portuguese discoveries down the West Coast of Africa were revolutionising geography, the information at the command, even of the learned, did not go beyond the fact that, somewhere in the Continent there was a potentate who professed the Christian faith. The imagination of Europe had been pleased by a fable, widely spread in the twelfth and thirteenth centuries, of a great Christian Emperor, in either Eastern Africa or Central Asia, the Preste John. This tale, which in Asia finally centred round a petty Mongol chief, flattered the hope that there was somewhere a great power to whom Europe could look for aid against the all-conquering Moslem. Gradually the central Asian Emperor faded away; but the fall of Constantinople, and the advance of new armies of Turks, only emphasised the need for the old hope; and around this unknown African Christian king, whose dominions lay somewhere on the flank of the Muhamedan advance, all the nebulous longings connoted by the name of Preste John collected.[2]

Simultaneously with their efforts to round the Southern Horn of Africa, the Portuguese sent expeditions overland, to discover trade routes, and to identify this Christian king. Covilham reached Abyssinia indeed, but he never returned; and when Albuquerque took up the problem he

---

[1] Alvarez, p. 210. Branca Leone was vigorously attacked by the Abyssinians for painting Jesus Christ carried on His mother's left arm, the left being the depreciated side in the East.

[2] In an English translation of the spurious travels of G. Baratti, published in 1670, this name appears as Precious John! Bruce (vol. iv, p. 457) says the common call of suppliants for justice in Abyssinia was "*Reie o jan hoi*" (which he translates, "Do me justice, oh my king"), which, said quickly, sounded like "Prete janni." The call was continual, for, failing suppliants, vagabonds were hired, lest the King should feel lonely. This explanation is fanciful, and Ludolf (*Commentary*, p. 263) gives the words differently, and adds the musical notation of the cry.

had nothing better than rumours to guide him. He speaks in his letters of two envoys whom he landed at Cape Guardafui, disguised as Muhamedan merchants, robbed by the Portuguese; one was actually a Muhamedan, and the other was circumcised in Melindi to keep up his assumed character.[1] Of the fate of these particular envoys little is known, but Matheus, the ambassador from Abyssinia, who reached India in 1512, knew their names.[2] Matheus was the first actual link between the Portuguese and Abyssinia—the knowledge Albuquerque acquired from him was supplemented by that given by Abyssinian captives in the hands of the Muhamedans, whom the Portuguese recaptured in the Red Sea and Zeila, and whom Albuquerque sent to Portugal.[3] The information gathered from all these sources was, however, even as late as 1520, very inconclusive, as one of the points the embassy under Dom Rodrigo de Lima had to solve was, whether the territory of the Preste John stretched as far south as the Cape of Good Hope.[4]

Matheus was himself an Armenian: in fact, no envoy could then hope to leave Abyssinia who could not assume the disguise of a Muhamedan. The Abyssinians, though often ready to temporarily change their faith in time of stress, have always shown themselves very averse to undertake missions outside their own country; possibly this may

---

[1] The Portuguese appears to have been called João Gomez (see Albuquerque, *Cartas*, p. 316), but on p. 427 there is the summary of a letter of Albuquerque of November 12th, 1510, in which he seems to refer to these men as landed, not by himself but by Tristão da Cunha; but both these leaders were in the same fleet. Alvarez mentions the envoys (p. 177), but they were dead when he reached Abyssinia.

[2] For the arrival of Matheus, see *Cartas* (p. 381), letter of December 6th, 1512. For Albuquerque's reply to the doubts thrown on the authenticity of this mission, see letter of October 25th, 1514, p. 314 to 318. This letter shows the extent of his knowledge of the country; there is a further account on p. 400.

[3] See letter of December 1st, 1513 (*Cartas*, p. 173).

[4] See instructions of Diogo Lopes de Sequeira to the ambassador of April 25th, 1520 (*Alguns Documentos*, p. 444).

be due to that indolence and self-satisfaction which show themselves in many other ways. Albuquerque's opponents used the fact that Matheus was not an Abyssinian to throw doubt on the authenticity of his mission, and the wretched man was subjected to indignities of every kind. Of his treatment after his return from Portugal, where he had been accepted as a genuine envoy, we have a very detailed account in a letter from Father Alvarez to the King, of January 9th, 1518, written with all the homely wit that makes his work on Abyssinia such pleasant reading.[1] This letter certainly brings before us the troubles of the unfortunate ambassador in a way no other existing document does; the man had probably but few qualifications for diplomacy. It may be also noted that in the instructions to Dom Rodrigo de Lima, quoted above, a special paragraph is devoted to the reply to be made if there were complaints of how the envoy had been treated. His death, however, soon after the embassy landed on Abyssinian soil, obviated any difficulty on this score.

Although it is not necessary to enter here in any detail into the history of the mission of Dom Rodrigo de Lima, all mention of it cannot be avoided.[2] Matheus had been sent to Europe by Queen Helena (Elēni), the widow, or rather one of the widows, of King Baeda Māryām (1468-78). This lady was the daughter of Muhamed, the Musalman Governor of Doaro, and although childless, still, partly owing to her private wealth, and partly to her natural ability, she became regent of the kingdom when

---

[1] *Alguns Documentos*, p. 413. Alvarez says in one place in this letter that the ambassador became "quiet as a lamb, instead of the raging lion that he usually was." He was, therefore, no diplomat.

[2] The *Narrative of the Portuguese Embassy to Abyssinia during the years 1520-27*, issued by the Hakluyt Society for 1881 (vol. 64), may be consulted.

Lebna Dengel, still a minor, was made king in 1508.[1] The policy of marrying as one of their wives (for they were polygamists though Christians) a daughter of one of the Muhamedan chiefs of frontier states, was a very favourite one in Abyssinia at this epoch: Alvarez indeed states that the Muhamedan wars of Lebna Dengel's reign began when he refused to marry a daughter of the chief of Adea (Hadia), because her front teeth were too large. She could not return as she had become a Christian, and a husband was found for her among the nobility; her family never forgave the insult.[2] However this may be, while Matheus was absent from Abyssinia, matters had considerably altered there. Helena had disappeared from local politics, and Lebna Dengel had taken the guidance of affairs into his own hands; he had been personally very successful in his campaign against the Muhamedans of the south, overrunning their territory, and killing Mahfuz, the powerful chief of Harar, whom Gabriel Andreas, an Abyssinian monk, slew in single combat in 1517.

There were matters, however, in the north that required consideration. The last of the comparatively tolerant Sultans of Egypt was displaced, in 1516, by the fanatical Ottoman Turk. This change might affect Abyssinia in two ways—the head of the Abyssinian church, the Abuna,

---

[1] Basset, *Études*, p. 249 *n*. Conti Rossini, *Storia di Lebna Dengel*, p. 631 and *n*. For the Abyssinian estimate of her worth after her death, see Alvarez, p. 329.

[2] Alvarez, p. 110. Hadia lies in the Sidama plateau on the east of the River Omo; it is now a very small province, but extended formerly far further; it has a peculiar language of its own. At this time the inhabitants were not allowed to carry arms, or ride saddled horses; and annually they had to send to the ruler of Abyssinia a sum of money and a young Muhamedan girl, over whom, on arrival at court, a funeral service was said by the Muhamedans, and who was then baptised. The rejected lady was a sister of the ruling Queen, but her grievances had nothing to do with the war. The Imam Ahmad overran Hadia early in 1532; it was retaken after his death by Galâwdêwos (Basset, *Histoire*, p. 188 *n*.).

was by the arrangements of Tecla Haimanaut, its organizer, never chosen from among the natives of the country, but was always nominated by the Patriarch of Alexandria—one question was, therefore, how far would the supremacy of the Turk interfere with the missions which periodically went with a heavy ransom to seek a new Abuna; the second way in which this change might affect Abyssinia was by causing a more active Muhamedan policy—a policy which would incite the Muhamedans of the Red Sea littoral against Abyssinia. Still, however much these considerations might be present to the minds of the Abyssinians themselves, there was nothing very pressing at the moment; and from their point of view it was natural that they should prefer to dally with De Lima's mission, and to keep the Portuguese amused, rather than to come to any definite conclusion which might hereafter prove embarrassing, it was always easy to say, as they did, that Matheus was only the envoy of Queen Helena. Dom Rodrigo de Lima, too, was entirely unsuited to be an ambassador, and the members of his suite injured their reputation by quarrelling violently with each other; it is not surprising, therefore, that the mission had no definite result. At the same time, as Alvarez' account of the embassy gives us a picture of the state kept by Lebna Dengel before the country was ravaged, and its stores of accumulated wealth swept off by the incursions of the Imam Ahmad, it must always retain its interest.

After some vexatious delays, the ambassador and his following left the country, taking with them a fresh envoy for Portugal, one Saga za Ab.[1] He was by birth an Abyssinian, and Alvarez states that he was a friar. Owing to a slight knowledge of Italian, acquired it is probable from the Italian painters, Saga za Ab was attached to the

---

[1] For Saga za Ab, see Alvarez, pp. 100, 115, 132, 159 *et seq.*

mission, and accompanied it on its marches; their progress was materially assisted by his energy, although their propriety was greatly shocked by his violence. Saga za Ab remained several years in Portugal, doing, as might be expected, absolutely nothing, and died at Cochin on his way home in 1540. Only two of the *personnel* of the first Portuguese mission appear again in connection with Abyssinia, both being then men of very small importance: one is Ayres Dias, or Diz, a mulatto, a servant of João Escolar, whose most notable exploit was getting his arm broken in a wrestling match with a converted Moor;[1] of him we shall hear much in the narrative of Bermudez; he is known also by his Abyssinian name of Marcos. The other was Bermudez himself, called by Alvarez Mestre João.

Mestre João was by some said to be a Gallician, and by others a Portuguese; this latter is the more probable. He tells us that he came originally to India in the fleet of Lopo Soares, who left Lisbon in April, 1515, and in this embassy he was the barber bleeder. His name does not often occur in Alvarez;[2] he got his head broken in a riot, and was one of six selected to accompany Alvarez to say Mass one Christmas Day before Lebna Dengel: the six being chosen because they understood church matters, and could sing well. Two of his claims may be mentioned as referring to this time, neither being supported by the evidence of any other person. He says that he remained on in Abyssinia as a hostage for Saga za Ab, and that he stood godfather to the eldest son of Lebna Dengel, Galâwdêwos, who was born in 1523, soon after the Portuguese ambassador reached the country. As male children must be baptized at forty days after birth, the ceremony must have taken place while the mission was in Abyssinia;

---

[1] Alvarez, pp. 216 and 300.
[2] Alvarez, pp. 9, 18, 113, 134, 221.

it is not only strange, therefore, that a subordinate like Bermudez should have been selected for so high an honour, but it is still more surprising that, if it is true, Alvarez is silent on so interesting an event. The life of Bermudez is much wrapped up in the history of the events of the next few years.

The[1] Portuguese mission left Abyssinia in 1526, and in 1527 the Imam Ahmad, surnamed Grañ, or the left-handed, began his incursions into the country. The coquettings between the Portuguese and the Abyssinians had not escaped the vigilance of the Muhamedans, whose attention had been previously arrested by the early proceedings of the Europeans in India. After the defeat of the Egyptian fleet off Diu, by Almeida in 1509, the survivors escaped to Jedda to form the nucleus of a new armada. The defeat of the Sultan of Egypt by the Ottoman Turk in 1516, caused a temporary break in the continuity of the Musalman policy; but the matter was never lost sight of. The action of the Portuguese in the Red Sea meanwhile had been irritating to their opponents, without at the same time striking any definite blow at their power. Both Albuquerque in 1513, and Lopo Soares in 1517, spent the summer months there, and lost a very large proportion of their men through the climate and unsuitable food.

---

[1] For this introductory notice I have used Conzelman, *Chronique de Galâwdêwos*; Basset, *Études sur l'histoire d'Éthiopie*; Perruchon, "Notes pour l'histoire d'Éthiopie" in the *Revue Sémitique*; Esteves Pereira, *Historia de Minas Ademas Sagad, Rei de Ethiopia*; Ignazio Guidi, *Di due frammenti relativi alla storia di Abissinia*; Conti Rossini, *Storia di Lebna Dengel*; Schleicher, *Geschichte der Galla*, all from the Ethiopic; Basset, *Histoire de la Conquête de l'Abyssinie* (from the Arabic); besides the usual Portuguese historians.

For maps, the French military map, on the scale $\frac{1}{2,000,000}$, is unrivalled for clearness, but shows few names. The Italian map, on the scale $\frac{1}{1,000,000}$ gives many place-names, and there is a skeleton contour map with few names on the same scale. The Italian contour map, scale $\frac{1}{250,000}$, only goes as far south as Aksum and Adigerat.

They retired thoroughly disorganised, and so alarmed were the Portuguese at the results of these expeditions that no fleet, until that of D. Estevão da Gama, even attempted again to spend any part of the year, after March, beyond the Straits of Babelmandeb. Albuquerque was defeated in his attempt to capture Aden; Lopo Soares was cajoled into not taking possession of it when it lay helpless at his mercy; and the Portuguese never had another opportunity to occupy it. They were thus reduced to a series of raids, burning coast towns and leaving ruined cities behind them to mark their track: proceedings which, if they singed the Muhamedan's beard, certainly never weakened his power for offence.

The expedition which Sulaiman Pasha, the Greek eunuch, commanded in 1538 was a complete failure, as far as regards the attack on Diu, but it secured to the Turks the command of the Red Sea. On his outward voyage Sulaiman established the Turkish power in all the ports on the Arabian coast, capturing even Aden, the key of the navigation of the Red Sea. On his return journey he left garrisons in all the more important towns. It is true that in 1541 D. Estevão da Gama took his lighter vessels as far as Suez, but his return thence, when he found the strength of the Turkish force, was very like a flight; and the audacity of his enterprise thoroughly aroused the Turks, whose galleys from that date patrolled the sea, and rendered communication between Abyssinia and India an enterprise of danger. Firearms had been introduced into Arabia in 1515, and Muhamedan merchants, aided by the policy of the Turks, brought these weapons to Zeila; as they had not at that time reached Abyssinia the relative power of Muhamedan and Christian was entirely changed, and the genius of the Imam Ahmad enabled him to take full advantage of the improved armament of his co-religionists. The Somali armies were accompanied by regular bodies of matchlock-men, who were usually Turks from Zebid, on the Arabian coast of the Red Sea. An olive tree standing in the Abyssinian centre was cut in two by the first cannon shot fired in one of the early battles; and then, as the Muhamedan chronicler puts it, "the Christians tumbled the one on the other," and the Imam's army by an immediate charge won the victory. By 1533 the Christians had got one or two cannon, which were worked by two renegade "Arabs," who from their names may have been a Turk and a Persian; the artillery opposed to them was managed, it is said, by Indians.[1]

Of the early history of the Imam Ahmad but little is known. He was the son of one Ibrahim el Ghazi, and both he and his father were common soldiers in the troop of the Garâd Aboun. Nothing even is said as to his nationality. He was certainly not an Arab: probably he was a Somali, for we find him closely connected with many who were Somalis. It is true that his early employer, the Garâd Aboun, was killed by a troop of Somalis, and that he refused to take service under their leader, and in fact fought and defeated him and them; but this does not appear decisive. His rise was very rapid, as in 1528, when his incursions into Abyssinia began, he was only twenty-one.[2] He married a remarkable woman, the second of the three notable women (Queen Helena being the first, and Ite Sabla Wângel, wife of Lebna Dengel, the third), that figure in this history; she was Bāti Del Wanbara, a daughter of Mahfuz, the well-known Emir of Harar, slain in single combat by the monk Gabriel Andreas in 1517.[3]

Del Wanbara was the constant companion of her husband in his raids in Abyssinia, but she was more than a

---

[1] Basset, *Histoire*, pp. 185 and 407.   [2] *Ibid.*, p. 44.
[3] The Emir Mahfuz had a son, Garâd Ahmadouch, one of Imam Ahmad's trusted lieutenants, as well as this daughter.

mere companion: her influence was frequently exercised on the side of mercy; so notorious was this, that even the Abyssinian chronicles, bitterly opposed as their writers were to her husband as the deadliest foe of Christianity, loudly praise her humanity. In 1539 the Muhamedans captured Minas, the fourth son of Lebna Dengel, and his two cousins; both the cousins were made eunuchs, but by the intercession of Del Wanbara, Minas was not only saved from this fate, but even married to her daughter: a unique instance of clemency. Minas was, however, subsequently utilised by his father-in-law, who sent him across to Zebid as a present to the Pasha, when the early victories of D. Christovão showed the necessity for reinforcements. At the battle of Wainadega, in February, 1543, when the Imam Ahmad was killed, Muhamad, his and Del Wanbara's eldest son, born in 1531, was captured. Through the influence of the two mothers, Del Wanbara and Sabla Wangel, an exchange of prisoners was effected, Muhamad being restored to the Muhamedans and Minas to the Christians. Minas lived to succeed his brother Galâwdêwos as ruler of Abyssinia.[1] But Del Wanbara's share in events was not ended with the death of the Imam Ahmad. She was sought in marriage by his successor, Nur, the son of Mujahid,[2] and she made it a condition of her

---

[1] See Esteves Pereira, *Historia de Minas*, p. 38, and following. The escape of Minas from emasculation was almost unprecedented; of course he turned Muhamedan temporarily. Del Wanbara was not always submissive to her husband, for she refused to leave him when all the army resented as an innovation her accompanying him on the Abyssinian raids (Basset, *Histoire*, p. 51). But her presence was not very obnoxious, for the soldiers soon after voted her a large share of the booty; it was refused as a private gift, however, but set aside as a war fund, and weapons purchased (*ibid.*, p. 65). Bermudez calls this lady Dinia Ambara, and in his chapter xxxviii (p. 202, below), with his usual inaccuracy, marries her to Ayres Dias. I follow the view taken by Bruce in preference to that of the editor of Bermudez, who is, I think, in error in defending his author.

[2] Mujahid was in command at the capture of Amba Geshen, and killed all the royal princes confined there.

INTRODUCTION.

consent that Nur should revenge on Galâwdêwos the death of her first husband, the Imam Ahmad.[1] Nur was eventually successful, and killed Galâwdêwos in battle, in 1559. Curiously enough, there seem to be no traditions now of the Imam Ahmad among the Muhamedans; but the Walasma Muhamad, Governor of Ifat, and head jailer under the King of Shoa, who appears in such an unpleasant light in the narratives of the Harris Mission, claimed to be his descendant.[2] Among the Christians on the other hand, traditions of the Gran are much more frequent; in Shoa he has assumed a fabulous character,[3] and, in Tigré, tradition says he was the son of a Christian priest, killed by his brethren on account of his intrigue with a Muhamedan woman.

It is unnecessary to detail at length the progress of the war between the Imam Ahmad and Lebna Dengel; it will suffice to give the dates of the chief events. The first great battle was that of Chembra Kouré, which the Ethiopian accounts place, some on March 7th, and others on March 9th, 1529; the Muhamedans merely date it early in March of that year.[4] The Futûh el Hâbasha gives the strength of the Abyssinians at sixteen thousand horse and over two hundred thousand foot, and that of the Muhamedans at five hundred and sixty horse and twelve thousand foot; the Ethiopian accounts, on the other hand, put the strength of their own army at over three thousand horse, and footmen innumerable; that of the Muhamedans at three hundred horse and very few foot; the figures then agree, in so far as they show that the relative strength of the two armies was very disproportionate. The result was a complete victory for the Muhamedans; the latter put

---

[1] Basset, *Études*, p. 113. [2] Johnston, vol. ii, p. 42.
[3] Harris, vol. ii, p. 255.
[4] Basset, *Histoire*, p. 115, and following; Basset, *Études*, p. 104 Conti Rossini, p. 637.

their own loss at five thousand men, as their left wing was defeated, but that of the Christians was enormous—over ten thousand leading men alone were killed. After this terrible defeat, the Christians could make but little organised resistance. On July 17th, 1530, Debra Libanos, the most sacred monastery in Abyssinia, was burned, and on October 28th, 1531, Lebna Dengel in person was routed and nearly captured near Amba Sel; after this he was never in a position to offer a pitched battle to his enemies. The spoliation of the churches followed, and the accounts of the rich booty they yielded almost exceed belief. In 1539 the Amba Geshen, the royal stronghold where all the royal family save the reigning sovereign and his wife and children were collected, was stormed; and here again the plunder that rewarded the conquerors was immense, for the hill was considered impregnable, and had been the royal storehouse for many generations.

When, on September 2nd, 1540, Lebna Dengel died at Debra Damo, he was a fugitive with no following, practically the whole of his territory was in the hands of the enemy. He left a widow, three sons, and two daughters; of his four sons the eldest, Fiqtor, had been killed in 1539; the youngest, Minas, was, as stated above, a prisoner; Galâwdêwos, the second son, succeeded his father; Yaekub, the third son, died during his brother Galâwdêwos' reign. The two daughters were Amata Giyorgis and Sabana Giyorgis. The widow, Ite Sabla Wangel, occupies a prominent place in the narrative of the events of the next few years; she lived until 1568, and died during the reign of her grandson, Sartsa Dengel.[1] The courtly historian celebrates her virtues in phrases that may seem conventional,[2] still, the picture which Castanhoso indirectly

---

[1] Basset, *Études*, p. 117.
[2] Conzelman, § 3.

draws of her, and of the chivalrous courtesy with which Dom Christovão da Gama (the *gentil homem*, the gentleman, of the writer) treated her, leaves an impression on the mind unusual from narratives of that time: her shrinking from the carnage of Baçanete, her kindness and attention to the wounded, her timidity when danger threatened, and her steadfast courage in adversity, all help to complete the picture. Even in the narrative of Bermudez some of this peeps through.

Gâlawdêwos, indeed, succeeded to a ruined kingdom. As the chronicler puts it: " Victory favoured the Muhamedans of Bar Saed ed din. They dominated the Ethiopian church; they had been conquerors in all the battles to the east, to the west, to the north, and to the south; they had destroyed all the churches whose walls were covered with gold, silver, and precious stones from India; they had put to the sword a great number of Christians, and taken away into bondage many youths and maidens and children of both sexes, and even sold them into the lowest slavery. Many believers had abandoned the faith of their church and embraced Muhamedanism; hardly one in ten maintained his religion."[1] Galâwdêwos collected some few followers; but he was quickly driven out of Tigré, and compelled to take refuge in Shoa. Tradition says that his headquarters there were in Tegulet,[2] where he remained with only sixty or seventy retainers, a mere spectator of events, until October, 1542, when he marched north, still with a mere handful of men, to join the Portuguese. Meanwhile his mother, brother, and sisters had stayed on

---

[1] Conzelman, § 4. The name, Bar Saed ed din, was given to the Muhamedan country south of Abyssinia in memory of Saed ed din, King of Adal, a dangerous enemy of the Christians, slain by them at Zeila, in 1402-03 (Basset, *Histoire*, p. 7, *n.*). See also p. 85 *n.*, below.

[2] *Combes et Tamisier*, vol. iii, p. 217. For a description of Tegulet, see Harris, vol. ii, p. 53.

the Amba of Debra Damo. The Imam Ahmad's strategy in this short campaign of the early months of 1541 was simple and effective. In March, 1540, a letter from India had reached Lebna Dengel through Massowa, referring to the approaching arrival of Bermudez. The Imam Ahmad must have known of this letter, for the country from Massowa inland was in his possession; and as Lebna Dengel told Bermudez in the letter he wrote to him, the coming of the Portuguese was well known.[1] Knowing, then, or suspecting, that aid for his opponent was at hand, the Imam Ahmad's endeavour was to drive Galâwdêwos as far south as possible, away from the base where reinforcements would land. Meanwhile he took up his own position at Darasgué, on the northern shore of Lake Tzâna, where he was about half way between Massowa and Shoa, and within easy striking distance of all the routes leading from the one place to the other.[2]

It is necessary now to go back somewhat, to marshal the events that brought the Portuguese to Massowa. We have only Bermudez' own account of what happened to him in Abyssinia for some years after the departure of Dom Rodrigo de Lima. He states that, in 1535, when Lebna Dengel's fortunes were at a low ebb, the Abuna Marcos lay on his death-bed, and that the King begged the dying Abuna to institute Bermudez, "according to custom," Patriarch of Abyssinia. This having been done, Lebna Dengel commissioned Bermudez to proceed overland and make his submission to the Pope, and obtain confirmation of his election as head of the Abyssinian Church. This done, he was to go on to Portugal and beg material help from the King. Bermudez says that he reached Europe

---

[1] Correa, vol. iv, p. 138. See p. 107, below.
[2] Basset, *Études*, p. 111: Basset says that Darasgué is five hours' march south-west from Gondar, that is, on or near the northern edge of Lake Tzâna (*ibid.*, p. 262, *n.*).

after a toilsome journey (one of the incidents of which was the loss of part of his tongue, cut off by the Turks); that the then Pope, Paul III, not only confirmed him in what he brought from Abyssinia, but also made him Patriarch of Alexandria. Not to interrupt the narrative, the criticism of this part of Bermudez' story must be deferred to a later part of this Introduction. Bermudez gives no dates after the one mentioned above; but Paul III became Pope after the death of Clement VII, in September 1534, so that he was Pope while Bermudez was in Europe, though the actual year of the latter's interview with the Pontiff is not stated. Bermudez went thence to Portugal, which he says he reached in the year the Evora water-works were completed. The Portuguese editor of Bermudez, on the authority of an unpublished manuscript, puts this in 1533; this is, in view of the date of Paul's election as Pope, and Bermudez' statement as to the year he left Abyssinia, impossible. Bermudez further says that, when he reached Portugal, Saga za Ab had been twelve years there. As Saga za Ab reached there in 1527, this gives us the impossible date of 1539 as that of Bermudez' homecoming.

These contradictions cannot be reconciled now, but under any circumstances Bermudez was ready to return to India with D. Garcia de Noronha, who left Portugal on April 6th, 1538; but he was taken ill, and did not sail until a year later, when he went out in the fleet commanded by Pero Lopez de Sousa. We have no copy of the instructions the Viceroy received concerning Bermudez; the latter claims that he was to be given both soldiers and mechanics under his own command; this seems doubtful. The Viceroy, D. Garcia, was ill at the time of Bermudez' arrival in India, and was therefore unable to fit out a fleet for the Red Sea; he, however, sent to Massowa, in February, 1540, one Fernão Farto, in a small vessel, with orders to land an

Abyssinian with letters for Lebna Dengel, to enquire if he wished to receive back Bermudez. Farto was in Goa again in May with the replies. Correa[1] gives the letter sent to Bermudez by Lebna Dengel, but not those sent to the Viceroy. D. Garcia de Noronha had died six weeks before Farto's return, and had been succeeded by D. Estevão da Gama, the second son of D. Vasco da Gama.

In one of his earliest councils the new Governor, in accordance with orders from Portugal, proposed an expedition to the Red Sea, the main object of which was, however, the burning of the Turkish galleys in Suez. This expedition having been determined on, it set sail when the season arrived, and reached Massowa on February 10th, 1541. At Massowa the Governor first heard of the death of Lebna Dengel, in the previous September. According to D. João de Castro,[2] he also received here letters from Abyssinia, more than pitiful and dejected (*mais que piadosas e miseraueis*), to which he replied with words of hope; making, however, no special arrangements for sending an expedition, he pressed on to Suez on February 18th. His heavy vessels were left in Massowa, under the command of his relative, Manuel da Gama, and, unfortunately for the new commander, Bermudez remained there also. The conditions of life for the Portuguese on board Da Gama's ships at Massowa were hard in the extreme; the country provided but little food, there were no fidalgos to provide messes for the sailors, and the men themselves had no money to buy the scanty necessaries that were obtainable; the bad climate of Massowa, too, had its effect, and the sick were soon numerous. All this while Bermudez poured out praises of the country of Abyssinia, and described the happy conditions of life there; the very hills of the paradise were in sight of the ships, but Manuel da Gama was

---

[1] Correa, vol. iv, p. 138. See p. 107, below.   [2] *Roteiro*, p. 70.

compelled to refuse permission to any to leave before the return of D. Estevão da Gama. The necessary result followed : one hundred men conspired together and agreed to desert in a body. Those not in the conspiracy so far sympathised with the seceders that they refused to fire on them when ordered, and the hundred men got away up country in an organised body. Unaccustomed, however, to African travel, they were enticed on until, exhausted by thirst, they were led into a trap, whence only two wounded men escaped to tell their comrades. Insubordination had infected the whole body of sailors, and Manuel da Gama had, against his better judgment, to head a futile expedition to try to avenge the death of these men. Even after this Bermudez contributed to the increase of the commander's difficulties, for he kept the agitation alive by showing to all the piteous letters begging for assistance that he received from Abyssinia.

The arrival of D. Estevão da Gama at Massowa, on May 22nd, did much to allay the rising discontent ; but he had to sacrifice, to some extent, his relative, Manuel da Gama, to his policy. He determined to send an expedition into Abyssinia, consisting of four hundred men under D. Christovão da Gama, his younger brother ; and in this number were included some seventy skilled mechanics, whom Bermudez had recruited in India under special written agreements. No other writer in any way supports Bermudez' story of his resistance to the appointment of D. Christovão da Gama ; neither are there extant the royal provisions which he says were passed for his benefit, empowering him to appoint the commander of any military force sent to Abyssinia. It may be that Bermudez had some special order in respect to these mechanics which he tried to twist into one affecting a military expedition, but this is mere conjecture. At the same time, although there is no external evidence that Bermudez raised any difficulties, there can be no doubt but that the appointment of D. Christovão da Gama, by his brother, did cause much discontent.[1]

In 1541 D. Christovão da Gama was twenty-five years of age; his eldest brother succeeded to his father's title, and never served in India; the next, D. Estevão da Gama, was at that time Governor of India; the third, D. Paulo da Gama, had been killed in Malacca in 1534. The two youngest brothers, D. Pedro da Silva and D. Alvaro de Athaide, do not come into this history. D. Christovão's first voyage to India was with his brother, D. Estevão, in the ship *Espirito Santo*, one of the fleet of 1532;[2] the vessel made an unlucky voyage: it did not touch at any of the usual halting-places, and was driven northwards in the Indian Ocean until it anchored off Shahr of Arabia. While watering, D. Estevão and several fidalgos being on shore, a sudden storm drove the ship from its moorings and down the east coast of Africa to Melindi. D. Christovão, though but a boy of sixteen, saved the vessel from destruction; and when she failed to get into Melindi harbour took her, though with great difficulty, to Mozambique. Either brother thought the other lost, but D. Estevão finally reached Mozambique in a hired vessel, and there found his brother refitting. D. Estevão had been appointed Captain of Malacca, and thither D. Christovão accompanied him, taking his share in the fighting that avenged his brother

---

[1] The family of D. Vasco da Gama is given here.

D. Vasco da Gama, Conde da Vidigueira. = D. Catharina de Athaide.

1	2	3	4
D. Francisco da Gama, Conde da Vidigueira.	D. Estevão da Gama, Governor of India, 1540-42.	D. Paulo da Gama, killed in Malacca in 1534.	D. Christovão da Gama.

5	6	7	
D. Pedro da Silva da Gama.	D. Alvaro de Athaide, the opponent of St. Francis Xavier.	D. Isabel de Athaide da Gama.	= Ignacio de Noronha, son of the first Conde de Linhares.

[2] See Couto, *Dec. IV*, Bk. VIII, chap. ii.

INTRODUCTION. xliii

D. Paulo da Gama's death. In 1535 D. Christovão was back again in Portugal, where, pending other advancement, he received some small appointments about the court. All the sons of D. Vasco da Gama who served abroad received, one after another, the patent of Captain of Malacca, the most lucrative appointment in the East; that of D. Christovão is dated January 12th, 1538, only to become operative when the appointment fell vacant. D. Garcia de Noronha went out as Viceroy, as we have seen, in April, 1538, and D. Christovão accompanied him as captain of one of the vessels of his fleet. He went with his superior in his progress to Diu, after the Turks had raised the siege, and in the violent storm the fleet encountered he distinguished himself greatly by saving the crews of some disabled ships: in these operations he showed not only humanity but seamanship. Of his period of service under D. Garcia there exist two gossipy letters to the King of Portugal, such as were then commonly written by aspiring young men in India to their sovereign: these letters, however, contain no malevolent stories, and some passages show a generous appreciation of his contemporaries.[1] After commanding a small force, sent by D. Estevão da Gama to punish the Arel of Porakkat, D. Christovão returned to Goa in time to take up his command of a vessel in the Red Sea fleet; he was with his brother in the voyage to Suez, and returned with him to Massowa.

It was natural that the selection of so young a man by his brother, the Governor, should have given rise to adverse comment; but it would be idle to contend that D. Christovão did not justify his brother's confidence. The work of Castanhoso is his monument, raised by the pen of a faithful follower: bold to temerity in action,

---

[1] These letters have been printed in the Portuguese edition of Castanhoso's book, published in 1898, pp. 119 to 126, but it has not been deemed necessary to add them to this volume.

chivalrous in his dealings with women, ready to share the burden of the common soldier, foremost in the fight, and willing, though wounded himself, to do the work of the wounded surgeon, Dom Christovão stands out through the book as a true leader of men; as the man to whom, when he died, his faithful followers would elect no successor, till they had exacted satisfaction for his death. It was no common man whom these soldiers, "with wounds still open," marched to avenge on the Shrove Tuesday of 1543; even the nameless John the Gallician, the man of foreign blood, pushed his way through the throng of enemies, regardless of the death that must inevitably come to him, if he might but shoot down the Imam Ahmad, by whose hand his old commander had fallen. The picture of Correa agrees with that of Castanhoso, save that he adds one or two strokes of that relentless cruelty to insubordination from which no son of D. Vasco da Gama could be quite free. In Bermudez' book, on the other hand, D. Christovão is a zany, irresolute and incompetent, with no attribute save personal courage; the success of the enterprise, where there was success, is due to the sagacity of Bermudez, the failure to the vices of D. Christovão. Later I will deal with the credibility of the two narratives of Castanhoso and Bermudez *seriatim*. I may merely say here that Bermudez is unsupported, and reaches his result, not so much by giving a new series of facts as to D. Christovão, as by suppressing everything that could redound to his credit, and by adding some statements on the foresight of Bermudez himself. There can be no doubt but that Castanhoso gives the true picture.

On Saturday, July 9th, 1541, D. Estevão da Gama and his brother parted for the last time; the fleet sailed for India, and D. Christovão and his four hundred men marched inland. The expedition was well found, both in arms and supplies, as they carried one thousand stand of matchlocks and several field pieces, while a number of the men were trained artificers recruited by Bermudez; in addition apparently to these four hundred men, who were all Portuguese, there were one hundred and thirty slaves, good fighting men, whose chief use was to act as supports to their masters in battle, and carry their supply of extra weapons; there was also a fife and drum band.

The route through Abyssinia of this expedition has never been worked out in England; there are objections to some of the suggestions of the Italian translator of Castanhoso; while, although no one can study the question without feeling his very great obligation to Esteves Pereira, the editor of the same work as published by the Lisbon Geographical Society in 1898, still, some of his identifications of places seem open to debate. The subject is, in fact, one which does not lend itself to a mathematical accuracy. Bermudez gives but the vaguest indications of localities, while, though there are no reasons to doubt the veracity of Castanhoso, still, omitting the names of places, such as Massowa, Zeila, and Zebid, outside the limits of Abyssinia, he only mentions eight or nine names; and of these some are corrupt and inexplicable, some corrupt and uncertain, about half remain regarding which there can be no reasonable question. Of Castanhoso's text there are two recensions: that printed recently by the Lisbon Geographical Society and translated here, which I will call A, and the early printed one, which I will call B. B has a few more names than A. There are, fortunately, some other authors from which Castanhoso's meagre list can be supplemented. Castanhoso published his account in 1564, after his return to Portugal; but twenty years before, in 1544, on his way home through India, he had given a copy of it to Correa, and that author, after enquiries from other Portuguese who had been in Africa, adopted the narrative, adding a few details. Couto got a copy of Castanhoso's book after it was printed, and he, too, made enquiries from other companions of D. Christovão, and included an abstract of the narrative in his *Decades*. He is at the best a careless writer. Pero Paez, who was in Abyssinia from 1603 to 1622, sixty years and more after D. Christovão's death, took some pains to identify the places connected with the events of this expedition, and the results of his enquiries will be found in Tellez' abridgment of Almeida. Sixty years is a long time, and local memory tends to become untrustworthy after such an interval, yet in Gondar Gobat found the traditions of Bruce still fresh in 1830, and Bruce had left Abyssinia in 1772. All other European authorities than these are of later date and less value. In addition to the above there are the Ethiopian chronicles, of which a list has already been given. From these materials an attempt will be made to indicate the route.

D. Christovão's force was accompanied by the Baharnagash, or ruler of the sea, the Abyssinian governor of the extreme northern province of that country. After a six days' march, partly over the hot lowlands, and partly over the rough ascent to the uplands, the expedition reached the Abyssinian table-land, and halted there for two days in a church destroyed by the Moors: no name is mentioned; the Italian translator identifies it with a ruined church near Asmara, and this seems probable. Three days' further march brought them to a town in the lordship of the captain who accompanied them, presumably Isaac the Baharnagash. Neither A nor Correa names this town; B calls it Baroa; Bermudez, Couto and Paez, Debarwa. The Ethiopian chronicles say the Franks passed the rains at Debaroua; presumably the identification of this place with Debarwa, still known by the same name, is inevitable. From July to December the expedition halted weatherbound at Debarwa. The position then was that the Portuguese with a small force were at Debarwa, the

Preste, Galâwdêwos, with a still smaller, was in Shoa, four hundred miles south, and the Imam Ahmad, with a force vastly superior to both combined, lay midway between them. From time to time communications from Galâwdêwos reached the Portuguese, all urging them to join him before fighting the Imam Ahmad, but it does not appear that Galâwdêwos himself started from Shoa.

The negociations for the Portuguese contingent had been carried on by Ite Sabla Wangel, the widow of Lebna Dengel, mentioned above, and the Baharnagash; the then King was no party to them, he was too far away. There can be no doubt but that the Portuguese had not in any way recognised how desperate the position of the Christian monarchy was; in fact, they did not recognise it until just before the fatal battle in which D. Christovão was killed. D. Christovão's first act on reaching Debarwa was to send for Ite Sabla Wangel, who was then on a neighbouring hill. Here we reach the first difficulty. In the previous September, Lebna Dengel had died and been buried on Debra Damo, and the Queen had taken refuge there. Castanhoso gives no name to the hill on which the Queen was, but his description of it agrees closely with that of Debra Damo. Couto calls it Dama, and Paez, Damo.[1] There can be no doubt then as to the hill; but it is especially stated that it was only one day's march from Debarwa, and the Portuguese escort sent to fetch the Queen marched there one day and returned the next. Debra Damo is sixty miles as the crow flies from Debarwa, and the ravines of the Mareb river intervene to make the road difficult. It is impossible that this distance should

---

[1] In modern times the summit of Debra Damo is, owing to the monastery, *taboo* to the female sex. Thus, after the death of Sabagadis in 1835, when his sons and their following sought refuge there, the males remained in safety on the impregnable plateau, while their women had to take their chance at the foot. Combes et Tamisier, vol. i, p. 232.

have been covered during the rains in one day; the question does not admit of a solution, though a guess at the truth is possible. The enforced leisure at Debarwa was spent in making carriages for the artillery and baggage. It seems probable that these carriages were sledges, not wheeled vehicles, as we are told that they were shod with iron, and that condemned matchlocks were used for the purpose. Oxen were captured in raids, and with difficulty broken to the yoke.

On December 15th, 1541, D. Christovão and his men, accompanied by the Dowager Queen and the Baharnagash, started from Debarwa. The order of the march as given seems to show that it was carried out with considerable military precaution. Up to February the complaints as to the road and the difficulties with the carriages were continuous; after that they cease. It seems probable that in February most of these carriages were discarded, and the depôt of surplus arms formed on Debra Damo. We know that there was a depôt there, from which, after the defeat of August, 1542, the remnant of the Portuguese were re-armed, though the date when the depôt was formed is not given.

At a gradually increasing distance from the sea, as they run from north to south, lies a chain of mountains which, close to the ocean at Massowa, is a considerable distance inland at Shoa. This chain forms the water-parting of this tract of country; the shed to the east is to the Red Sea, to the west to the river Nile. Along this water-parting lies the natural highway from the north to the south of Abyssinia, where the rivers are at their smallest, and the river valleys at their shallowest. It seems clear that the Portuguese expedition of 1541 followed this water-parting. The westerly line from Debarwa to Shoa, whether longer or shorter, crosses all the great water systems of the country, and would have led the Portuguese into the very jaws of the Imam Ahmad. It was along the line of this natural highway that Krapf made his adventurous journey in 1842, and the English expedition to Magdala of course followed it.

Distance measured on the map is no guide in a country like Abyssinia, intersected by mountains and deep river valleys. Thus, the approach to Shoa from the north is barred by the ravines of the Wancheet, the Jemma, and their tributary streams, over these there is one very bad road only. Alvarez describes these gates, as he calls them, in his chapter lxv. Krapf, too, speaks of the passage, and points out that the difficulty of the approaches explained why the King of Shoa feared so little the attack of any enemy from the north.[1] On the north-west of Shoa the country is more open, but the journey by that route to Lake Tzana, which is the one taken by Combes and Tamisier on their way north, is more circuitous for a traveller from Shoa to Debarwa, than the eastern road.

After marching for eight days, from December 15th, the Portuguese reached a mountain, in the territory of the Baharnagash, where they spent Christmas. There is a name here in Castanhoso, the Portuguese editor is uncertain whether grammatically it refers to the place they were in, or to the festival they spent there; it does not become a foreigner to hazard a suggestion. In A the word is Cabelaa, in B Cabeda, in Correa Caboa; Couto's account is hopelessly confused, the word is irrecoverable. The

---

[1] Alvarez calls the worst part of the crossing *aqui afagi*, or "death of the asses," and says the gates and ravines are called Badabaxa. Krapf (p. 313) calls the village at their southern entrance, Amadwasha, which perhaps is the same word. Another account of the difficulties of the passage through this country will be found in Combes et Tamisier (vol. ii, pp. 284 and 330); they passed it on their way south, and call the village Ouacha, or the grotto. Probably this name refers to the King's treasure grotto located here by Alvarez in his chap. cxxvii. See also Wylde (p. 392, and following). When he crossed this piece of country, the Italian prisoners were making a road under Abyssinian superintendence.

INTRODUCTION.

Italian translator considers that the mountain where they spent Christmas was that south of Gundet; that in the next two marches the river Mareb was crossed; that they ascended the Tigré mountains between Amba Krestos and Amba Beesa, and that they thus reached the plains of Dara Takle. None of these names are given in any authority, and the suggestion fails entirely to place the hermitage, with the bodies of the three hundred martyrs from the time of the Romans, which we shall see they soon reached. As long as the carts were a drag on them, the Portuguese marches were rather short (after February they seem to have been much longer); it appears probable, too, that in the earlier marches they were not only hampered by this unsuitable transport, but that they intended to put heart into the people, long under the Muhamedan yoke, rather than to push south to join Galâwdêwos; perhaps also the delay was intentional, in the hope of receiving reinforcements through Massowa. D. Estevão da Gama had promised that these reinforcements should be sent, and one vessel under Manuel de Vasconcellos did certainly reach Massowa in February, 1542, and land there a messenger to get news of D. Christovão, to learn his urgent wants, but Vasconcellos was driven from the coast by Turkish galleys before a reply could reach him. The supersession of D. Estevão da Gama by Martim Afonso de Sousa in the Indian government, in May of the same year, effectually prevented any further attempt to communicate with the Portuguese who, cut off in Abyssinia, and abandoned by their fellow-countrymen, could only trust to their own right arms.

After the octave of Christmas was ended, the Portuguese marched by a very rough road to the top of a high hill, where was a hermitage with the bodies of three hundred martyrs. Here we reach more certain ground; there can be no doubt but that Sir Clements Markham is right when he identifies this place with the church of St. Romanos, and the adjoining cell, where the bodies of these three hundred martyrs are still shown to visitors through a hole. This church is near Barakit, close to Senafé.[1] In a note with which he has favoured me, Sir Clements Markham has described the place thus: "The church of St. Romanos is on a ledge 500 feet above the valley, perpendicular precipice above and below. Behind the church, on an almost inaccessible ledge, there is a clump of date palms, and a cell is hewn in the rock as a hermitage." Through his kindness a reproduction of a photograph of this place is included in this volume. Not only does the description agree with that of Castanhoso, but those of the surroundings agree also: coming from the west the rise from the valley of the Mareb is abrupt; going towards the south Agamé would be reached in two days' march over fairly level ground; to the Portuguese, also, ignorant of a saint called Romanos, the interpretation of martyrs, dating from the time of the Romans, would be the natural explanation of an ill-understood exposition in a foreign tongue. No other site has ever been suggested for this church, and the only objection urged to the one near Senafé is, that it lies further east than the line of Portuguese advance usually adopted by commentators. At the same time there is no specific fact urged that renders this an impossible identification, and, if it be accepted, certain points in the narrative are cleared up. The line, for instance, from Debarwa to Senafé crosses the Mareb nearer its source than that suggested by the Italian translator; the river there is insignificant, and the omission of any mention of it in Castanhoso is explicable; once near Senafé, also, the expedition was on a well-known route, and the rest of its march can be easily followed.

---

[1] *Abyssinian Expedition*, pp. 23 and 195.

After a short rest near the hermitage, the Portuguese marched for two days, over a level plain, till they came, as Castanhoso tells us, to Agamé, where they halted eight days and spent the Epiphany ;[1] as stated above, Agamé is two days' march from the church of St. Romanos. After the Epiphany the advance southward was continued until they reached a detached solitary hill on a plain, held by the Moors, before which they camped on February 1st, 1542. The name of the hill was Baçanete ; the summit was flat, a league in circuit, and a high peak rose from it ; at the foot of this peak was a spring of water. To the hill there were only three approaches, all difficult. It was garrisoned by Moors, who had no firearms, and who raided the country round. Castanhoso states that the hill was very high ; but, in his account of the assault, he says the Moors on the summit dared not show themselves to hurl down rocks, owing to the artillery and matchlock fire. It does not follow that this was an aimed fire : the garrison would have been cowed by random discharges provided the bullets struck the rocks. Still, knowing what firearms were then, the hill could not have been very lofty. Castanhoso says the Kings of Abyssinia were crowned on the summit ; this is a confusion : they were, of course, crowned at Aksum. Paez gives the name of the hill as Amba Sanait, and says the three approaches were called Amba Sanait, Amba Shembat, and Amba Gadabat. On the Italian map is a place called Sanaiti, fifty kilometres east of Aksum, which may be the place Paez means. The Italian translator says the name has disappeared from modern maps, but places the hill in Haramāt. Haramāt lies somewhat east of Sanaiti, and it is in it that I think Baçanete must be searched for. The name occurs in two authors : in neither

---

[1] There seems some difficulty in this. The Epiphany should have been spent at the hermitage, but all the authorities agree in the statement.

case were they referring in any way to this expedition; in fact, when one wrote it had not even started. In his chapter xli Alvarez speaks of reaching Bacinete; unfortunately, his route has not been entirely worked out. In chapter xxxv he speaks of crossing a river, which is clearly the Mareb, and marching to Abafazem; this is undoubtedly the ancient Ava, the modern Yeha, some twenty miles north-east of Aksum. From there they went to the church of St. Michael, which is, he tells us, two days' journey east of Aksum,[1] and after leaving there they reached Bacinete in two marches. It was on a high hill above a large river, and Abacinete was the name of the country and lordship. A day's march is a varying quantity, depending on the weather and the roads; it could not have been less than three leagues a day, and was possibly more;[2] four journeys of this length, east from Aksum, would bring the traveller to Haramāt. The other author who mentions Basanate is Pearce;[3] he speaks casually of "Ito Musgrove of Basanate, and the whole of Arramat." Ito Musgrove was a man, and the context seems to show that Basanate was in Haramāt.[4] The Italian map gives a name, Amba Sourat in Haramāt, east of the road, and the contour map shows that it is an isolated hill; it seems a likely place for banditti, but, connecting it with Baçanete is merely a guess, though a plausible one.

---

[1] There is a large church dedicated to St. Michael, close to Adowa on the north-east. If this be the one referred to, it is not two days' march east of Aksum, but only some fourteen miles. Between this place and Bacinete, Alvarez and his party halted one night at Angueha. This name is not on modern maps. Bruce (vol. iv, p. 305) says that in coming from the north-east, at a day's journey from Adowa, he crossed the Angueah river, a tributary of the Mareb; this must be the Unguia river of the Italian map. If, as is probable, the place Angueha was near this river, then the route of the mission lay not south but east from Adowa, that is, towards Haramāt.

[2] Alvarez says that his last march into Bacinete was three or four leagues in length.   [3] Vol. i, p. 179.

[4] Ludolf (Lib. I, cap. iii) gives Amba Sanet as one of the districts of Tigré, but does not indicate its position.

On February 2nd, 1542, the Portuguese stormed the hill and put all the garrison to the sword; their loss was eight killed and several wounded. As a feat of arms this capture was notable; but the Queen was probably justified in opposing D. Christovão's intention to attack, for the news aroused the Imam Ahmad. It is possible, though not probable, that marching quickly D. Christovão could have joined Galâwdêwos before meeting the Imam Ahmad in person. All February the Portuguese remained encamped on the hill, and at the end of the month came the news that a Portuguese vessel had touched at Massowa; forty men were sent to communicate with her, and bring back her lading of stores. As mentioned above, they never succeeded in even getting speech of her; they rejoined the expedition on April 17th, just too late to participate in the important events that had happened in the interval.

After the men had started for Massowa, D. Christovão continued his progress towards the south, marching but slowly, and only changing his ground to obtain the necessary supplies. Castanhoso says their destination was Jarte. Paez and the Italian translator suggest Sahart, which is possible. Adjoining Sahart, and in the same line of country, is Wajárat, and the Portuguese editor suggests that Campos do Jarte, in the original, should be Campos d'Ojarte or Wajárat; both these places are on the water-parting line, but Wajárat is, in view of the site of the two succeeding battles with the Imam Ahmad, by far the more probable. On the way came news that the Imam Ahmad was near at hand, and on the Saturday before Palm Sunday (April 1st), D. Christovão pitched his camp, selecting the site with especial care in view of the expected attack.[1] The army of the Imam Ahmad was very numerous; the numbers given by the Portuguese are of course

---

[1] They made what would now be called a "zariba."

mere estimates; they say fifteen thousand foot, fifteen hundred horse, and two hundred Turkish matchlockmen—they themselves numbered three hundred and fifty, and there were no Abyssinians of any fighting value with them. The tactics of the Imam Ahmad were simple: he held the Portuguese closely invested, both night and day, and advanced his matchlockmen to worry the besieged, which they did effectually from behind some low stone breastworks. With his supplies cut off, D. Christovão had to fight in the open, or starve, and on the morning of Tuesday, April 4th, 1542,[1] he marched out; his troops were formed in a square, with the Queen and the non-effectives in the centre. The square moved slowly over the plain, until stopped by the advance of the Turks, musquetry and artillery playing from each of its faces. D. Christovão was himself wounded, and the Portuguese were for some time hard pressed, until a lucky shot struck the Imam Ahmad, wounding him in the leg; when he was carried from the field the Muhamedan force gave way; the Portuguese were too weary to follow, but selected a new camp where some supplies could be obtained. D. Christovão desired, of course, the return of the Portuguese detached to Massowa before engaging again; but having no news of them, and finding that the forces of the Imam Ahmad increased daily, as troops from the more distant provinces came pouring in, he was compelled to move out again, and offer battle on Sunday, April 16th, 1542. This second battle was more obtinately contested than the first; the Muhamedan leader was present at the fight, but carried in a litter, and his followers must have missed the exhilaration of his more active presence; his horse, however, nearly succeeded in breaking the Portuguese square: they were only hindered by the opportune explosion of some gun-

---

[1] The Ethiopian chronicles date this battle March 25th.

powder, which the horses could not face. This time the Muhamedans definitely retreated in disorder, and their camp was captured. In the two battles the Portuguese lost about thirty killed.

It remains to determine where these battles were fought. Castanhoso gives no name, nor does Correa, or Couto. Paez says the fighting took place on the banks of the Afgol stream. In one of Markham's maps the Afgol spur and valley are shown to the east of Antalo and Chelicut, just where the Italian map shows the hill of Afgol-Giyorgis. Salt, in his first journey,[1] mentions the large village of Afgol, between Antalo and Chelicut; and in his second he speaks of crossing the Mai Afgol stream after leaving Antalo for Aksum;[2] Portal took leave of King John in the village of Afgol.[3] Lobo (not a good authority) speaks of the battles as occurring on the plains of Bellet; these may be the same as the plains of Bellisart, between Antalo and Chelicut, casually mentioned by Pearce. Bruce says that the fighting took place at the village of Ainal, in the country of the Baharnagash; where that is I cannot say. The Ethiopian chronicles place the actions in the country of Anasa, or Aynaba, wherever that may be; the names of Antalo and Anseba found near the supposed site of the battles seem reminiscent of these words. The site of these battles may be taken as approximately fixed, and as being close to Antalo, which is on the direct line between Haramāt and Wajárat; this having been determined from other sources, it is satisfactory to know that the reference of Bermudez in his chapter xvii (p. 160 *n.*) to the monastery of Nazareth confirms the identification.

After the battle the Imam Ahmad retreated to a "strong hill opposite the straits," eight days' march away. A gives no name to the hill, B calls it Măgadafo, which I

---

[1] *Lord Valentia's Travels* (vol. iii, p. 35).
[2] Salt (p. 347).
[3] Portal (p. 182).

INTRODUCTION. lvii

cannot explain, Lobo calls it Membret, equally unintelligible. The Ethiopian chronicles say that the Imam Ahmad wintered in Zabl, or Zobl. There can be no doubt that the place referred to is Zabul, which is a hilly region at the right distance from Antalo, south-east of Lake Ashangi. The expression "opposite the straits" clearly means that no higher land intervened between it and the Straits of Bab-el Mandeb, which is correct with reference to Zabul. This place was selected with the Grãn's usual discernment; he had hitherto found that a body of two hundred Turkish matchlockmen was sufficient to defeat any force the Abyssinians could bring against him, and this number he kept regularly in his pay, but they were quite inadequate when opposed to a large body of disciplined Europeans; the only supply of matchlockmen that could be obtained was from the Turkish garrisons of the Red Sea ports. A return to his old base near Lake Tzâna would have cut him off entirely from this necessary reinforcement, and have left him exposed to destruction. The move to Zabul, on the other hand, gave him the command of the line of communication with Zebid to the east, where the main garrison of the Turks was. This line the Europeans could not threaten, both because of their small number, and because of the climate between Zabul and the sea. The command of the sea itself had passed from the Portuguese to the Turks.

After D. Christovão had been joined by the returning Portuguese from Massowa, he marched to Ofala: Castanhoso calls the place Ofala, the Ethiopian chronicles Ofla. This is Wofla, a district south of Lake Ashangi, and west of Zabul. As this point of the itinerary is of considerable importance, it is fortunate that there can be no doubt in its identification; at the same time it is rather strange that Castanhoso never mentions Lake Ashangi. D. Christovão's selection of a place for wintering showed little skill. He was indeed in sight of his enemy, but where he was posted he had no means of knowing what went on behind the screen of hills, and this was, in fact, the cause of his destruction. The Imam Ahmad, unknown to him, obtained large reinforcements from Zebid, on the Arabian coast of the Red Sea, amounting to nine hundred matchlockmen and several field pieces. By the end of August the Muhamedan force was so strong that it could at pleasure overwhelm the handful of Portuguese.

After the Portuguese were hutted in for the rains at Wofla, there occurred certain events, whose record forms one of the most difficult passages of the narrative of this campaign. A Jew came to D. Christovão and told him of a mountain stronghold, of which he had formerly been the commander, but which had been captured by the Muhamedans since Galâwdêwos had retreated to Shoa. When driven south Galâwdêwos had of necessity crossed this mountain, as the only road lay over it; and now, unless the Muhamedans were driven from it, he could not join the Portuguese, as his following was too small to force a passage. It was this information that first opened D. Christovão's eyes to the extreme weakness of the titular King of Abyssinia. The mountain itself is described as four leagues across and twelve leagues long, inhabited by ten thousand or twelve thousand Jews, with only two paths giving access to it.[1] The Jew further told D. Christovão that the garrison of Muhamedans then on the hill was weak, that he could guide him by an unsuspected access, and that among the booty would be several good horses, a bait that was very attractive. The distance and direction of this hill are not given; it is described as near, and that on the road the river Tagacem (Takazzé) would have to be

---

[1] The description seems inconsistent with the statement that Galâwdêwos *crossed* it; probably the hill commanded the only road.

INTRODUCTION. lix

crossed. D. Christovão determined to undertake the expedition, and, after providing for the guard of his camp, he started secretly at night with one hundred men; they carried a supply of skins to inflate, in order to make rafts for the crossing of the river Takazzé. The time occupied in reaching the hill is not stated;[1] but the expedition was successful, the Muhamedans were taken by surprise and routed; those who escaped the Portuguese falling at the hands of the Jew inhabitants. The spoil was very considerable: goods and slaves, besides horses, mules, and cattle. It is not clear how long D. Christovão took in returning to Wofla from the hill; it would almost seem as if he and seventy of his men covered the distance in one forced march; but it is clear from the narrative that thirty men, with the horses, came on more slowly than he did, and took at least two days longer on the road. D. Christovão was driven to a very hurried return by a presentiment of coming trouble at his camp. Before continuing the story, it is necessary to discuss the site of this feat.

The text of Castanhoso translated here gives no name to the hill. B calls it Gimen, which may be Semien, Geshen, or Gideon. Couto gives it the name Caloa, which, as his text often omits cedillas under capital C's (Canet, a little earlier for Sanet), may be Saloa. Paez calls it Amba Wati of Cemen: Amba Wati I cannot trace. Bruce identifies the hill with Amba Gideon, eighty miles west of Wofla, and says that the Portuguese alone mention this exploit. The Italian translator seems to consider that the Muhamedans were driven out of the whole province of Semien, which would be a very considerable undertaking;

---

[1] The time spent must have been longer than the condensed narrative of Castanhoso would lead us to believe, because D. Christovão, after capturing it, had to obtain the Queen's consent before making it over to its old commandant, the Jew, now turned Christian.

Massaia, a late Italian writer, puts the hill considerably over one hundred miles west of Wofla. All these conjectures assume that the hill lay west of Wofla; but, although the indications are so very slight that no solution can be entirely free from doubt, I think the position of this hill must be sought in the south and not in the west. The Takazzé river flows both south and west of Wofla; no other river is mentioned, and yet if the Portuguese had to march to the west they must have crossed the Tellaré, a river nearly as large as the Takazzé, before reaching the latter. In the rainy season, which was then on, both are large rivers, and both unfordable for days together.[1] Towards the south no large river intervenes before the Takazzé is reached; it is there at its nearest point to Wofla, and although the road crosses it near its head, still, as Markham points out, the Abyssinian expedition, who were on this road, could see that in the rains a very considerable body of water passed down it. These considerations lead to the conclusion that the outward march of the Portuguese lay towards the south; but there is still another very strong reason. Shoa, where Galâwdêwos then was, lies south of Wofla, and any hill that he would have to cross to reach the Portuguese in Wofla must also lie to the south, and not to the west of the latter place. In that direction, and not very far south from the river Takazzé, lies the great hill of Amba Sel,[2] adjoining the royal Amba Geshen; this Amba, both in size and difficulty of access, agrees with Castanhoso's description. It lies some sixty-five miles south of Wofla, that is, nearer than Amba Gideon, and its name, Sel, is not very unlike Couto's, if the latter be indeed Saloa. Krapf, in his journey, took from April 10th to April 16th, 1842, to march from Amba Sel to Wofla; but

---

[1] Wylde, pp. 189 and 341.
[2] Magdala is only a few miles distant.

he travelled on foot, and his maximum was twelve miles a day. The Falashas, or Jews, are usually connected with Semien, and possibly this may have led to a search for the amba in that direction; but there were Jews on this hill also.[1] Amba Geshen, which adjoins Amba Sel, was captured by the Muhamedans in 1539, when, as the Ethiopian chronicles put it, "they slew the Israelites by the edge of the sword."[2] Basset, it is true, explains this term by saying that it was applied to the members of the royal family, as descendants of Solomon. Ápropos of quite another matter, MacQueen, in his Introduction to Isenberg and Krapf, derives Amba Sel from Amba Israel; of course MacQueen was not a philologist. There is another point to be noticed. Castanhoso says the hill lies nearly west from the straits (Bab-el Mandeb), and may be forty or fifty leagues distant from it. The direction is about correct, but the distance is nearer eighty leagues; the point, however, to be noticed is that the hill and the straits are brought into connection at all. This would be done in a case where the hill stood up looking over lower ground, as Amba Sel does over the lowlands to the east, but would hardly be done where high hills intervened, as they do between the Semien peaks and the sea; as we have seen, the same expression is applied to Zabul. That the hill was not more securely held was due partly to the withdrawal of troops by the Imam Ahmad to repel the Portuguese incursion, and partly to the peculiarity of the Muhamedans, who never made much use of these ambas. The Muhamedan commander of the hill, who was killed, is called Cide Amede, or Cide Hamed. The Jew inhabitants,

---

[1] It throws no light on this particular problem, but it is curious that there was a belief current among the Portuguese, before the expedition left Massowa, that the Preste John had taken refuge from the Grañ in the hill of the Jews (D. João de Castro, *Roteiro*, p. 69).

[2] Basset, *Études*, p. 109.

astonished at the feat of arms, became Christians. If the hill of the Jews be Amba Sel, there are difficulties in the route followed by the remnant of the Portuguese some months later; these will be adverted to subsequently.

D. Christovão's presentiment was correct. When he returned he found that the Imam Ahmad had moved his army from Zabul, and was in position in close proximity to the camp; he had that day opened fire, disclosing his full force. During the rains some palisades had been erected between the Portuguese camp and the foot of the hill on which it stood, and the Muhamedans were on the other side of the palisades, at the foot of the same hill. There was, perhaps, still time to have escaped by a hurried flight, but D. Christovão considered that the risks to be run in a retreat were greater than those to be run in accepting battle; and at this distance of time, and in ignorance of many of the facts, it is impossible to say that he was wrong; his error, as pointed out before, lay in camping where he did at all. The following day, August 28th or 30th (accounts differ), the Muhamedans advanced to the attack. The Portuguese tactics appear to have consisted in a series of rushes of small bodies of men, to drive the assailants from a threatened point. Such a course could have but one ending: the enemy gave way to the rush, and then shot down the Portuguese in the retreat, and the tiny army wearied itself in useless efforts. By the evening D. Christovão was himself helpless with two wounds, his standard was captured, four out of his five captains had been killed, together with more than half their men, many of the remainder were wounded, the palisades had been captured, and the camp entered. As evening fell, the wearied remnant of the Portuguese force escaped up the hill in company with the Queen. Bermudez seems to have fled early. The pursuit at first was slack, as the camp was being looted, and the Portuguese had time before morning to put some distance between themselves and the battlefield. During the night, however, D. Christovão and a few companions became separated from the rest, and hid in a thicket, where they were discovered at dawn by the Muhamedans. D. Christovão was taken to the Imam Ahmad, who, after torture, slew him with his own hand. Bermudez states that D. Christovão had appropriated the widow of Cide Hamed, killed on the Jew's hill, and he intimates, rather than says, that this woman betrayed his hiding-place. It would almost seem from Castanhoso's own narrative, that D. Christovão was betrayed by a woman, and that this is the foundation of the semi-miraculous account he gives of an old woman, an account invented to cover his leader's weakness. There were very few Abyssinians on the Portuguese side in this battle, and the Imam Ahmad directed all his energy to destroying the Portuguese, who were his really dangerous opponents, and it would naturally appear to him that he had succeeded. Not only had he killed nearly all their leaders, and some two hundred of the rank and file, but he had captured their artillery, their small arms, their camp, and all their ammunition; it might well seem that the few fugitives, with no weapons, and defenceless in an unknown country, were enemies he could afford to neglect. He, therefore, after dismissing the Turkish contingent, and retaining only his ordinary complement of two hundred matchlockmen, betook himself to his old camping ground on the Tzâna lake.

Before continuing the history of the fugitive Portuguese it will be well to conclude with D. Christovão. The miraculous stories connected with his death were possibly suited to the then Portuguese taste, but it is bootless to examine them in the hope of finding truth. D. Francisco da Gama, fourth Conde da Vidigueira, was Viceroy of India from 1597-1600. He does not seem to have taken steps at that time to recover the remains of his great uncle, D. Christovão, but, after his return to Portugal, he entered into correspondence on the subject with Ruy Lourenço de Tavora, Governor of India from 1608-10. Nothing came of this correspondence, but when D. Francisco went back for a second term as Viceroy, 1622-27, he commissioned D. Afonso Mendes, who went out as Patriarch of Abyssinia in 1625, to make a search, at the same time writing to the King of Abyssinia, asking for his help. Lobo was deputed by Mendes, and his account will be found commencing on p. 95 of Le Grand's book. The expedition was organised on a large scale in 1626, for with Lobo was joined Tecla Giyorgis, Viceroy of Tigré, and brother-in-law of the then king, who took with him a considerable army. The site of the battlefield was occupied by the Gallas, and the journey, which was of fifteen days from the Jesuits' head-quarters at Fremoña, near Aksum, was considered a dangerous undertaking. Their guides were, firstly, an old Muhamedan—so old that he had to be carried—who professed to have been an eye-witness of D. Christovão's death; in this case he must have been very old, for that event had occurred more than eighty years previously; and secondly, a Christian who had heard the story from his father.

Certain Portuguese[1] were guided to a large heap of stones from under which they claim to have recovered "ces prétieuse Reliques;" what they were is not stated; from a neighbouring spring, where the guides said that D. Christovão's head (with that of a dog) had been thrown, were recovered some teeth and a jaw-bone. During the whole halt at this place they were very hurried, and in

---

[1] Lobo's narrative would lead to the belief that he accompanied the searchers. Almeida, in his *Lettre dell' Ethiopia* (p. 59-62), makes it clear that Lobo did not accompany them. They, after a search of all one night and part of the next day, brought back whatever they did bring to Lobo.

continual fear of a Galla attack. The remains were taken to India, on their way to Europe, in 1627, by P. Thomé Barreto, together with a helmet and suit of mail, said to have been D. Christovão's, and an image of the Virgin he always carried: the two former had been captured from the Muhamedans in battle in 1577. The Conde da Vidigueira was accused of parsimony in not rewarding the finders of these remains; we can understand his reasons.

This story might perhaps have been allowed to fall by its own weight, but there are two remarks pertinent to it: the first, that D. Christovão's head was taken to Zebid directly after his death, and not thrown into a spring with the head of a dog; consequently, the jaw-bone and the teeth were not genuine. The second is, that as to whatever was found under the stones, Lobo and his companions proceed on the assumption that the Abyssinian custom is like that of some other countries, namely, that every passer-by throws a stone on the place where anyone dying a violent death has been buried, but this is quite incorrect; in Abyssinia heaps of stones are certainly frequent, but they are made by every passer-by adding a stone to the heap at the spot where a particular church is first visible.[1] The existence of a heap of stones, then, proves nothing as to D. Christovão's relics.[2]

Of the Portuguese who escaped the battle, fifty fled with Manuel da Cunha, and, believing themselves to be the only survivors of the engagement, made their way through Tigré to Debarwa, intending to get shipping at Massowa

---

[1] See Pearce, vol. i, p. 328. Bent (p. 70) cites a similar Greek custom; see also Harris, vol. ii, p. 254.

[2] See Esteves Pereira's edition of *Castanhoso* (p. xxxvi), for an account of the sword, apparently a genuine relic of the expedition of D. Christovão, obtained by Dr. Paulitschke in Harar, and presented by him to the Geographical Society of Lisbon.

for India. In this they failed. One hundred and twenty Portuguese, with the Queen, took refuge in the Jew's hill, recently captured by D. Christovão, where they were hospitably received by the commander, whom he had made a Christian. They were soon after joined by Galâwdêwos, who was accompanied by a few followers (far too small a force to have fought their way past the hill if uncaptured), and by the mulatto Ayres Dias, known to the Abyssinians as Marcos, whom D. Christovão had sent to the King as an envoy soon after he himself had reached Wofla. The date of Galâwdêwos's arrival at the hill of the Jews is not mentioned by Castanhoso, but it would appear that he puts it about the middle of September, as he states that Galâwdêwos got there ten days after the Portuguese. According to the Ethiopian accounts, however, Galâwdêwos joined his mother and the remnant of the Portuguese in Semien, in October (*teqemt*).[1] From this point indeed, onwards, until the final battle of Wainadega is reached, the account in the Ethiopian chronicles differs considerably from that of the Portuguese, and I cannot but think that the former is rather confused and is less probable than the latter. For instance, the abridged chronicle[2] makes Galâwdêwos start on a raiding expedition from the Imam Ahmad's headquarters (Darasgué). It also implies that Galâwdêwos was, shortly after his arrival from Shoa, strong enough to face the Muhamedan force without the help of the Portuguese. The latter, after losing all their weapons at the battle in Wofla, required time to re-arm themselves from Debra Damo, and to make gunpowder from the raw materials locally obtained. By dating the action of Woggera (which is mentioned below), November 8th, the

---

[1] Basset, *Études*, p. 111. See also Conzelman, § 15; the statement here is not so definite.
[2] Basset, *Études*, p. 111.

Ethiopian chronicles do not give time for the Portuguese to refit, and allow little time for Galâwdêwos' forces to collect. These dates further imply that the Imam Ahmad was cognisant of the existence of a fighting force in his vicinity as early as the beginning of November; this would have given him considerably over three months to prepare before the decisive battle at the end of February, 1543. Had he had this leisure, he would certainly have been more ready to crush his opponent than he was. The Portuguese accounts, on the other hand, describe the whole campaign as short and sharp, and as a surprise for the Muhamedans—as indeed to be successful it must have been.

The difficulty in the Portuguese account is, that if their final advance began from Amba Sel, there is hardly time enough allowed for the march from there to the shores of Lake Tzâna, between February 6th, when they started, and February 21st, the date of the battle of Wainadega. It requires the Portuguese and Abyssinians to have marched sixteen to twenty miles a day, and also to have fought two actions in that time, and we know of no other instance of their having accomplished this rate of marching. It may be that in October, either before or after the junction of the Portuguese force with Galâwdêwos, the headquarters moved to Semien. If this had been the case, the conflicting narratives, except as to the date of the battle of Woggera, could have been reconciled, and almost all difficulties removed. This course, too, would have been a very natural one, because Galâwdêwos had more adherents in Semien than elsewhere in Abyssinia, and the Portuguese would have been rather closer to their real base on Debra Damo. The discrepant accounts may mean this, but it is a mere guess, and cannot be definitely adopted as fact. It may, however, be pointed out that Bermudez, in his chapter xxiv, says, that the Portuguese did leave the hill of the Jews, and did march to other hills in another district, where Galâwdêwos joined them.

There is a point on which Castanhoso and Bermudez differ, in which the latter is to some extent supported by a letter of Galâwdêwos. Castanhoso says that, after the death of D. Christovão, the Portuguese refused to appoint any new commander; they determined to fight under the banner of *Sancta Misericordia* until they had avenged their loss. Bermudez, on the other hand, says that, even before he heard that D. Christovão was dead, he appointed one Afonso Caldeira (of whom little is known)[1], and that, on his death from an accident a few weeks later he, at the request of Galâwdêwos, appointed Ayres Dias. He allows that there were several of the Portuguese to whom this appointment was very distasteful. Galâwdêwos, in his letter to the King of Portugal, of December 6th, 1550, says that he appointed Ayres Dias commander of the Portuguese, and he repeats this in a letter to the Governor of India. Ayres Dias was a man of no family, a mulatto, a mere servant: it is hardly conceivable that any Portuguese could have committed the blunder of suggesting him as a fit commander of his countrymen, many of them fidalgos of position. At the same time, the disabilities of Ayres Dias were disabilities which Galâwdêwos, unaccustomed to Portuguese class distinctions, would be unable to appreciate. Ayres Dias knew the language, and was well known to the Abyssinians as Marcos. As the bearer of D. Christovão's letter he would be thrown much into Galâwdêwos' company, and would have many opportunities of ingratiating himself. That Galâwdêwos made, or wanted to make, him captain, is certain; it is at the same time equally certain that the

---

[1] According to Couto (*Dec. V*, Bk. VIII, chap. xiii), D. Christovão put this man in charge of the convoy of horses, when he hurried back from the hill of the Jews just before the battle in Wofla.

Portuguese, or at least those of the better sort, refused to accept him, and preferred to fight under their banner of *Sancta Misericordia*. So much is, indeed, clear between the lines of Castanhoso's narrative; for the dissensions reached such a pitch that as many as fifty Portuguese, under the banner of the Holy Compassion, accompanied Castanhoso to Massowa, in the hope of getting shipping there, under a promise to return if the Governor of India sent someone whom they could recognise as captain over the whole band. Bermudez' statement that he appointed Ayres Dias is merely one of the many reckless assertions in his book, made to enhance his position and support his pretensions.

Taking the Portuguese account, then, we find that by the commencement of February, Galâwdêwos had obtained as many adherents as he could hope for, before defeating the Imam Ahmad. The Portuguese under Manuel da Cunha had not yet joined, but the other survivors of the battle of the previous August were re-armed, and straining at the leash to be allowed to revenge their leader's death. On the Shrove Tuesday of that year, February 6th, 1543, the allies started. Before getting far they heard of a force, under the orders of some of the Imam Ahmad's generals, which was stationed at Woggera, a little south-west of Semien; this they attacked and defeated, killing the Muhamedan commander, Mir Ezman.[1] From the prisoners they learned that the Imam Ahmad was only five days' march away on the banks of the Tzâna lake. Pressing on, the rival forces came in sight of each other at Wainadega. Neither Castanhoso nor Correa preserves this name for us; Couto calls it "Oenad," and Paez "Oinadaga." Bruce[2] passed through a village on the south-west corner of the

---

[1] The Ethiopian accounts mention Talila and Sid Muhamed as well as Ezman among the slain. This is the battle they date November.

[2] Vol. v, p. 210.

lake, which he says was called Wainadega or Granber: that is, Grañ's defile, from the Grañ's death there. Lobo tells us[1] that the Grañ, feeling death near, struck a tree with his sabre, which Lobo had seen, which tree had since that time been called "Grangniber," or "Jaaf Gragné," Grăn's defile or tree. The Ethiopian chronicles say that the Grañ fell on the slopes of Zăntâra[2] at a place called Grañbar. It is allowed by nearly all authorities that this decisive battle took place in Dembya.

Bruce's identification is very circumstantial, and it seems presumption to question the decision of such an authority. The difficulty that presents itself to my mind is, to understand by what possible strategy one army starting from Darasgué, and the other from Woggera, neither desiring to avoid an engagement, and both starting-places being north of Lake Tzâna, the decisive battle could have taken place at its south-west corner. The place referred to by Bruce is marked Uendighe on modern maps, but it is not in Dembya at all. Some old maps place some mountains in Dembya north-east of Lake Tzâna and east of Gondar, called Wainadega, just where we should expect the two armies to have met. The French map shows Mount Wehni, south-east of Gondar, just where the Italian map has Ueni, and the latter has also Mount Ueene just north of this and east of Gondar, on the 38 deg. of E. lon., but neither has the name Wainadega.[3] Combes

---

[1] Legrand, p. 94.

[2] Is Zăntâra connected with the Tzâna lake?

[3] Rohlfs (p. 282) says the Abyssinians divide their country into: (a) Kolla, the lowlands; (b) Deka Woina, the country from fifteen hundred to three thousand metres above the sea; (c) Deka simply, that is the country above three thousand metres. Although (b) usually only ranges to three thousand metres, in places in the south, and even in the north, where the land has a south or south-west aspect, it may range to four thousand metres. As Woina is the Greek οἶνος, wine, the name really means the country where vines grow, and the derivation of the word shows that Greeks introduced

and Tamisier crossed this mountainous country northeast of Lake Tzâna in 1835, and they call it Ouenadega.[1] It was here, I think, that the decisive engagement occurred. Tellez says,[2] that after the battle the Emperor "coming down from the high ground of Oinadega, encamped near the great lake." The battle, therefore, was fought among the hills.

The Christians and Muhamedans remained for some days in sight of each other; there were skirmishes, but, knowing the importance of the engagement, neither side cared to risk a decisive battle. The Christians, too, had hopes of the arrival of the Portuguese under Manuel da Cunha, who they heard were coming after them by forced marches. In these preliminary encounters Azmach Keflo, who appears to have been the Fitauraris, or leader of the vanguard of the Abyssinian forces, distinguished himself, and inflicted such losses by cutting off convoys, that the Imam Ahmad determined on his destruction; he effected it by a misuse of the white flag. This event put an end to the procrastination, for Azmach Keflo's death so greatly discouraged the Abyssinian forces that Galâwdêwos was compelled to offer battle before his army entirely melted away. On the 21st February, 1543, the Abyssinians and Portuguese advanced to the attack. The little band of Portuguese cared nothing for the main body of the Imam Ahmad's army: their quarrel was with the Imam Ahmad himself, and with his two hundred Turkish matchlockmen; one of them, John the Gallician, pressing through the throng, levelled his matchlock and shot the Imam Ahmad in the breast; his own life was the price he paid for his

---

the vine. Wainadega is merely, therefore, Deka Woina, not the specific name of a country, but given to certain tracts. As the cultivation of the vine has died out, the name would seem to have disappeared from modern maps.

[1] Vol. ii, p. 36. [2] Bk. II, chap. xvii, p. 137.

success.[1] The dying leader rode away from the field, and his fall decided the fortunes of the day; only forty of the two hundred Turks survived the defeat, but in their flight they carried off Del Wanbara, the Imam Ahmad's widow, and the treasure he had amassed by the spoliation of Abyssinia. This victory was decisive; Galâwdêwos had much fighting before him, but during his lifetime Abyssinia was never again prostrate before an alien conqueror.

The special task of the Portuguese in Abyssinia was now ended, but their country had abandoned them to their fate, and the Indian government was unable, even if it had been willing, to send ships to the Red Sea to bring them back, without a display of force that would have severely taxed its resources. Castanhoso came away in a chance vessel in 1544, but its commander, Diogo de Reynoso, got into serious difficulty with the authorities in consequence of his conduct in the Red Sea, where he was guilty of various piratical acts. Correa tells us of five other Portuguese who escaped, he does not say how, in 1550. Bermudez got a vessel to take him back in 1556, and there were probably a few others, such as those of whom Couto speaks, who returned while D. Constantine de Bragança was Viceroy (1558-61); but the main body remained in the country, married Abyssinian women, and were by degrees merged in the population.[2] From the date of the death of the Imam Ahmad the Ethiopian chronicles, which never say much of the Portuguese and their exploits lest a reflection should be cast on Abys-

---

[1] Bermudez' tale of Pero de Lião and the Grañ's ear, which has crept into even the fragment of the Ethiopian chronicle translated by Guidi, is, I think, an undoubted fable.

[2] The Iteghe, or Queen, who befriended Bruce was proud of the Portuguese blood in her veins. The Portuguese who escaped in 1550 probably brought with them Galâwdêwos' letter of that year, which is translated in this volume (p. 115, below); if so, Diogo Dias would have been one of them.

sinian glories, only mention them intermittently. They give us, however, to understand that they had numerous disputes about religious matters with the representatives of the Abyssinian church, thus confirming the statements of Bermudez. Couto, in his *Decades*, and the letters from missionaries in Abyssinia, somewhat fill up the gap.

Altogether, one hundred and seventy Portuguese escaped from the battle in Wofla, namely, one hundred and twenty with the Queen, and fifty with Manuel da Cunha; of these, apparently, ninety-three were still living in Abyssinia in 1555,[1] that is, thirteen years after the battle, but there were, if Bermudez is correct,[2] other Portuguese there also. His story is, that while he was in Debarwa—and he appears to have been there from 1554 till he left the country—there came to Abyssinia from Egypt a Venetian, whom he calls Micer Çunkar, to arrange for the ransom of forty Portuguese prisoners in the hands of the Turks; that Galâwdêwos duly ransomed them, and that they were brought to Abyssinia. This story may possibly be true, for we know, from other sources, that several Portuguese were captured by the Turks in Pir Beg's attempt to drive them out of the Persian Gulf in 1552, when the fort of Muscat and several vessels were captured.[3] There is a tradition, mentioned by Salt, that the Wajárat province was peopled by the descendents of the Portuguese, and that these descendants were noted for their physique and their fidelity. If this be true, it is contrary to the general experience regarding cross-breeds.

Bermudez made his claim to be the head of the Abyssinian Church, and to receive the submission of Galâwdêwos to the Latin Church, even before the Imam

---

[1] Couto, *Dec. VII*, Bk. 1, chap. viii.   [2] Chap. lv.
[3] Four contemporary letters describing this incursion will be found in India Office MSS. (*Corpo Chronologico*, vol. ii).

Ahmad's death, and that in the most haughty and offensive way. The demand both irritated and astonished Galâwdêwos, who, as we shall see later, sent a letter by Castanhoso to the King of Portugal asking who Bermudez was, and what was the foundation for his claims. In the meantime the Portuguese were kept in a ferment by Bermudez' exhortations, until they had recourse to arms.[1] Galâwdêwos quieted this mutiny with considerable tact, and then banished Bermudez to the country of Gafat, which lies south of Gojame, on the right bank of the Nile. Bermudez was here, on his own showing, guilty of considerable violence; and after some months' detention he effected his escape under the terror caused by his actions. By the time he returned to Galâwdêwos, Ayres Dias, who through all the disputes had sided with Galâwdêwos against Bermudez, was dead, and Gaspar de Sousa had been made commander of the Portuguese. Meanwhile, after an interregnum of several years, a new Patriarch, Abuna Yusaf, had been sent from Alexandria, and the pretensions of Bermudez to be Patriarch of the Abyssinians received their final blow. On the pretext of defending the frontier, Galâwdêwos deported the Portuguese, and Bermudez with them, to the hot and unhealthy provinces of Doaro, Bali, and Fatagar, from which they were expelled a few months later by the Gallas, when those provinces became separated from the Abyssinian empire. Bermudez afterwards settled in a place he calls Bethmariam : there appear to be several places called Beyt Mariam in Abyssinia, and it is to one of these presumably that he refers, though to which it is not clear; he by this time had lost whatever credit he possessed. An anecdote preserved by several writers seems to be connected with this place, and his departure

---

[1] It is allowed that the influence of Sabla Wangel, widow of Lebna Dengel, was always used in softening the anger of both Galâwdêwos and Minas against the Portuguese.

from it, though Bermudez does not himself mention it.[1] It is said that Bermudez was accused of appropriating a certain gold church vessel, which on search was found in his house, having been placed there by his accusers. Bermudez after this made his way to Debarwa, and waited in the neighbourhood of that town until he heard of the arrival of a vessel under João Peixoto; when going down to Massowa, on a subterfuge, he says, he obtained a passage, and left in March, 1556. He remained for a year, on the way home, in St. Helena, and reached Portugal in 1558. In Portugal he lived in retirement, in S. Sebastião da Pedreira, where Couto saw him. The publication of Castanhoso's book aroused him, and in 1565 he published his own short account, which has been translated here; he intended it apparently as a reply to Castanhoso. Five years later, on March 30th, 1570, he died. He was buried at the door of the hermitage in which he lived, but in 1653 his body was transferred to the parish church of S. Sebastião, where, under the arch of the main chapel, his tomb may yet be seen.[2] It is recorded that his articulation was indistinct, as the Turks had cut off part of his tongue.

Meanwhile, as the attention of the Jesuits had been drawn to Abyssinia as a hopeful field for their enterprise, their influence both in Rome and Portugal had been exerted to start a missionary crusade in that country.[3]

---

[1] For this story see Couto, *Dec. VII*, Bk. I, chap. i, and Gouvea, Bk. I, chap. vii. *Oriente Conquistado Conq.* 5, Div. 2, § 15, has an account rather hostile to Bermudez' claims; but this story is not given.

[2] See Preface to the edition of his book, published 1875, from which the date 1653 is taken.

[3] This short sketch of the end of the Portuguese force in Abyssinia is taken from Couto's *Seventh Decade*. He is rather prolix; the following places may be consulted: Bk. I, chaps. i, vii, viii; Bk. III, chaps. iii, vi, vii; Bk. IV, chaps. iv, vi; Bk. VII, chaps. iv, v, xii; Bk. VIII, chap. ix; Bk. X, chaps. iv, vi. Much valuable assistance has been obtained from Esteves Pereira, *Historia de Minas*, especially from the notes on p. 73 and following pages.

The matter was referred to Ignatius Loyola, and in 1555, on his nomination, João Nunez Barreto was consecrated Patriarch, and André de Oviedo, Bishop *in partibus*, while Belchior Carneiro was directed to proceed to India to be there consecrated Bishop; all these were, of course, Jesuits. It is very significant that in the proceedings regarding these men there is no mention of Bermudez, or of any powers conferred on him by the Pope. The final orders as to these appointments were passed by Pope Paul IV; they had been for some time under consideration, but had been delayed by the successive deaths of Pope Julius III and Pope Marcellus II; consequently, information of what was impending had gone out in the ships of 1554, with instructions to send an envoy to Abyssinia to report on the actual state of affairs in that country. These orders led to the despatch of Mestre Gonçalo, a Jesuit, with another Jesuit, Fulgencio Freire, and Diogo Dias do Prestes, one of the followers of D. Christovão da Gama, who had returned from Abyssinia; their instructions were to sound the disposition of Galâwdêwos, and to discover whether he was inclined to abandon the customs of the Abyssinians, and submit himself to the Latin Church. This expedition left Goa in February, 1555, in a vessel commanded by Fernão Farto, and landing at Arkiko proceeded up country.[1] Mestre Gonçalo found before long that Galâwdêwos had no intention of abandoning the customs of his ancestors to adopt the Latin ritual. He consequently returned to the coast, and picking up Bermudez at Massowa, was back in Goa in May, 1556. In the ships that reached India at the end of 1556 there arrived the episcopate and the Jesuit missionaries selected for Abyssinia, as well as an ambas-

---

[1] Conzelman (§ 47) refers to their arrival in Abyssinia. In Ludolf's *Commentary* (p. 474) will be found a letter purporting to be Mestre Gonçalo's report on this journey. Ludolf states that he has brought together the substance from more than one source.

sador from the King of Portugal. The King's orders required that this mission should be sent to its destination, accompanied by a force of five hundred men, and a fleet corresponding to its importance. Francisco Barreto, the then Governor of Portuguese India, however, not only knew from Mestre Gonçalo's report the futility of the proposed mission, but also found himself, from lack of men and money, entirely unable to comply with the royal command. At the pressing instance of the ecclesiastics a council of local theologians and a few fidalgos was called, and at this it was decided that as it was impossible to send at that time the force the King had ordered, that the person of the Patriarch should not be risked, but that André de Oviedo and a few companions should proceed to Abyssinia: as a matter of fact, the so-called Patriarch never landed in that country.

Early in 1557 Oviedo reached Arkiko, to find an advanced guard of the Turks in possession of Massowa. The garrison was, however, small, and made no attempt to intercept his party.[1] Oviedo's mission had the success that Mestre Gonçalo's report predicted: Galâwdêwos sturdily refused to depart from the faith of his ancestors, and Oviedo's violence would have led a less politic prince to stern measures of repression: that Bishop, for instance, directed the Portuguese to no longer obey the heretic and contumacious Emperor Galâwdêwos. Apparently, however, while that King was alive, Oviedo did not proceed to the extremities of which he was guilty in the time of that King's successor. Soon after Oviedo arrived in Abyssinia very large Turkish reinforcements reached Massowa, and access to the country by that route was closed to the Portuguese; the Turks advanced as far as Debarwa, which they captured after defeating Isaac the Baharnagash; but

---

[1] Conzelman (§ 54) refers to the Bishop's arrival in Abyssinia.

their further progress was temporarily stayed, and their success neutralised, by an epidemic that destroyed practically the whole force. In March, 1559, Galâwdêwos marched in person against Nur, the successor of the Imam Ahmad, already mentioned as the candidate for the hand of Del Wanbara, who had invaded his country from the south. In the battle that ensued, on the 23rd of the month, Galâwdêwos was killed, as were also nearly all the few Portuguese who accompanied him in the campaign. The Muhamedan force was recalled by troubles within its own frontier, and Minas, the brother of Galâwdêwos, ascended the throne of Abyssinia. Minas had been a convert to Muhamedanism while in the power of the Imam Ahmad, but had on his return to Abyssinia reverted to Christianity. His policy towards the Latin Bishop was the same as that of his brother Galâwdêwos, but he appears to have been an overbearing and harsh ruler. He forbade Abyssinians to enter the Latin churches, banishing those who disobeyed, whether converts or not; even the wives of the Portuguese were not allowed to join their husbands' communion. The bishop was banished for opposing these regulations. A cabal, which included Isaac the Baharnagash, was soon formed among the Abyssinians against him. Oviedo, the bishop, undoubtedly fomented these troubles, and intrigued against Minas, and several of the Portuguese openly joined the rebels, and were involved in the defeat that Isaac suffered at the hands of Minas on July 2nd, 1561; but the Portuguese who had sided with Minas obtained his consent to the return of the bishop from exile. Isaac, escaping from the battle in which he was overthrown, made peace with the Turks, who through him again—and this time more or less permanently—obtained possession of the northern provinces of Abyssinia; their combined forces, assisted by a body of malcontent Portuguese, defeated Minas in a pitched battle on April

22nd, 1562.[1] The bishop and missionaries remained from this time until Minas' death, on January 30th, 1563, with the insurgents into whose hands they had fallen. The only result of the intrigues of the Portuguese was the entire destruction of their credit, and from this time they disappear as a separate body: an ignominious ending for the gallant companions of D. Christovão. As the Portuguese historian Couto puts it, "Our men being discredited so that none of the Emperors would afterwards trust them, or ask more help of men from the Viceroys."[2]

Of Castanhoso not much is known beyond what we learn from his book;[3] he was a native of Santarem, and sprung from a noble Spanish family. The date of his original departure for India is unknown. On his return to Portugal from Abyssinia, King D. João III made him, on July 13th, 1548, a knight of the Order of Christ, and at some unknown date made him commander of S. Romão de Fonte cuberta, a village in the archbishopric of Braga, of the value of seventy thousand reals annually. There is a receipt for his contribution to the expenses, dated January 6th, 1551, so that he was then in enjoyment of it. He married D. Violante da Serra, and had one son, D. Afonso de Castanhoso. Castanhoso was captain of the *Conceição*, one of the six ships of the fleet which started on April 2nd, 1554, convoying D. Pedro Mascarenhas when he went as Viceroy to India. The date of Castanhoso's return is not known; he was certainly in India in October,

---

[1] This battle was fought in Enderta. The Turkish pasha is called Zemur pasha.

[2] Couto, *Dec. VII*, Bk. x, chap. vi.

[3] For the few facts of Castanhoso's life I am indebted to Esteves Pereira's edition of Castanhoso's book, in which the original documents are printed.

1555. The date of his death is equally unknown. The printer of the early edition of his work speaks of him as still alive on July 27th, 1564; he was dead before July 1st, 1565, as his commandership was vacant on that date. D. Violante da Serra was daughter of Afonso Lopes, a clerk in the Lisbon custom house, and of Branca da Serra. On August 23rd, 1563, the King D. Sebastião granted Afonso Lopes a pension of forty thousand reals; and with the royal permission he gave his daughter one half from February 19th, 1567. On July 26th, 1567, the King granted this pension to her personally, and on September 27th, 1571, the King confirmed a grant of September 13th, 1568, to Afonso de Castanhoso of the twenty thousand reals vacant by his mother's death.

Castanhoso's book was first published in Lisbon in 1564, with the title: " Historia | Das cousas que o muy esforça | do capitão Dom Christovão da | Gama fez nos Reynos do Pre | ste Ioão, com quatrocẽtos Por | tugueses que consigo leuou | Impressa por Ioã da Barreyra | E por elle dirigida ao muyto | magnifico & illustre señor Dõ | Francisco de Portugal." |

It was dedicated to the son of the then Conde da Vidigueira. Copies of this edition became very rare, and in 1855 it was reprinted by the Royal Lisbon Academy as No. 2 of vol. i of their Collection of reprints of works connected with the History of the Navigations, Voyages, and Conquests of the Portuguese. In 1888 it was translated and published, with notes in Italian, with the title " Storia della spedizione Portoghese in Abissinia narrata da Michele de Castagnoso. Corpo do estado Maior Italiano." The notes are curiously uneven in value. The British Museum has neither the first edition nor this Italian translation. Finally, another text, from which the translation here given has been made, was published in 1898 by the Lisbon Geographical Society, among their quarcentenary publications, with the title "Dos feitos | de | D. Christovam da Gama | em | Ethiopia." | It is hard to over-estimate the value of this edition. The text differs in certain small particulars from that of the earlier printed edition; omitting mere verbal changes, these differences have been mentioned in the notes to this translation. The numbering of the chapters in the two texts differs, as what in the earlier printed edition is chapter one becomes in this an unnumbered introduction—the earlier printed text has therefore twenty-nine chapters while this has twenty-eight; in other respects the division is the same. The manuscript from which this text was printed gives, it is believed, the text as it was before the printer of the first edition revised it. It is considered to be a copy made in the eighteenth century, and as at regular intervals blanks have been left for words, it is probable that the old manuscript from which the copy was made had become worn. In the Geographical Society's reprint these blanks have been marked by brackets, and the omissions supplied from the early printed text; it has not been considered necessary to mark these in the translation. It is conjectured that the original manuscript from which this copy was made was that presented by Miguel de Castanhoso to King João III. The copy has been preserved in the Royal Library of Ajuda. The Portuguese editor detects in the language of the treatise traces of Castanhoso's Spanish ancestry.

The other complete work, of which a translation is given here, is that of D. João Bermudez. It was first published in 1565, with the title, "Esta he hũa breue re | lação da embaixada q̃ o Patri | archa dõ Ioão Bermudez trou | xe do Emperador da Ethiopia, chamado | vulgarmente Preste Ioão, ao christianisſi | mo, & zelador da fee de Christo Rey de | Portugal dom Ioão o terceiro deste no | me: dirigida ao muy alto & poderoso, de | felicissima esperança,

f

Rey tãbem de Por | tugal dom Sebastião o primeiro deste no | me. Em a qual tãbem conta a morte de | dom Christovão da gama: & dos suceſſos | que acontecerão aos Portugueſes que fo | rão em ſua companhia | q Em Lixboa en caſa de Fran | ciſco Correa Impreſſor do Cardal | Inffante | Anno de | 1565" | Copies of this edition are very rare indeed; the British Museum has one of the very few known. A picturesque but incomplete, and in some respects unfaithful, translation of this was published by Purchas in his *Pilgrimes*[1] in 1625.

It ill becomes a translator, who is liable to blunder himself, to carp unadvisedly at his predecessors' work; still the unfaithfulness of the work in Purchas must be pointed out, and the criticism made must be justified. It was only a peculiarity of spelling, perhaps, to translate the last words of chapter i, *Patriarcha e Pōtifice daq̃lla See*, as Patriarch and Bishop of the Sea. But it misled Bruce, who wondered of what ocean Bermudez could be bishop, and through Bruce it has misled certain modern scholars. "Sea" should of course be "see;" but to translate in chap. xiv, "*hũ ouo de prata dos pègus*," as "a silver egg of Pegu," is unpardonable; Pègu is a sort of bird (Latin, *picus*), not the country Pegu. The last instance I will quote is from chapter xxviii, where he translates "*hum gomil rico dauentagem*" as a "Rich   of advantage," omitting the difficult word and mistranslating another. It is not only, however, in mistranslations that Purchas errs; he has abstracted Bermudez, and done it without showing that there have been omissions, and in such a way that it is impossible to judge from the abstract the trustworthiness of the original. As a consequence Bermudez has, for a long series of years, obtained a credit that, if the full text had been available, would not have been his. Owing to

---

[1] Purchas, Bk. VII, chap. vii, p. 1149, and following.

the extreme rarity of the original, this translation of Purchas has been widely used: thus even the erudite Ludolf never obtained a sight of Bermudez in the original, but had to trust to Purchas; and also Veyssière de la Croze could not obtain a copy of the book in Portuguese when writing his *Histoire du Christianisme d'Ethiopie et d'Armenie*, but had to trust the English translation.[1] In 1875 the Royal Academy of Lisbon published a reprint of the edition of 1565. From a copy of this reprint the translation here given has been made; in any case of doubt the edition of 1565 has been consulted; but the reprint appears to be exact.

Bermudez' claim to have been invested with considerable powers in the Abyssinian Church, both by delegation from the Abuna Marcos and by investiture by the Pope of Rome, requires some consideration. Gibbon, who had only before him the translation of Purchas, considered, following Ludolf, that "the author may be suspected of deceiving Abyssinia, Rome, and Portugal. His title to the rank of Patriarch is dark and doubtful."[2] Bermudez' own statement as to Abyssinia, in his chapter i, is that in 1535, when the Abuna Marcos was at the point of death, the then Preste, Lebna Dengel, begged him to institute Bermudez "in accordance with his use as his successor, and as Patriarch of that country as he had heretofore been;" this the "Patriarch" did, "first ordaining me in all the sacred orders." He goes on to say that, after numerous adventures he reached Rome, where Pope Paul III "confirmed me in what I had brought thence, and at my request rectified all, and ordered me to be appointed to the Chair of Alexandria,

---

[1] His book was published in 1739. He failed to obtain access to either Bermudez or Castanhoso, even in Portugal (see pp. 265 and 267). The latter he could not obtain in any shape, the former he obtained in Purchas. Ludolf also never saw Castanhoso's book (*Com.*, pp. 6 and 13). [2] Chap. xlvii.

and be called Patriarch and Pontifex of that see."[1] He was, he says, given the usual authenticated documents, which were examined and approved in Portugal, but were afterwards lost at the defeat of D. Christovão. The obvious objection to this is that, even though the originals may as alleged have been lost, copies of them must have existed in Rome, and traces of the verification in Portugal. No proofs founded on such papers have been produced, and whenever any statement as to Bermudez' position is examined, it can always be traced back ultimately to his own assertions as the sole authority.

Judging from contemporary narratives, we find that before he reached Abyssinia in 1541, Bermudez was known in India as the Patriarch of Abyssinia appointed by the Pope: this is what Correa calls him. The claim to have been made head of their Church by the Abyssinians themselves does not seem to have been made until after he had learned the death of Lebna Dengel. The final claim to be Patriarch of Alexandria, under the orders of the Pope, was advanced after the year 1555, when Barreto had been created Patriarch of Abyssinia, which excluded him from that dignity. Bermudez adhered to this final claim to the last: it appears in his book and it is inscribed on his tombstone.

First, as to exactly what Bermudez claims happened in Abyssinia. He says he was appointed by the Abuna, *in accordance with his use (côforme ao seu costume)*, his successor and Patriarch of that country. It is not a merely verbal criticism to say there never had been a "Patriarch of that country:" the only Patriarch recognised by the Abyssinians was he of Alexandria.

It will be well, before going further, to explain the con-

---

[1] In chapter lviii he says that the Pope gave him personal possession of the See of Alexandria, whatever that means.

stitution of the Abyssinian Church. The local head of that church was called the Abuna, and it was a fundamental rule—dating from at least as far back as the time of Tecla Haimanaut, in the late thirteenth or early fourteenth century, and probably from an earlier date even than that— that the Abyssinians should never elect one of their own countrymen as Abuna, but should obtain one nominated and appointed by the Patriarch of Alexandria. It was never the custom, therefore, for the Abuna, as Bermudez asserts, to nominate his successor; he was, as a matter of fact, strictly debarred from doing so. Of course, in 1535, Lebna Dengel was sorely pressed by his Muhamedan enemies, and he may have been glad to adopt even desperate measures to secure his own safety; but although the King of Abyssinia was supreme in ecclesiastical matters in Abyssinia, it would have been a desperate measure indeed to set aside, of his own motion, the whole constitution of the Abyssinian Church, and thus alienate the few followers who then adhered to him. Since 1516, however, the tolerant government of the Mamelukes had been superseded in Egypt by that of the Turks; and Alvarez tells us that a few years before he reached Abyssinia, as the Abuna Marcos was growing old, 2,000 ounces of gold had been sent to Egypt for a new Abuna, but the Turks had taken the gold and not sent the official asked for;[1] one

---

[1] Alvarez, p. 252. This payment of money for the Abuna gave rise to the sneer that the head of the Abyssinian Church was a slave who had been bought and sold. In Le Grand (p. 367) is a statement of De Maillet, French Consul in Cairo, that in his time (1700) the Copts held Abyssinia in such abhorrence, that the one selected to be Abuna had to be sent in chains to prevent him escaping. In Quatremere's *Mémoires sur l'Egypte*, vol. ii, p. 267, will be found his "Mémoire sur les relations des Princes Mamlouks avec l'Abyssinie." He states that the Arabic historians mention that from A.D. 1427 the kings of Abyssinia ceased to send tribute to the Coptish Patriarch. On the authority of an Arabic MS. history of Ibn Aias, he relates at length the reception of a body of five hundred Abyssinian pilgrims, who reached Egypt in 1516 on their way to Jerusalem; it had taken them nine months to get thus far on their journey. Although their presents

Abuna Joseph, younger than Abuna Marcos, and his understudy, had died while Alvarez was in the country. The Abyssinians may have despaired of getting a new Abuna from Egypt; but whether they did or not, neither Lebna Dengel nor the Abuna Marcos had the power to select the successor to the latter's post, and it is very improbable that such a revolution in the Abyssinian Church should have been the subject of the death-bed intrigue which Bermudez describes. Correa, who was in India when D. Estevão da Gama started on his Red Sea expedition, always speaks of D. João Bermudez as the ambassador of the Preste, and he sometimes adds, whom the Pope made Patriarch of Abyssinia. D. João de Castro, in his log of the voyage to the Red Sea, says a good deal about Abyssinia, but not one word to show that he had ever heard that he was travelling with so interesting a personage as a Portuguese who had been elected by the Abyssinians themselves as head of their own Church; yet, had he known it, his eager, curious mind would have seized with avidity on so remarkable a circumstance. There does not, indeed, seem to be any contemporary record of any claim to have been elected by the Abyssinians to the headship of their Church, made by Bermudez before his arrival at Massowa. It was at Massowa that Bermudez heard of the death of Lebna Dengel six months before; thus the Abuna Marcos was dead, Lebna Dengel was dead, and there was a free course for the exercise of his imagination, in an account of what had passed at an interview of which he was the only survivor.

Not only had the Abuna no power to select his successor, but he had no power to consecrate a bishop: he could merely ordain to the orders of deacon and priest, and

---

were considered inadequate, they were treated with consideration and allowed to proceed. This was not apparently the embassy referred to by Alvarez.

possibly Bermudez was ordained deacon and priest by the Abuna. In fact, his expression "all the sacred orders" would as applied to Abyssinia mean these orders only. Judging from the accounts of different authorities, it was not very difficult to obtain them; thus Alvarez saw the Abuna Marcos confer them. For deacons there was no examination; many of the candidates were babes in arms, who were taken from their mothers who could not enter the church.[1] "Their lamentations resemble those of kids in a yard without the mothers, when they are separated and are dying of hunger, because they finish the office at the hour of vespers; and they are without food, because they have to receive the communion . . . . . . it is an amazing thing the danger of the little ones, for even by the force of water they cannot make them swallow the sacrament, both on account of their tender age, and their much crying." The account of Bruce[2] is to the same effect, though told more in the style of a dinner-table *raconteur*. "A number of men and children present themselves at a distance, and there stand, from humility, not daring to approach him. He then asks who these men are? and they tell him they want to be deacons. On this, with a small iron cross in his hand, after making two or three signs, he blows with his mouth twice or thrice upon them saying, 'Let them be deacons.'" Bruce says there was an examination for the order of priest, which was that the candidate had to read a chapter of St. Mark in a language which the Abuna did not understand. Alvarez says, there were very few who did not pass; and as the latter saw two thousand three hundred and fifty-seven priests ordained

---

[1] Alvarez, p. 250.

[2] Bruce, vol. v, p. 5. He adds that on one occasion the whole Tigré army, with about one thousand women, were in the direction towards which the Abuna waved his cross and blew, and that he presumes that these became good deacons also.

by the Abuna on a particular day, it must have been easy work to become a priest—the more so as the Preste informed Alvarez that there were very few ordinations that day, the average, per ordination day, being between five thousand and six thousand. It is quite possible, therefore, that Bermudez received ordination by the Abyssinian rites from the Abuna.

There exists a letter of Leo X, of which Bermudez was possibly aware, that would at least have suggested to him that the idea of Rome supplying a head to the Abyssinian Church would be warmly received by the Pope. The letter was addressed to the King of Portugal, when the news of the arrival of the Abyssinian ambassador, Matheus, reached the Pope, and is dated 1514,[1] the subject-matter being the reconciliation of the Abyssinians with the Latin Church. In this it is suggested that, on the death of the Abuna Marcos, a Latin Patriarch should become head of the Abyssinian Church. The words used are: "peterque propterea ut interventu mortis ipsius Marci patriarche, ne christifideles patiantur apud ipsos detrimentum, eligamus successorem, interim cum nostrum et apostolice sedis legatum deputemus quo, maiore devotione populorem accepta ab apostolica sede auctoritate, que necessario ad fidem pertinent, pro animarum salute, prestare et exercere possit."

Bermudez' claim implies, of course, that he was consecrated a bishop, because, in his chapter xxix, he speaks of an archbishop whom he had made; and one of the points he most strongly urged on Galâwdêwos was the necessity of allowing him to reordain all the clergy of the Abyssinian Church according to the Latin rite. Hitherto, Bermudez' claims have been admitted, though with hesitation, and it has been agreed that they are based on some substratum of truth, though only his word can be adduced

---

[1] *Alguns Documentos*, p. 357. The reprint of the Latin is exact; it contains obvious mistakes, but the sense is clear.

in proof. It is clear from his own narrative that Galâwdêwos always steadily repudiated his pretensions, only temporarily conceding them on one occasion when very sorely pressed. If, however, Bermudez had any claims whatever to the position he assumes, there were certainly three persons who must have been cognisant each of at least part of the facts. They are first, Lebna Dengel, second the Pope, third the King of Portugal. It is fortunate that we have something, whether a letter or an act of each of these three personages to guide us; and all these indications are, it appears to me, hostile to Bermudez' claims. Of Lebna Dengel we have the letter to Bermudez, preserved for us by Correa, which was brought to India by the Fernão Farto mentioned by Bermudez in his chapter v.[1] This letter is an ordinary one from an employer to a factor; it mentions the commission of Bermudez to get soldiers and artificers, but there is not an expression in it to lead any one to believe that it was addressed by Lebna Dengel to the head of the Abyssinian Church. There is no distinct utterance of the Pope on the subject of Bermudez, and in fact none could be expected; but, while Bermudez was still in Abyssinia, the Pope appointed to that country a Patriarch and a bishop, and in their patents there is no reference to any previous appointment: a silence that seems, under the circumstances, to be conclusive that no appointment had been made of Bermudez to the Patriarchate of Abyssinia; this Patriarch and bishop are mentioned by Bermudez in his chapter lvi.

This act of the Pope in appointing a Patriarch to Abyssinia during the lifetime of Bermudez, without mentioning the latter's name, disposes of his claim to have ever received that appointment from the Pope; but there still remains his definite statement that the Pope made him

---

[1] P. 107, below.

Patriarch of Alexandria. Now it is evident, from what has been stated, that, if this claim has any foundation whatever, Bermudez must have been appointed between 1535, when he left Abyssinia, and the early part of 1538, by which time he had returned to Portugal, and was only prevented by a sharp attack of illness from leaving in the Indian ships that sailed on April 6th of that year. This point could, clearly, only be finally settled by a search in the records of the Vatican, and this search has been very kindly made by Mr. W. Bliss. The result is so far negative, that during the years mentioned above no trace whatever of the name of Bermudez can be found; but important and significant as this negative result is, there came to light in this search a document of very great interest, that almost eclipses in value the silence of the records. It is a missive of Pope Paul III, dated January 3rd, 1538—that is, at the very end of the period during which Bermudez could have been made Patriarch—addressed to another person (one Cæsar), calling him Patriarch of Alexandria.[1] It runs :—

"Venerabili fratri Cesari patriarchæ Alexandrino . . . . Cum tempus celebrandi universale concilium dudum per nos indictum appropinquat . . . . necessarium putamus ut tu qui patriarchali dignitate præditus . . . . . . Fraternitatem igitur in domino hortamur eique nihilominus in virtute sanctæ obedientiæ . . . . distincte percipiendo mandamus quatinus infra xx dierum spatium . . . . . ad nos in eo loco in quo tunc erimus omnino venias . . . . . .

"Datum Roma iii Januarii 1538 anno quarto."

At the time, then, covered by Bermudez' claim to have been appointed Patriarch of Alexandria, Pope Paul III recognised this Cæsar as the Patriarch, and the last shred

---

[1] The reference is Pauli III Brev. Minut. 1538, tom. i, No. 7.

of Bermudez' pretensions to a superior ecclesiastical dignity has disappeared.

Having dealt with the facts as to the first two personages, we shall now find that the writings of the third are equally conclusive. Galâwdêwos, alarmed and astonished at the actions and claims of Bermudez, wrote to the King of Portugal a letter, which he sent by Castanhoso; this letter does not appear to be extant, but the reply to it of the King of Portugal, dated March 13th, 1546, has been preserved.[1] In it he says that João Bermudez was sent as ambassador from Abyssinia to Portugal; that all the King knows of him is that he is a mere priest (*cleriguo simpres*); that he knows nothing of any powers he claims to have received from the Pope, but that he will send the Preste a Patriarch with whom he can discuss the matter of João Bermudez. He goes on to suggest discretion in dealing with Bermudez, for if he assumes the dignity of Patriarch, " which he wishes to usurp, though no one has given it to him," and is punished with death, Christianity will be discredited. The view thus expressed by the king has governed all action taken with respect to Bermudez. Bermudez himself evidently rather dreaded the return to Portugal, as his halt on St. Helena shows; when he reached home eventually, he remained in obscurity, until the publication of Castanhoso's book, followed quickly by the author's death, led him to print his own narrative. The internal affairs of Portugal during the reign of King Sebastian were not in a condition to lend themselves to any orderly investigation of events in a far-away corner of the globe. Bermudez was an old man; there were no charges against him; thus there is no evidence that Bermudez ever assumed any episcopal dignity in Portugal, and there was nothing to be gained by any inquiry. An

---

[1] P. 110, below.

inquiry might, in fact, be harmful, and end in discredit to Christianity: a result to be avoided at all hazards. It is certainly strange how scarce Bermudez' book became; it has been suggested by a recent Portuguese writer[1] that its disappearance was due to the action of the Da Gama family, who considered that it reflected on the reputation of D. Christovão; but it is just as possible that the disappearance was due to the feeling that Bermudez was a person who was no credit to the Christian Church.[2] It is, however, noteworthy that the imperfect abstract of Purchas has kept alive the memory of Bermudez, and given him a vogue not conceded to him by his contemporaries.

Bermudez calls himself ambassador from the King of Abyssinia, and such in a sense he undoubtedly was; it remains to examine what status this employment denoted, and how far the office gave a standing to its holder. An Abyssinian ambassador has but little in common with the dignified official of the same name in Europe. For many hundred years the Abyssinians were cut off from all intercourse with the world; with other countries they had neither treaties nor commerce. An Abyssinian dared not leave his own country, lest he should be enslaved or slain by the Muhamedans that hemmed him in.[3] When the King, therefore, desired to communicate with another

---

[1] Innocencio Francisco da Silva, *Diccionario bibliographico*.

[2] That Bermudez was a grossly ignorant man can be seen from his book, as by his education indeed he must have been. In his chap. xxxiv he gives some fortunate persons both God's blessing and his own, as if he had some private fountain of grace other than that derived from God.

[3] Among some Muhamedan tribes a man cannot marry until he has slain his Christian; and it is on record that, when the supply has not equalled the demand, a loving couple has set out for a Christian village. In the early morning there are heard the cries of a maiden in distress, the first chivalrous Christian who runs up is killed by the lover in ambush, and the happy pair return contented with blushing honours.

country, he was driven to select as the bearer of his letter —that is, as his messenger—either some Muhamedan[1] or some stray European or Levanter, who was found either in Abyssinia itself or on the neighbouring sea coast. The history of these so-called Embassies, some genuine, some forged, starting from Matheus, whose adventures we have in part followed, would form an entertaining volume. Not the least entertaining part would be the story of the Armenian who had been a cook (Murat the younger), at the end of the seventeenth century, which is such delightful reading in the pages of Bruce and Le Grand.[2] It is among these messengers or factors that Bermudez must take his place.

It remains, then, to determine whether the narrative of Castanhoso or that of Bermudez be the more trustworthy, for the two accounts vary very considerably the one from the other. There are printed in this volume translations of both these narratives; extracts, also, from that of Correa are given, so far as he adds anything to the facts. These, then, may be called the only contemporary narratives of the events of 1541-1544 in Abyssinia, though of course Correa was not, like the other two authors, an actor in them.

---

[1] Bruce calls the local Muhamedans Gibberti, and speaking of them (vol. iii, p. 45), says: "These are the people who at particular times have appeared in Europe, and who have been straight taken for and treated as ambassadors, although they have generally turned out to be thieves and sharpers."

[2] See Bruce, under reign of Yasous I, 1680-1704 (vol. iii, commencing p. 480, Le Grand, p. 157 and following, and p. 359 and following). Le Grand gives the original documents out of which Bruce has evolved the story with great skill. All the characters are comic: the irascible De Maillet, consul in Egypt, who received the hint from Paris that an embassy from Abyssinia would please Louis XIV; the ex-cook Murat, with the dried elephant's ear, all that remained of the so-called present of the King of Abyssinia, to prove his mission; the pasha who forces the ex-cook to give up the pretended letter of the Abyssinian King; the French ambassador at Constantinople, who brings on the pasha's head the thunder of the Porte for violating diplomatic correspondence, only to find that his French consul had instigated the pasha's action to reduce the puppet Murat to pliability, followed by the squabble as to who should pay the pasha's fine. At the background lies ecclesiastical intrigue, the whole ending with the dark murder of Du Roule.

To these have been added translations of the letters of the King of Portugal and of the King of Abyssinia bearing on these events, as far as they are available. This exhausts what may be called the first-class evidence as to the expedition of D. Christovão into Abyssinia. Taking, then, the two narratives of Castanhoso and Bermudez, we find that the latter stands in this class of evidence alone; Correa, who had received from Castanhoso a copy of his narrative, which he had compared with the statements of Portuguese returning from Abyssinia, follows that writer very closely. There is nothing, however, to show that he was acquainted with Bermudez' book; he probably wrote before it was published, but he knew something of the man; more important than this, the original letters, as far as they support either narrative, are distinctly in favour of Castanhoso. We must, however, carry the matter further, and discuss all other evidence that exists, in addition to merely that of the first class.

For an inquiry of this character two methods of investigation are available: the first to discover what view of the events other authors have taken; and the other, the more difficult, to examine the relative probability of the two narratives.[1] To take the first method, it is obvious that all authors have not the same value; we have exhausted above the evidence of those of the first class, namely, the actual contemporaries of the events, and we find that it favours the credibility of Castanhoso. All other authors may be divided into two classes: the second and third. In the second class fall all those who, though not contemporaries, were in a position to inquire from actors in the events, or if they visited Abyssinia, did so at a time when the traditions of those events were fresh. In the second class then

---

[1] The narratives of the Ethiopian chronicles have not been included in this inquiry; they are too fragmentary.

fall all authors, not contemporaries, who wrote before 1600; or, where they had special knowledge acquired in Abyssinia, before 1610 or 1620. In the third class fall all other writers who, proceeding only on an examination of documents or traditions trustworthy and untrustworthy, are less able perhaps than modern authors, who have more published evidence at their command, to take a correct view of the events. Thus, take the case of Tellez, who wrote in 1660: he finds it most difficult, in the face of the silence of the Bull appointing Barreto Patriarch of Abyssinia, to believe that Bermudez had been previously appointed to the same office; still, judging from his tombstone and his book, he thinks that he must have been Patriarch of Alexandria. Here Tellez' opinion must be taken for what it is worth; we, with the evidence from the Vatican and the letter of the King of Portugal of 1546 before us, are in a better position to judge the evidence. Again, as an example of untrustworthy tradition, take the case of Gouvea. Gouvea went to Goa in 1597, and his *Jornada*, which describes the progress of the Archbishop through Malabar, was published in 1606; he was therefore an ecclesiastic in touch with ecclesiastics, and in a position to know the facts; yet he makes Bermudez a young man of great prudence, and well educated in both lay and theological literature, who was taken captive by the Turks from some Italian galleys and sent to Cairo, whence he was forwarded as a present to the King of Abyssinia, with whom he ingratiated himself.[1] This class of evidence is to be avoided.

There are three writers who fall into the second class, namely, Diogo de Couto, who wrote the *Decadas*; Maffœus the Jesuit, who was never in India, whose volume, *Historiarum Indicarum Libri XVI*, was published in 1574; and Pero Paez, a Jesuit, who went to Abyssinia in 1603—a man

---

[1] *Jornada*, Bk. I, ch. vii.

of singularly active and inquiring mind, who devoted much attention to the subject, and whose account will be found preserved by Tellez.[1] Maffœus may be at once dismissed; his account is an abstract of Castanhoso, and, ecclesiastic though he is, he never once mentions Bermudez. Paez, also an ecclesiastic, who investigated the narrative on the spot, follows Castanhoso even more closely than Correa, using in many cases his very expressions. He adds some very valuable topographical details of his own. Couto, in his account, also follows Castanhoso, giving as his reason that he had met in Goa two men, Simão Fernandes and Diogo Dias do Prestes, who had been companions of D. Christovão, and who had returned to India in the time of D. Constantine de Bragança (1558-61); these men informed him that Castanhoso's account was very accurate.[2] Couto had also seen Bermudez in the flesh, and was acquainted with his narrative, which he accepted as far as it stated that Bermudez was made patriarch by the Abyssinian Abuna, and confirmed by the Pope.[3] The writers of the second class, like those of the first, are then unanimous in considering Castanhoso's account the more trustworthy.

---

[1] See Tellez (Bk. II, chap. vii), for an account of Pero Paez. Paez' account of D. Christovão's expedition will be found in Bk. II, chaps. viii to xvi. In Part iv of Guerreiro's *Relaçam Annual das Cousas*, etc., there is more concerning Paez. For a letter of his, dated July 3rd, 1617, see p. 126 of the Italian translation of Jesuit Letters, published at Milan in 1621.

[2] Couto, *Dec. V*, Bk. x, chap. iv.

[3] Couto, *Dec. VII*, Bk. I, chap. i. Ludolf handles Bermudez very carefully, prefacing his account with the words "ut ipse de se scribit." See also p. 473 of his *Commentary*, where he sums up the evidence, as far as it was then known, entirely against Bermudez' pretensions. The work of Ludolf is a mine of erudition, in which subsequent writers have of necessity quarried. His informant Gregory was learned and trustworthy, but found at times his pupil's scientific enthusiasm embarrassing, as when to one question: "pudibundus exclamabat *Phy phy* .... nec quidquam respondere volebat." Ludolf quotes Chaucer in the original, which is remarkable.

An examination of the two books leads to the impression that contemporary opinion is in this case correct. Dealing as they do with events so unfamiliar and a country so remote, very little of the narrative can be checked by any historical work ; still, Bermudez at the beginning and end of his story does make statements that can be compared with those of independent writers ; in these cases what he puts forward is frequently inaccurate. Discrepancies are noted in the translation as they occur ; here I only propose to mention two misstatements which, even leaving out of account his great cardinal misstatement as to his own position, seem to mark a loose, inaccurate habit of mind in the writer, and thus throw doubt on the whole work.

The first misstatement is as to the year of Bermudez' own return to Portugal; when he wrote this event was comparatively recent, and there was absolutely no object to be gained by misstating it. He very rarely gives a date, but in his chapter lvii he says that he reached Lisbon in August, 1559. Now, it is as certain as such a thing can be, that he reached Lisbon on August 16th, 1558; the steps of the argument are these. He says he left Massowa with Mestre Gonçalo in the vessel of João (not Antonio, as he says) Peixoto ; we know from independant sources that Mestre Gonçalo left Massowa in March, 1556, and reached Goa in May. Bermudez tells us that he stayed nine months in Goa, and then sailed for Europe in the fleet of João de Menezes. We know that this fleet left India late in 1556 or early in 1557 (thus agreeing with Bermudez), and that it would reach St. Helena about April, 1557. Bermudez says that he landed at St. Helena, and remained there a year, and then went to Portugal in the ship *São Paulo*. Now we know from Falcão[1] that, although the

---

[1] Falcão, p. 166.

fleet of Menezes did return in August 1557, one ship belonging to it (the *São Paulo*) was delayed a year, and did not reach Lisbon until August 16th, 1558. The facts, therefore, fit in with Bermudez' statement, but he errs by one year.

The second misstatement I will mention is more serious. In his chapter xxii, Bermudez tells us that after the battle in Wofla, in which D. Christovão was killed, forty Portuguese were found wanting. Now the other sources give the loss of the Portuguese at about two hundred killed, while fifty under Manuel da Cunha had separated off from the rest and gone to Debarwa; this makes two hundred and fifty missing. Originally there were about four hundred Portuguese. Of these thirty had been killed near Antalo, and some eight at Baçanete, which, with two hundred killed and fifty missing, would leave about one hundred and ten or one hundred and twenty fugitives with the Queen, Sabla Wangel. Castanhoso gives no exact figures, but says that the Imam Ahmad had one hundred and sixty Portuguese heads before him when D. Christovão was brought to him a prisoner. In addition, there were some forty Portuguese blown up by gunpowder, and possibly all their heads could not be discovered. He says one hundred and twenty collected with the Queen, and fifty were with Manuel da Cunha. The Ethiopian chronicles say the greater number of the Portuguese were killed, which would not agree with a loss of forty men. Galâwdêwos, in both his letters, of December 1550 and December 1551, says that one hundred and thirty Portuguese were collected with the Queen after the battle. But Bermudez' own statement of forty men missing is refuted from his own book. Of course, he does not mention the death of every single man; but adding up those he does mention, and including the men he says went to Debarwa, over forty can be totalled from his own narrative. Bermudez, then, is a man of loose inaccurate habit of mind, whose statements individually require verification before they are accepted.

The two narratives themselves can be further considered from another point of view: in which narrative do the events best hang together, and in which do the actors behave as we may expect human beings, actuated by ordinary human motives, to behave? Such an enquiry touches on the domain of opinion rather than on that of fact, but a few considerations may be given. The narrative of Castanhoso is direct and soldierly; events follow each other in their natural sequence. D. Christovão and Galâwdêwos correspond, with the intention of—if possible—joining forces before the Imam Ahmad has an opportunity of defeating them in detail. The Imam Ahmad, like a capable general, sees through their intention, and throws himself in the way of D. Christovão, who marches with all proper precaution; the former is defeated by the superior arms and organisation of the Portuguese, whose tactics in the action are simple and effective. Recognising the impossibility of contending with the foreigners unless supplied with a large body of troops similar to theirs, he purchases the assistance of the Turks in the Red Sea, and, having encamped at a suitable base, collects an irresistible force. At the head of this he defeats the Portuguese, and recognising that they were the enemies to be dreaded, and not the Abyssinians, concentrates all his energies on destroying them, and nearly succeeds; less than half escape the rout, throwing away all their arms. This remnant would have been useless had not D. Christovão (apparently unknown to the Imam Ahmad) left his surplus weapons on Debra Damo. Galâwdêwos collects his forces, and he and the Portuguese engage the Imam Ahmad on the shores of Lake Tzâna, before he has had time to collect reinforcements, where a lucky shot decides the campaign. Castanhoso's account is then intelligible.

Bermudez' narrative, on the other hand, is confused and contradictory; it was written over twenty years after the event, when the author had no papers, and could only re-write Castanhoso by the light of a failing memory and unfailing malice. There is nothing to be gained by following his numerous contradictions; take an example: in chapter xiv he learns that the Queen intends to fly, and, recognising the danger of such a course, prevents her flight. A few days later, in chapter xvi, on the other hand, he starts to fly with her, and, stopped by a sharp message from D. Christovão, justifies himself with reasons that would be farcical in the stage comic coward. Take his narrative of the fighting with the Imam Ahmad round Antalo (Bermudez, chapter xiv to xvii), and compare it with Castanhoso (chapter xii to xv). In Castanhoso, D. Christovão, like a man governed by ordinary motives, delays fighting a general action as long as he can, in the hope of being reinforced; but, when compelled to risk one, he forms his troops into a square, and their musketry and artillery mow down the enemy, until by good fortune the Imam Ahmad is wounded. In Bermudez, D. Christovão, knowing that there is a vastly superior force at hand, fires his guns generally to advertise himself; and when the Imam Ahmad in consequence comes in sight, does not know what to do. Bermudez suggests that some wile or stratagem should be thought of, and that, pending the birth of this wile or stratagem, they should march up a hill, which they do—it is perhaps unnecessary to continue. One other instance I will notice: we have seen how, in Castanhoso's narrative, the Imam Ahmad retires to the shores of Lake Tzâna to his family, when he knows that he has killed the Portuguese leader and more than half his men, captured all their arms, munitions, stores and camp, and dispersed the survivors. In Bermudez' account, on the other hand, we find only forty Portuguese missing in all, and the Imam Ahmad actually enters into correspondence with the survivors, whom he knows to be a military body in being; and yet, leaving them unmolested, he dismisses his Turkish matchlockmen, and retires with his ordinary guard to his family on the banks of Lake Tzâna. Perhaps no more instances are needed.

It may be objected that, if Bermudez' narrative is so untrustworthy it need not have been translated here; but Bermudez was in Abyssinia during the time of the Portuguese expedition, and his book has, owing to the abstract in Purchas, attained a notoriety to which Castanhoso's far superior work can lay no claim. Neither book has before been translated in full into English, and Castanhoso's narrative could hardly command the credit it deserves had it not that of Bermudez with it as a foil.

LISTS FOR REFERENCE.

LIST OF ABYSSINIAN KINGS DURING THIS PERIOD.

Name.	Royal Name.	European Name.	Dates of Reign.
Lebna Dengel	Wanag Sagad	David	1508 to 1540
Galâwdêwos	Asnáf Sagad	Claudius	1540 to 1559
Minas	Además Sagad	—	1559 to 1563

LIST OF POPES.

Name.	Elected.	Died.
Leo X	March 11th, 1513	December 1st, 1521
Adrian VI	January 9th, 1522	September 24th, 1523
Clement VII	November 19th, 1523	September 25th, 1534
Paul III	October 13th, 1534	November 10th, 1549
Julius III	February 8th, 1550	March 23rd, 1555
Marcellus II	April 9th, 1555	April 20th, 1555
Paul IV	May 23rd, 1555	August 18th, 1559
Pius IV	December 25th, 1559	December 9th, 1565

KINGS OF PORTUGAL.

Emmanuel	1495 to 1521
John III	1521 to 1557
Sebastian	1557 to 1571

DATES OF EASTER DAY.

In 1541 Easter Day fell on April 17th
In 1542 ,, ,, ,, 9th
In 1543 ,, ,, March 25th
In 1544 ,, ,, April 13th

THE ABYSSINIAN CALENDAR.

The Abyssinian system of computation of time differs considerably from that used in Europe. The year is divided into twelve months each of thirty days, and at the end of the year there are, in ordinary years, five intercalary days; in Leap Year there are six.[1] The years are arranged in cycles of four, each year being called after an evangelist; the year of St. John is always Leap Year. The era in use is that of the creation of the world, 5500 B.C., but there is a difference of eight years in the date of the Incarnation, as accepted in Europe, so that 1540 A.D. European is 1532 A.D. Abyssinian. I give here the dates of the commencement of each month in the European nomenclature (O. S.). For the New Style the comparative dates will differ; this information is taken from Ludolf's *Commentary*.

Name of Abyssinian Month.	English Date of Commencement of Abyssinian Month.
1. Maskaram	August 29th
2. Teqemt	September 28th
3. Hedâr	October 28th
4. Tahsâs	November 27th
5. Ter	December 27th
6. Yakâtit	January 26th
7. Magâbit	February 25th
8. Miyâzyâ	March 27th
9. Genbot	April 26th
10. Sene or Sane	May 26th
11. Hamle	June 25th
12. Nahase	July 25th

After August 23rd come the intercalary days. Apparently the year of St. John is the year before our Leap Year, so that between the end of August and the end of February in one year of the cycle, the above Table would be wrong by one day. There is now a difference of thirteen days from the above, due to the change in the European style.

---

[1] These days are called by Pearce *Pogme*, by Rohlfs *Pagumiehne*, by Isenberg and Krapf *Pagmie*, and by Ludolf *Paguemen*.

BIBLIOGRAPHY OF *ABYSSINIA*,

GIVING

THE BRITISH MUSEUM PRESS-MARKS.

Abbadie (Antoine Thompson d').
    See Ahmad Ibn 'Abd Al-Kādir.

Abbadie (Antoine Thompson d').—L' Abyssinie et le roi Théodoros. *Paris*, 1868. 8°. [Not in the British Museum.]

Abbadie (Antoine Thompson d').—Catalogue raisonné des manuscrits éthiopiens appartenant à A. d'Abbadie. [By A. T. d'A.] pp. xv. 235. *Imprimere Impériale: Paris*, 1859. 4°. (11900. k. 7, 8.)

Abbadie (Antoine Thompson d').—Dictionnaire de la langue Amariñña. (vol. 10. Actes. Société Philologique). Pp. xlvii. coll. 1336. *F. Vieweg: Paris*, 1881. 8°. (Ac. 9808,)

Abbadie (Antoine Thompson d').—Géodésie d'Ethiopie . . . verifiée et rédigée par R. Radau. pp. xxxii. 502. *Gauthier-Villars: Paris*, 1873. 4°. (10095. i. 13.)

Abbadie (Antoine Thompson d').—Géographie de l'Ethiopie. *Paris*, 1890. 8°. [Not in the British Museum.]

Abbadie (Arnauld d').—Douze Ans dans la Haute-Ethiopie (Abyssinie). Tom. I. *L. Hachette et Cie.: Paris*, 1868. 8°. (10097. e. 23.)

Aboulféda.
    See Ismail Ibn Ali.

Abu Sālih, *al-Armanī*.—The Churches and Monasteries of Egypt and some neighbouring Countries . . . Edited and translated by B. T. A. Evetts . . . With added notes by A. J. Butler. (Anecdota Oxoniensia. Semitic. Pt. 7.) pp. xx. 382. *Clarendon Press: Oxford*, 1895. 4° (12204. f. 11 | 7.)

Abyssinia.—L'Abyssinie et sa grande mission. Par un catholique français pp. 44. *A. Rey: Lyon* [1900.] 4°. (8027. k. 3.).

Abyssinia.—Les Abyssiniennes et les femmes du Soudan Oriental. d'après les relations de Bruce, Browne, Cailliaud, Gobat, Dr. Cuny, Lejean, Baker, *etc.* pp. 126. *Jean Gay: Turin*, 1876. 8° (8416. d. 31.)

Abyssinia.—Abyssinische Kirchen-Geschichten von anno 1698 biss 1703. Beschreibung des Reichs Abyssinia oder Ethiopien. (J. Stoecklein's Allerhand . . . Reis-Beschreibungen. Vol. i, pt. 8. pp. 43-59.) *P. Martin: Augspurg*, 1728. fol. (4767. g. 3.)

Abyssinia.—Corpus Juris Abessinorum. Textum aethiopicum arabicumque . . . cum versione latina et dissertatione juridico-historica edidit J. Bachmann. *F. Schneider & Co.: Berolini*, 1889. 4°. (754. c. 7.)

Abyssinia.—The Ethiopic Didascalia, or, The Ethiopic Version of the Apostolical Constitutions, received in the Church of Abyssinia. With an English translation, edited and translated by T. P. Platt. (Oriental Translation Fund.) pp. xvi. 131. *R. Bentley: London*, 1834. 4°. (14003. f. 16.)

Abyssinia.—Il "Fetha Nagast," o "Legislazione dei Re." Codice ecclesiastico e civile di Abissinia, pubblicato da Ignazio Guidi. (Pubbl. Scient. del R. Istit. Orient. in Napoli. Tom. 2, 3.) 2 vols. *Roma,* 1897, 99. 8°. (754. c. 8.)

Adamus, *Bremensis.*—Gesta Hammaburgensis ecclesiae pontificum. ed. J. M. Lappenberg. *Hannover,* 1876. 8°. [Not in the British Museum.]

Africa.—Recueil de divers Voyages faits en Afrique et en l'Amérique, qui n'ont point éste' encore publiez... Avec des Traitez curieux touchant la Haute Ethyopie... la mer Rouge, & le Prete-Jean. [Illustrated.] 6 pts. *L. Billaine: Paris,* 1674. 4°. (214. a. 11. 1684: 566. h. 1.)

Ahmad Ibn 'Abd Al-Kādir (Shihāb al-Dīn).—Histoire de la conquête de l'Abyssinie, XVIe. siècle. Texte arabe publié avec une traduction française et des notes, par René Basset. (Publications de l'Ecole Supérieure des Lettres d'Alger. Nos. 19-22.) Fasc. 1-6. *E. Leroux: Paris,* 1897-1901. 8°. (Ac. 5350 | 2.)

Ahmad Ibn 'Abd Al-Kādir (Shihāb al-Dīn).—Futûh el-Habacha des conquêtes faites en Abyssinie au XVIe. siècle. Version française de la chronique arabe du Chahâb ad-Din Ahmad. Publication commencée par A. d'Abbadie, terminée par P. Paulitschke. pp. xxviii. 394. *E. Bouillon: Paris,* 1898. 8°. [Not in the British Museum.]

Ahmad Ibn 'Alī, al-Makrīzī.—Macrizi historia regum Islamiticorum in Abyssinia. Interpretatus est et una cum Abulfedae descriptione regionum Nigritarum... Arabice edidit F. T. Rinck. pp. x. 36. 41. 15. *Lugduni Batavorum,* 1790. 4°. (14555. b. 11.)

Alamanni (Ennio Quirino Mario).—La Colonia Eretrea, e i suoi commerci. pp. xxxii. 911. *Frat. Bocca: Torino,* 1891. 8°. (08227. h. 8.)

Albuquerque (Affonso de) *Governor of India.*—Cartas de Afonso de Albuquerque seguidas de documentos que as elucidam publicadas... sob a direcção de R. A. de Bulhão Pato. 3 tom. (Collecção de Monumentos.) *Academia das Sciencias: Lisboa,* 1884, 85, 4°. (9056. i.)

Albuquerque (Affonso de) *the Younger.*—Commentarios de Afonso Dalboquerque... collegidos por seu filho Afonso Dalboquerque das proprias cartas que elle escreuia ao... Rey dõ Manuel o primeyro deste nome, em cujo tempo gouernou a India, *etc.* ff. cccv. *Joam de Barreyra: Lixboa,* 1557. fol. (9057. c. 1.)

Albuquerque (Affonso de) *the Younger.*—Commentarios do grande Afonso Dalboquerque, capitam geral que foy das Indias Orientaes, em tempo do Rey dom Manuel o primeiro deste nome. Nouamente emendados & acrescentados pelo mesmo auctor. pp. 578. *por João de Barreira: Lisboa,* 1576. 4°. (582. h. i.)

—— [Another edition.] 4 tom. *Regia Officina Typografica: Lisboa,* 1774. 8°. (148. a. 3-6.)

Albuquerque (Affonso de) *the younger.*—The Commentaries of the great Afonso Dalboquerque... Translated from the Portuguese edition of 1774... by W. de G. Birch. 3 vols. *Hakluyt Society: London,* 1875-80. 8°. (Ac. 6172 | 47.)

Alguns Documentos do Archivo Nacional da Torre do Tombo acerca das navegações e conquistas portuguezas publicados... ao celebrar-se a commemoração quadricentaria do descobrimento da America. [With a preface by José Ramos-Coelho.] pp. xvii. 551. *Academia das Sciencias: Lisboa,* 1892. fol. (Ac. 191 | 2.)

Almeida (Manoel de), *Jesuit.*
    See Thévenot (Melchisedech).

Almeida (Manoel de), *Jesuit.*—Historia de Ethiopia a alta, ou Abassia, imperio do Abexim, cujo Rey vulgarmente hecha mado Preste Joam; composta pelo Padre Manoel de Almeida da Companhia de Jesus, natural de Viscu. [MS. Map dated 1662.] [1665?] fol. (Add. MSS. 9861.)

Almeida (Manoel de), *Jesuit.*—Historia geral de Ethiopia a alta ov Preste Joam e do que nella obraram os Padres da Companhia de Jesus: composta na mesma Ethiopia ... Abreviada com nova releyçam e methodo pelo Padre Balthezar Tellez. 2 vols. *Manoel Dias: Coimbra,* 1660. fol. (984. f. 15 and 566. d. 2.)

Almeida (Manoel de), *Jesuit.*—Lettere dell' Ethiopia ... 1626 fino al Marzo del 1627 [by M. de Almeida] e della Cina ... 1625 fino al Febraro del 1626 [by M. Dias]; con una relatione del viaggio all regio di Tunquim, nuovamente scoperto [by G. Baldinotti]. Mandate al molto Rev. Padre Mutio Vitelleschi, Generale della Compagnia di Giesu. pp. 133. *B. Zannetti: Roma,* 1629. 8°. (867. i. 41. 295. g. 44.)

Almeida (Manoel de), *Jesuit.*—Victorias de Amda Sion, rei de Ethiopia (1494). Traducção abreviada pelo P. M. de Almeida ... com uma versão franceza por M. J. Perruchon. Memoria apresentada por F. M. Esteves Pereira. P. 40. *Imprensa Nacional: Lisboa,* 1891. 8°. (9007. g. 22. | 2.)

Almeida (Manoel de), *Jesuit.*—Vida de Takla Haymanot. ed. F. M. Esteves Pereira. *Lisboa,* 1899. 8°. [Not in the British Museum.]

Alvares (Francisco), *Priest.*—Ho Preste Joam das indias. Verdadeira informaçam das terras do Preste Joam. G. L. ff. 136. *Luis Rodriguez: Coimbra,* 1540. (493. i. 1. G. 6829.)

Alvares (Francisco), *Priest.*—Ho Preste Joam das indias. Verdadeira, etc. *Lisboa,* 1889. 4°. [Not in the British Museum.]

Alvares (Francisco), *Priest.*—The Voyage of Sir Francis Alvarez ... made unto the Court of Prete Janni, the ... Emperour of Ethiopia.
See Purchas (Samuel) *the Elder.*—Purchas His Pilgrimes, *etc.* Lib. VII, ch. 5, pp. 1026-1121. 1625. fol. (679. h. 12.)

Alvarez (Francisco), *Priest.*—Narrative of the Portuguese Embassy to Abyssinia ... 1520-27 ... Translated from the Portuguese and edited with notes ... by Lord Stanley of Alderley. pp. xxvii. 416. 18. (Vol. 64.) *Hakluyt Society: London,* 1881. 8°. (Ac. 6172 | 56.)

'Amda Sĕyon, *King of Ethiopia.*—Histoire des guerres d' 'Amda Syôn, roi d'Ethiopie (1494). Traduite de l'Ethiopien par M. Jules Perruchon. (Extrait du "Journal Asiatique.") pp. 205. *Imprimerie Nationale: Paris,* 1890. 8°. (754. b. 14. Ac. 8808.)

Andrade (Jacinto Freire d').
See Freire de Andrade (J.).

Anglerius (Petrus Martyr).
See Barthéma (Lodovico).

Annesley (George Arthur) *Earl of Mountmorris.*—Drafts and copies of papers relating to the History and Geography of India, Egypt, and Abyssinia, collected by Viscount Valentia. Paper. 19th cent. Fol. (Add. MSS. 19, 348.)

Annesley (George Arthur) *Earl of Mountmorris.*—Voyages and Travels to India, Ceylon, the Red Sea, Abyssinia ... 1802-06. 3 vols. *London,* 1809. 4°. (10058. l. 13, and 10056. l. 16.)

Antinori (Orazio) *Marquis.*—Viaggio nei Bogos. *Roma,* 1887. 8°. [Not in the British Museum.]

Apel (Ferdinand H.)—Drei Monate in Abyssinien und Gefangenschaft unter König Theodorus II. pp. 104. *C. Meyer: Zürich*, 1866. 8°. (10096. bb. 30.)

Arbousse-Bastide (Antoine François).
   See Blanc (Henry).

Bachmann (Paulus Johannes).
   See Abyssinia.

Bachmann (Paulus Johannes).—Aethiopische Lesestücke. Inedita Aethiopica ... herausgegeben von Dr. J. Bachmann. pp. 50. *J. C. Hinrichs: Leipzig*, 1892. 8°. (754. b. 18.)

Badger (George Percy).
   See Barthéma (Lodovico).

Baker (*Sir* Samuel White).—The Nile Tributaries of Abyssinia and the Sword-Hunters of the Hamran Arabs. 4th edition. pp. xix. 413. *Macmillan and Co.: London*, 1871. 8°. (2358. a. 4.)

Baker (*Sir* Samuel White).—Die Nilzuflüsse in Abyssinien. Herausgegeben von Friedrich Steger. 2 vols. *Braunschweig*, 1868. 8°. [Not in the British Museum.]

Baldinotti (Giuliano).
   See Almeida (Manoel de) Lettere, &c.

Baratti (Giacomo).—The Late Travels of S. Giacomo Baratti, an Italian gentleman, into the remote countries of the Abissins, or of Ethiopia Interior ... Translated by G. D. pp. 238. *B. Billingsley: London*, 1670. 12°. (979. b. 30.)

Baratti (Giacomo).—Reis-Beschreibung Sig. Giacomo Baratti, eines edlen Italiäners, in die entlegenen Länder der Abyssiner oder Innere Aethiopia, etc. ("Asiatische und Africanische Denckwürdigkeiten dieser Zeit." pp. 407-480). *W. M. Endter: Nürnberg*, 1676. 4°. (790. f. 19.)

Barbier de Meynard (Charles Adrien Casimir).—Notice sur l'Arabie Méridionale d'après un document turc. (Publications de l'Ecole des Langues Orientales Vivantes. Ser. 2. vol. 9. Mélanges Orientaux. pp. 87-123.) *E. Leroux: Paris*, 1883. 8°. (752. f. 22.)

Barros (João de).—Da Asia de J. de Barros e Diogo de Couto nova edição. 24 vol. *Regia Officina Typografica: Lisboa*, 1778. 8°. (978. c. 1-24.)

Barthéma (Lodovico).—The Navigation and Voyages of Lewes Vertomannus, Gentelman of the citie of Rome, to the regions of Arabia, Egypt ... Ethiopia ... 1503 ... Translated ... by Richarde Eden ... 1576. fol. 354-421 of P. M. Anglerius's "The History of Travayle," &c. *R. Jugge: London*, 1577. 8°. (304. d. 10.)

Barthéma (Lodovico).—The Travels of Ludovico di Varthema in Egypt, Syria ... and Ethiopia, A.D. 1503 to 1508. Translated from the original Italian edition of 1510 ... by J. Winter Jones ... and edited ... by G. P. Badger. pp. cxxi. 320. *Hakluyt Society: London*, 1863. 8°. (Ac. 6172 | 30.)

Barthéma (Lodovico).—Les Voyages de Ludovico di Varthema ou Le Viateur en la plus grande partie d'Orient, traduits de l'Italien en français par J. Balarin de Raconis ... publiés et annotés par M. Ch. Schefer. (No. 9. Recueil de Voyages.) pp. lxxi. 406. *E. Leroux: Paris*, 1888. 8°. (10024. i.)

Basset (René).
   See Ahmad Ibn 'Abd Al-Kādir.

Basset (René).—Les Apocryphes Ethiopiens, traduits en français par R. Basset.—I. Le Livre de Baruch & la Légende de Jérémie, 1893.—II. Mas' H'Afa T'Omar. Livre de l'Epitre, 1893.—III. L'Ascension d'Isaïe, 1894.—IV. Les Légendes de S. Tertag et de S. Sousnyos, 1894. —V. Les Prières de la Vierge à Bartos et au Golgotha, 1895.—VI. Les Prières de S. Cyprien et de Théophile, 1896.—VII. Enseignements de Jésus Christ à ses Disciples et Prières Magiques, 1896.—VIII. Les Règles attribuées à St. Pakhome, 1896.—IX. Apocalypse d'Esdras, 1899.—X. La Sagesse de Sibylle, 1900. 10 vols. *Bibliothèque de la Haute Science: Paris*, 1893-1900. 8°. (754. a. 8.)

Basset (Rene).—La Bordah du Cheïkh El-Bousiri, *Paris*, 1894. 12°. [Not in the British Museum.]

Basset (René).—Deux Lettres ethiopiennes du XVIe. siècle, traduites du portugais de M. F. M. Esteves Pereira. *Rome*, 1889. 8°. [Not in the British Museum.]

Basset (René).—Etudes sur l'Histoire d'Ethiopie. (Chronique éthiopienne, d'apres un manuscrit de la Bibliothèque Nationale de Paris.) pp. 318. *E. Leroux: Paris*, 1882. 8°. [Not in the British Museum.]

Basset (René).—Les Inscriptions de l'île de Dahlak. (Journal Asiatique, ser. 9. vol. 1. pp. 77-111.) *E. Leroux: Paris*, 1893. 8°. (Ac. 8808. and 2098. d.)

Basset (René).—Notice sur le Magsaph Assetat du P. Antonio Fernandes, traduite du portugais de M. F. M. Esteves Pereira. *Alger*, 1886. 8° [Not in the British Museum.]

Basset (René).—Rapport sur les études berbères, éthiopiennes et arabes (1887-91). pp. 41. *Oriental University Institute: Woking*, 1892. 8°. [Not in the British Museum.]

Basset (Rene).—Vie d'Abbâ Yohanni. (Texte éthiopien du MS. 132, Bibliothèque Nationale, & traduction française par R. Basset). "Bulletin de Correspondance Africaine," 1884. pp. 433-453. *P. Fontana & Cie,: Alger*, 1884. 8°. (Ac. 5350.)

Battell (Andrew).—The Strange Adventures of Andrew Battell, of Leigh, in Angola and the adjoining regions. Reprinted from "Purchas His Pilgrimes." Edited . . . by E. G. Ravenstein. pp. xx. 210. *Hakluyt Society: London*, 1901. 8°. (Ac. 6172 | 82.)

Beke (Charles Tilstone).—The British Captives in Abyssinia . . . Second edition. pp. xxvi. 398. *Longmans, Green and Co.: London*, 1867. 8°. (10095. cc. 28.)

Beke (Charles Tilstone).—Christianity among the Gallas. (In "The British Magazine," Dec. 1847, pp. 660-667.) *T. C. Smith: London*, 1847. 8°. (P. P. 326. d.)

Beke (Charles Tilstone).—An Enquiry into M. Antoine d'Abbadie's Journey to Kaffa . . . 1843 and 1844, to discover the Source of the Nile . . . Second edition. pp. xvi. 63. *J. Madden: London*, 1851. 8°. (10095. c. 10.)

Beke (Charles Tilstone).—Journal of Travels in Southern Abyssinia, vocabularies of native dialects, water-colour sketches by Dr. Beke, Abyssinian artists, and others, maps, etc., 1840-67. Paper. 4° and fol. (Add. MSS. 30, 247-258.)

Beke (Charles Tilstone).—On the Languages and Dialects of Abyssinia. (Proceedings of the Philological Society. vol. 2. No. 33. pp. 89-107). *The Society: London*, 1845. 8°. (Ac. 9930. & 739. b. 33.)

Beke (Charles Tilstone).—The Sources of the Nile, *etc.* pp. xv. 155. *J. Madden: London*, 1860. 8°. (10095. e. 30.)

Bent (James Theodore).—The Sacred City of the Ethiopians. Being a record of travel and research in Abyssinia in 1893 . . . With a chapter by Prof. H. D. Müller on the Inscriptions from Yeha and Aksum, and an Appendix on the morphological character of the Abyssinians by J. G. Garson. Illustrated. pp. xv. 309. *Longmans, Green and Co.: London*, 1893. (010096. ee. 40.)

Bermudez (João).—Esta he huã breve relação da embaixada q̃o Patriarcha dõ João Bermudez trouxe do Emperador da Ethiopia, *etc.* ff. 80. *F. Correa: Lisboa*, 1565. 8°. (790. g. 29.) 1875 edn. [Not in the British Museum.]

Bermudez (João).—Breve relação da embaixada que o patriarcha D. João Bermudez trouxe da Emperador da Ethiopia, vulgarmente chamado Preste João, dirigida a El-Rei D. Sebastião. *Lisboa*, 1855. 4°. [Not in the British Museum.)

Bermudez (João).—A Briefe Relation of the Embassage which the Patriarch Don John Bermudez brought from the Emperour of Ethiopia . . . to . . . Don John, the third of this name, King of Portugall, *etc. See* Purchas (Samuel) *the Elder*. Purchas His Pilgrimes, *etc.* Lib. VII, ch. 7, 8. pp. 1149-1188. 1625. fol. (679. h. 12.)

Berridge (Frederic), *of the British Museum*.
See Hotten (John Camden).

Bianchi (Gustavo).—Alla Terra dei Galla. Narrazione della spedizione Bianchi in Africa nel 1879-80. pp. 543. *Trat. Treves: Milano*, 1884. 8°. (10097. m. 7.)

Birch (Walter de Gray).
See Albuquerque (Affonso de) *the Younger*.

Blanc (Henry).—A Narrative of Captivity in Abyssinia, with some account of the late Emperor Theodore (1855-1868), his country and people. pp. xii. 409. *Smith, Elder and Co.: London*, 1868. 8°. (10095. bb. 33.)

Blanc (Henry).—Ma captivité en Abyssinie, traduite par M. Arbousse-Bastide. *Paris*, 1870. 12°. [Not in the British Museum.]

Blanford (William Thomas).—Observations on the Geology and Zoology of Abyssinia, made during the progress of the British Expedition . . . 1867-68. pp. xii. 487. *Macmillan and Co.: London*, 1870. 8°. (7001. b. 16.)

Blundell (Herbert Weld).—A Journey through Abyssinia to the Nile. ("Geographical Journal," vol. xv, pp. 97-121, 264-272.) *Royal Geographical Society: London*, 1900. 8°. (Ac. 6170, & 2058. aa.)

Bonchamps (C. de).—Une Mission vers le Nil blanc. (Bulletin de la Société de Géographie de Paris. Ser. 7. Vol. 19. pp. 404-431.) *Paris*, 1898. 8°. (Ac. 6035.)

Borelli (Jules).—Ethiopie Méridionale. Journal de mon voyage aux pays Amhara, Oromo et Sidama, Sept. 1885 à Nov. 1888. pp. 520. *May & Motteroz: Paris*, 1890. fol. (10095. i. 9.)

Botta (Paul Emile).—Relation d'un voyage dans l'Yémen, entrepris en 1837, &c. pp. 148. *B. Duprat: Paris*, 1841. 8°. (10076. d. 10.)

Bottego (Vittorio).—Viaggi di scoperta nel cuore dell' Africa. Il Giuba esplorato sotto gli auspici della Società Geographica Italiana. pp. xviii. 537. *Ermanno Loescher & Co.: Roma*, 1895. 8°. (010096. m. 29.)

Bourke (Dermot Robert Wyndham) *Earl of Mayo*.—Sport in Abyssinia. Mareb and Tackazzee. *John Murray: London*, 1870. 8°. (7907. bbb. 5.)

Bricchetti (Luigi Robecchi).
    See Robecchi-Bricchetti (L.).

British Museum.—Catalogus Codicum Manuscriptorum Orientalium, qui in Museo Britannico asservantur. Pars Tertia; Codices Aethiopicos amplectens [By C. F. A. Dillmann.] pp. viii. 78. *Impensis Curatorum: Londoni*, 1847. fol. (Cat. Desk A.)

British Museum.—Catalogue of the Ethiopic MSS. in the British Museum acquired since ... 1847. [By W. Wright. 13 plates.] pp. xiii. 366. *The Trustees: British Museum*, 1877. 4°. (Cat. Desk A.) [The Preface contains a List of the Kings of Abyssinia, 1270-1877, compiled in 1873 by Prof. Alfred von Gutschmid.]

Bruce (James) *of Kinnaird.*—Voyages en Abyssinie. Trad. par J. H. Castéra. 5 vols. *Paris*, 1791. 4° (10096. gg. 19.)

Bruce (James) *of Kinnaird.*—Travels [in Abyssinia and Nubia] to discover the Source of the Nile ... 1768 to 1773 ... Third edition, corrected and enlarged. Illustrated. 8 vols. *A. Constable and Co.: Edinburgh*, 1813. 8° and 4°.

Bulhão Pato (Raymundo Antonio de).
    See Albuquerque (Affonso de), *Governor of India.*

Burnell (Arthur Coke.)
    See Linschoten (Jan Huygen van).

Burton (*Sir* Richard Francis), *K.C.M.G.*—First Footsteps in East Africa, or, An Exploration of Harar. pp. xl. 648. *Longmans: London*, 1856. 8°. (2358. e. 3.)

Bury (John Bagnell).
    See Gibbon (Edward).

Butler (Alfred Joshua).
    See Abu Sālih.

Cartas Annuas.
    See Jesuits.

Castanhoso (Miguel de).—Historia Das cousas que o muy esforçado cápitão Dom Christovão da Gama fez nos Reynos do Preste Ioão, com quatrocetos Portugueses que consigo leuou Impressa por Ioã da Barreyra E por elle dirigida ao muyto magnifico & illustre señor Dõ Francisco de Portugal. *J. da Barreyra: Lisboa*, 1564. fol. [Not in the British Museum.]

Castanhoso (Miguel de).—Historia Das cousas que o muy esforçado capitão Dom Christouão da Gama fez nos Reynos do Preste Ioão, com quatrocetos Portugueses que consigo leuou, Impressa por Ioã da Barreyra. (Collecção de Opusculos reimpressos relativos a Historia das Navegações, Viagens, e Conquistas dos Portuguezes. Tom. I. pt. 2.) pp. 93. *Academia Real das Sciencias: Lisboa*, 1855. 8°. [Not entered in the British Museum Catalogue, but at 1298. g. 15.]

Castanhoso (Miguel de).—Dos Feitos de D. Christovam da Gama em Ethiopia ... publicado por F. M. Esteves Pereira. (Quarto Centenario do Descobrimento da India. Contribuições da Sociedade de Geographia de Lisboa). pp. xlvii. 152. *Imprensa Nacional: Lisboa*, 1898. 8°. (09057. dd.)

Castanhoso (Miguel de).—Storia della spedizione Portoghese in Abissinia narrata da Michele de Castagnoso. Corpo do estado Maior Italiano. *Roma*, 1888. 8°. [Not in the British Museum.]

Castenheda (Fernam Lopes de).
  See Lopes de Castenheda (F.).

Castro (João de), *Viceroy of India.*—Roteiro em que se contem a viagem que fizeram os Portuguezes... 1541, partindo da nobre cidade de Goa atee Soez, etc. [Portrait of J. de Castro.] Atlas. 2 vols. *Baudry: Paris,* 1833. 8° and fol. (1047. k. 21 ; 563. g. 34.)

Cecchi (Antonio).—L'Abissinia Settentrionale e le strade che vi conducono da Massaua. Notizie. pp. vi, 48. *Fratelli Treves: Milano,* 1887. 8°. (10097. df. 19.)

Cecchi (Antonio).—Da Zeila alle frontiere del Caffa. Viaggi... pubblicati a cura e spese della Società Geografica Italiana. 2 vols. *E. Loescher & Co.: Roma,* 1886, 87. 8°. (10097. h. 27.)

Chahab Eddin Ahmed, *surnamed Arab-Faqih.*
  See Ahmad Ibn 'Abd Al-Kādir (Shihāb al-Dīn).

Cicero (Marcus Tullius) [*Somnium Scipionis.—Latin*].—M. Tulli Ciceronis Somnium Scipionis. Edited by W. D. Pearman. (Pitt Press Series.) (V. 10, 11, p. 17.) *University Press: Cambridge,* 1883. 8°. (2322. b. 42.)

Citerni (Carlo).
  See Vannutelli (Lamberto).

Claudius, *King of Ethiopia.*—Chroniques de Galâwdêwos (Claudius), roi d'Ethiopie (1540-1559). Texte ethiopien traduit, annoté... par W. E. Conzelman. (Bibliothèque de l'Ecole des Hautes Etudes, fasc. 104.) pp. xxxi. 190. *E. Bouillon: Paris,* 1895. 8°. (Ac. 8929.)

Claudius, *King of Ethiopia.*— Confessio Fidei Claudii, Regis Aethiopiae (1540-1559), cum versione Latina, notis et prefatione Iobi Ludolfi, primum in Anglia, deinde in Commentario Historiae eius Aethiopicae edita. Nunc vero aliquot in locis revisa, et denuo impressa, cura I. H. Michaelis. Aeth. et Lat. pp. 20. *Sumtibus Orphanotrophii: Halae Magdeburgicae,* 1702. 4°. (4376. i. 19 | 1).

Coffin (William), *Traveller in Abyssinia.*—Mr. Coffin's Account of his visit to Gondar.
  See Pearce (Nathaniel).—The Life, etc., 1831. 8°.

Coffin (William), *Traveller in Abyssinia.*—Notes respecting Abyssinia, made during a residence in the country, 1810-15, with copies of letters from Capt. H. Rudland, agent for E. I. Co. at Mocha, addressed to W. Coffin and Nathaniel Pearce. Paper. 4°. (Add. MSS. 19,421.)

Colizza (Giovanni).—Lingua Afar nel nord-est dell' Africa. Grammatica, testi e vocabolario. pp. xii. 153. *A. Hoelder: Vienna,* 1887. 8°. (12904. df. 36.)

Combes (Edmond) and Tamisier (Maurice).—Voyage en Abyssinie, dans le pays des Galla, de Choa, et d'Ifat... 1835-37. 2nd edition. 4 vols. *L. Desessart: Paris,* 1839. 8°. (790. g. 25, 1838. G. 15756-9, 1843.)

Combes (Paul).—L'Abyssinie en 1896. pp. 179. *J. André et Cie.: Paris,* 1896. 12°. (9061. aa. 18.)

Conzelman (William El.).
  See Claudius, *King of Ethiopia.*

Cook (Thomas).—Routes in Abyssinia, *London,* 1867. 8°. [Not in the British Museum.]

Cooley (William Desborough).—Mémoire sur le Tacuy de Barros. trad. par Antoine d'Abbadie. (Bulletin de la Société de Géographie. Ser. 5. Vol. 18. pp. 191-216). *La Société: Paris,* 1869. 8°. (Ac. 6035.)

Correa (Gaspar).—Lendas da India. 4 vols. (Collecção de Monumentos ineditos para a Historia das Conquistas dos Portuguezes em Africa.) *Academia Real das Sciencias: Lisboa*, 1858-64. 4°. (9056. i.)

Cosmas, *Indicopleustes*.—The Christian Topography of Cosmas, an Egyptian monk. Translated from the Greek and edited . . . by J. W. McCrindle. pp. xxvii. 398. *Hakluyt Society: London*, 1897. 8°. (Ac. 6172 | 76.)

Couto (Diogo de).
  See Barros (João de).

Crooke (William).—Rural and Agricultural Glossary for the N. W. P. & Oudh. *Calcutta*, 1888. 8°. [In the India Office Library, but *not* in the British Museum.]

Danvers (Frederick Charles).—The Portuguese in India, *etc.* 2 vols. *W. H. Allen and Co.: London*, 1894. 8°. (9056. cc. 19.)

Danvers (Frederick Charles).—Report to the Secretary of State for India . . . on the Portuguese Records relating to the East Indies, contained in the Archivo da Torre do Tombo, and the Public Libraries at Lisbon and Evora. pp. xi. 209. *India Office: London*, 1892. 8°. (9057. b. 21.)

Dāwīt II, Wanāg Sagad I, *King of Ethiopia*.
  See Lebna Dengel.

Debra Sina.—Ein Besuch in abessinischen Kloster Debra Sina. ("Bibelblätter." 1901. pp. 49-55.) *Leipzig*, 1901. 8°. [Not in the British Museum.]

Decken (Carl Claus von der), *Baron*.—Baron Carl Claus von der Decken's Reisen in Ost-Afrika in den Jahren 1859 bis 1865. Bearbeitet von O. Kersten, &c. 4 vols. *C. F. Winter: Leipzig*, 1869-79, 70. 8°. (10097. i. 35.)

De Cosson (Emilius Albert).—The Cradle of the Blue Nile. A Visit to the Court of King John of Ethiopia. 2 vols. *John Murray: London*, 1877. 8°. (2358. c. 5.)

Deflers (A.).—Voyage au Yemen. Journal d'une excursion botanique faite en 1887 dans le montagnes de l'Arabie heureuse. *P. Klincksieck: Paris*, 1899. 8°. [Not in the British Museum.]

Defrémery (Charles François).
  See Muhammad Ibn 'Abd Allāh.

Deramey (J.).—Les Inscriptions d'Adoulis & d'Aksoum. (Revue de l'histoire des religions. Vol. 24, pp. 316-365.) *E. Leroux: Paris*, 1891. 8°.

Deramey (J.).—Introduction & Restauration du Christianisme en Abyssinie, 330-480. (Revue de l'histoire des religions. Vol. 30.) pp. 33. *E. Leroux: Paris*, 1895. 8° (4530. dd. 10. (4.))

Des Vergers (A. Noel).—Abyssinie. (L'Univers. Histoire et description de tous les peuples). pp. 48. *Firmin Didot Frères: Paris*, 1847. 8°. (10024. dd. 9.)

Des Vergers (A. Noel).—Arabie, *etc.* (L'Univers. Histoire et description de tous les peuples.) pp. 522. *Firmin Didot Frères: Paris*, 1847. 8°. (10024. dd. 17.)

Devic (L. Marcel).—Le Pays des Zendjs, ou La Côte Orientale d'Afrique au Moyen-Age . . . d'après les écrivains arabes. pp. 280. *Hachette & Cie: Paris*, 1883. 8°. (010096. f. 21.)

Diaz (Manuel).
  See Almeida (Manoel de).—Lettere, &c.

Didier (Charles).—Cinquante Jours au désert. *Hachette & Cie: Paris*, 1857. 16°. [Not in the British Museum.]

Dietel (R. W.)—Missions-stunden. Heft 5. Abessinien. 2te Auflage, neu bearbeitet von C. Paul. pp. v. 148. *Richter: Leipzig*, 1901. 8°. [Not in the British Museum.]

Dillmann (Christian Friedrich August).
See British Museum.

Dillmann (Christian Friedrich August).—Catalogus Codicum Manuscriptorum Bibliothecae Bodleianae. Pars. VII. Codices Aethiopici. Digessit A. Dillmann. pp. 87. *E. typ. Acad.: Oxonii*, 1848. 4°. (Cat. Desk A.)

Dillmann (Christian Friedrich August).—Chrestomathia aethiopica. Edita et glossario explanata ab A. Dillman. pp. xvi. 290. *T. O. Weigel: Lipsiae*, 1866. 8°. (753. g. 26.)

Dillmann (Christian Friedrich August).—Die Kriegsthaten des Königs Amda-Sion gegen die Muslim. *Berlin*, 1884. 8°. [Not in the British Museum.]

Dillmann (Christian Friedrich August).—Lexicon linguae Aethiopicae, cum indice Latino. Adiectum est vocabularium Tigre dialecti septentrionalis compilatum a Werner Munzinger. 2 pt. *T. O. Weigel: Lipsiae*, 1865. 4°. (12907. h. 6.)

Dillmann (Christian Friedrich August).—Ueber die Anfänge des axumitischen Reiches. pp. 64. *Ferd. Dümmler: Berlin*, 1878. 8°. [Not in the British Museum.]

Dillmann (Christian Friedrich August).—Ueber die geschichtlichen Ergebnisse der Th. Bent'schen Reisen in Ost Afrika. *Berlin*, 1894. 8°. [Not in the British Museum.]

Dillmann (Christian Friedrich August).—Ueber die Regierung insbesondere die Kirchenordnung des Königs Zar'a-Jacob. pp. 79. *G. Reimer: Berlin*, 1884. 8°. [Not in the British Museum.]

Dillmann (Christian Friedrich August).—Zur Geschichte des abyssinischen Reiches. pp. 338-364 of the "Zeitschrift der Deutschen morgenländischen Gesellschaft." vol. 7. *F. A. Brockhaus: Leipzig*, 1853. 8°. (Ac. 8815 | 2.)

Dimotheos.
See Saprichian (Dimoteos.)

Dolganev (E. E.)—Strana Efiopov (Abissinija). pp. 200. 39. *St. Petersburg*, 1896. [Not in the British Museum.]

Dresser (Matthaeus).—De Statu Ecclesiae et religionis in Aethiopia, sub Praecioso Ioanne. pp. 25. *G. Defnerus: Lipsiae*, 1586. 12°. (568. b. 7. (2.)).

Drouin (Edmé Alphonse).—Les Listes royales éthiopiennes, et leur autorité historique. Extrait de la "Revue Archæologique." pp. 54. *Didier & Cie.: Paris*, 1882. 8°. (7704. cc. 23 | 1.)

Duensing (Hugo).—Liefert das äthiopische Synaxar Materialien zur Geschichte Abessiniens? Für den zweiten, die Monate Magābit bis Pāguemēn enthaltenden Teil des Synaxars untersucht. pp. 56. *Kästner: Göttingen*, 1900. 8°. [Not in the British Museum.]

Dufton (Henry).—Narrative of a Journey through Abyssinia in 1862-3. With Appendix on "The Abyssinian Captives Question." pp. xiv. 337. *Chapman and Hall: London*, 1870. 8°. (10095. bb 32, 1867.)

Eden (Richard).
>   *See* Barthéma (Lodovico).

Esteves Pereira (Francisco Maria).
>   *See* Almeida (Manoel de) *Jesuit.*

Esteves Pereira (Francisco Maria).
>   *See* Castanhoso (Miguel de).

Esteves Pereira (Francisco Maria).
>   *See* Susenyos, *King of Ethiopia.*

Esteves Pereira (Francisco Maria).—Canção de Galavdevos. *Lisboa*, [1895?] 8°. [Not in the British Museum.]

Esteves Pereira (Francisco Maria).—Historia de Minas Ademas Sagad, rei de Ethiopia (1559-63). [Translated from the Ethiopic with text.] pp. 87. *Lisboa*, 1888. 8°. [Not in the British Museum.]

Ethiopia.—La Conquista Mussulmana dell' Etiopia nel secolo XVI. Traduzione d'un manoscritto arabo con prefazione e note di Cesare Nerazzini e una carta geografica del 1636. [An imperfect translation of Futûh el-Habacha.] pp. xxxviii. 174. *Forzani e C: Roma*, 1891. 8°. (14555. e. 10.)

Ethiopia. — Notizie del Viaggio d'un Etiopico dall' Etiopia all' Italia in vero Tigrai, etc. pp. 16. *Roma*, 1895. 8°. (754. b. 28.)

Ethiopic, Amharic, and Arabic Letters, written to Henry Salt by Ras Waldá Selasé and others. With English translations and specimens of Coptic writing, 1810-27. Paper. Fol. (Add. MSS. 19,343.)

Fenzl (Eduard).—Bericht über die von Herrn Constantin Reitz auf seiner Reise von Chartum nach Gondar gesammelten geographisch-statistischen Notizen. *Wien*, 1855. 4°. [Not in the British Museum.]

Ferrand (Gabriel).—Le Çomal. *Alger*, 1884. 8°. [Not in British Museum.]

Ferrand (Gabriel).—Notes de grammaire çomalie. *Alger*, 1886. 8°.

Ferret (Pierre Victor Adolphe) and Galinier (Joseph Germain).—Voyage en Abyssinie dans les provinces du Tigre, du Samen, et de l'Amhara. 3 vols. & Atlas. *Paulin: Paris*, 1847-48. 8°. & fol. (10095. e. 2. & S. 263. (18.))

Fetha Nagast.
>   *See* Abyssinia.

Fialho (Manoel.)
>   *See* Fonseca (Francisco da.)

Fialho (Manoel).—Evora Illustrada com as noticias antigas e modernas... pello padre Manoel Fialho. [Not in the British Museum.]

Ficalho (— de) *Count.*—Viagens de Pedro da Covilhan. pp. xvii. 365. *A. M. Pereira: Lisboa*, 1898. 8°. (10024. k. 1.)

Figueiredo Falcão (Luiz de).—Livro em que se contém Toda a Fazenda e Real Patrimonio dos Reinos de Portugal, India e Ilhas adjacentes e outras particularidades... Copiado fielmente do Manuscripto Original, &c. (1607). pp. 270. *Imprensa Nacional: Lisboa*, 1859. Fol. (8225. ff. 24.)

Flad (Johann Martin). — Kurze Schilderung der Abessinischen Juden. *Kornthal*, 1869. 16°.

Flad (Johann Martin).—The Falashas (Jews) of Abyssinia... Translated from the German by S. P. Goodhart. pp. xiv. 75. *W. Macintosh: London*, 1869. 8°. (4765. aa. 21.)

Flad (Johann Martin).—Notes from the Journal of F. [*i.e.*, J.] M. Flad, one of Bishop Gobat's pilgrim missionaries in Abyssinia. Edited with a brief sketch of the Abyssinian Church by . . . W. D. Veitch. pp. iv. 88. *J. Nisbet & Co. : London*, 1860. 8° (4765. a. 44.)

Flad (Johann Martin).—Zwölf Jahre in Abessinien ; oder, Geschichte des Königs Theodoros II. und der Mission unter seiner Regierung. pp. iv. 176. *C. F. Spittler : Basel*, 1869. 8°. (10095. b. 29.)

Flad (Johann Martin).—Zwölf Jahre in Abessinien, oder, Geschichte des Königs Theodorus II. und der Mission unter seiner Regierung. (Institutum Judaicum Schriften. Nos. 12,-15.) *Dörffling & Franke : Leipzig*, 1887. 8° (4034. dd.)

Fonseca (Francisco da).—Evora Gloriosa, epilogo dos quatro tomos da Evora Illustrada, que compoz o R. P. M. Manoel Fialho . . . escritta, acrecentada e amplificada pello P. Francisco da Fonseca. *Na Officina Komarekiana : Roma*, 1728. fol. (4625. f. 7.)

Freire de Andrade (Jacinto).—Chronica d'El Rei Dom Joao III. 4 vols. *Coimbra*, 1726. 8°.

Freire de Andrade (Jacinto).—Vida de Dom João de Castro, quarto Viso-Rey da India. pp. 444. *Na Officina Craesbeeckiana : Lisboa*, 1651. fol. (582. i. 19 | 1.)

Freire de Andrade (Jacinto).—The Life of Dom John de Castro, the fourth Vice-Roy of India . . . Translated into English by Sir Peter Wyche . . . Second edition. pp. 272. *H. Herringman : London*, 1699. fol. (612. 1. 22.)

Friederici (Karl).—Bibliotheca Orientalis, oder, Eine volständige Liste der im Jahre 1876-83, in Deutschland, Frankreich, England, und den Colonien erschienenen Bücher, Broschüren . . . über die Sprachen, Religionen, Antiquitäten Literaturen, Geschichte und Geographie des Ostens. 8 pts. *O. Schulze : Leipzig*, [1877-84.] 8°. (BB. T. d. 4.)

Fumagalli (Giuseppe).—Bibliografia Etiopica. pp. xi. 288. *Ulrico Hoepli : Milano*, 1893. 8°. (011900. h. 12.)

Futuh el-Habacha.
 See Ahmad Ibn ' Abd al-Kādir.

Gadla Aragâwî.—Il "Gadla Aragâwî," Memoria del socio J. Guidi letta nella seduta del 21 giugno 1891. (Atti della R. Accademia dei Lincei. Anno CCXCI, 1894. Ser. 5. Classe di Scienzi Morali, *etc.* Vol. ii. Pt. ia, Memorie. pp. 54-96). *V. Salviucci : Roma*, 1896. 4°. (Ac. 102 | 10.)

Gadla Takla Hāymānot.—Relazione dei soci Guidi, relatore, e Teza, presentata al Presidente durante le ferie accademiche del 1895, sulla Memoria del dott. C. Conti Rossini intitolata : "Il Gadla Takla Hāymānot," secondo la redazione waldebbana." (Atti della R. Accademia dei Lincei. Anno CCXCI, 1894. Ser. 5. Classe di Scienzi Morali, *etc.* Vol. ii. Pt. ia, Memorie. pp. 97-143.) *V. Salviucci : Roma*, 1896. 4°. (Ac. 102 | 10.)

Galinier (Joseph Germain).
 See Ferret (Pierre Victor Adolphe).

Galla.—Geschichte der Galla . . . Bericht eines Abessinischen Mönches über die Invasion der Galla im sechzehnten Jahrhundert. Text & Ubersetzung herausgegeben von A. W. Schleicher. pp. 42. *T. Fröhlich : Berlin*, 1893. 8°. (754. b. 26.)

Garstin (*Sir* William Edmund), *K.C.M.G.*—Report on the Irrigation of Egypt. (Report upon the Administration of the Public Works Department.) June 7, 1901. pp. 58 and 12 maps. 8°. [Not in the British Museum.]

Geddes (Michael).—The Church-History of Abyssinia. pp. 488. *R. Chilwell: London*, 1696. 8°. (677. d. 9. 201. c. 7.)

Ghika (Nicolas D.), *Prince.*—Cinq mois au pays des Somalis. pp. vi. 223. *Georg and Co.: Genève and Bâle*, 1898. 8°. (10094 f. 4.)

Gibbon (Edward) *the Historian.*—The History of the Decline and Fall of the Roman Empire... Edited... by J. B. Bury. L. P. (vol. iv, c. xlii. pp. 384-387. Vol. v, ch. xlvii. pp. 165-168.) *Methuen and Co.: London*, 1896-1900. 8°. (9039. de. 1.)

Girard (Jules).—Souvenirs d'un Voyage en Abyssinie. *Le Caire*, 1873. 8°. [Not in the British Museum.]

Glaser (Eduard).—Die Abessinien in Arabien & Afrika, auf Grund neuentdeckter Inschriften. pp. xii. 210. *H. Lukaschik: München*, 1895. 8°. (07703. g. 5.)

Gleichen (Albert Edward Wilfred) *Count.*—With the Mission to Menelik, 1897. Illustrated. pp. xi. 363. *E. Arnold: London*, 1898. 8°. (010095. g. 16.)

Glen (Jean Baptiste de).
   See Gouvea (Antonio de.)

Glyn (Frederick), *4th Baron Wolverton.*—Five Months' Sport in Somali-Land, etc. pp. 108. *Chapman and Hall: London*, 1894. 8°. (07905. i. 2.)

Gobat (Samuel), *Bishop.*—Journal of a Three Years' Residence in Abyssinia, in furtherance of the objects of the Church Missionary Society... To which is added, A Brief History of the Church in Abyssinia, by... Samuel Lee... Second edition. pp. xxxix. 383. *Seeley and Co.: London*, 1847. 8°. (4765. c. 45.)

Gobat (Samuel), *Bishop.*—Journal d'un sejour en Abyssinie. *Paris* [1844?] 8°. [Not in the British Museum.]

Goj (Luigi).—Adua e prigionia fra i Galla. 10 Genn. 1896. 6 Maggio, 1897. pp. 176. *Scuola tip. Silesiana: Milano*, 1901. 8°. [Not in the British Museum.]

Gouvea (Antonio de), *Bishop of Cyrene.*—Jornada do Arcebispo de Goa Dom Frey Aleixo de Menezes, primaz da India Oriental... quando foy as Serras do Malavar & lugares em que morão os antigos Christãos de S. Thome, &c. ff. 152. *D. Gomez Loureyro: Coimbra*, 1606. fol. (1124. k. 4. (1.))

Gouvea (Antonio de), *Bishop of Cyrene.*—Histoire Orientale des Grans Progres de l'Eglise Cathol. Apost. & Rom. en la reduction des anciens Chrestiens, dits de S. Thomas... composée en langue Portugaise... & puis mise en Espagnol par... François Munoz, & tournee en François par F. J. B. de Glen. pp. 748. *H. Verdussen: Anvers*, 1609. 8°. (867. f. 3. | 1.) [The Spanish translation is not in the British Museum.]

Guerreiro (Fernão).—Relaçam annal das cousas que fizeram os Padres da Companhia de Jesus nas partes da India Oriental... commais huã addiçam á relaçam de Ethiopia, *etc.* 4 vols. *P. Crasbeeck: Lisboa*, 1603-11. 8°. (1369. g. 68 and 295. k. 8.) [In Woolmer's Catalogue, Sept. 2, 1799, this book was described as "Fizeramo's Relaçam and Annal"!]

Guidi (Ignazio).
   See Abyssinia.

Guidi (Ignazio).
   See Gadla Aragâwî.

Guidi (Ignazio).
   See Gadla Takla Hāymānot.

Guidi (Ignazio).—Di duo frammenti relativi alla storia di Abissinia. [Translated from the Ethiopic with text.] pp. 29. *Roma*, 1893. 8°. [Not in the British Museum.]

Guidi (Ignazio).—Le Liste dei Metropoliti d'Abissinia. *Roma*, 1899. 8°. [Not in the British Museum.]

Guidi (Ignazio).—Uno squarcio di storia ecclesiastica di Abissinia. *Bessarione*. vol. 8. pp. 10-25.) *Direzione: Roma*, 1900. 8°. (P. P. 23. eb.)

Guidi (Ignazio).—Vocabulario amarico italiano. *Roma*, 1901. 8°, [Not in the British Museum.]

Guillain (Charles).—Documents sur l'histoire, la géographie, et le commerce de l'Afrique, orientale, recueillis & rediges par M. Guillain. (Album lithographié . . . d'après des épreuves daguerriennes et les dessins de MM. Caraguel et H. Bridet.) 2 vols. *Paris*, [1856-57.] 8°. and fol. (1425. k. and 1853. h. 13.)

Gwynn (Charles William). — Surveys on the proposed Sudan-Abyssinian Frontier. (Geographical Journal, vol. 18. pp. 562-573.) *Royal Geographical Society: London*, 1901. 8°. (2058. aa.)

Haggenmacher (G. A.).—G. A. Haggenmacher's Reise im Somali-Lande, 1874. (Ergänzungsband 10. Petermann's Mitteilungen.) pp. 45. *J. Perthes: Gotha*, 1876. 4°. (P. P. 3946.)

Hakluyt (Richard).—Hakluyt's Collection of the Early Voyages, Travels and Discoveries of the English Nation. A new edition, with additions. L. P. 5 vols. *R. H. Evans: London*, 1809-1812. 4°. (208. h. 10-14.)

Halévy (Joseph).—Essai sur la langue agaou. *Paris*, 1873. 8°. [Not in the British Museum.]

Halévy (Joseph).—Excursion chez les Falachas d'Abyssinie. (Bulletin de la Société de Géographie. Ser. 5. Vol. 17. pp. 270-294.) *Arthus Bertrand: Paris*, 1869. 8°. (Ac. 6035.)

Halévy (Joseph).—Prières des Falashas, ou Juifs d'Abyssinie. Texte éthiopien publié pour la première fois & traduit en Hébreu par J. Halévy. *J. Baer & Ce.: Paris*, 1877. 8°. (754. a. 2.)

Halls (J. J.)
   See Pearce (Nathaniel).

Harris (*Sir* William Cornwallis).—The Highlands of Aethiopia, described during 18 months' residence of a British Embassy at the Christian Court of Shoa. Second edition. 3 vols. *Longman, Brown & Co.: London*, 1844. 8°. (1425. h. 4-6.)

Hartmann (Johann Melchior).—Edrisii Africa. Curavit J. M. Hartmann. Editio altera [of "Commentatio de Geographia Africae Edrisiana," 1791.] pp. cxxiv. 530. *Sumtibus J. C. Dieterich: Gottingae*, 1796. 8°. (14565. b. 5.)

Hasan Ibn Ahmad, *al-Khaimi*.—Der Gesandtschaftsbericht des Hasan ben Ahmed El-Haimî. Herausgegeben von F. E. Peiser. (Zur Geschichte Abessiniens im 17. Jahrhundert. . . . uebersetzt von F. E. Peiser.) 2 vols. *Wolf Peiser: Berlin*, 1894, 98. 8°. (14565. c. 24, 28.)

Heeren (Arnold Hermann Ludwig).—Historical Researches into the Politics, Intercourse, and Trade of the Carthaginians, Ethiopians, and Egyptians . . . Translated from the German [by D. A. Talboys.] 2 vols. *D. A. Talboys: Oxford*, 1832. 8°. (2067. a.)

Henri Philippe Marie [d'Orléans], Prince.—Une Visite à l'Empereur Ménélick. Notes et impressions de route. pp. 264. *Dentu: Paris*, [1898.] 8°. (10095. bbb. 38.)

Henty (George Alfred).—The March to Magdala. [Letters reprinted from "The Standard."] pp. vii. 431. *Tinsley Bros.: London*, 1868. 8°. (10095. cc. 23.)

Hertslet (*Sir* Edward).—The Map of Africa by Treaty. 2nd edition. Vol. i. *Stationery Office: London*, 1896. 8° (8028. e. 38.)

Heuglin (M. Theodor von).—Reisen in Nord-Ost-Afrika . . . Tagebuch einer Reise von Chartum nach Abyssinien . . . 1852 bis 1853. pp. x. 136. *J. Perthes: Gotha*, 1857. 8°. (10095. d. 26.) [1878 edn., not in the British Museum.]

Holland (Trevenen James), and Hozier (Henry Montague).—Record of the Expedition to Abyssinia. 3 vols. *Stationery Office: London*, 1870. 4°. (9061. g. 9.)

Hotten (John Camden).—Abyssinia & its People; or, Life in the Land of Prester John. [Selected from various narratives.] Edited by J. C. Hotten. pp. 314. (pp. 369-384 contain a good Bibliography by F. Berridge.) *J. C. Hotten: London*, 1868 [1867]. 8°. (2358. b. 4.)

Hozier (Henry Montague).—The British Expedition to Abyssinia. pp. xi. 271. *Macmillan & Co.: London*, 1869. 8°. (2358. f. 6.)

Ibn Batoutah.
 See Muhammad Ibn 'Abd Allāh, called *Ibn Batūtah.*

Isenberg (Carl Wilhelm) and Krapf (Johann Ludwig).—Journals of the Rev. Messrs. Isenberg and Krapf . . . detailing their proceedings in the kingdom of Shoa, and journeys in other parts of Abyssinia . . . 1839-42. To which is prefixed a Geographical Memoir of Abyssinia . . . By J. M'Queen, *etc.* pp. xxvii. 95. 529. *Seeley & Co.: London*, 1843. 8°. (1369. f. 14.)

Ismail Ibn Ali (Imad Al-Din Abu Al Fida) *Prince of Hamat.*—Géographie d'Aboulféda traduite de l'Arabe en Français . . . par M. Reinaud (tom. i, ii. pt. 1; et par M. S. Guyard. tom. ii. pt 2). 2 tom. *Imprimerie Nationale: Paris*, 1848, 83. 4°. (14566. c. 13, 14.)

Jackson (James) *Archiviste-Bibliothécaire, etc.* Liste Provisoire de Bibliographies Géographiques Spéciales. (Afrique.—Nos. 532-36, 538-9, 542-4, 585-7.) pp. 340. *Société de Géographie: Paris*, 1881. 8° (BB. I. a. 8.)

Jesuits.—Cartas Annuas dos Padres da Companhia de Jésus. [Portuguese MS., Academia Real das Sciencias de Lisboa.]

John, *Bishop of Nikiou.*—Chronique de Jean, Eveque de Nikiou. Texte éthiopien publié et traduit par H. Zotenberg. Extrait des Notices des Manuscrits, vol. 24, pt. 1. pp. 48. *Imprimerie Nationale: Paris*, 1883. 4°. (753. k. 18.)

John, *Prester.*
 See British Museum Catalogue. Forty-seven entries from 1478 to 1879.

John, *Prester.*—Description de l'empire du Prete-Jean. (Recueil de divers voyages faits en Afrique). pp. 35. *L. Billaine: Paris*, 1674. 4°. (214. a. 11.)

Johnson (Samuel), *LL.D.*
 See Rasselas, *Prince of Abyssinia.*

Johnston (Charles) *M.R.C.S.*—Travels in Southern Abyssinia, through the country of Adal to the kingdom of Shoa. 2 vols. *J. Madden and Co.: London*, 1844. 8°. (1425. h. 7.)

Johnston (Sir Henry Hamilton) *K.C.B.*—A History of the Colonisation of Africa by alien races, *etc.* (G. W. Prothero.—Cambridge Historical Series.) pp. xii. 319. *University Press: Cambridge*, 1899. 8°. (2378. b.)

Jomard (Edmé François).—Remarques à l'occasion de la notice de M. Fresne sur les sources du Nil. (Bulletin, Société de Géographie.. Ser 3. Vol. 10. pp. 304-309.) *Arthus-Bertrand: Paris*, 1849. 8°. (Ac. 6035.)

Jones (John Winter).
    See Barthéma (Lodovico).

Katte (A. von).—Reise in Abyssinien im Jahre 1836. (E. Widenmann & H. Hauff's Reisen & Länderbeschreibungen. Pt. 15.) pp. xii. 180. *J. G. Cotta: Stuttgart*, 1838. 8°. (1294. c. 4.)

Keane (Augustus Henry).—Man, Past and Present. Second edition, revised. (Cambridge Geographical Series.) pp. xii. 584. *University Press: Cambridge*, 1901. 8°. (Not in the British Museum. 1899 at 2352. c. 16.)

Keltie (John Scott).—The Partition of Africa. 2nd edition. pp. xv. 564. *E. Stanford: London*, 1895. 8°. (2386. d. 1.)

Kebra Nagast.—Fabula de Regina Sabæa apud Æthiopes. [An extract from the Ethiopic Chronicle: Kebra Nagast.] Dissertatio inauguralis quam ... defendet ... F. Prætorius. *Eth. and Lat.* pp. x. 44. *Halis*, [1870.] 8°. (754. b. 4,) [The copy of Kebra Nagast, written A.D. 1682-1706, British Museum, Or. MSS. 819, was generously restored by the Trustees of the British Museum to Prince Kasa, afterwards King John of Abyssinia, on Dec. 14, 1862.]

Klöden (Gustav Adolph von).—Beiträge zur neueren Geographie von Abissinien. *Berlin*, 1855. 8°. [Not in the British Museum.]

Koettlitz (Reginald).—A Journey through Somaliland and Southern Abyssinia to the Berta or Shangalla country and the Blue Nile, and through the Sudan to Egypt. (Journal of the Tyneside Geographical Society. Vol. 4. pp. 323-343.) *Newcastle-on-Tyne*, 1901. 8°. [Not in the British Museum.]

König (Friedrich Eduard).—Neue Studien über Schrift, Aussprache und allgemeine Formenlehre des Aethiopischen, &c. pp. xii. 164. *J. C. Hinrichs: Leipzig*, 1877. 8°. (12904. bbb. 13.)

Krapf (Johann Ludwig).
    See Isenberg (Carl Wilhelm).

Krapf (Johann Ludwig).—An Imperfect outline of the elements of the Galla Language ... Preceded by a few remarks concerning the ... Gallas ... by ... C. W. Isenberg. pp. xiv, 16. *Church Missionary Society: London*, 1840. 8°. (829. d. 17.)

Krapf (Johann Ludwig).
    See Mayer (Johann).

Krapf (Johann Ludwig).—Vocabulary of the Galla Language. pp. ii. 42. *Church Missionary Society: London*, 1842. 8°. (12907. b. 30.)

Krapf (Johann Ludwig).—Reisen in Ost-Afrika ... 1837-55. 2 pt. *Im Selbstverlage des Verfassers: Kornthal*, 1858. 8°. (10396. e. 30.)

Krapf (Johann Ludwig).—Travels, Researches, and Missionary Labours during an 18 years' residence in Eastern Africa, together with journeys to ... Shoa, Abessinia ... With an appendix respecting ... the languages and literature of Abessinia ... by E. G. Ravenstein. pp. li. 566. *Trübner & Co.: London*, 1860. 8°. (2358. e. 10.)

Kuhn (Ernst).—Literatur-Blatt für Orientalische Philologie ... Herausgegeben von Prof. Dr. Ernest Kuhn. 4 vols. *O. Schulze: Leipzig*, 1844-88. 8°. (P. P. 5044. cb.)

Lafitau (Joseph François).—Histoire des découvertes et conquestes des Portugais dans le Nouveau Monde [East Indies]. 2 vols. *Saugrain Pere: Paris*, 1733. 4°. (145. c. 11, 12.)

Lālībalā, *King of Ethiopia*.—Vie de Lalibala, roi d'Ethiopie. Texte éthiopien, publié d'après un manuscrit du Musée Britannique (Or. MSS. 718, 719) et traduction française. Avec un resumé de l'histoire des Zagüés et la description des églises monolithes de Lalibala, par Jules Perruchon. (Publ. de l'Ecole des Lettres d'Alger., vol. 10.) pp. xlvii. 164. *E. Leroux: Paris*, 1892. 8°. (Ac. 5350 | 2.)

Lauribar (Paul de).—Douze Ans en Abyssinie. Souvenirs d'un officier. pp. vi. 648. *E. Flammarion: Paris*, 1898. 8°. (10096. e. 38.)

Lebna Dengel, Dāwīt II, Wanāg Sagad I.—Storia di Lebna Dengel (1508-1540). [Translated from the Ethiopic with text by C. Conti Rossini.] *Roma*, 1894. 8°. [Not in the British Museum.]

Lee (Samuel).
 See Muhammad Ibn 'Abd Allāh.

Lefebvre (Théophile).—Voyage en Abyssinie ... 1839-43, par une Commission Scientifique, *etc.* 6 vols., and Atlas 3 vols. *A. Bertrand: Paris* [1845-54]. 8° and fol. (1294. f. 15-20, and 1295. k. 4-6.)

Le Grand (Joachim).
 See Lobo (Jeronymo).

Le Jean (Guillaume) Théodore II., le nouvel empire d'Abyssinie, et les intérêts français dans le Sud de la Mer Rouge. pp. xii. 300. *Amyot: Paris*, [1865.] 12°. (10095. aa. 30.)

Le Jean (Guillaume).—Voyage en Abyssinie exécuté de 1862 à 1864. (Atlas.) 2 vols. *Hachette & Cie: Paris*, 1872. fol. (1854. a. 15, d. 4.)

Le Roux (Hugues).—Ménélik et Nous. *Paris*, 1901. 8°. [Not in the British Museum.]

Linschoten (Jan Huygen van).—The Voyage of John Huyghen van Linschoten to the East Indies ... Edited ... by ... A. C. Burnell ... P. A. Tiele. 2 vols. (Nos. 70, 71.) *Hakluyt Society: London*, 1885. 8°. (Ac. 6172 | 59.)

Littmann (Enno).—Abyssinian Folk-Lore. (Princeton University Bulletin. Vol. 13. pp. 14-16.) *The University: Princeton*, 1900. 8°. [Not in the British Museum.] *See also:* Theodore II.

Lobo (Jeronymo).
 See Thévenot (Melchisedech).

Lobo (Jeronymo).—P. Hieronymi [*i.e.* J. Lobo] eines Jesuiten in Portugal Neue Beschreibung & Bericht von der wahren Beschaffenheit. 1. Des Mohrenlandes sonderlich des Abyssinischen Käyserthums. 2. Des Ursprungs Nyli. 3. Wo das Einhorn zufinden. 4. Warumb der Abyssiner Käyser Priester Johannes genefiet werde, &c. ... die Teutsche Sprache übersetzt. pp. 106. *J. H. Kunsth: Nürnberg*, 1670. 12°. (1052. a. 2.)

Lobo (Jeronymo).—Voyage Historique d'Abissinie ... Traduite du Portuguais, continuée et augmentée ... [*sic*] par M. [Joachim] Le Grand. pp. xiv. 514. *P. Gosse: Paris*, 1728. 8°. (982. f. 23.)

Lopes de Castenheda (Fernam).—Historia do descobrimento e conquista da India. 7 vols. *Na typographia Rollandiana: Lisboa*, 1833. 4°. (C. 33. m. 803. k. 26.)

Ludolf (Hiob), *the Elder.*
    See **Claudius.**—Confessio, &c.

Ludolf (Hiob), *the Elder.*—Iobi Ludolfi, alias Leut-holf dicti Historia Aethiopica. *J. D. Zunner: Francofurti ad Moenum*, 1681. Fol. (583. k. 13. G. 6643 | 1.)

Ludolf (Hiob), *the Elder.*—Iobi Ludolfi ... ad suam Historiam Aethiopicam antehac editam Commentarius. pp. 632. *Sumptibus J. D. Zunneri: Francofurti ad Moenum*, 1691. Fol. (583. k. 13. G. 6643 | 2.)

Ludolf (Hiob), *the Elder.*—Appendix ad Historiam Aethiopicam Iobi Ludolfi illiusque Commentarium, ex nova relatione de hodierno Habessiniae statu concinnata. Additis Epistolis Regiis ad Societatem Indiae Orientalis ejusque responsione cum notis necessariis. pp. 32. *Sumptibus J. D. Zunneri: Francofurti ad Moenum*, 1693. Fol. (583. k. 13. G. 6643 | 3.)

Ludolf (Hiob), *the Elder.*—A New History of Ethiopia ... second edition ... Made English by J. P. Gent. pp. 398. *Samuel Smith: London*, 1684. fol. (983. h. 8.)

Luzzato (Filosseno).—Mémoires sur les Juifs d'Abyssinie ou Falashas [Edited by S. Cahen.] (Extrait des Archives Israelites. pp. 120. *Paris*, [1853.] 8°. (10095. bbb. 11.)

MacCrindle (J. W.).
    See **Cosmas.**

MacQueen (James).
    See **Isenberg** (Carl Wilhelm).

Macrizi.
    See **Ahmad ibn 'Alī.**

Major (Richard Henry).—Memoir on a Mappemonde by Leonardo da Vinci ... now in the Royal Collections at Windsor, etc. (*Archæologia.* vol. 40. pp. 1-40.) *Society of Antiquaries: London*, 1866. 4° (Cat. Desk I.)

Maltzan (Heinrich von), *Baron.*—Reise nach Süd-Arabien, &c. pp. xvi. 422. *F. Vieweg & Sohn: Braunschweig*, 1873. 8°. (10075. cc. 6.)

Marcian, *of Heracleia.*—Périple de Marcien d'Héraclée, épitome d'Artemidore [both with the Latin version of J. Hudson], Isidore de Charax, *etc.*, ou Supplément aux dernières éditions des Petits Geographes [of J. Hudson and J. B. Gail] d'après un manuscrit grec de la Bibliothèque Royale avec une carte par E. Miller. pp. xxiv. 363. *Imprimerie Royale: Paris*, 1839. 8° (793. i. 4.)

Markham (*Sir* Clements Robert) *K.C.B.*—A History of the Abyssinian Expedition, *etc.* pp. xii. 484. *Macmillan & Co.: London*, 1869. 8°. (2358. f. 11.)

Martial (Fr.).—Un Peuple antique, ou, Une colonie gauloise au pays de Ménélik. Les Galla, grande nation africaine. pp. xx. 427. *Plantade: Cahors*, 1901. 8°. [Not in the British Museum.]

Mashafa Tomār (Mazhafa Tomâr).—Das Aethiopische Briefbuch nach drei Handschriften [in the University Libraries of Berlin and Tübingen, and in the British Museum, Or. MSS. 710] herausgegeben und übersetzt von F. Praetorius. pp. 31. *F. A. Brockhaus: Leipzig*, 1869. 8°. (752. h. 18.)

Massaja (Guglielmo) *Cardinal.*—I miei Trentacinque anni di Missione nell' Alta Etiopia. Memorie storiche. 7 vols. *Tipografia Poliglotta di Propaganda Fide: Roma*, 1885-89. fol. (4767. g. 6.)

Massaja (Guglielmo), *Cardinal.*—Mes trente-cinq années de mission dans la Haute-Ethiopie. *Lille*, [1890.] 8°. [Not in the British Museum.]

Massaja (Guglielmo), *Cardinal.*—In Abissinia e fra i Galla. Dalle memorie del Cardinal Massaja. Pubblicazione dell' Associazione Nazionale per soccorrere i Missionarj Cattolici Italiani a benefizio delle Missioni dell' Eritrea. pp. xv. 387. *E. Ariani: Firenze,* 1595. 8°. (4765. eee. 5.)

Massaja (Guglielmo), *Cardinal.*—Lectiones grammaticales pro missionariis qui addiscere volunt linguam Amaricam, seu vulgarem Abyssiniae, &c. pp. xix. 501. *In Typographeo Imperiali: Parisiis,* 1867. 8°. (12906. e. 5.)

Mathuisieulx (H. de).—L'Omo. Voyage d'exploration dans les pays des Somalis et de l'Ethiopie méridionale. La Mission Bottego. Adapté par M. H. de Mathuisieulx. *Tour du Monde,* N. S. vol. 6. pp. 313-336.) *Hachette & Cie: Paris,* 1900. 4°. (2058. d.)

Matteuci (Pellegrino).—In Abissinia. Viaggio di P. Matteuci. pp. vii. 316. *Fratelli Treves: Milano,* 1880. 12°. (10097. aa. 17.)

Mayer (Johann).—Kurze Wörtersammlung in englisch, deutsch, amharisch, gallanisch, guraguesch. Herausgegeben von Dr. L. Krapf. pp. 28. *Pilgermissions-Buchdruckerei: Basel,* 1878. 8°. [Not in the British Museum.]

Mayo, Dermot Robert Wyndham, *Earl of.*
See Bourke.

Meynard (Charles Adrien Casimir Barbier de).
See Barbier de Meynard (C. A. C.).

Michel (Charles) De la Mer Rouge au Nil, à travers l'Ethiopie. (Bulletin de la Société d' Anthropologie de Lyon. Vol. 19. pp. 31-40.) *H. Georg: Lyon,* 1901. 8°. (Ac. 6244.)

Michel (Charles).—Vers Fachoda à la rencontre de la mission Marchand à travers l'Ethiopie. Mission de Bonchamps. pp. 560. *Plon-Nourrit & Cie.: Paris,* 1901. 8°. (10094. de. 6.)

Mitchell (L. H.).—Report on the seizure by the Abyssinians of the geological and mineralogical reconnaissance Expedition attached to the General Staff of the Egyptian Army . . . Containing an account of the subsequent treatment of the prisoners and final release of the Commander. pp. x. 125. *General Staff: Cairo,* 1878. 8°. (9061. ff. 5.)

Muhammad Ibn 'Abd Allāh, called *Ibn Batūtah.*—The Travels of Ibn Batūta. Translated from the abridged Arabic MS. Copies . . . in the Public Library of Cambridge, with notes . . . by . . . Samuel Lee. (Oriental Translation Fund.) pp. xviii. 243. *John Murray: London,* 1829. 4°. (14003. f. 2.)

Muhammad Ibn 'Abd Allāh, called *Ibn Batūtah.*—Voyages d'Ibn Batoutah. Texte arabe, accompagné d'une traduction par C. Defrémery et . . . B. R. Sanguinetti. (Collection d'Ouvrages Orientaux publiée par la Société Asiatique.) 4 vols. *Imprimerie Impériale: Paris,* 1853-59. 8°. (14003. b. 3.)

Muhammad Ibn Muhammad (Abū 'Abd Allāh), *Al-Idrīsī.*—Description de l'Afrique et de l'Espagne par Edrisi. Texte arabe publié pour la première fois d'après les mains de Paris et d'Oxford avec une traduction, des notes, et un glossaire par R. Dozy et M. J. de Geoje. 2 pt. *E. J. Brill: Leyde,* 1866. 8°. (14565. a. 23.)

Müller (David Heinrich).—Epigraphische Denkmäler aus Abessinien nach Abklatschen von J. T. Bent, Esq. (Denkschriften der Phil. hist. Cl. Vol. 43. Pt. 3.) pp. 82. *Kais. Akademie der Wissenschaften: Wien,* 1894. 4°. (Ac. 810 | 12.)

Müller (Friedrich), *Professor, of Vienna.*—Uber die Harari-Sprache im östlichen Afrika. (Sitzungsberichte der phil. hist. Classe der kais. Akademie der Wissenschaften, vol. 44. pp. 601-613.) *K. Gorold's Sohn: Wien*, 1864. 8°. (Ac. 810 | 6.)

Müller (Friedrich August) *Orientalist.*—Orientalische Bibliographie. *Reuther & Reichard: Berlin*, 1898, *etc.* 8°. (P.P. 6522, and BB. T. d. 14.)

Münzenberger (Ernest Franz August).—Abessinien und seine Bedeutung für unsere Zeit. Aus dem Nachlasse von E. F. A. Münzenberger... Herausgegeben von Joseph Spillmann. [Illustrated.] pp. xi. 161. *Herder: Freiburg im Breisgau*, 1892. 8°. (010096. i. 17.)

Munzinger (Johann Albert Werner).—Ostafrikanische Studien . . . Mit einer Karte von Nord-Abyssinien, &c. pp. viii. 584. *Fr. Hurter: Schaffhausen*, 1864. 8°. (10095. d. 14.)

Munzinger (Johann Albert Werner).—Ueber die Sitten und Recht der Bogos. pp. xiv. 96. *J. Wurster & Co: Winterthur*, 1859. 4°. (10096. h. 14.)

Munzinger (Johann Albert Werner).—Vocabulaire de la langue Tigré. pp. x. 93. *T. O. Weigel: Leipzig*, 1865. 8°. (12903. dd. 22 | 6.)

Nerazzini (Cesare).
   See Ethiopia.

Nerazzini (Cesare).—Itinerario in Etiopia, 1885, con una carta, &c. (Estratto dal Bollettino della Società Geografica Italiana, 1889-1890.) pp. 78. *La Società: Roma*, 1890. 8°. (10095. dd. 8.)

Ortroy (F. van) *Capitaine, 4e. Regt. de Lanciers.*—Conventions Internationales définissant les limites actuelles des Possessions, Protectorats et sphères d'influence en Afrique, publiées, d'après les textes authentiques. pp. xix. 517. *O. Schepens: Bruxelles*, 1898. 8°. (8156. f. 10.)

P., J., *Gent.*
   See Ludolf (Hiob).

Paëz (Gaspar).—Lettere Annue di Ethiopia del 1624, 1625, e 1626, scritte al M. R. P. Mutio Vitelleschi, Generale della Compagnia di Giesu [by G. Paëz and A. Mendes]. pp. 232. *Herede di B. Zannetti: Roma*, 1628. 12°. (4767. b. 14.)

Paëz (Gaspar).—Histoire de ce qui s'est passé au royaume d'Ethiopie es années 1624, 1625, and 1626. Tirées des letres écrites & addressées au R. P. Mutio Viteleschi, Générale de la Compagnie de Jésus. Traduite de l'Italien en Françios par un Père de la mesme Compagnie. pp. 252. *S. Cramoisy: Paris*, 1629. 12°. (4767. c. 2. (1).)

Paris.—*Bibliothèque Nationale.* Catalogue des manuscrits éthiopiens (Gheez & Amharique) de la Bibliothèque Nationale. (Par H. Zotenberg.) Manuscrits Orientaux. [especially § X. Histoire. pp. 211-249.] pp. v. 283. *Imprimerie Nationale: Paris*, 1877. 4°. (Cat. Desk G.)

Parkyns (Mansfield).—Life in Abyssinia. Being notes collected during 3 years' residence and travels ... Second edition. pp. xxviii. 446. *J. Murray: London*, 1868. 8°. (2358. b. 10. 1853. 2 vols. 10096. g. 24.)

Paulitschke (Philippe).
   See Ahmad Ibn 'Abd Al-Kādir.

Pearce (Nathaniel).—The Life and Adventures of N. Pearce, written by himself, during a residence in Abyssinia ... 1810 to 1819. Together with Mr. Coffin's Account of his visit to Gondar. Edited by J. J. Halls. 2 vols. *H. Colburn & R. Bentley: London*, 1831. 8°. (613. f. 16.)

Pearce (Nathaniel).—A Small but true Account of the ways and manners of the Abyssinians. For ... Sir Evan Nepean ... Governor of Bombay ... Oct. 1814. [Literary Society of Bombay. Trans. II. 15, 1820. 4°. (T. C. 14, b. 3.)] Paper. Fol. (Add. MSS. 19,336.)

Pearce (Nathaniel).—Vocabulary of the Languages of Tigré and Amhara. Paper. 19th cent. 4°. (Add. MSS. 19, 337.)

Peiser (Felix Ernst).—Zur Geschichte Abessiniens. (Text & Übersetzung von MS. Glaser 147 Königl. Bibliothek, Berlin. Mit dem Vortrag von A. Ilg. über Abessinien.) *Orientalische Litteraturzeitung*, vol. 4. pp. 129-138. *Wolf Peiser: Berlin*, 1901. 4°. (P. P. 4750. ba.)

Perruchon (Jules).
    See Almeida (Manoel de) Victorias, &c.

Perruchon (Jules).
    See 'Amda Sĕyon, *King of Ethiopia*.

Perruchon (Jules).
    See Lālībalā, *King of Ethiopia*.

Perruchon (Jules).
    See Zara Ya 'ḳob, *King of Ethiopia*.

Perruchon (Jules).—Notes pour l'Histoire d'Ethiopie. ("Revue Sémitique," 1893, pp. 274-86, 359-72; 1894, pp. 78-93, 155-166, 263-270; 1896, pp. 177-185, 273-278, 355-365; 1897, pp. 75-80, 173-189, 275-285, 360-372; 1898, pp. 84-92, 157-171, 267-271, 366-372; 1899, pp. 76-88, 166-176, 251-266, 364-369; 1900, pp. 176-179; 1901, pp. 176-179; 1901, pp. 71-78, 161-167.) *E. Leroux: Paris*, 1893-1901. 8°. (P. P. 37. cf.)

Platt (Thomas Pell).
    See Abyssinia. The Ethiopic Didascalia, &c.

Plowden (Walter Chichele).—Travels in Abyssinia and the Galla country. With an account of a Mission to Ras Ali in 1848 ... Edited by ... T. Chichele Plowden. pp. xv. 485. *Longmans: London*, 1868. 8°. (10095. cc. 15.)

Polo (Marco).—The Book of Ser Marco Polo, the Venetian, concerning the Kingdoms and Marvels of the East. Newly translated and edited ... by Col. Henry Yule. Second edition, revised, *etc.* 2 vols. *J. Murray: London*, 1875. 8°. (2354. f. 14.)

Poncet (Charles Jacques).—Relation abrégée du Voyage que M. C. J. Poncet ... fit en Ethiophie [*sic*] en 1698, 1699, & 1700. (Lettres édifiantes et curieuses, edited by Ch. Le Gobien. Rec. 4.) *J. Barbou: Paris*, 1713. 8°. (295. f. 2.)

Portal (*Sir* Gerald Herbert) *K.C.B.*—My Mission to Abyssinia [1888.] Illustrated. pp. vi. 261. *E. Arnold: London*, 1892. 8° (010096. f. 24.)

Purchas (Samuel) *the Elder*.—Purchas His Pilgrimes. In five Bookes. 4 pts. *H. Fetherstone: London*, 1625. fol. (679, h. 11-14. G. 6838-41.) [Mr. Grenville's copy contains the very rare cancelled p. 65 in Part 1, which contains a variation of the Map of the World, by H. Hondius.]

Quatremère (Etienne Marc).—Mémoires géographiques et historiques sur l'Egypte, et sur quelques contrées voisines . . . extraits des MSS. Coptes, Arabes, *etc.*, de la Bibliothèque Impériale. 2 vols. *F. Schoell: Paris,* 1811. 8°. (1298. c. 11.)

Raconis (J. Balarin de).
    See Barthéma (Lodovico).

Raffray (Achille).—Abyssinie. (Afrique orientale.) [Illustrated.] pp. xii. 395. *E. Plon et Cie.: Paris,* 1876. 8°. (10095. de. 5.)

Raffray (Achille).—Les Eglises Monolithes de la ville de Lalibéla (Abyssinie). [20 plates.] pp. 14. *Ve. A. Morel et Cie.: Paris,* 1882. fol. (1734. b. 16.)

Raffray (Achille).—Voyage en Abyssinie et au pays des Gallas Raias. (Bulletin de la Société de Géographie. Ser. VII, Tom. 3, pp. 324-352.) *Société de Géographie: Paris,* 1882. 8°. (Ac. 6035.)

Rassam (Hormuzd).—Narrative of the British Mission to Theodore, King of Abyssinia (1865-1868). With notices of the country traversed from Massowah, through the Soodân, the Amhâra, and back to Annesley Bay, from Mágdala. 2 vols. *John Murray: London,* 1869. 8°. (2358. f. 13.)

Rasselas, *Prince of Abyssinia.*—The Prince of Abissinia. A Tale. [By Samuel Johnson. 1st edition.] 2 vols. *R. & J. Dodsley: London,* 1759. 8°. (635. a. 7.)

Reclus (Elisée).—Nouvelle Géographie Universelle. La terre et les hommes. Tom. x. L'Afrique Septentrionale. Première partie, Bassin du Nil . . . Ethiopie, *etc.* ch. 5. pp. 195-337. *Hachette et Cie.: Paris,* 1885. 8°. (2056. e.)

Rink (Friedrich Theodor).
    See Aḥmad ibn 'Alī.

Robecchi-Brichetti (Luigi).—Lingue parlate Somali, Galla e Harari. *Roma,* 1890. 8°. [Not in the British Museum.]

Robecchi-Bricchetti (Luigi).—Nell' Harrar. Seconda edizione. pp. viii. 409. *C. Chiesa: Milano,* 1896. 8°. (010095. gg. 3.)

Robecchi-Bricchetti (Luigi).—Testi Somali. *Roma,* 1889. 8°. [Not in the British Museum.]

Rochet d'Héricourt (C. E. X.).—Mémoire sur l'état constant de soulèvement du sol du Golfe Arabique et de l'Abyssinie, et sur un abrégé des résultats scientifiques de mon voyage. (Bulletin, Société de Géographie. Ser 3. Vol. 12. pp. 291-302.) *Arthus-Bertrand: Paris,* 1849. 8°. (Ac. 6035.)

Rochet d' Hericourt (C. E. X.).—Voyage sur la côte orientale de la Mer Rouge, dans le pays d'Adel et le Royaume de Choa. pp. xxiii. 439. *A. Bertrand: Paris,* 1841. 8°. (10095. cc. 12.)

Rochet d' Héricourt (C. E. X.).—Second Voyage sur les deux rives de la Mer Rouge, dans le pays des Adels, *etc.* (Atlas.) pp. xlviii. 406. *A. Bertrand: Paris,* 1846. 8°. (1425. k. 8.)

Rohlfs (Gerhard).—Land und Volk in Afrika. Berichte aus den Jahren 1865-1870. pp. 240. *J. Kühtmann: Bremen,* 1870. 8°. (10095. de. 27.)

Rohlfs (Gerhard).—Meine Mission nach Abessinien . . . im Winter, 1880 | 81. Illustrated. pp. xx. 348. *F. A. Brockhaus: Leipzig,* 1883. (10097. df. 9.)

Rossini (Carlo Conti).
    See Gadla Takla Hāymānot; *see also* Lebna Dengel.

Rossini (Carlo Conti).—Appunti ed osservazioni sui Re Zague. *Roma*, 1895. 8°. [Not in the British Museum Catalogue.]

Rossini (Carlo Conti).—Catalogo dei nomi proprî di luogo dell' Etiopia, contenuti nei testi gitiz ed amhariña finora pubblicato, *etc.* (Atti del primo Congresso geografico italiano, *etc.* Vol. 2. pt. 1.) pp. 387-439. *R. Istituto Sordo-Muti: Genova*, 1894. 8°. (Ac. 6007.)

Rossini (Carlo Conti).—Di alcune recenti publicazioni sull' Etiopia. *Roma*, 1897. 8°. [This, and the following works by the same author, are not in the British Museum Catalogue.]

Rossini (Carlo Conti).—Di un nuove codice. *Roma*, 1893. 8°.

Rossini (Carlo Conti).—Donazioni reali alla cattedrale di Aksum. *Roma*, 1895. 8°.

Rossini (Carlo Conti).—Note etiopiche. *Roma*, 1897. 8°.

Rossini (Carlo Conti).—L'Omelia di Abba Yohannes, vescovo d'Aksum. *Paris*, [1895.] 8°.

Rossini (Carlo Conti).—Rapport sur le progrès des études éthiopiennes. *Paris*, 1894-97. 8°.

Rossini (Carlo Conti).—Ricerche e studi sull' Etiopia. *Roma*, 1900. 8°.

Rossini (Carlo Conti).—Sulla dinastia Zague. *Roma*, 1897. 8°.

Routes in Abyssinia. Compiled at the . . . War Office by Lieut.-Col. A. C. Cooke. With a map. Presented to the House of Lords by command of Her Majesty. Parl. Papers. 1867-68. [3964.] Vol. 44. pp. 1-252. *Stationery Office: London*, 1867. fol. (N. R.)

Rüppell (Wilhelm Peter Eduard Simon).—Reise in Abyssinien. F. P. 2 vols. & Atlas. *S. Schmerber: Frankfurt am Main*, 1838-40. 8° and fol. (790. k. 22, and 789. h. 7.)

Russ (Camill).—Abessinien's gegenwärtige Lage. (Deutsche Geographische Blätter. Vol. 2, pp. 141-169.) *G. A. von Halem: Bremen*, 1878. 8°. (Ac. 6059.)

Russel (Stanislas), *Count.*—Une Mission en Abyssinie et dans la Mer Rouge, 23 Octobre, 1859—7 Mai, 1860. pp. xxvii. 306. *E. Plon et Cie.: Paris*, 1884. 8°. (10097. b. 37.)

Saineano (Marius).—L'Abyssinie dans la seconde moitié du XVIe. siècle, ou le règne de Sartsa-Dengel (Malak-Sagad), 1563-1594, d'après des annales éthiopiennes inédites. pp. 54. *Leipsig-[F. Göbl Fiu] Bucharest*, 1892. 8°. (754. b. 41.)

Salt (Henry).—Memorandum-Book, containing notices of Abyssinia, grammatical notes, vocabularies, *etc.* Paper. 19th cent., small 4°. (Add. MSS. 19,420.)

Salt (Henry).—Notes of Travels in Mozambique and Abyssinia, 1809 and 1810. Paper. fol. (Add. MSS. 19,419.)

Salt (Henry).—Original Journal by H. Salt, Secretary to George Annesley, Viscount Valentia, of his proceedings at Massowah and Arkiko, previous to his expedition into the interior of Abyssinia, 28th June to 20th July, 1805, *etc.* Paper. 8°. (Add. MSS. 19,338.)

Salt (Henry).—A Voyage to Abyssinia . . . 1809 and 1810. [Illustrated.] pp. xi. 506. lxxv. *F. C. & J. Rivington: London*, 1814. 4°. (146. g. 12.)

Sanguinetti (Benjamin Raphaël).
    See Muhammad Ibn 'Abd Allāh.

Sapeto (Giuseppe).—Etiopia. *Roma,* 1890. 8°. (Quoted in "Encyclopædia Britannica," vol. 25, 1902, but not in the British Museum.)

Sapeto (Giuseppe).—Viaggio e Missione Cattolica fra i Mensâ i Bogos e gli Habab, con un cenno geografico e storico dell' Abissinia . . . Volume unico. pp. xxxix. 528. *S. Congreg. di Prop. Fide: Roma,* 1857. 8°. (10095. f. 20.)

Saprichian (Dimoteos).—Deux ans de séjour en Abyssinie, ou, Vie morale, politique et religieuse des Abyssiniens, par le R. P. Dimothéos. 2 vols. *Couvent de St. Jacques: Jerusalem,* 1871. 8°. (890. l. 15.)

Schefer (Charles Henri Auguste).
    See Barthéma (Lodovico).

Schleicher (Adolf Walter).
    See Galla.

Schreiber (J.).—Manuel de la Langue Tigraï parlée au centre et dans le nord de l'Abyssinie. pp. vii. 93. *Alfred Hoelder: Vienne,* 1887. 8°. (12910. dd. 33.)

Seckendorff (Götz Burkhard von) *Graf.*—Meine Erlebnisse mit dem englischen Expeditionscorps in Abessinien, 1867-1868. *R. Cabos: Potsdam,* 1869. 8°. (10095. cc. 21.)

Silva (Innocencio Francisco da).—Diccionario bibliographico portuguez. Estudos de J. F. da Silva applicaveis a Portugal e ao Brasil. 16 vols. *Imprensa Nacional: Lisboa,* 1858-93. 8°. (2050. d.)

Simon (Gabriel).—L'Ethiopie, ses moeurs, ses traditions, le Négouss Iohannès, les églises monolithes de Lalibéla. (Voyage en Abyssinie et chez les Gallas-Raias.) [Illustrated.] pp. vii. 368. *Challamel aîné: Paris,* 1885. 8°. (10096, ff. 9.)

Simpson (William).—Abyssinian Church Architecture. (Sessional Papers of the Royal Institute of British Architects, June 21, 1869. pp. 234-246.) *The Institute: London,* 1869. 4°.

Simpson (William).—Ancient Coptic Churches of Egypt [and Abyssinia. A review of the work of this name by Alfred J. Butler, 2 vols. Oxford, 1884. 8°.] (Journal of the Royal Institute of British Architects, vol. 4. 3rd Series. pp. 232-237.) *The Institute: London,* 1897. 4°. (Ac. 4880 | 4.)

Sonnenschein (William Swan).—The Best Books. (Abyssinia, pp. 354, 426, 511, 530, 550, 553, 853.) pp. cix. 1009. *Sonnenschein and Co.: London,* 1896. 4°. (Cat. Desk C.)

Sousa (Francisco de) *Jesuit.*—Oriente conquistado a Jesu Christo Pelos Padres da Companhia de Jesus da Provincia de Goa. 2 pts. *V. da Costa Deslandes: Lisboa,* 1710. Fol. (1232. g. 1, 2.)

Sousa Coutinho (Manoel de).—Annaes de el rei Dom João Terceiro por Fr. Luiz de Sousa. Publicados por A. Herculano. (Indice.) pp. xxiii. 469. *Sociedade Propagadora dos Conhecimentos Uteis: Lisboa,* 1844. 8°. (9195. e. 13.)

Spillman (Joseph).—*See* Münzenberger (Ernst Franz August).

Stanley (Henry Edward John) *Baron Stanley of Alderley.*
    See Alvarez (Francisco) *Priest.*

Stanley (*Sir* Henry Morton) *G.C.B.*—Magdala. The Story of the Abyssinian Campaign of 1866-67 ... Second Part of ... "Coomassie and Magdala." pp. vi. 190. *Sampson Low & Co.: London*, 1896. 8°. (9061. aaa. 12.)

Steger (Friedrich).
    See Baker (*Sir* Samuel White).

Stern (Henry Aaron).—Wanderings among the Falashas in Abyssinia. Illustrated. pp. viii. 322. *Wertheim & Co.: London*, 1862. 8°. (10025. cc. 27.)

Susenyos, *King of Ethiopia.*—Chronica de Susenyos, rei de Ethiopia. Texto ethiopico segundo o Manuscripto da Bibliotheca Bodleiana de Oxford e traducção de F. M. Esteves Pereira. 2 vols. *Imprensa Nacional: Lisboa*, 1892, 1900. 8°. (754. b. 42.)

Tamisier (Maurice).
    See Combes (Edmond).

Tellez (Balthazar).
    See Almeida (Manoel de) *Jesuit.* Historia geral, *etc.* 1660. Fol.
    See Thévenot (Melchisedech).

Tellez (Balthazar).—The Travels of the Jesuits in Ethiopia ... now first translated into English. (Index.) pp. 264. 1710. *See* Collection.—A New Collection of Voyages and Travels ... None of them ever before printed in English. Vol. 7. *J. Knapton: London*, 1708-10. 4°. (566. d. 1, 2.)

Theodore II, *Emperor of Abyssinia.*—The Chronicle of King Theodore, of Abyssinia. Edited from the Berlin MS., with translation and notes by Enno Littmann. *University Library: Princeton, N. J.*, 1902, *etc.* 8°. *In progress.* (754. b. 45.)

Thévenot (Melchisedech).—Relations de divers voyages curieux, qui n'ont point esté publiées ... Nouvelle edition. (Histoire de la Haute Ethiopie écrite sur les lieux ... Extraite et traduite de la copie portugaise du R. P. Baltazar Tellez.—Remarques sur les Relations d'Ethiopie des RR. PP. Jeronimo Lobo et Balthazar Tellez, Jesuites.—Relation du R. P. J. Lobo de l'Empire des Abyssins, *etc.*—Découverte de quelques pays qui sont entre l'Empire des Abyssins et la coste de Melinde.) Tom. 2. *T. Moette: Paris*, 1696. fol. (566. k. 5.)

Treaties between the United Kingdom and Ethiopia, and between the United Kingdom, Italy, and Ethiopia, relative to the frontiers between the Soudan, Ethiopia, and Eritrea. Signed at Adis Ababa, May 15th, 1902. Ratifications delivered at Adis Ababa, Oct. 28th, 1902. With a map. Presented to both Houses of Parliament by command of His Majesty, Dec., 1902. (Treaty Series, No. 16, 1902.) Ed. 1370. p. 6. *H. M. Stationery Office: London*, 1902. 8°. (N. R.)

Umārah Ibn 'Alī, al *Hakami.*—Yaman. Its early mediæval history. By Najm Ad-Din ' Omārah al-Hakami. Also the abridged history of its dynasties by Ibn Khaldūn, and an accouunt of the Karmathians of Yaman, by Abu 'Abd Allah Baha Ad-Din al-Janadi. The original texts, with translations and notes by H. C. Kay. 2 pt. *E. Arnold: London*, 1892. 8°. (14555. a. 21.)

Valentia (George Arthur) *Viscount.*
　　See Annesley (G. A.) *Earl of Mountmorris.*

Vanderheym (J. G.).—Une Expédition avec le Nēgous Ménélik. Vingt mois en Abyssinie... Deuxième édition. [Illustrated.] pp. v. 203. *Hatchette et Cie.: Paris*, 1897. 8°. (010097. f. 21.)

Vannutelli (Lamberto) and **Citerni** (Carlo).—L'Omo. Viaggio d'esplorazione nell' Africa Orientale. (Seconda Spedizione Bòttego.) pp. xvi. 650. *Ulrico Hoepli: Milano*, 1899. 8°. (010095. i. 25.)

Varthema (Ludovico di).
　　See Barthéma (Lodovico).

Veitch (Sophie Frances Fane).—Views in Central Abyssinia, with portraits of the natives of the Galla Tribes, taken in pen and ink... by T. E., a German traveller, believed at present to be one of the captives there. With descriptions by S. F. F. Veitch. 40 plates. *J. C. Hotten: London*, 1868. obl. 4°. (1780. a.)

Veitch (William Douglas).
　　See Flad (Johann Martin).

Veyssière de la Croze (Mathurin).—Histoire du Christianisme d'Ethiopie et d'Arménie. pp. 402. *La Veuve Le Vier: La Haie*, 1739. 8°. (295. k. 31.)

Vignéras (Sylvain).—Une Mission Française en Abyssinie. pp. xiv. 224. *Armand Colin et Cie.: Paris*, 1897. 18°. (010097. e. 11.)

Vigoni (Pippo).—Abissinia. Giornale di un viaggio. pp. viii. 246. *Ulrico Hoepli: Milano*, 1881. 8°. (10097. g. 24.)

Vigoni (Pippo).—Massaua e il Nord dell' Abissinia, *etc.* (Esplorazione Commerciale. Suppt. Jan. 1888.) pp. 18. *P. B. Bellini & Co.: Milano*, 1888. 4°. (Ac. 2503.)

Vito (Lodovico de).—Esercizi di lettura tigrigna. *Roma*, 1894. 8°. [Not in the British Museum.]

Vito (Lodovico de).—Grammatica elementare della lingua tigrigna. pp. 85. *S. C. de Propaganda Fide: Roma*, 1895. 8°. (012904. h. 25.)

Vito (Lodovico de).—Vocabulario della lingua tigrigna. *Roma*, 1896. 8°. [Not in the British Museum.]

Vivian (Herbert).—Abyssinia. Through the Lion-Land to the Court of the Lion of Judah. pp. xvi. 342. *C. A. Pearson: London*, 1901. 8°. (10094. de. 4.)

Vivien de St. Martin (Louis).—Le Nord de l'Afrique dans l'antiquité grecque et romaine. Etude historique & géographique, *etc.* pp. xix. 519. *Imprimerie Impériale: Paris*, 1863. 8°. (10095. i. 29.)

Waldmeier (Theophil).—The Autobiography of T. Waldmeier, Missionary: being an account of ten years' life in Abyssinia, and sixteen years in Syria. pp. xiv. 339. *S. W. Partridge & Co.: London*, [1886.] 8°. (4766. ff. 14.)

Waldmeier (Theophil).—Erlebnisse in Abessinien in den Jahren 1858-1868. ... Bevorwortet von Dr. L. Krapf. pp. viii. 138. *C. F. Spittler: Basel*, 1869. 8°. (10095. aaa. 22.)

Waldmeier (Theophil).—Wörter-Sammlung aus der Agau-Sprache. pp. 29. *Pilgermission: St. Crischona*, 1868. 8°. (12907. bbb. 19. (6.))

Wanāg Sagad I, *King of Ethiopia.*
    See Lebna Dengel.

Wellby (Montagu Sinclair).—'Twixt Sirdar and Menelik. An account of a year's expedition from Zeila to Cairo through unknown Abyssinia. pp. xxv. 409. *Harper Bros.: London & New York,* 1901. 8°. (010095. g. 26.)

Whiteway (Richard Stephen).—The Rise of Portuguese Power in India (1497-1550). pp. xvi. 357. *A. Constable & Co.: Westminster,* 1899. 8°. (09057. bb. 3.)

Wilkins (Henry St. Clair) *Lieut.-General.*—Reconnoitring in Abyssinia ... prior to the arrival of the main body of the Expeditionary Field Force [1869. Illustrated.] pp. xi. 409. *Smith, Elder & Co.: London,* 1870. 8°. (10095. bbb. 6.)

Winstanley (William).—A Visit to Abyssinia. An account of travel in Modern Ethiopia. 2 vols. *Hurst & Blackett: London,* 1881. 8°. (10097. de. 11.)

Wolverton, Frederick, *Baron.*
    See Glyn.

Wright (Thomas), *M.A., F.S.A.*—Early Christianity in Arabia. An historical essay. pp. vi. 198. *B. Quaritch: London,* 1855. 8° (4532. d. —No third-mark is given in the British Museum Catalogue.)

Wright (William) *Professor of Arabic in the University of Cambridge.*
    See British Museum.

Wylde (Augustus Blandy).—'83 to '87 in the Soudan. With an account of Sir William Hewett's Mission to King John of Abyssinia. 2 vols. *Remington and Co.: London,* 1888. 8°. (10816. cc. 24.)

Wylde (Augustus Blandy).—Modern Abyssinia. [Map.] pp. 506. *Methuen & Co.: London,* 1901. 8°. (010095. ee. 13.)

Yule (*Sir* Henry).
    See Polo (Marco).

Yule (*Sir* Henry) and **Burnell** (Arthur Coke).—Hobson-Jobson. Being a Glossary of Anglo-Indian Colloquial Words and Phrases, and of kindred terms. 2nd edn. by W. Crooke. pp. xlviii. 870. *John Murray: London,* 1903. 8°. (2274. e. 7.)

Zara Ya 'ḳōb, *King of Ethiopia.*—Les Chroniques de Zar'a Yâ'egôb (1434-1468) et de Ba'eda Mâryâm (1468-1478), rois d'Ethiopie de 1434 à 1478. Texte éthiopien (Brit. Mus. Or. MSS. 821) et traduction ... par Jules Perruchon. (Bibl. de l'Ecole Pratique des Hautes Etudes. Fasc. 93.) pp. xl. 206. *E. Bouillon: Paris,* 1893. 8°. (Ac. 8929. No English translation has yet been published by the British Museum.)

Zenker (Julius Theodor).—Bibliotheca Orientalis. Manuel de Bibliographie Orientale. 2 vols. *Chez G. Engelmann: Leipzig,* 1846, 61. 8°. (BB. T. d. 11.)

Zotenberg (Hermann).
    See John, *Bishop of Nikiou.*
    See also Paris: *Bibliothèque Nationale.*

ADDENDA.

Abbadie (Antoine Thompson d'). —Extrait d'une Lettre de M. A. d'Abbadie sur les Falacha ou Juifs d'Abyssinie. (Bulletin Société de Géographie. Ser. 3. Vol. 4. pp. 43-57, 65-74.) *Arthus-Bertrand: Paris*, 1845. 8°. (Ac. 6035.)

Abyssinia. —Geldwesen in Abessinien. (Zeitschrift für Socialwissenschaft. vol. 4. pp. 673, 674. *G. Reimer: Berlin*, 1901. 8°. (P. P. 1423. hcc.)

Aubry (Alphonse). —Une Mission au Choa et dans les pays Gallas. (Bulletin de la Société de Géographie. Ser. 7. Vol. 8. pp. 439-485.) *Société de Géographie: Paris*, 1887. 8°. (Ac. 6035.)

Basset (René). —Contes d'Abyssinie. (Contes Arabes & Orientaux. No. IX. Revue des Traditions Populaires. Vol. 7. pp. 391-409.) *Librairie de l'Art Indépendant: Paris*, 1892. 8°. (Ac. 9798|2.)

Basset (René). —Notice sur le Magsaph Assetat du P. Antonio Fernandes, traduite du portugais de M. F. M. Esteves Pereira. (Bulletin de Correspondance Africaine. 1886. pp. 69-80.) *Association Ouvrière: Alger*, 1886. 8°. (Ac. 5350.)

Berghold (Kurt). — Sŏmâli-Studien. (Zeitschrift für Afrikanische und Oceanische Sprachen. III. pp. 1-16). *D. Reimer: Berlin*, 1897. 8°. (P. P. 4991. ha.)

Berkeley (George FitzHardinge). —The Campaign of Adowa and the Rise of Menelik ... With maps. pp. xiv. 403. *A. Constable & Co.: Westminster*, 1902. 8°. (09061. b. 35.)

Freire de Andrade (Jacinto). —Vida de Dom João de Castro ... notas por D. Fr. Francisco de S. Luiz. pp. 514. *Academia Real das Sciencias: Lisboa*, 1835. 8°. (1199. h. 24, but *not* entered under the Academy.)

Godinho (Nicolao). —De Abassinorum rebus. deque Æthiopiae Patriarchis, I. N. Barreto et A. Oviedo, libri tres. *H. Cardon: Lugduni*, 1615. 8°. (583. b. 25.)

Guidi (Ignazio). —Due Notizie istoriche sull' Abissinia. (Giornale della Societa Asiatica italiana. Vol. 3. pp. 176-181.) *R. Accad. dei Lincei: Roma*, 1888. 8°. (Ac. 8804.)

Hirsch (Leo). —Reisen in Süd-Arabien, Mahra-Land und Hadramūt. Mit Karte. pp. xii. 232. *E. J. Brill: Leiden*, 1897. 8°. (10076. f. 32).

Hoyos (Ernst) *Count.* —Zu den Aulihan. Reise und Jagderlebnisse im Somâlilande, *etc.* pp. 190. *Gerold & Co.: Wien*, 1895. 4°. (010096. i. 28.)

Hunter (Frederick Mercer). —Grammar of the Somali Language. pp. xxviii. 181. *Education Society: Bombay*, 1880. 8°. (12906. a. 34.)

Isenberg (Karl Wilhelm). —Dictionary of the Amharic Language. 2 pt. *Church Missionary Society: London*, 1841. 4°. (621. k. 10.)

Issel (Arturo). —Viaggio nel mar Rosso e tra i Bogos. ... Quarta edizione riveduta. p. 213. *Fratelli Treves: Milano*, 1885. 8°. (10096. g. 9.)

Maffei (Giovanni Pietro). —J. P. Maffeii ... Historiarum Indicarum Libri XVI. pp. 465. *Apud P. Junctam: Florentiae*, 1588. fol. (148. f. 13.)

Maffei (Giovanni Pietro).—L'Histoire des Indes Orientales et Occidentales . . . traduite de Latin en François par M. M[ichel] De P[ure], &c. 2 pts. *R. de Ninville: Paris,* 1665. 4°. (454. a. 15.)

Paez (Pero).—Lettera scritta d'Etiopia. . . . 1617, dal Pietro Paez. (pp. 126-157. Lettere Annue del Giapone, *etc.*) *P. Pontio & G. B. Piccaglia: Milano,* 1621. 8°. (867. e. 13 | 1.)

Shepherd (A. F.).—The Campaign in Abyssinia. pp. xxvi. 388. L. "*Times of India*": *Bombay,* 1868. 8°. (9061. cc. 2.)

Smith (Arthur Donaldson).—Through unknown African Countries. First expedition from Somaliland to Lake Lamu. pp. xvi. 471. *E. Arnold: London,* 1897. 8°. (10094 e. 3.)

Smith (Horace Francis Harrison).—Through Abyssinia. An Envoy's Guide to the King of Zion. pp. 263. *T. F. Unwin: London,* 1890. 8°. (010096. e. 6.)

ERRATA.

Page cv, Albuquerque (A. de).—Cartas, *for* 3 tom., *read* pp. xxiii. 448.

,, cvi, l. 2, *for* hecha mado, *read* he chamado.

,, cix, Bermudez (J.).—Esta, etc., *dele* 1875 . . . Museum.]

,, cix, Bermudez (J.).—Breve, etc., *for* 1855. 4°., *read* 1875. 8°.

NOTE.—The compilation of this Bibliography, by Mr. Basil H. Soulsby, has been a somewhat difficult task, as the British Museum Catalogue of Ethiopic Printed Books is still in MS., and as translations of the Magdala MSS. have not been printed. The Editor regrets that there is no mention of this Bibliography in the Preface, but it was only after the latter was printed off that Mr. Soulsby undertook the preparation of what is a great addition to the volume.

CASTANHOSO.

A DISCOURSE OF THE DEEDS

of the very valorous

Captain Dom Christovão da Gama

in the

KINGDOMS OF THE PRESTE JOHN,

with

The four hundred Portuguese, his Companions.

Written by MIGUEL DE CASTANHOSO, *who was present through all.* 1541.

INTRODUCTION.[1]

WHILE D. Estevão da Gama, Governor of India, was anchored off Massowa with all the fleet which he had brought to the Straits of Meca,[2] there came to him a captain of the Preste, who was called the Barnaguais,[3] with letters asking him to consider that his king-

---

[1] B numbers this chapter i, and heads it, "Of how the Preste John sent to seek help of Dom Estevão da Gama, Governor of India." In A it is introductory. A in these notes is the text here translated; B, the text printed in 1564. Words in the text between [ ] have been added by the translator.

[2] B adds, "after burning and destroying the city of Suakin and the port of Alcocer, and the city of Tor, two leagues from which is the body of the blessed St. Catherine of Mount Sinai. And many other exploits that he did on this expedition: burning ships and destroying all the straits occupied by Moors and Turks."

[3] Baharnagash, or ruler of the sea, the title of the Governor of the

doms had been for fourteen years occupied by the Moors, and that the main of his people were in captivity; that, as the King [of Portugal], his brother, was accustomed to assist the impotent, he besought him for his own sake to send some help; for those kingdoms belonged to his highness, and he [Preste John] held them in his name. When the governor had read these letters he summoned the captains of his fleet and fidalgos to take counsel with them as to what should be done in this case; and they agreed that it would be to the service of God and his highness to send them help in their great necessity. This enterprise was much desired of all the captains, and was sought for by those who considered that it would be given to them. The Governor, moved by his great importunity, gave it to his brother, D. Christovão. He immediately prepared himself with all his men, and landed to begin his journey.

Northern frontier of Abyssinia, which originally came down to the sea. This Baharnagash was called Isaac. He revolted against Minas the king in 1561, and subsequently made over Debarwa, his capital, to the Turks. He was killed fighting against the then King of Abyssinia, Sartsa Dengel, on December 13th, 1579. Tellez says that he was accompanied to Massowa by another lord called Robel (Bk. II, chap. viii): that is Robel, Governor of Tigré (see Alvarez, p. 329, for his appointment as Tigré Makuanam). It is worthy of note that Ras Michael Sahul, who plays such a part in Bruce's journey, was fifth in lineal descent from this Robel (Bruce, vol. v, p. 422).

CHAPTER I.

Of how Dom Christovão began his March, and of his Reception in the Country of the Barnaguais.

ON Saturday, on the 9th day of July, 1541,[1] late in the day, taking leave of the Governor and all his people, he marched with his camp, conveying artillery and munitions for the war. All the soldiers had double sets of arms, and started very carefully provided and very well found. They slept that night and rested by some brackish wells. The next day (Sunday), they did not march before sunset: for the country was very hot and very rugged, and they could only travel by night; then they marched and halted at some wells, sweeter than the last, in a plain full of wild fowls.[2] Here we had to set a watch for the remainder of the night, because of the many wild beasts

---

[1] B gives the date as Saturday, June 9th; Correa and Couto as July 6th. Neither of these dates was on a Saturday in 1541. Bermudez and Pero Paez agree in saying that D. Christovão started inland the day the fleet sailed. D. João de Castro, in his *Roteiro*, puts this on July 9th, which was a Saturday. It would appear that on July 6th D. Christovão moved from Massowa to Arkiko, and the advanced force mentioned by Correa must have started about June 6th, as letters announcing their safe arrival on the uplands were received in the fleet on June 28th.

[2] Alvarez constantly refers to the quantity of game and its tameness, thus (p. 67): "All the game is almost tame, because it is not pursued. Without dogs we killed and carried away twenty hares

on the plain—very terrible. Thus we marched for six days, always by night; for the country was very hot and water very scarce, which troubled the people much. D. Christovão marched with all on foot, as there were no riding animals. The artillery, munitions, and supplies were carried on camels and mules, which the Barnaguais had brought with him; but we often unloaded them and carried the baggage, and even the artillery, on our backs, through very rugged defiles, where laden camels and mules could not pass. In this labour, which was very heavy, D. Christovão showed the great zeal and fervour that animated him in this holy enterprise: for he was the first to shoulder his burden, giving orders to bring on the rest. By this energy and zeal he doubled that of the soldiers, who did double tides without feeling it; for the labour was such that had not this been done we could never have got through.[1] As we have said, we marched in this way for six days, and on the last of these days we ascended so lofty a mountain that we spent from morning till evening in getting to the top. When we reached the summit, we found extensive plains, and a country very level and very cool, with good air and good water. Here D. Christovão rested for two days in a church—a very large one that had been destroyed by the Moors, and the country wasted;[2] from here we could see the sea. On the following day we continued our march through this cool country, which we enjoyed more than the other,[3] and over it we

---

with nets in an hour, and as many partridges with springes, just like piping goats to a fold or hens to the roost. So we killed the game that we wanted."

[1] B has: "we could not so easily have passed through so mountainous a country."

[2] The Italian translator identifies this ruined church with some remains found near Asmara, which seems probable.

[3] B, "more than the warm one."

marched for three days, crossing several streams of very good water, till we reached a large place with stone houses, flat-roofed like the Moors have.[1] This city was in the lordship of that captain who marched with us;[2] on one side it is bounded by a very fine river, in which there is much fish, and on whose banks on both sides there are many villages of cultivators, with numerous herds, all in sight of the city. At that time these villages were depopulated, through fear of the Moors, and the inhabitants had taken refuge with their herds on a mountain, where they lay hid, abandoning their husbandry; but, on our arrival, they all returned to their homes. There came out of this city to receive D. Christovão, many monks with crosses in their hands, in solemn procession, praying God for pity. When they met D. Christovão, they told him that God had brought him to that country in the time of great trouble, when for fourteen years the enemies of our holy faith had lorded over it, and destroyed the churches and monasteries; that they saw that he was the apostle of God come to deliver them from captivity and subjection, and they called on him for vengeance against this evil people; this they demanded with such clamour, that truly there was none who heard them but was ready to weep a thousand tears. Thence

---

[1] B, "with terraces and platforms as roofs." In Hamasen, around Asmara, the houses are all flat-roofed, being generally partially excavated from a hill, not round and thatched as over a large part of Abyssinia. Bruce saw the first thatched round houses near Debra Damo.

[2] B calls it Baroa; Couto and Tellez, Debarwa. Debarwa was then the capital of the Baharnagash, and the name occurs frequently in travels of the period. Bent (p. 87) speaks of it as now a place of abject squalor and misery. The Ethiopian chronicle says: "This year the Franks arrived, who came from their country Bertegual (Portugal); their captain was Dengestobou (Dom Christovão); they slew Aba Esman Nour; they passed the winter at Debaroua and Grañ at Darasgé" (Basset, *Études*, p. 110). Absama Nur, who is apparently the Aba Esman Nur mentioned, was a distinguished Muhamedan leader. There is possibly a confusion, and Sharif Nur, Governor of Arkiko, is meant (see Basset, *Histoire*, p. 75, *n.*).

we went to their monastery, which had been destroyed, to pray. What of it was still standing was built with pillars and masonry, and had an altar decorated after the manner of one in a poor hermitage, and thatched with straw, for more they dared not do for fear of the Moors. D. Christovão took his leave of them, consoling them much that with the help of our Lord they would quickly return to prosperity, as he had come to that land only to expel the Moors, and die for the faith of Christ: the monks were much comforted by this reply. D. Christovão went, accompanied by his soldiers, to his tents, which the Barnaguais had had pitched for him on a plain close to the city. Here we dwelt comfortably, and by the orders of the Barnaguais the cultivators brought in what supplies they could; but they were not plentiful, for they had been much despoiled and for long had neither ploughed nor sown.[1]

CHAPTER II.

Of the Counsel taken by D. Christovão with the Barnaguais and the People of the Country as to what should be done.

THE next day, in the morning, D. Christovão sent for the Barnaguais, and the two Abyssinian captains who had

---

[1] Correa (vol. iv, p. 346) adds here: "D. Christovão proclaimed to the sound of trumpets that all who left the royal standard would be punished as traitors; that if a slave he would be burned alive; this the Barnegaes, by order of D. Christovão, proclaimed in the country language, ordering his followers that if any of them found a Portuguese escaped from the camp, they should bring him to the camp tied up like a wild beast, and should it be an escaped slave they should kill him and bring his head to the camp. But, although it was thus proclaimed, still three slaves ran away, whose heads three days later were brought to the camp. This caused such terror that none else afterwards tried to escape, which was a very good thing. A Portuguese fled, desiring to go to the Preste, to receive from him handsel (*alviçara*) of the news of the arrival of help. He was captured, and brought prisoner to the camp. D. Christovão had both his hands cut

now joined us,[1] to inform himself of the country and learn what had to be done, how far distant the Preste was, and whether we could join him before fighting with the King of Zeila.[2] When they had assembled and had learned what D. Christovão wanted, they replied that then was not the season proper for marching, as the winter had begun there, which in those parts is very violent and causes the rivers to swell, and that the country was very cold, with much mist;[3] that therefore for this, and because we were in that city which was under his [the Barnaguais] rule, we should spend the winter there till the end of October, for then was the season to begin marching;[4] that as to what he asked them about the Preste, and if it were possible to join him before meeting the King of Zeila, to that they replied, that two months previously the King of Zeila and the Preste had fought a great battle, in which the Preste was defeated, and that he had retired back so far that he had taken refuge in some mountains three hundred leagues inland, which were strong, and that he was there quite safe from his enemies;[5]

---

off, which was considered a heavier punishment than death, and told him to go where he pleased, as, if he was found in the camp he would be hanged; after that no one else dared to leave the camp."

[1] Correa (vol. iv, p. 346) adds: "and the patriarch D. João Bérmudez, who was the Ambassador that had returned from the kingdom" (Portugal).

[2] The personage called the King of Zeila is the Imam Ahmad, surnamed Grañ, or the left-handed, the Emir of Harrar. His history has been traced in the Introduction.

[3] B has *neve*, snow, for the *nevoa*, mist, of A, clearly a misprint; snow is unknown, except on the highest peaks of Semien. The term "winter" is used here by the Portuguese as it was in India, for the rainy season (see Yule's *Glossary*, *s.v.* "Winter").

[4] Bruce puts the beginning of the marching season at Hedar St. Michael, that is, November 8th (Bruce, vol. iv, p. 492).

[5] "Reached the country of Sard, where he celebrated Easter in remembrance of the resurrection of our Saviour Jesus Christ. He was in this country when Garad Emar marched against him. They met at Salf, and fought on the 29th of Miyazya (April 24th, 1541); the enemy said we have never seen or known anyone so valiant or courageous as this young man, who fears not death though he has

that they had learned that he had very few men with him, because the majority had gone over to the Moors; that as all the country was held by the Moors we should of necessity have to fight frequently with his captains; and that they thought that the King of Zeila in person would await us on the road, for he had his captains with their garrisons in the greater part of the country; that at one day's journey away was the Queen, Mother of the Preste, in a very strong mountain, to which she had retreated with her women and servants on the death of her husband, then Preste,[1] and that D. Christovão should send for her, as her presence was necessary by reason of the country people, that they should bring supplies of food, and necessaries. When he heard this, and learnt how near the Queen was, he was very joyful, and at once sent to inform her that he had arrived with the Portuguese for the service of herself and her son, and that he would send one hundred soldiers to return as her guard, as it was very necessary that Her Highness should personally live among her people; because in this way she would be better obeyed and we better received.[2]

---

but few men with him. He then returned to the province of Samen" (Basset, *Études*, p. 110). Sard is probably Sahart. Conzelman (§§ 8 and 9) speaks of this fighting, saying Galâwdêwos was defeated by Abbas, and continues: "Mar Galâwdêwos then crossed two rivers to pass from Tegraye" (Tigré) "to Shewa" (Shoa), "in order to see his flock who lived there in equity, and to visit his people who had stayed there in peace. He reached the country he wished to attain in the month of Haziran, which is the month of Sane, the first winter month of the Abyssinians." Haziran is the Syrian month corresponding to June, while Sane is the Ethiopian month beginning May 26th. It was the tradition in Shoa that Galâwdêwos took refuge in Tegulet of Shoa (Combes et Tamisier, vol. iii, p. 217). For a description of Tegulet, see Harris (vol. ii, p. 53).

[1] Reference is here made to Ite Sabla Wangel, widow of Lebna Dengel; for her virtues see Conzelman, § 3. Lebna Dengel died at Debra Damo on the 5th Maskaram (September 2nd, 1540), and was buried in the monastery of Abba Aragawi (Basset, *Études*, p. 109). Castanhoso does not name the mountain where the Queen was; both Couto (*Dec. V*, Bk. VII, chap. x), and Tellez (Bk. II, chap. viii, p. 118) call it Damo.

[2] Couto (*Dec. V*, Bk. VII, chap. x) adds: "The Queen, who was called Sabani and by her other name Elizabel, chose this hill (Debra Damo),

CHAPTER III.

Of how D. Christovão mustered his People, and divided them as seemed best to him.

AFTER D. Christovão had sent this message to the Queen, he mustered his followers, because, considering the excitement and the desire to join the expedition when he left Massowa, it appeared to him that more men followed than the Governor gave him; still, it was not found that there were more than four hundred men[1] very well armed, and among them over six hundred matchlocks.[2] He appointed five captains from among them in this way: he told off fifty soldiers to each captain, which makes two hundred and fifty, and he appointed one hundred and fifty to the royal standard.[3] After this, each captain had charge of his own men and catered for them, with whatever was obtainable in the country.[4] The Barnaguais, as lord of the country, gave daily to the camp ten very fat cows, larger than those of Portugal, and many cakes of millet and of a

---

with her women and family and the Barnagais, because it was strong and safe, and also in order not quite to abandon that part, where indeed there was nothing more for the Moors to conquer save it. Thus the kingdom of the Christians was in the most miserable condition in which it ever was, for there was no church standing or religious person in safety, for all wandered over the deserts homeless and in misery."

[1] Correa (vol. iv, p. 347): "And in the count found 400, less 3 men; there were 130 slaves, good men to help their masters, and with trumpets, kettledrums, and bagpipes, played by slaves whom the commander took with him."

[2] For the word *espingarda*, translated "matchlock," the contemporary equivalent is caliver; but that term savours of pedantry.

[3] Correa (vol. iv, p. 347): "The most honourable men and fidalgos delighted to accompany him on this expedition, many of whom were his relatives."

[4] Correa (vol. iv, p. 348): "To each of these" (the captains) "his men were allotted by list, with these under their ancients they separated off, and the great royal banner of damask with the cross of Christ on both sides in crimson satin. This done, each captain separated with his men and lodged among them, each in his own tent, for all were supplied with tents by the Barnegaes; each captain provided a mess for his men of the best that could be procured."

grain called Dachery.[1] With this, and with some rice which we had brought from the fleet, we lived through the winter, until the Lord in his pity was pleased to succour us.[2] And the names of the captains were these: Manuel da Cunha, João da Fonseca, Inofre de Abreu, Francisco de Abreu, and Francisco Velho;[3] all the other fidalgos, and servants of His Majesty's household, remained with the royal standard, and with them Luiz Rodriguez de Carvalho,[4] to whom D. Christovão gave charge of those under the royal standard.

CHAPTER IV.

Of how D. Christovão sent for the Queen, and of her Reception of the Portuguese who went to fetch her.

THAT day passed in completing the arrangements, and on the next, D. Christovão sent Manuel da Cunha and Francisco Velho, with their men, to fetch the Queen.[5] They

---

[1] B, dacheni; Correa, nachenym. These are corruptions of the Sanskrit name *Natchenny*. The Abyssinian name is *dagousha*—the *Eleusine coracana*. The Northern Indian proverbs (in that part it is called *Manrua*) are not complimentary to it—one runs: "Manrua got up on a height, and said I am a very pimp among grains. If a strong man eat me for eight days, he will not be able to get up" (Crooke, *Rural Glossary, s. v.*). Mansfield Parkyns says much the same; he considers *dagousha* rather a grass than a corn; the taste of the bread made from *teff* is like that of chewing a sour sponge; that of *dagousha* is even worse, with a gritty and sandy flavour. "Its virtues may be judged of from the fact that it undergoes but little change in passing through the stomach" (vol. i, p. 368). The tone of Castanhoso's remarks seems justified.

[2] B adds: "For in this winter we suffered much misery, because we had to take by force of arms what we required for food; for the cows the Barnaguais gave us lasted but for a short time, as he had but few, and after they were ended we had to act as I have said."

[3] B adds: "and to me with 50 soldiers, all arquebusiers, he gave charge of the Queen, to guard her on our marches."

[4] Correa (vol. iv, p. 348) calls him Luiz Fernandes de Carvalho.

[5] Correa (vol. iv, p. 348) adds: "if she would come."

started at once, and arrived the same day late at the foot of the hill, where they pitched their tents, and notified to the guard of the hill that the Portuguese had arrived to be the [Queen's][1] guard and attendants; she was greatly pleased, and with much content ordered the guards to allow the two captains to ascend the hill. When they arrived at the entry to the hill, there were lowered to them very strong thongs of leather, to which was attached a contrivance like a large basket,[2] and they were told that the Queen ordered them both to ascend, as she wished to see them while she was getting ready to start. They obeyed, each ascending by himself in the basket; they were taken to the Queen's lodgings, who received them very hospitably, and talked much with them, asking them of the coming of D. Christovão, and of the Portuguese her children, for so she called us. She got ready immediately, with all her women and servants, leaving on the mountain

---

[1] Some words seem to have dropped out of the manuscript here.

[2] B, "who arrived at the foot of the hill, and ascended by a very narrow path, until there were let down very strong thongs of leather, to which was attached a large basket that would hold one man."

Correa (vol. iv, p. 348) has: "The hill on which the Queen was, was of solid rock, so precipitous that it seemed cut with a pickaxe. It was about 80 fathoms high, up which there was a path with many turns, by which only one man at a time could ascend, who could with difficulty climb two-thirds of the way up, where was a small level space; from this point they could only ascend in a basket, which was let down from above through a hole made in the rock, for above the rock turned outwards like the fighting-top of a man-of-war . . . . . . she (the Queen) sent to the captains to tell them to ascend, who in full dress went up by the basket, that was worked by an engine."

The basket is connected with one of the miracles of Tecla Haimanaut, the Abyssinian saint. He was going up in the basket to the monastery, when some one, who did not share the general belief in his holiness—it is said to have been the devil in person—cut the thongs. Tecla Haimanaut would have been dashed to pieces on the rocks below, had he not immediately, while in the air, developed three pairs of wings. He is frequently drawn fully-fledged. During the civil wars of 1832, Samuel Gobat lived for several months on Debra Damo for security. He stayed in the monastery, and, considering his missionary zeal, was very well treated. As already said, only males may now visit the top. The ascent, pulled up by ropes, is so severe a trial, that many reach the summit insensible.

her second son and two very beautiful daughters[1] with her mother, grandmother of the princesses, carefully guarded. I will tell later why she did not bring the prince with her to help us in the war, although he was of age to do so. When the Queen found herself away from the hill, she gave many thanks to God, weeping with pleasure for His great mercy in allowing her to leave that hill, where she had been imprisoned for so many years;[2] since God had sent for her help the Portuguese, who were so desired of all the dwellers in that country, she trusted to His pity to have very soon vengeance on her enemies. Thus passed the day in preparations to begin the march on the morrow.

CHAPTER V.

Of how the Queen arrived at D. Christovão's Camp, and of her Reception there.

WHEN the morning came, the Queen, whose name was Sabele Oengel,[3] with all her ladies and her women, got ready for the march, and the Portuguese with her; and

---

[1] Lebna Dengel and Sabla Wangel had four sons and two daughters.

Sons.	*Daughters.*
1. Fiqtor, killed 1539.	1. Amata Giyorgis.
2. Galâwdêwos, King 1540-1559.	2. Sabana Giyorgis.
3. Yaekub, died in 1558.	
4. Minas, King 1559-1563.	

Yaekub, the second living son, must be the one who remained on the hill.

[2] Correa (vol. iv, p. 349) gives the length of the "imprisonment" as four years.

[3] B, "was in the Chaldean language Sabele o Engel, that is, in Portuguese, Isabel do Evangelho." The name Sabla Wangel is said to really mean the "corn spike of the Gospel," a name of the Virgin Mary.

because this mountain is the strongest there is in the country, and the most precipitous that ever was seen,[1] I will explain here the manner of its fortification, for it appears constructed by the hands of God to preserve this lady and her following from captivity, and to prevent the destruction of the monastery of friars on the summit, in which the service of God is constantly performed. For the King of Zeila came against it with all his power for a year, but could never capture it; and this not out of desire for the treasures that were in it, for there were none there and he knew it well, but to get the Queen into his hands, whom he much desired, as she is very beautiful. When at the end of the year he found that he could not capture it by starvation, he struck his camp and marched away, for he discovered the manner of the fortification, which is in this wise.

The summit is a quarter of a long league in circumference, and on the area on the top there are two large cisterns, in which much water is collected in the winter; so much that it suffices and is more than enough for all those who live above, that is, about five hundred persons.[2] On this summit itself they sow supplies of wheat, barley, millet, and other vegetables.[3] They take up goats and fowls; and there are many hives, for there is much space for them; thus this hill cannot be taken by hunger or thirst. Below the summit the hill is of this kind. It is squared and scarped for a height double that of the highest tower in Portugal, and it gets more and more precipitous near the top, until at the end it makes an umbrella

---

[1] B, "because this mountain is the strongest in the country; nor do I think that in any other can one so steep and so strong be found."

[2] Correa (vol. iv, p. 348) says "1,000 persons," and adds ducks and geese to the live stock enumerated.

[3] B, "millet and other seeds, such as beans, lentils and peas; and everything sown here grows."

all round, which looks artificial, and spreads out so far that it overhangs all the foot of the mountain, so that no one at the foot can hide himself from those above; for all round there is no fold or corner, and there is no way up save the one narrow path, like a badly-made winding stair *(caracol)*, by which with difficulty one person can ascend as far as a point whence he can get no further, for there the path ends. Above this is a gate where the guards are, and this gate is ten or twelve fathoms above the point where the path stops, and no one can ascend or descend the hill save by the basket I have above mentioned.[1] Thus this hill cannot be captured if even only ten men guard it; as for the fortress, it is the custom of the country[2] that the princes who are not the first in succession

---

[1] "The spectator, standing at the foot of the Focada amba and looking to the westward, has before him, at his own level, an apparently interminable plateau, with peaks and hills, such as that of Focada, rising out of it. But the plateau is also deeply cut into by valleys of considerable width and great depth . . . . . . But the most remarkable feature of the landscape remains to be described. Just as peaks rise from the surface of the plateau, so hills rise up out of the valley itself, with sides exactly like those descending from the plateau, and with flat top summits corresponding exactly with the plateau level. One of these valley-hills is the amba of Debra Damo, famous in the history of Da Gama's expedition" (Markham, *History of the Abyssinian Expedition*, p. 176).

[2] In Castanhoso's account which follows there are numerous errors. Debra Damo was formerly the royal prison, but had been given up several centuries before this, after the massacre of the royal family there by Judith, one of the Falasha queens. The next choice was Amba Geshen, south of the Tacazzé, where it was in Alvarez's time (chapters 58 to 61); it in its turn was abandoned after the massacre of the *détenus* by the Vizir Mujahid, in 1539. There was no further selection until the reign of Sultan Segued (1632-65), when Wechne, near Emfras, was used; it was retained as late as Bruce's time. The Harris mission found the relations of the Shoa king imprisoned in a dungeon, and obtained their release. Johnson's idyllic pictures in "Rasselas" (Ras Sela Christos) had no foundation in fact. Our knowledge is but fragmentary, but there can be no doubt but that the unfortunate captives were starved and ill-treated by their guards, who embezzled what was set aside for their maintenance. On the summit of Amba Geshen, at least, the climate was very rigorous. None but the selected heir was ever allowed out of the mountain, and even he had to leave his wife and children behind, and begin life afresh. Only

are at birth taken to this hill, and remain there and are brought up as king's sons, but never leave it or see any other country; unless the heir who accompanies his father dies, when they take the eldest from the hill; the others remain until the heir marries, and has sons, and sits on the throne, which he cannot do save on his father's death. Therefore, when the heir has sons, the princes leave the hill and go to their lordships, which have been already defined for them. These precautions are taken because the people are so evil that, on any dispute with the heir, if one of the princes were at large they would rebel under him; thus this custom I describe has arisen because they meet with so little loyalty among them.

After the Queen had descended with her women and servants (of the women there were about thirty, and of the men fifty) she and her ladies mounted the mules which were at the foot of the hill, which the Barnaguais had sent her, and started for D. Christovão's camp, where she was received by him and his troops very nobly, for by his order all were in full dress and in ranks, the captains with their soldiers, all matchlockmen, with their banners of blue and white damask with red crosses, and the royal standard of crimson and white damask, with the cross of Christ, heading the rest of the troops. The commander, a great gentleman (*muito gentilhomem*),[1] clothed in hose and vest of red satin and gold brocade with many plaits, and a French cape of fine black cloth all quilted with gold, and a black cap with a very rich medal, the captains and fidalgos and others with the best equipments they had, which were very fine. We saluted her twice with all the artillery and matchlocks, when we certainly made a show of being more than one thousand

---

kings' sons were imprisoned—not his daughters—but the sons and their descendants were retained for successive generations. The details in Bruce are scattered over several references.

[1] Correa (vol. iv, p. 351): "of the age of about 25 years."

Portuguese.[1] After the review we drew up in two ranks, and the Queen with all her women remained between; she was all covered to the ground with silk, with a large flowing cloak (*oparlandas*),[2] and some men bore a silk canopy (*esparavel*) that covered her and the mule to the ground, with an opening in front for her to see through.[3] She was clothed in very thin white Indian cloth and a burnoose (*albornoz*) of black satin, with flowers and fringes of very fine gold, like a cloak (*bedem*), her head dressed in the Portuguese manner, and so muffled in a very fine cloth that only her eyes could be seen. The Barnaguais, lord of that country, walked on foot naked to the waist, with a lion or tiger's skin on his shoulders as a covering, with the right arm exposed,[4] and he led her by the bridle; for it is the custom, whenever the Preste or his Queen makes a state entry, for the lord of the land to lead them by the bridle in the manner I describe, as a sign of submission; and for twenty days they remain at court dressed as I have described. There came also with the Queen two lords like marquises, whom they call Azayes,[5] and no one else can

---

[1] B, "Matchlocks."

[2] B, "She came on a very handsome black mule, all covered with silk to the ground."

[3] B, "She and the mule were covered entirely by a canopy, and she journeyed so that no one could see her save when she desired—then she ordered the door to be opened in the canopy."
"Some men carried a silk canopy (*docel*), which covered her so that except from the front she could not be seen" (Tellez, *Historia*, Bk. II, chap. vii, p. 118). "They covered her with a canopy (*esparaval*) of white cloth, which covered her mule to the ground; men carrying high rods bore this canopy, which was open in front for her to see out when she desired" (Correa, vol. iv, p. 350). Cf. account in Alvarez of the Preste's "canopy," p. 232.

[4] Baring the shoulders is a custom noticed by most travellers. Alvarez (pp. 53 and 59) may be consulted.

[5] Azaj is a judge. The preface to Bruce's *History of Abyssinia*, which is not by Bruce, says there were four from whom the bench was formed in all cases (Bruce, vol. iii, p. 24). Basset (*Études*, *note*, p. 256), however, says that this word is connected with the root to order, and means an intendant or major-domo; this appears to be the meaning in this passage.

wear their uniform in the way they do, and by it they are recognised; this is a garment (*sobre camiza*) to the ground, tunics of silk garnished with silk of its own colours, reaching to the ground, with a train of two palms behind like a woman's; these tunics laced, and over them cloaks.[1] They accompanied the Queen one on one side and the other on the other, near her, with their hands on the mule; the Queen rode on a saddle with a low pommel, with a stirrup for the left foot, and the right leg doubled over the pommel, but so covered with her garments that no one could see the manner of her sitting, and her ladies all riding properly on mules muffled in their cloaks. When the Queen arrived among the Portuguese she stopped, astonished at what she had never seen before. D. Christovão, the captains and the fidalgos, went near to speak with her; and to welcome them with honour and good grace she ordered the canopy in which she travelled to be opened, and she lowered her muffling a little, showing much pleasure while he spoke. The words which he spoke are these:—

Speech of the Commander to the Queen.

Most Christian Queen. The Governor of India was with his fleet in the Red Sea, defeating the infidels of our holy faith in the service of the most Christian King of Portugal, my lord; after he had wasted many towns and places, he was in the port of Massowa, on his return to India, when there arrived this captain, who holds your highness's bridle, on an Embassy from the Preste your son, and bringing letters from you, begging the Governor, in the name of God and the King of Portugal, to take pity on this Christian kingdom, so wasted and tyrannized over by the enemy; begging him to send some aid, as it was his custom to assist the helpless, because for fourteen years the enemy had occupied his country, doing much harm and injury. When the Governor learned what need this kingdom had of help, and what service he would do to God and the King in helping it at this time, he sent him (me) and these soldiers for the moment; in the coming year he will send more men, so that with the help of our Lord God, that kingdom

---

[1] In the copies of Castanhoso, both A and B, the words of this description have become displaced. In Correa (vol. iv, p. 350), however, they are arranged rightly.

will soon again be prosperous; and that trust can be placed in his (my) words, for all the Portuguese who were there had come ready to die for the faith of Christ and the salvation of that kingdom.[1]

All these words were translated by an interpreter we had with us, a Portuguese, who knew the language well, who knelt before the Queen.[2] She was very content and joyful at the words, and gave her thanks to D. Christovão as the one who desired to undertake the enterprise; and she also thanked all the Portuguese much for their coming, saying that neither she nor any other prince could repay the King of Portugal, her brother, for the great help he had given: only the Lord of Heaven who is over all. That the help which the Governor had sent her and her son, he had sent to the King of Portugal, because those kingdoms were his, and they held them for him. The speeches finished, we conducted the Queen to her tents, for they had already been pitched on the plain near the city.[3]

CHAPTER VI.

Of how D. Christovão visited the Queen, and of how the Winter was spent till the beginning of marching.

Two days later, D. Christovão visited the Queen, to enquire her pleasure, and ask what she wished done. He went with all his troops, armed with glittering and shining weapons, with fife and drum, and all in ranks with lances and matchlocks. We went through our drill (*soiça*)[4] twice

---

[1] The form of the speech changes suddenly to the oblique at the end.

[2] Possibly Ayres Dias.

[3] Correa (vol. iv, p. 351) adds: "there remained with her the Barnegaes and the patriarch, with whom the Queen delighted to talk, and hear the things he told her of Portugal."

[4] *Soiça* is connected with Suissa (Switzerland), and shows that this drill was learnt from the Swiss companies. It came through Italy.

in front of the Queen's tent, both with closed and open *caracol*; the Queen watched this through an opening in the circuit of her tent, astonished to see the Portuguese with this new instrument of war, especially the closing and opening of the *caracol*, in which her people fail. She was very pleased, giving many thanks to God for such delight as this, for it gave her a hope of renewed prosperity. When this was concluded, D. Christovão entered with the patriarch and the captains, to speak with her of those things which touched the service of herself and of her son. When this conversation was finished, leave was taken, and we returned to our camp.[1] D. Christovão determined to spend the winter in getting ready for the war by preparing carts for our artillery and munitions, and for fortifying our camp wherever we might be; we made these with much labour, for we cut the wood and sawed it, as the natives of the country have not the wit for anything.[2] D. Christovão was the master of the works; he arranged them as if he had been a carpenter all his life, and it was his pleasure to spend all his days at it. When we had been in this camp a month, there arrived an Ambassador from the Preste, with letters for his mother and for D. Christovão, in which he wrote pleasant words: that he was not astonished at the great help his brother had sent him, as he was sure that he should receive it from so renowned a King; that the people of his country had a prophecy, made many years before

---

Littré explains the French word *caracole* as a term used when a squadron turned by ranks and not by files. The Italian translator seems to have mistaken the sense; *caracol* is indeed a winding stair, but the word here does not denote a device for scaling fortified places—there were none in Abyssinia. *Caracol* seems to have been a movement by which the front rank retired after delivering their volley, to allow the rear rank to deliver theirs.

[1] Correa (vol. iv, p. 352): "After this they made many houses of wood and straw, which was in plenty, where all the people were housed."

[2] Apparently these were sledges and not wheeled conveyances; old matchlocks were used to make runners.

the kingdom was overrun, that it would be recovered by white men come from far, who were true Christians; that they would free all Ethiopia from the bondage of the enemies of our holy faith, who for fourteen years had possessed it with absolute power, and dwelt in it as if it were their own country; that the Lord God had done him the great favour that in his time had come what was desired of so many; that he begged D. Christovão to march towards him, and that he would do the same; that in no other way could they so quickly meet, as the length of road between them was great; finally, he sent greetings to all the Portuguese. On this letter D. Christovão agreed with all that, when the spring came they would start and endeavour to join the Preste; with this hope we worked harder at the carts, so that twenty-four were completed before the end of winter, with much labour, as I have already said. We also made eleven racks for the carts that were to carry the hundred swivel guns,[1] for our artillery consisted of these I have mentioned, six half-bases and two bases; these eight pieces had each its own cart, and in the other five carts were powder and ball. In the middle of the winter, with the permission and by the order of the Queen, we made two attacks on certain places near our camp, which were in rebellion and refused to submit; there we captured several mules for our riding, for, up to here, as I have said, we had marched on foot as we had nothing to ride; we also took many bullocks and cows, which we trained and broke to the yoke (*canga*) to drag the carts, which cost us great labour. All the winter we watched our camp carefully, as was necessary, and kept our quarter-guard armed, for we heard that the King of Zeila had sent his spies to discover how we were placed,

---

[1] Correa (vol. iv, p. 353): "Mosquetes, which were long matchlocks that the patriarch had brought from the kingdom."

and how many we were, and what watch we kept; for this reason, therefore, and also to inure ourselves to labour, we armed ourselves each night, as we expected that the labour of the next winter would be even greater than that of this. Watching in this way we took two spies of the King of Zeila, who were among us, clothed like Abyssinians; from them we learned where the enemy was, and how numerous he was, and what else we wanted. When D. Christovão had learned this from them, he ordered them to be pulled to pieces by the carts: at which sentence the Abyssinians were terrified, so that no one would again run into this danger.

CHAPTER VII.
Of how D. Christovão began to march, and of the Order of his March.

ON December 15th, 1541, when the winter had ended, and all preparations were completed, we began to march with the Queen and her women and attendants, and two hundred Abyssinians, who helped us to convey the baggage and transport.[1] Our force marched with the most complete discipline, and the order of our rout was this. Every day two captains, with their soldiers, accompanied the carts on foot to guard them, for we had no other men of the country with us to help, save the two hundred Abyssinians I have mentioned, and they looked after the droves of cattle, for there were many laden oxen with the goods of the army; while these two captains went on foot, the remainder marched armed, guarding the whole; in the rear followed

---

[1] "In the month of Tahsas (December) Grañ went to Tigré; the Franks left Debaroua, having with them Ite Sabla Wangel, mother of the King, who sent them assistance with prudence and wisdom." (In Perruchon's version (p. 264) this last sentence is translated, "strengthened them by his wise advice") "and supplied them with the necessary food stuffs" (Basset, *Études*, p. 111).

the Queen, and I was on guard over her with fifty Portuguese, all arquebusiers, with their arms loaded and matches lighted, for such were my orders. D. Christovão inspected all the army twice a day accompanied by four horsemen, saw how matters were progressing, and if anything were needed; for this purpose he kept fast free-trotting mules, of which there are very good ones in that country. Each day the two captains changed from foot to horse, and two others left their mounts to go with the carts. We marched in this order, experiencing much trouble with the carts; for in many places where the oxen could not drag them, we lifted them by main strength and on our shoulders, and they were all shod with iron. In this labour D. Christovão showed himself very earnest; we marched thus with two men on horseback, and three or four Abyssinians also on horseback, scouting in front, besides other spies which the Queen had sent in advance to learn news of the Moors.[1] We marched in this way eight days, and everywhere we passed, the country people, who were all cultivators, put themselves under the protection of the royal standard; some Moors, who were collecting rents in the villages, fled on hearing news of us. At the end of eight days we reached a mountain in the lordship of the Barnaguais, which submitted to us; here we passed Christmas: they call it *Cabelaa*.[2] D. Christovão had a large tent fitted up

---

[1] Correa (vol. iv, p. 353): "D. Christovão had four horses, on which four men always accompanied him in visiting the line, from the van to the rear; the two captains who were in front with the carts, half a league in advance, were changed every day, for the work was hard, as in places they found the roads such that the cattle could not drag the carts, and our men had to carry them over their shoulders. Two Portuguese on horseback, with four Abyssinians also on horseback, scouted the route for half a league in front of the captains with the carts, while still further in front were men of the country spying; if they saw Moors, they returned with the news."

[2] B has *Cabeda*; Correa, *Caboa*. Couto's account is very confused. The Portuguese editor is unable to say whether the name refers to the place or the festival. Parkyns (vol. ii, p. 82) calls Christmas Day *Liddet*; speculation is useless.

with an altar, with a very reverential picture of the birth of our Lord Jesus Christ, where Mass was said by the patriarch and the Portuguese Mass-priests, who were in our company. We remained all night armed before the altar, and the matins were very solemn for such a country, as we had bagpipes (*charamellas*), kettledrums (*atabales*), flutes, trumpets, and the full Mass ; that night we all confessed, and at midnight Mass received the holy sacrament. The Queen looked on at all this from her tent, which was pitched in front ; she was much astonished at our customs, which appeared to her very fitting ; she was so delighted to see them and our Mass that, to get a better view, she and one of her ladies, both muffled, left the tent so secretly that her own servants did not miss her, for those who knew what had happened made the greater fuss ; thus the ladies in the tent, as well as those outside, kept moving the people from the line of sight of the tent. Thus she went about, seeing all that passed, as several other ladies did, and in this had much pleasure. They celebrated the same feast on the same day ; many friars came in from the country around, and there were several in the Queen's train, some priests and some friars, for they said Mass wherever she happened to be ; and all these joined in celebrating the birth with all joy and solemnity.[1] At the end of the octave of Christmas we marched for two days[2] by a very rough road, where the carts travelled with great trouble to us. At the end of these days we reached a very high hill, so extended that it borders all that country : to follow our road we had of necessity to cross it. The Queen and her people were very doubtful whether we could get more than ourselves across it, in fact, they were certain we

---

[1] According to Harris (vol. iii, p. 198), Christmas in Shoa was rather a saturnalia.

[2] Correa (vol. iv, p. 354) says six days. He must include the ascent of the hill.

could not. D. Christovão, seeing that the carts could not be dragged over it, ordered us to take every cart to pieces, and remove the artillery and munitions from them. We then carried all these things on our backs, little by little, with the very greatest labour; D. Christovão was the first to carry on his back whatever he could. It took us three days to get to the top of this hill; and such was our labour that, had it happened at any other time, as much could have been written of it as of the labour of Hannibal in crossing the Alps: for, few as we were, it was much more for us to get to the top in three days than for Hannibal with his army to cross in a month. After this, the Queen believed that there were no people equal to the Portuguese, for she had considered it very difficult for us to reach the summit. On the top was a city, which from the outside looked very fine, with windows and white walls; the houses were terraced above and inside arranged after the Moorish fashion.[1]

CHAPTER VIII.

Of how D. Christovão examined the top of this Mountain, and of what he found there.

ABOVE this city, on the highest point, was a hermitage, very white, and of such steep ascent that it was with great difficulty that any one could reach it, for the pathway was very narrow and twisting. Close to this hermitage was a small house (*casinha*), in which were some three hundred men, more or less, all desiccated (*mirrados*), sewn up in

---

[1] This part of the march has been discussed in the Introduction. There seems to be good ground for not accepting the line suggested by the Italian translator. The indications in this chapter are vague; but in the next a point is reached which admits of identification.

very dry skins, the skins much decayed[1] but the bodies entire.[2] The people of the country said that these men had come to that country many years before, and had conquered it in the time of the Romans; others said they were saints; the patriarch, Dom João Bermudez, said also that they were saints, who had been martyred here, and that he had heard this said when he had passed there on another occasion. Some men took some relics from them, but there were none of the country who could say how it had happened, nor had they any writing showing who they were; but of necessity there must be something, since for so many years these three hundred white men have been here together all dried up, although the country is so cold and so dry that it is nothing for dead bodies to dry up on that hill, for the living run much risk; I was never in such another country, for it was so cold, and the air so dry, that we thought that we should all die.[3] After we had rested

---

[1] *Cosidos com couros mui secos e os couros mui gastados.*

[2] B adds: "save that they wanted the tips of their noses, and, in some cases, fingers." Correa (vol. iv, p. 355) describes the bodies as follows: "over three hundred desiccated corpses of men enclosed in hides sewn up (*metidos en coiros coseytos*), much decayed, but the bodies were sound and whole."

[3] Sir Clements Markham (*History of the Abyssinian Expedition*, pp. 23 and 195) identifies this place with the church of St. Romanos, at Barakit, near Senafé. In a MS. note with which he has favoured me, he describes the place thus: "Church of St. Romanos, on a ledge, 500 feet above the valley, perpendicular precipice above and below. Behind the church, on an almost inaccessible ledge, there is a clump of date palms, and here a cell is hewn in the rock as a hermitage." This hermitage is Castanhoso's *casinha*. Wilkins (p. 279) says he saw the bodies through a hole in the side, the outlines of the figures being perceptible through the cloths in which they were enshrouded. There can be no doubt that the identification made by Sir Clements Markham is correct. Apart from the name, the march up to Senafé on the west is a sharp rise, such as Castanhoso describes, and the province of Agamé is, as he says, only some 25 miles distant. As a negative argument, it may be noted that the route of Alvarez, as far as can be ascertained, took him west and south of Senafé, nearly along the line the Italian translator suggests for D. Christovão, yet he never mentions these bodies, as he certainly would have if he had seen or heard of them. Through the kindness of Sir Clements Markham a photograph of the *casinha* is reproduced in this volume.

from our past labours, and were all armed and ranged in ranks, we again began our march. Beyond the hill the the ground was flat, with no descent, and thence onwards all plain, over which we marched for two days, when we reached the lordship called Agamé, of which the Captain was an Abyssinian who had sided with the Moors, and who had, from fear of our arrival, recently fled. The cultivators came out to receive us, bringing much food; they excused themselves to the Queen, saying they could do nothing else, that they had obeyed under compulsion. Among them came a Captain, brother of the Captain of that land, whom the cultivators brought as their leader, who was always for the Preste, and who had always separated himself from his brother, seeing the great treason he had committed to his King. When he heard that the Portuguese had arrived with the Queen, he came to visit D. Christovão, and gave an account of himself, begging him to consent, having respect to his past when he had always remained loyal, to help him to obtain from the Queen a grant of those lands as his ancestors had held them; all the people of the country also desired him for their Captain and lord. D. Christovão, seeing the disposition of the people, and understanding that it was true, arranged with the Queen to give him a grant of it; it was immediately made over to him with all the ceremonies usual in such cases. We stayed here eight days, arranging the administration of the districts, and from all of them persons came to yield obedience. We passed here the Epiphany,[1] during which the Abyssinians hold a great festival; and as it is very different from that of our country, I will explain it.

On the day of the Epiphany, before sunrise, the Queen

---

[1] This must be an error; as they recommenced their march from "Cabelaa" after the octave of Christmas, they must have passed the Epiphany at the hermitage.

and her ladies, and all the other people, went to the bank of a stream hard by, where several tents had been pitched ; one was for the Queen to hear Mass. The patriarch and all the ecclesiastics went to the river, and the patriarch blessed the water where the Queen and the others were to bathe ;[1] after the blessing, the Queen, all covered with many cloths, so that she could not be seen, went undressed into the water and bathed, and thence went to her tent, and her ladies did likewise. The patriarch and all the friars and priests went a little apart and washed themselves, and then went to say Mass with great music and festivity, in which the whole day was passed ;[2] on the following we marched. On the march there joined D. Christovão the Captains who had escaped into the strong mountains, and who, hearing the news of the Portuguese who were marching through their country with their Queen, left the mountains and came to meet us ; but they brought no following to help us, only themselves and their immediate relatives. We marched in this way very slowly, not being able to advance more than two or three leagues a day.[3]

---

[1] The share of Bermudez was certainly easier than that of "the old priest master of the Preste," whom Alvarez saw, who had to remain "naked as when his mother bore him (and quite dead of the cold, because it was a very sharp frost), standing in the water up to his shoulders."

[2] The account of the celebration of the Abyssinian Epiphany varies greatly in different writers. Alvarez (p. 241) describes what he saw in South Abyssinia, which verged rather on an orgie. Bruce, who knew only North Abyssinia, attacks Alvarez as guilty of a libellous caricature (Bk. v, chap. xii). Krapf, however (Isenberg and Krapf, p. 184), and Harris (vol. iii, p. 200), who saw the celebration in Shoa, agree very closely with Alvarez. On the other hand, Castanhoso's account (he saw it in the north) agrees with Bruce, as do those of Parkyns (vol. ii, p. 78), and Pearce (vol. ii, p. 18), who were both in the same part. The ceremonies, then, vary in the north and south. The most informed and informing account will be found in Bent, p. 53. As he was also in the north, his account differs little from Castanhoso's.

[3] A Portuguese league is said to equal 3.858 English miles.

CHAPTER IX.

Of how D. Christovão, on his March, found a very strong Hill, and made arrangements to attack it.

NEAR this, D. Christovão learned that there was a hill standing in the middle of a plain which we had to cross, that was held for the King of Zeila, and on it one of his Captains, a Moor, with fifteen hundred archers and buckler men. The hill was naturally very strong, standing alone, and very lofty. There were only three passes to it, all easily defended; each pass lay a matchlock shot distant from the other. At the beginning of the rise, in the first pass, was a very strong stone wall with its gate. Leaving the gate, the ascent is very steep, and by a very narrow path easily commanded by those on the summit. At the top is a gate in the living rock, through which is the entry. At this point of the pass was a Captain with five hundred men. The second pass is not so strong, but any way the path is a very difficult one; for it is also commanded from the summit, as I have explained, and at the top is another door, where was another Captain with five hundred men to defend the ascent. The third pass is the strongest of all, as from all outward appearance it is impregnable; for there is no path save over slippery rocks entirely exposed to the summit, so that any stone would do great damage. Men can only climb up with naked feet to a projection; from this up is four fathoms,[1] and the rock is scarped with only a few holes chiselled out and some chinks, and over this one must proceed, or clamber by help of spears. Above was another Captain with five hundred men, who defended the pass.[2]

---

[1] Braça translated "fathom" as a measure of length equal to 2.2 metres, or rather over seven English feet.

[2] Correa (vol. iv, p. 356): "Above, on the edge of the hill, were certain holes and breaches in the rocks, by which they entered."

The top of the mountain is very flat, with a few hillocks. In the centre is a very high peak, visible for a long distance, and from its foot there gushes a fountain of very excellent water, so copious that it irrigates the whole hill; thus they sow on it food grains in sufficiency, and maintain numbers of cows and all kinds of cattle. The circumference is about a league. They kept there nine horses, with which they used to raid the country. They captured many people from the skirts of the hill, and did such damage that the very inhabitants, who were subject to them, dared not pass that way. On the summit was a large church, which they had turned into a mosque. Before the hill was captured, it was the custom of the kingdom for all the kings of the country to be crowned here, like the Emperors in Rome; and nowhere else could it be done save here. The Moors captured it by treachery in this way. The King of Zeila sent several of his men, disguised as merchants, to start a fair at the foot of the hill, which they did; and when they saw the people immersed in the fair, and in the desire of buying, selected men, under colour of desiring to obtain lodgings, ascended, and when there captured the hill.[1] This was the first step the King of Zeila took to conquer the country; for when he knew that the hill was held for him, he marched with his army, and subdued all the more defenceless country between his own and the hill. As the Preste was at that time some distance away he could not easily assist; still he would never have been defeated had his men been as loyal as the Portuguese, even although they were much weaker than they are. When D. Christovão heard that this hill lay on his road he enquired about it, and determined to take it in order not to

---

[1] Correa (vol. iv, p. 356): "which the Moors had held for eight years, when our men reached there and camped at the foot of the hill, that is, February 1st, 1542, the eve of the Purification of Our Lady."

leave any danger behind him. When the Queen heard of D. Christovão's intention she sent for him, and told him that he should not think of daring such a great deed with so small an army; that they should march and join the Preste, and then they could do everything—that it was less difficult to fight twelve thousand men in a plain, and destroy them, than to capture that hill. To this D. Christovão replied that she should fear nothing, as they were Portuguese, and they hoped to be able, with the help of God, to capture it with very little loss; that she should be at ease, for they would all die before any harm came to her. With these words she and hers were somewhat pacified, and agreed that D. Christovão should act in the matter as he pleased, but very doubtful that the attempt could be satisfactorily prosecuted. All this while we were approaching the hill.[1]

---

[1] Correa (vol. iv, p. 356): "The country people and the Abyssinian captains, who all knew it well, gave information as to the hill, and D. Christovão determined not to go further without capturing the hill. Having settled this in his heart, he discussed it with the patriarch, the Barnegaes and his captains, saying that it did not appear to him right to advance, leaving these Moors behind, passing their very gate. That it would seem a cause for mockery (*judaria*), and that they refused to fight them through fear; that it would greatly hearten the Moors and greatly depress the Portuguese: seeing that, although they came to aid the Preste and to drive the Moors out of the kingdom, they still passed without attacking and capturing that hill. All considered that D. Christovão spoke well, but their judgment was opposed to what he suggested, more especially as the Queen had often said to him that she would prefer, and that it would be the best plan for D. Christovão to adopt, to undertake nothing against the Moors, unless they sought him, until he had joined and seen the Preste; that when they were united they could do what seemed right. Further, if they did attack this hill now, and some disaster happened to D. Christovão and he died, all would be lost, and she would have to return and fly to the hill where she had been. D. Christovão weighed these reasons, and replied that in no way whatever could he forego attacking that hill, as the Moors were in his very road; that he had great hopes in the Passion of our Lord that He would give him victory over the unbelievers in His holy faith, as He always did; that everywhere where Portuguese fought Moors, even though they were few, they defeated many Moors. This he hoped in His holy pity would now be the case."

The position of this hill has been fully discussed in the Introduction,

CHAPTER X.

Of how D. Christovão pitched his Camp on the skirts of the Hill, and of how he took Order to attack it.

ON the morning of the next day, February 1st, 1542, the eve of the day of the Purification of Our Lady, we pitched our camp, and as D. Christovão came with full knowledge of the approaches, as soon as we were in sight he allotted them to the Captains: to Francisco Velho and Manuel da Cunha, with their people and three pieces of artillery, the first approach, with the wall at the foot, the attack to be made at a given signal; to the second he appointed João da Fonseca and Francisco de Abreu, with three other pieces of artillery, and with the same instructions as to the signal; as the last approach was the strongest and most dangerous, he selected it for himself with the remaining people. There remained on guard over the Queen sixty soldiers with matchlocks and pikes,[1] who were angry and discontented that they were excluded from the attack. That day also, late, D. Christovão made a feint of attacking, signalling to the Captains and bringing his artillery close, drawn up in order (*posse em ordem*);[2] he did this to learn where it would be better to attack with matchlocks, and where the artillery would cause greater damage; and also to induce them to expend their munitions and magazines, which would help us on the following day. It is

---

and Castanhoso's mistake in calling it the hill on which the Kings of Abyssinia were crowned has been pointed out. Castanhoso is correct as to the time the Muhamedans must have held the hill, as the Imam Ahmad began his advance on Tigré about 1533. From Basset (*Histoire*, p. 422), it would appear that "Ambâ Sanét" was the Muhamedan headquarters to which the Imam returned with his booty after a raid in the direction of Aksum.

[1] B, "there remained with the Queen a few Portuguese and the Barnagaes and his men to guard her."

[2] B omits these three words.

difficult to believe how thick the stones and arrows fell when we got near; and they let fall rocks from the hill above, which caused us great fear and damage. When D. Christovão had seen all he wanted[1] he retired. When the Moors saw this, it appeared to them that we could not attack them, and their delight was so excessive that all night they made great clamour with many trumpets and kettledrums. The Queen, too, became very sad and distrustful, for it seemed to her as it appeared to the Moors, that there was no more determination in us than that, for she had watched all. As D. Christovão, from what he was told, understood her distrust, he sent to tell her why he had advanced and retreated; and that in the morning her highness would see how the Portuguese fought, and what men they were.[2] That night we spent in careful guard.[3]

CHAPTER XI.

Of how the Portuguese attacked this Hill and captured it, with the Death of some.

AT dawn, on the following day, we all commended ourselves to Our Lady, and made a general confession before a crucifix, held in his hands by a Mass priest, and received absolution from the patriarch; when this was done[4] we fell into our ranks, and marched to the hill, each to his own pass, as had been before arranged. At D. Christovão's

---

[1] Correa (vol. iv, p. 358) adds: "he signalled with a trumpet and"

[2] Correa (vol. iv, p. 358) has: "D. Christovão went to see the Queen, who told him this; but D. Christovão told her that he had not ascended then, but that he would the following day, which was a very holy one."

[3] B adds: "both on the camp and on the approaches, lest the Moors should attack us, as we suspected they would do."

[4] Correa (vol. iv, p. 358): "when all had breakfasted."

signal we all attacked together, and our artillery helped us greatly, for it all fired high,[1] and caused the Moors great fear, so that they dared not approach close to the edge of the hill, whence they could have wrought us much damage with a vast store of rocks; had it not been, as I say, for the artillery and matchlocks, which searched every place, they had killed many from the top, this helped us greatly.[2] All the same, they treated us very badly, and killed two men of ours before we began to climb the hill. D. Christovão, seeing the evil treatment they gave us, attacked the ascent very briskly, and we all followed him with our lives in our hands; when we got under shelter of the hill the stone-throwing did us less harm, and then we began to ascend the pass. D. Christovão headed the climb by the help of his pike, and of fissures in the rocks; here many were wounded, and all twice beaten back,[3] but our matchlocks kept off the Moors from approaching the pass.[4] With this help we forced our way in, D. Christovão being among the first, and he certainly gave this day proof of his great courage, and it was his valour that rendered the capture of the pass easy. The Moors were so hard pressed that the commander had not time to mount his horse; when he saw the Portuguese on the summit, he prepared, with his five hundred companions, to defend themselves, animating and urging them to advance; but with all they could not await the impetuosity of the Portuguese. At the time these Moors gave way, Manuel da Cunha and Francisco Velho were already on the top with their following, the forcing costing them much labour. They suffered a good deal, and many Portuguese were wounded before they

---

[1] B, "our artillery fired very quickly."
[2] Correa (vol. iv, p. 358): "the Moors . . . . merely throwing stones from the inside at hazard."
[3] B adds: "having nearly reached the top."
[4] B, "Our artillery helped us, as it fired at the Moors on the top, who, through fear, dared not come too close."

entered the outer gate; between the two gates the Moors slew two Portuguese. The Moors would not close the last gate, thinking they could take better vengeance inside. When our men did get in, they found them formed up in one body, with the commander and three others on horseback. Our men, seeing them collected together, attacked with the shout of "St. James!" falling on with lance-thrusts and sword-cuts, and the battle[1] raged. The commander at this pass fought like a very valiant man. He ran a Portuguese through with a javelin he carried, transfixing him through his armour; then he drew his sword, and delivered such a blow on another's head that he dashed his helmet into his skull and felled him to the ground senseless. Seeing then the destruction that Moor wrought, three attacked him at once, threw him down, and he died the death he deserved. While this was in progress, the third pass of João da Fonseca and Francisco de Abreu was entered, with the same opposition as the others; and in the forcing they slew two of their men. When the Moors saw the passes were occupied they retreated, the one body on the other, neither knowing of the other's defeat; thus they all collected under our swords and pikes, and remained in a trap whence none escaped. Those who had fled early hid in the houses, and were all killed by the Abyssinians, who delighted in doing it. Some Moors preferred to throw themselves from the summit, hoping they might escape; but they were all dashed to pieces. After the capture of the hill, we searched the houses, where we found many captive Christian women and many other Moor women.[2] We also captured nine horses and ten

---

[1] A has *baralha*, a shuffling as of cards. B has *batalha*, a battle.

[2] Correa (vol. iv, p. 359): "Many Moor women were also captured, but D. Christovão ordered that all the Moor men should be slain, so that only a few fitted for service were retained. The Moor women he sent to the Queen, but she refused to see them, and ordered all to be killed."

very handsome mules, besides many others, perhaps seventy or eighty. When we mustered, we found a loss of eight Portuguese, who had been killed in the attack, and over forty wounded.[1] D. Christovão went straight to the mosque after the victory, and directed the patriarch and the padres who had followed to consecrate it, in order that Mass might be said the next day. They gave it the name of Our Lady of Victory, and we buried there the eight Portuguese. D. Christovão next sent to ask the Queen if she wished to see the hill in the condition in which the Moors had held it. She was astonished at the ease with which we had carried it; she considered that all the Moors who were on the summit could not possibly be killed. When she was told by her people that it was true, she said that indeed we were men sent of God, and she thought all things were possible to us, but that she did not wish to ascend the hill, as the road was so full of dead bodies that it would pain her. When everything had been arranged, D. Christovão came to the Queen, leaving on the summit those wounded who could not be moved, as they were weary and their wounds cold. The Queen gave the hill to one of her Captains, whose ancestors had held it. The name of the hill is Baçanete. We spent the whole month here resting, in order to cure the wounded. As the news spread over the country, the inhabitants came to us with ample supplies, and with all that we needed. At the end of February, before we left here, there joined us two Portuguese with six[2] Abyssinians to guide them, sent by Manuel de Vasconcellos, who was in Massowa in command of five ships, sent by D. Estevão from India, to learn what had happened to us; whether we needed any help or anything,[3] as we should be provided with all.

---

[1] B, "Fifty wounded."   [2] B, "two Abyssinians."
[3] B, "whether we were dead or living."

D. Christovão, in particular, and we all were much pleased at this news;[1] and Francisco Velho was at once ordered to get ready with forty men, to go to Manuel de Vasconcellos and give him letters for the Governor, his brother; and in the same bundle were enclosed letters for the King, our lord, in which he reported to him the country he had reduced to obedience to the Queen, that is, about forty leagues, and this merely through dread of the Portuguese name. They also went to the fleet, to bring back the powder and the munitions necessary for the war.[2] When Francisco Velho had started, the Queen and D. Christovão determined to shift their camp to eight leagues away: to some plain country where supplies were very abundant, as the lord there was a Christian, and had become subject to the Moors against his will. He wrote to the Queen to invite her, as she would be better supplied there, for he was and always had been hers. He explained his obedience to the Moor as extracted from him by force, and asked her pardon. We marched there to await the Portuguese, who should not take more than fifteen days in

---

[1] B, "to get news of India."

[2] Correa (vol. iv, p. 360): "Early in March there arrived two Portuguese, who came from the Straits, with men of the country to guide them, sent by Manuel de Vascogoncellos, who had passed the Straits with five foists, who had been very strictly commissioned by the Governor, D. Estevão, to learn news of D. Christovão. As they brought many letters from India for all, the arrival of these men caused great pleasure, chiefly to D. Christovão, who showed his letters to the Queen, in which his brother told him that if he required more men he would, on the arrival of his message, send him as many as he required; which caused great joy to the Queen and all the camp. As Manuel de Vascogoncellos said that he would wait a month for the men who brought the letters to receive his answer, and that as for the many things he brought—garments and Cambay cloths—he would not land them till he had received his reply, D. Christovão told off Francisco Velho with his fifty men, to proceed to Massowa to bring all these things, and those entrusted to the men in the foists; they were also to bring four bases, and powder and bullets as much as they could; not to delay, but to return immediately. Francisco Velho started at once with men of the country as guides."

coming and going,[1] as they travelled on very free-going mules, and only carried their arms, and there was no reason for longer delay.

CHAPTER XII.

Of how D. Christovão, in nearing the plains of Jarte, met an Ambassador from the Preste, and of the Warning received that the King of Zeila was near.

WE had marched for two days towards Jarte (*para o Jarte*), which is the lordship of that Captain I mentioned, when, while we were pitching our camp, there arrived an envoy from the Preste, with a message for the Commander to march as quickly as might be, while he did the same, in order to join before meeting the King of Zeila, who had a large force, and with whom a fight by one alone would be perilous. Thus we marched on until we reached the plains, where came the Captain of the country, to ask pardon and pity of the Queen, who pardoned him, for she had had many communications from him, and knew that he was always a Christian. He visited D. Christovão, and presented him with four very handsome horses, and told him that he knew that the King of Zeila was coming in search of us,[2] and that many days could not elapse before we met him; that he should make what arrangements were necessary, and that he himself would send out spies to discover what was occurring. D. Christovão asked him to do this, and determined to march slowly,

---

[1] Pearce (vol. ii, p. 284) puts the time of going from Adowa to Massowa and back at fourteen days. This estimate agrees very closely with the above, if Baçanete be in Haramat.

[2] Correa (vol. iv, p. 361): "That the King of Zeila ... had started at once when he heard of the capture of the hill." I have already stated that Jarte, to which the Portuguese were marching, is probably Wajarat.

awaiting our men, fearing lest the King of Zeila should come on us before we joined the Preste. We marched forward in this way, with many spies ahead of us, who two days later returned to us with the news that the Moors' camp was near, and that we should meet before the next day. When D. Christovão found that he could not avoid a battle with the Moors without losing the reputation we had gained, he determined to accept it; for he felt, concerning the country people, that if he retreated to the hill they would disobey him, and would not assist him with any supplies; and that it was far the greater risk to chance famine, and losing our prestige, than to fight the Moors, for victory is in the hands of God. With minds made up we continued our march, and when we reached some wide plains two horsemen, who had been ahead scouting the plain, returned, saying that the King of Zeila was a league away. We at once pitched our camp, and it was the Saturday before Palm Sunday.[1] D. Christovão, as the Queen came in the rear, and had heard how near the enemies were, went out to receive her with great parade and joy, for she was a woman, and came filled with fear at the news. Encouraging her greatly, he placed her in the centre of our camp, which was this same day pitched in proper order,[2] and arranged to await in it the Moors; for the ground was very suitable, as we occupied the best site on the plain, for we were on a hillock in it. All the night

---

[1] April 1st, 1542. Castanhoso's narrative does not lead us to expect that a month had elapsed since leaving Baçanete. Following the Ethiopian chronicles, Bruce (vol. iii, p. 205) dates the battle March 25th. Where he got his statement that there were 12,000 Abyssinians with the Portuguese, I cannot discover. In chap. xiv Castanhoso says there were 200 only.

[2] Tellez (Bk. II, chap. x, p. 122): "D. Christovão at once pitched his camp on a hillock, which was in the middle of the plain, very proper for our purpose, near a beautiful stream called Afgol." In his chap. xvii, Bermudez, in this connection, mentions the monastery of Nazareth. As already pointed out in the Introduction, this supports the identification founded on the statement of Paez.

we watched vigilantly, and the following morning, at dawn, there appeared on the summit of a hill five Moorish horsemen, who were spying the plain; when they saw us they retired to give the news to the King. Then D. Christovão sent two Portuguese on good horses to ascend the hill, and discover how large the enemy's camp was, and where pitched; they returned directly, saying that they covered the plains and were halted close to the hill. While his camp was being pitched, the King of Zeila ascended a hill with several horse and some foot to examine us; he halted on the top with three hundred horse and three large banners, two white with red moons, and one red with a white moon, which always accompanied him, and by which he was recognised;[1] thence he examined us, while the rest of his army, with its bannerets, descended the hill and surrounded us. Such was their trumpeting, drumming, cries, and skirmishing, that they appeared more numerous and stout-hearted [than they were]. D. Christovão, thinking they meant to attack us, visited all the defences. We were ready for the fight; but they did no more than hold us surrounded all that day and that night, lighting many fires everywhere, and with the same noise and music. We feared them greatly that night, for every moment we thought they would attack us. We stood ready and armed, with powder-pots in our hands, matches lighted for the artillery and matchlocks, firing from time to time the bases as a guard, for we feared much their horsemen. We learned afterwards, from the Abyssinians who were with them, that they dared not attack us at night because our camp appeared from the outside very formidable, both because of the shots we fired from time to time, and

---

[1] A very detailed description of the Imam Ahmad's standard, some few years earlier than this, with all the mottoes on it, will be found in Basset (*Histoire*, p. 88). It is there said to have been white, with a red border.

because of the many matches they saw lighted, of which they had great fear; they said it could not be we were so few as we appeared by day.

CHAPTER XIII.

Of the Embassy the King of Zeila sent to D. Christovão.

AFTER this night, passed in trouble, as I tell, on the morning of the next day, the King of Zeila sent a king-at-arms[1] to D. Christovão with a message: that he marvelled greatly how he had the audacity to appear before him with so small a force; that indeed he seemed to be a mere boy, as rumour said, and innocent without experience. As he had been so deceived, he did not blame him, but the people of the country, who knew the truth. That they, indeed, were of small account, for they were disloyal to their own King. That he knew in fact that that woman had beguiled him, but that he should pay no more attention to her. That he, as a pitiful King, wished to have compassion on him, and for his boldness in facing him (a thing which had not happened in fourteen years[2] in that country), he would pardon his great temerity, on condition that he came over to him with all his Portuguese. That if he did not care to join him, that he could return to his own country. That he assured him no evil should befall him. That he treated him with this magnanimity because of his age and inexperience, and because he was sure that the woman had deluded him, by telling him that in those countries there was some other King than himself; but, since he now knew the truth, that he should do as he

---

[1] Correa (vol. iv, p. 363): "A Moor, who came on horseback, with his boy, who carried a white flag on a lance in front of him."

[2] Correa (vol. iv, p. 364): "Thirteen years."

was ordered. With this he sent him a friar's cowl and a rosary of beads, making us all out friars—for so they call us.[1] After D. Christovão had heard the King's message, he gave great honour and welcome to him who brought it, and gave him a red[2] satin garment, and a scarlet cap with a valuable medal; and told him to return and he would send a reply to the King. Dismissing him, he had him accompanied out of the camp, and then discussed with the Captains and fidalgos what reply he should send to the Moor, and who should take the answer. It was agreed not to send a Portuguese—as there was no trusting a Moor—but a boy of a Portuguese, his slave and white.[3] He was clothed finely, and given a mule to ride. His answer was a few lines written in Arabic, that the King might read it. This said that he had come here by order of the great Lion of the Sea, who is very powerful on land; whose custom it is to help those who are helpless and need his assistance. That as he was informed that the most Christian King, the Preste, his brother in arms, had been defeated and driven from his kingdom by the infidels and enemies of our Holy Catholic Faith, he had sent the small succour that was here, which still sufficed against such evil and bad persons; that reason and justice, which were on his side, were enough to defeat them, as they only conquered that country because our Lord desired to chastise the Abyssinians for their sins. That he trusted that in future they would be free, and would recover possession of what they had had. That the following day he would see what the Portuguese were worth, and that was not to go over to him; for they obeyed no lord save the King of Portugal,

---

[1] The play is on *frades* and *frangis*; the statement is repeated in chap. xv. There may have been a confusion in the Abyssinian mind between the two terms, but not, as a commentator suggests, in Castanhoso's. The words were common enough in India.

[2] B, "Dark coloured."

[3] B adds: "from India." Correa (vol. iv, p. 364) calls him a free man.

whose vassals all the Kings of India, Arabia, Persia, and the greater part of Africa were; and the same, by the help of our Lord, he hoped to make him. With this he sent him small tweezers for the eyebrows, and a very large looking-glass—making him out a woman. The slave carried this message, but it did not please the Moor; still, he said that people of such stomach, who though few yet wanted to fight him, were worthy that all Kings should do them much honour and favour. With this the slave returned. The Moor determined to continue the blockade, to see if he could not reduce us by famine. That day he did no more than hold us besieged, and creep somewhat closer to us. There were fifteen thousand foot, all archers and bucklermen; fifteen hundred horse, and two hundred Turkish arquebusiers, of whom they thought a great deal, and with whom they had conquered all that country. They were indeed men of greater determination, for they came closer to us than any of the others, and helped him a good deal. They got so close that they made some breastworks of loose stones very near us, whence they did us some hurt. D. Christovão had to send Manuel da Cunha and Inofre de Abreu with seventy men to dislodge them, which they did. The horsemen tried to support the Turks, and here some Portuguese were wounded. From the camp our artillery killed some horsemen, and wounded many Moors.[1] D. Christovão, finding that this engagement increased, ordered a trumpet to sound the recall, and they obeyed; thus the day passed. That night D. Christovão determined (as our supplies were failing, and the Captain of the country who was with us was unable to help us, as we were blockaded) to join battle next morning early, as they refused to attack. Thus we passed the night with careful watch, and before dawn we began to get ready.

---

[1] B, "killed with the artillery, four horse and some foot."

CHAPTER XIV.

Of how D. Christovão fought the first Battle with the King of Zeila, in which the Moor was defeated, and wounded by a matchlock Bullet.

AFTER the artillery had been mounted on the carriages,[1] and the tents and all the baggage loaded on mules, D. Christovão arranged his forces: the Captains with their men were in advance, the Queen with her women and all the transport in the centre, and the royal standard, with the rest of the force, in the rear; thus we made a circle as we were surrounded on all sides; the arrangements were completed before dawn without our being discovered.[2] At break of day, on Tuesday, April 4, 1542, we began to march towards the enemy. D. Christovão, with eight mounted Portuguese and four or five Abyssinians, visited every part of the force, arranging the men. When the Moors saw us advancing towards them, they raised such a noise of shouting, trumpets, and kettledrums, that it seemed as if the world were dissolving; they showed great joy, thinking they had us already in their net. At this we began to do our duty with matchlocks and artillery, which played continually on all sides, so that we cleared the plain as we advanced.

---

[1] A uses here the word *carretoens*; B has *carros*, which is the word used previously in chap. vi.

[2] "They" (the Franks and Ite Sabla Wangel) "met Grañ in the country of Anasa, and fought him on 29th of Magabit" (March 25th, 1542). "They fired at him with fire-arms, but he did not die" (Basset, *Études*, p. 111).

"During this same year (the second of Galâwdêwos' reign) the children of Tubal, sons of Japhet, who were strong and valiant men, eager for battle like wolves and hungering for the fight like lions, landed from the sea. They helped the church in her wars against the Muhamedans, and began with a success; but when they thought their victory was complete it was not granted to them" (Conzelman, § 12, p. 130).

The inhabitants of the Spanish peninsula were traditionally said to be descended from Tubal.

The Turks, who were in our front, seeing the damage we caused, advanced close to us, and the battle began to rage. When the Moor found that the Turks were those who helped him most, he came in person against us with more than five hundred horse, and with the three standards that were always with him. Here we found ourselves in great trouble; but our artillery stood us in good stead, for those in charge behaved like valiant men without fear, and fired so rapidly that the horse could never get near us, because the horses feared the fire; still the Moors did us much harm, especially the Turks with their matchlocks. D. Christovão, seeing this, halted the force, ordering us not to fight save with the artillery, with which we did them much hurt; and as one hundred Turks advanced very close to us, D. Christovão sent Manuel da Cunha to attack them with his men, that is, about fifty Portuguese. He obeyed, and the engagement waxed so fierce that the Turks seized the banner and slew the ensign and three other Portuguese; they also killed and wounded many of the Turks; Manuel da Cunha retired, wounded in the leg with a matchlock bullet. All this while D. Christovão was encouraging our people, always present where danger was greatest, many of ours being wounded; he himself was wounded by another bullet in the other leg,[1] which was a great disaster for all, but for him an honour, for, wounded as he was, he behaved himself and acted as we find no example of any notable Captain in ancient or modern histories. The battle going thus, as I say, and it being now midday,[2] it pleased the Lord God to remember His servants, as He always does in times of such dire distress, when He is merciful. It

---

[1] B omits both "another" and "other," which, indeed, make no sense.

[2] Correa (vol. iv, p. 367): "Our men were in great trouble, for the Moors wounded them from all sides, and there was a great cry in the force, so that all thought that their last day had come."

appeared to us that we had the worst of the battle, and it appeared to the King of Zeila, who saw it from the outside, the opposite. He therefore advanced to encourage his men, and came so close to us that he was wounded in the thigh by a matchlock bullet; that pierced his horse, which fell dead under him. When they saw him fall, his ensigns lowered the three banners which accompanied him: this was the signal of retreat; they lowered them three times, and then took him up in their arms and bore him away. When D. Christovão saw this he knew that the Moor had been wounded; then sounding the trumpets and kettle-drums, we shouted "St. James!" and charged, with the Abyssinians who were with us, in number about two hundred. We slew many and followed them a space, where the Abyssinians avenged themselves on the Moors, slaying them as if they had been sheep. D. Christovão, as he had no horse to pursue, and as we were all very weary, and as we feared lest the Moorish horse should turn on us, contented himself with the victory our Lord had given him that day, which was not a small one. While we were in pursuit, the Queen had had a tent pitched and placed the wounded in it; she and her women went about binding up the wounded with their own head-gear, and weeping with pleasure at the great mercy our Lord God had done them that day, for truly she had found herself in great fear and tribulation. Meanwhile, D. Christovão returned to where the tent was pitched, and had all the others pitched also. The dead on the battle-field were examined, to bury the Portuguese who had fallen. There were eleven, and among them Luiz Rodriguez de Carvalho, with a musket-ball through the head, the first man killed, Lopo da Cunha fidalgo, and a foster-brother of D. Christovão;[1] there were

---

[1] Correa (vol. iv, p. 367) calls the foster-brother Fernão Cardoso; but this must be wrong. The man of that name survived the great defeat of D. Christovão, in the following August. For his bravery see chap. xx.

over fifty wounded, chiefly by matchlock bullets; but the enemy paid heavily, for the field was full of them; among them the Abyssinians recognised four of the principal Captains of the King of Zeila; there lay dead on the field forty horses and thirty Turks.[1] After we had buried the dead we wanted to rest; but the Captain of that country said to D. Christovão that we should not stay on that spot, as water was scarce, and there was little grass for the mules; that we should approach the skirts of a range of hills two matchlock shots away, where water was plentiful, and where we should be lords of the country, through which abundant supplies could come from his territory, and the enemy unable to interfere. This was agreed to, and, after eating, we left that spot and went there. This day D. Christovão laboured much, for he attended to all the wounded himself; for the surgeon we had with us was wounded in the right hand. After attending to all the others, he tended his own wound last of all. When night fell, he sent a man very secretly, to travel night and day until he came up with the Portuguese who were in Massowa, to tell them of the victory and of the King's wound, and to direct them to hasten, as he hoped in God to be able, on their arrival, to finish the conquest. We stayed here, curing the wounded and resting, until the first Sunday after Easter,[2] both because the wounded could not carry arms, and in order to see if the Portuguese came. After Easter and its octave had passed, D. Christovão, seeing that there was delay, and that the enemy would meanwhile be enabled to recruit their army, determined to fight a second battle on the Sunday, for we were in sight of each other.[3] It was

---

[1] B, "over forty Turks." Correa (vol. iv, p. 367) puts the number of Moors killed at over three hundred.

[2] B, "*Domingo de Quasi modo*," April 16th, 1542.

[3] Correa (vol. iv, p. 368): "Their camp was pitched in sight of ours, and the Queen and the patriarch sent men in disguise to spy what the

in this battle that the patriarch and others first saw the blessed St. James help us, in the shape in which he always does;[1] there can be no doubt but that without his help, and chiefly that of our Lord, we should never have been victorious.

CHAPTER XV.

Of the Second Battle which D. Christovão fought with the King of Zeila, in which the King was defeated.

THUS, when the Sunday after Easter came, the camp was struck before dawn, and all were drawn up in order, with the artillery in its place, and the Queen with her women in the centre. After the patriarch had said the general confession and absolved us,[2] we marched against the Moors, who when they saw us also advanced. The King, still suffering from his wound, lay on a bed carried on men's shoulders. He came to encourage his men, but this was hardly necessary, for they were so numerous that merely seeing how few we were encouraged them; besides, there had joined him a Captain with five hundred horse and three thousand foot; and had we delayed longer many more would have come to him; for his Captains were scattered over the country, and, when he was wounded, he called them all in, and they joined him daily. The Captain

---

Moors did, which they reported to D. Christovão, who was always on guard. By the spies D. Christovão had among the Moors, he learned that the Moor King was getting ready, and was calling in reinforcements to give him battle, while his men did not return from Massowa."

[1] Bermudez did not see him. See his chap. xvi, where he says that D. Christovão, some Portuguese, the Baharnagash, and an aunt of the King's, saw him. Correa, vol. iv, p. 368, says he was seen in the first battle. Bermudez refers to the second battle, as also apparently does Castanhoso.

[2] Correa (vol. iv, p. 368): "told the patriarch to make a general confession, and give plenary absolution, under a bull of the Pope's which he had."

who had come in was called Grada Amar,[1] and it was he who was the first to attack us. He, too, urged on the others, saying, how could so few as we were endure long against such a force. In his pride he attacked us with five hundred horse, and had all his men followed his example they would indeed have done us much hurt; but from dread of the artillery, which slew many, they could not break our ranks; but the Captain with four or five valiant Moors threw themselves on our pikes and died like brave cavaliers. D. Christovão all this time kept everything in the best possible order, and everyone fought with great courage; but had the horse broken our ranks then our destruction was a certainty: for when this Captain attacked with his horse, all the others who were on horseback did the like from all sides. By the will of our Lord, at this time, a little powder accidentally caught fire in the part where we were weakest. Truly we thought we should all be burned when we saw the fire in the powder, but as it told for our victory, we did not notice the loss it caused: that is, two Portuguese killed and eight burned, who were very badly injured.[2] The horsemen could not

---

[1] B, Gordamar. Correa, Gradamar. The name would be Garâd Amar. "Garâd," among the Muhamedans south of Abyssinia, means the governor of a district. Apparently this is the man whose defeat of Galâwdêwos is referred to in the extract from Basset, quoted in the note to chap. ii, p. 9, above.

[2] Correa (vol. iv, p. 369): "But the Moors, those who were horsemen, being at push of spear with our men, and our men at push of pike with them, the Moors broke in at one place, where the line was weak and there was none to resist them; but God in His pity helped, and fire caught in a little powder that was there, and killed two men and burned six others, who were at the point of death. This fire was so great that it frightened the horses, who fled over the plain without the Moors being able to master them. This was the salvation of the force, among which the Moors had already forced their way; and above all, the firing of the guns and the matchlocks, which the horses dreaded so much, that even the Turks did not dare to fire from among them. In this battle, D. Christovão, and the eight Portuguese horsemen with him, performed wonders, especially among the Turks who approached nearest, of whom many were killed and wounded. The horsemen drove them off, so that they could not come close, and

break in because of the fire I mention, as the horses were so frightened that they bolted over the plain with their riders. Meanwhile, we did our duty both with the artillery and the matchlocks, and the whole field was strewn with corpses. Eight Portuguese who were mounted did such deeds, that had they been done at any other time, they would have been held in remembrance. I will not name them, because the footmen would have done the same had they had horses; their deeds while on foot prove this, for they went out to the Turks who came near us, and fought grandly: so that they drove them back far, leaving many dead and wounded on the field. When the Turks retired, and the horse no longer came on, D. Christovão saw that they were shaken; and we attacked them briskly, and drove them before us till they took flight. The victory would have been complete this day had we had only one hundred horses to finish it: for the King was carried on men's shoulders on a bed, accompanied by horsemen, and they fled with no order. D. Christovão pursued them for half a league, and killed many Moors, who in their haste took no thought of their camp and tents, which spoil fell to our lot. When we could no longer pursue the Moors, as we were very weary, we returned, and when we were mustered fourteen Portuguese were found missing, who were sought out and buried. As the grass on this plain was destroyed, D. Christovão and the Queen agreed to advance to camp by a stream that was near, to rest there, where there was more refreshment for the wounded, of whom there were more than sixty, and of these four or five subsequently died. We began our march, leaving the plain strewn with dead.

---

retreated. When D. Christovão saw this, he ordered the trumpets to sound, and charged before all, with his companions on horseback, shouting 'St. James!' At this our men acquired fresh heart and strength, and the Abyssinians mingled with our men, attacked the enemy briskly, and dislodging them from the plain put them to flight."

There was killed in this fight an Abyssinian Captain who was with us: a very valiant man. When we arrived in sight of the stream we saw the Moors halted on its banks, because, when they had crossed it the King thought that we were not in pursuit; and as it was late and the place suitable, he desired to rest there. They fled when they saw us; and an Abyssinian who joined us there, and who had been with them, told us afterwards that the King said "these *frades* will not let me long alone"—for thus they call us.[1] The Moors started on their way, travelling all that night and eight days,[2] without resting, and many who were wounded died on the march. As D. Christovão would not pursue he went no further, but we pitched our camp there, tending our wounded. Two days later, the Portuguese who had gone to Massowa returned, and with them the Barnaguais, with thirty horsemen[3] and five hundred foot, whom we welcomed with much joy; but the Portuguese returned sadder than can be believed, because they were absent from the battles, and because they had not succeeded in the business on which they had gone, nor had even seen our fleet, because of the Turkish galleys who guarded the harbour, in order that our foists should learn nothing of us, nor we of them.

CHAPTER XVI.

Of how, on the Arrival of the Barnaguais and of the Portuguese, D. Christovão followed in Pursuit of the King of Zeila.

D. CHRISTOVÃO was much rejoiced at the arrival of these men, and determined to pursue the Moor. He began his preparations at once, sending fourteen very badly wounded

---

[1] See note, p. 43, chap. xiii, above.
[2] B, "that night and the next day." Correa (vol. iv, p. 370) says the same. Paez (Tellez, Bk. II, chap. xi, p. 127) gives eight days.
[3] B, "forty horsemen."

Portuguese (of whom, as I have said, four or five died) to a hill governed by a Captain who was with us, called Triguemahon,[1] who is like a Viceroy; he went with us to the hill, and we were all on beds (*catres*),[2] which was a heavy labour to those who carried us. Truly, the hospitality and honour we received from his wife and from himself cannot be expressed: for we were all so well provided and so well tended that in the houses of our own fathers we should have had no better, and I enlarge on this, for I was present.[3] When, a month later, some of us were better, we returned to D. Christovão, for, directly he sent us to recover, he started in pursuit of the Moor. It took him ten days[4] to reach where he was, which was in a great and strong hill, opposite the entrance to the straits, because he did not dare to retire elsewhere, for the country people after his defeat refused to obey him or give him supplies; and hence it suited him to retire to this hill, where he could recuperate, and could get assistance from the skirts of the sea, either from his own people or from the Turks, as it happened. Here, then, D. Christovão came up with him, and that with great labour, by reason of the rains and the mire, for the winter begins here at the end of April until September, as in India.[5] And because, as I have said, the winter was beginning, it appeared better to the Queen to occupy another hill, which is called Ofala,[6] in

---

[1] B, Tigremahō. This is Tigre makuanam, or Governor of Tigré, the name of the office, not the man. The then holder was called Degdeasmati Robel.

[2] B, "carried on the shoulders of Abyssinians."

[3] B, "as I was one of the wounded."

[4] B, "eight days."

[5] B, "the opposite of our Spain and the rest of Europe."

[6] "He" (Grañ) "passed the winter at Zabl" (Perruchon, Zobl), "and the Queen, Sabla Wangel, at Afla" (Perruchon, Ofla) "with the Franks" (Basset, *Études*, p. 111). Couto (*Dec. V*, Bk. VIII, chap. xiii) calls it the city of Offar. Paez, in Tellez, Bk. II, chap. xi, p. 126, calls it Ofla. It is now called Wofla.

sight of this one,[1] and winter there, for now all the country people obeyed her, and in that country there were ample supplies; further, it was on the road by which the Preste would come, and it might be that he would arrive soon. This seemed good to D. Christovão, and he determined to send a man to the Preste to acquaint him with the victory in the battles, that with this encouragement he might march more quickly. And when he had written he sent a mulatto,[2] called Ayres Dias,[3] who knew the language of the country well, for he had been there in the time of D. Rodrigo de Lima, the Ambassador; he sent this man because by reason of his colour and of his tongue he might pass for a Moor.[4] He reached the Preste, who was very pleased to hear what had occurred. The Queen collected many cultivators to make straw huts to winter in, which they made very diligently, for there are plenty of materials for this in the country, namely wood and straw; they also brought all the necessary supplies in great abundance, for the soil is very fertile and the produce great. The King of Zeila finding that, by reason of his defeat, those of the country refused to obey him or give supplies, had of necessity to send to take them by force; but his people returned each time fewer than they started, thus his only resource was what came to him from the skirts of the sea,[5] which was very little. We could not intercept this, for the hill is very extensive, bounding all that country, so that he was the lord of the further side. He made up his mind,

---

[1] B, "The hill where the King was is called Māgadafo." This name I cannot trace, nor can I Lobo's Membret (see his p. 91). The Imam Ahmad was camped at Zabul.

[2] B, "dark man."

[3] This embassy is referred to in the Abyssinian chronicles (see below at the end of chap. xx, p. 73). Marcos was the Abyssinian name of Ayres Dias.

[4] B softens this into "might pass through easily."

[5] B, "From the other slope of the hill by the side of the sea."

finding the straits he was in, with his people dead or cowed, to send secretly to demand help from the Captain of Azebide,[1] who was under the Turk, with three thousand Turks under him, sending to inform him of his defeat, and to tell him to regard him as a vassal of the Grand Turk, and not allow him to lose what he had already gained;[2] with this he sent him much money, both for himself and for the Turks, of whom on this inducement there came nine hundred, all arquebusiers, very fine and good men; he also sent him ten field bombards, knowing that what damage he had received from us was by artillery and matchlocks, for hitherto he had had no field pieces.[3] There also came to him many Arabs, sent by an Arabian lord, his friend; among these were twenty Turkish horsemen, with gilt stirrups, and their horses shod with iron, for in the Preste's country the horses go unshod.[4] All this help came in the course of the winter without its being known.

---

[1] B, "A port in the straits of Mecca under the Grand Turk." Zabid is on the Arabian coast of the Red Sea. The Italian translator suggests that Jedda is meant, but that lies over 600 miles north. As to Zabid, Basset, *Histoire*, p. 43 *n.*, may be consulted.

[2] B, "with much labour and brought into subjection to the Grand Turk; and if now he sent no help, all the country would return to the Christians; and with this he sent him much gold, silver, and jewels."
In the history of Minas, who was captured in 1539, there occurs this reference to this embassy (Esteves Pereira, *Minas*, p. 37): "In the third year of his (Minas) captivity, the Gran heard of the coming of the Franks, whose Captain was D. Christovão; then his hatred was devilish; as he desired to obtain Turks, he sent an embassy to the Pasha of Zabid; and he sent also the son of the King (Minas) with his servants, to be made over to the Pasha as his present." The year 1542 is correctly given.

[3] The Imam Ahmad used some field-pieces in the earlier battles against the Christians; they are mentioned in several places in the *Fath-ul-habsha*, but apparently he had not brought any against the Portuguese before this.

[4] Correa (vol. iv, p. 372) gives eight hundred matchlockmen, six hundred fighting Arabs and Persian bowmen, and thirty Turkish horsemen of good standing. Their stirrups are particularly mentioned, as Abyssinians ride only with a ring for the big toe. Readers of Bruce will remember the capital he made out of his knowledge of riding in the Moorish manner with stirrups.

CHAPTER XVII.

Of what D. Christovão did that Winter, and of how he Captured a very strong Hill which had belonged to a Jew Captain.

ABOUT this time D. Christovão learnt that there was near us a hill of the Jews,[1] by which the Preste must of necessity pass as there was no other road; that it had been captured by the Moors; and that the Captain of it, who was a Jew, was a fugitive because he obeyed the Preste; he put himself on the defensive when the Moors attacked the hill, and when he found they had captured it he fled. D. Christovão desired greatly to see him, to enquire what Moors were on the hill, and to discover if it could be recaptured. While in this mind the Jew, who had heard that he was wintering there with the Queen, determined to visit him to see if he could recover his country; because, from the information which he had of us, it seemed to him that this might be the case. Besides, our Lord chose to arrange matters thus, because the restoration of the kingdom was to be brought about by this means; when he came, the Jew informed D. Christovão about the hill, and told him that there were but few Moors on it, and that he would guide him to an approach where he would not be discovered until he was at the top, and that it was easy to capture, if the people of the country helped; that he would find on it many and good horses that were bred on the hill; and that it was quite impossible for the Preste in any manner to pass save over it, and that he had with him so

---

[1] B, "by name the Hill of Gimen." Couto (*Dec. V*, Bk. IX, chap. iv), "the Hill of the Jews, which by another name was known as Caloa." Paez (Tellez, Bk. II, chap. xii, p. 127), "a very strong hill called Oaty, in the province of Cemen hard by." The Italian translator quotes Massaia, a late Italian writer, who calls it Jalaka Amba or Houza, near the head-waters of the Ensea river. Bruce (Bk. V, chap. vii) identifies it with Amba Gideon. I have discussed the situation of the hill in the Introduction.

little strength that he could not capture it; when he had retired thence to the part whence he was now about to return, the hill had not yet been occupied by the Moors: had it been, he could not have escaped. When D. Christovão learnt how small a force the Preste had with him, he became very dispirited and disquieted, and went to the Queen to learn if it was true that her son had so small a force; when it was confirmed by her he became still more downcast, without, however, letting her know it, because until then he had not heard this, but had hoped that the Preste would quickly join him, as the winter was already verging to an end. That he [the Preste] might not find that obstacle in the way, and because he himself wanted the horses, he determined to go there personally, as the Jew told him that with one hundred good followers he might with skill recover the hill; that he required but few days for this, and that he could return to his camp with many horses without his absence being noted. D. Christovão did not wish to take all his force to capture that hill, lest the King of Zeila should think we were raising the siege and leaving. If he did this, the Moors would advance and capture the hill on which they [we] then were, and collect supplies of which they had need; and it might be that they would pursue him, thinking he was retreating; and, encouraged by this, they might have a confused and ill-timed battle; it would allow them, too, to recover their boldness, which had been much diminished by their late fear. That events might not so fall out, he determined to carry out the expedition in another way—to leave the camp well guarded, and to go so secretly as not to be discovered, taking with him Manuel da Cunha and João da Fonseca and one hundred men at the outside. He started at midnight, and travelled very secretly, carrying with him many skins necessary for crossing a river near the hill. They marched thus until they reached it, when they found it much swollen.

They quickly cut a quantity of wood and branches, and with these, and the skins filled with air, made rafts (*jangadas*), which they bound strongly together, and for this they had brought the necessaries. They crossed a few at a time, taking their matchlocks, powder, and matches inside other skins, lest they should be wetted; thus they all got over, some by swimming. When they and the mules had all crossed, they began to climb the hill,[1] not being discovered until they were at the top. When the Moors saw them they armed quickly; there were about three thousand foot and four hundred horse.[2] D. Christovão, who rode with the other eight Portuguese who were mounted, Manuel da Cunha on the one flank, with thirty matchlockmen, João da Fonseca on the other, with another thirty, and the remaining forty in the centre with the royal standard, attacked with great vigour. The Captain of the Moors, by name Cide Amede,[3] advanced in front of his men and encountered D. Christovão, in which encounter he died; the other horsemen with D. Christovão also overcame each his man. By this time the foot had all collected into one body, and did nothing save slay the Moors; who, seeing their Captain dead, and that there was none before whom they could feel shame, nor from whom they could receive orders, took to flight, and many died, for the very Jews slew them, and few escaped. When the hill was cleared, D. Christovão collected the spoil, which was rich in goods

---

[1] Couto (*Dec. V*, Bk. VIII, chap. xiii): "All that day" (day he left the camp) "he marched, guided by the Jew, and crossed a large river on rafts, and lodged on the other side. They marched again in the third watch, and before dawn reached the hill."

[2] Correa (vol. iv, p. 373): "Three hundred horse and four thousand foot;" also twelve mounted Portuguese, not eight.

[3] B, "Cide hamed." Basset (*Études*, p. 111) puts the death of Sid Mahamad, or Sidi Mohammed, on 13th Hedar (November 9th) of this year, at Woggara. Perruchon (*Revue Sémitique*, p. 265) puts it at same place on 16th Hedar (November 12th). The name is not an uncommon one, and possibly there may have been two persons with similar, if not identical, appellations.

and slaves[1] all very valuable. There were eighty excellent horses, with which he was more pleased than with anything else, and more than three hundred mules, with many cattle without number. When this was ended, he made over the hill to the Jew who had held it before, as he had always obeyed the Preste. When that Jew saw this great deed, and how God favoured us, he become a Christian, with twelve of his brethren, all Captains of places on that hill, which is twelve leagues long and all very fertile, with many populous places and villages and very strong; there are only two passes to it, all the rest is scarped rock. There are about ten thousand or twelve thousand[2] Jews on it; it is four leagues across; on the summit are very pleasant valleys and streams, and by the skirts of the hill runs a river as large as the Douro,[3] called Tagacem,[4] the one crossed by D. Christovão; it runs all round the hill, which is almost made an island by it. It is the most fertile hill that can be, and they may boast that they still enjoy manna, since they are in such luxury that they can get honey from the rifts in the rocks, and there is so much that there is no owner, and whoever likes collects it. This hill lies nearly due west of the Straits,[5] and may be forty[6] leagues distant. When D. Christovão had made over the hill to the Jew, he left him an order to send to the Preste to inform him of its capture. He started for the camp, and as the way after passing the river was rough, he left thirty men with the horses to come on slowly,[7] while he went on very quickly with the other seventy, dreading lest some disaster

---

[1] B, "female slaves."

[2] Correa (vol. iv, p. 374): "twenty thousand Jews."

[3] B, "Tejo."

[4] B, "Tagazē"—that is, the Tacazzé.

[5] Bab el Mandeb.

[6] B, "fifty." At this point the sea is nearly double this distance.

[7] Couto (*Dec. V*, Bk. VIII, chap. xiii) says that he left Afonso Caldeira in command of the escort.

should have befallen us, travelling both night and day. The very night he returned, the Turks arrived to reinforce the King of Zeila, and on the following day they mustered over one thousand matchlockmen. They came at once to the foot of our hill, and pitched their camp close to ours; thence they saluted us with their artillery and matchlocks, and pitched some balls into our camp. When D. Christovão saw this, he knew what succour had reached them, and took counsel with all as to what should be done. It was agreed to wait until the following day, when they could see the power of the Moor, but that they should not fight before the arrival of the horses, which could not be delayed more than two days: that, should the Moor attack us, we should defend ourselves the best we could, as our camp was somewhat fortified by some palisades erected during the winter. D. Christovão agreed to this, for he knew that, if we struck our camp that night, the very people would rise against us, and we should have nothing to eat; for this reason we were bound to fight and retain what we had gained. He sent an urgent message to those with the horses, to march as quickly as possible, as the Moors had been reinforced by the Turks, and a battle appeared imminent. We kept careful watch all that night, which was not good refreshment for those who came weary from their journey. All that night we were under arms.

CHAPTER XVIII.

Of how there was a Battle between D. Christovão and the King of Zeila, in which D. Christovão was defeated.

THE next day, in the morning, Wednesday, August 28th, 1542, the day of the beheadal of St. John the Baptist,[1] the

---

[1] In 1542 this date fell on a Monday, not a Wednesday, and the beheadal of John the Baptist is commemorated by the Latins on

Moor came out with all his power, with one thousand Turks in advance, to give us battle : the artillery was in the van, all prepared. D. Christovão, seeing his intentions, manned the positions in the best way he could, and stood on the defensive. At daybreak the artillery began to play, for at that hour they advanced against us; by it and the matchlocks many on both sides were wounded. The Turks, as they were many and but recently arrived, advanced very proudly, doing us much hurt. When D. Christovão saw the great hurt they did us, and that the palisades of our camp were not strong enough to be defended, especially from the Turks, he decided to sally out frequently and attack them, and then retreat. It appeared to him that in this way he would secure victory, for they could not await the very first onset of any body of Portuguese. He acted accordingly: he being the very first who, with fifty soldiers, with matchlocks and pikes, attacked over one hundred Turks who were on that flank. He drove them back a considerable way, killing and wounding many. He began to retreat when he met the main body of the enemy, and in the retreat they killed four of his men; the remainder all returned wounded, including D. Christovão himself, with a matchlock bullet in one leg. When he had returned, Manuel da Cunha, as he had been ordered, attacked on the other side, and drove the Turks back for another space: for they were those who came closest to us and pressed us hardest. He, too, killed and wounded many, but in the retreat they killed five or six of his men, and wounded several. The other

---

August 29th, and by the Abyssinians on August 30th, but by neither on the 28th. Correa (vol. iv, p. 375) gives the same date as Castanhoso. Couto (*Dec. V*, Bk. VIII, chap. xiv), says August 29th, the day of the beheadal, but does not name the day of the week. Paez gives August 28th only. The Ethiopian accounts (Basset, *Études*, p. 111; Perruchon, *Revue Sémitique*, 1894, p. 265) give the date 3rd Maskaram, that is, Thursday, August 31st. The saint's day would be more easily remembered than the date, and therefore the probable date of the battle is Tuesday, August 29th, 1542.

captains of the positions, as one retreated another attacked, but always in the retreat they killed some of our men. The affair became so confused that they killed some of our men in the very camp. In this way we continued for a great part of the day; the followers of the Moor were pleased enough, seeing the Turks on their side, and the hurt we received. D. Christovão, wounded as he was, went round the positions, encouraging the men : for these are the days when leaders are recognised; I have no words wherewith even to express his courage, when looking at the positions and the camp, he saw his men very weary, and the greater number wounded. The Queen was in her house in the direst trouble, weeping for the hour that had come to her. The house was filled with men too wounded to fight, and she, with her women—who that day did their duty in this well—bound up their wounds. They fired many shot into her house, and wounded two of her women. When D. Christovão saw this, and the great hurt the Turks were causing, and that in each retreat men were killed, he ordered Francisco de Abreu to attack with his men on his side, and his brother, Inofre de Abreu, to follow on his flank, so that when the first retreated the other should support, that they might not have the opportunity of doing so much hurt. He attacked, killing many of them, but in the retreat his fortune willed that they killed him by a matchlock bullet. When his brother saw this, he ran to bring him in, forcibly driving them off; lifting his brother to carry him, a shot struck him and stretched him on the other; thus they both lay.[1] Our men retreated with difficulty, for here they met the main body of the

---

[1] B explains that the men driven off by force were the Moors, who were carrying off the brother's body. Correa (vol. iv, p. 376) says the Moors were running to cut off Inofre de Abreu's head, and his brother, thinking him alive, ran to his assistance. Castanhoso's account is involved. The head is not the trophy sought in Abyssinia, but the word is used euphemistically.

Moors, who slew many of them. D. Christovão, seeing that they had slain the greater part of his people, collected whom he could—and they but few—round the royal standard: for there were not many now to fight, for midday was past. When they were collected, he left word with Manuel da Cunha to attack the Moors with his men during his retreat, to hinder their harming him; and he charged them straight, driving them back over the field a great space. Truly, had we had the horses, which were on the way, the victory was ours; but we deserved for our sins that this should befall us, to happen what did happen. While our men attacked they drove them like sheep, but they were now so weary they could not bear the fatigue. When D. Christovão turned to retreat he was so far in the field, that in the retreat they killed many of his men and wounded him with another bullet that broke his right arm;[1] and he returned in great pain. Here Manuel da Cunha helped greatly, for he attacked the Moors, and then retreated with him; they also slew and wounded many of his. João da Fonseca, who had sallied from his position to drive off the Moors, was, after two or three sallies, killed, and Francisco Velho the same. When D. Christovão found that they had killed four of his Captains, and that the rest of his people, as well as himself, were so badly wounded, he determined to sally out no more, but continued encouraging his men, and trying to induce them to return to the positions, which now had none to guard them, and none to fight in them, for it grew very late. At this time the Turks entered the positions, and twice they were driven out; but, as matters stood, there was none to rally to the royal standard. When the patriarch saw affairs in this state, he mounted a mule, and retreated to a hill on our flank. The Queen wanted to do

---

[1] B, "above the elbow."

the same, but D. Christovão ordered her to be restrained, lest the Portuguese should accompany her. By now many of the Moors were inside the palisades, and of ours there was none to fight, the greater part being wounded or dead. We were compelled to retreat up the hill, which D. Christovão refused, being determined to die. Our men, seeing that it served no purpose to delay, as there was none to fight, made him retreat, telling him that he could see that all the Portuguese were withdrawing, and that those around him were too few to resist the enemy ; that, for all this, they would all die with him, as honour bade them, but that it would be wiser to join his own men, as the Lord God was pleased to give them that punishment for the sin of all. With this they made him retreat, riding a mule ; the Queen preceding him, ready to share whatever fate befell us. With great labour we retreated up the hill, for we were all wounded, each one going as he could. The steepness of the hill was our safeguard, as horsemen could only follow us slowly ; but the foot did us much hurt, as numbers followed us, and slew many who could not travel with arrows and stones. When night fell, some went one way, some another, without waiting the one for the other. D. Christovão went one way with the fourteen Portuguese,[1] who always accompanied him, and the Queen another, with the rest of us ;[2] we continued our retreat in this confusion, and in these difficulties. The Turks staying in the camp to collect the spoil, they entered the Queen's houses, where they found more than forty wounded, who

---

[1] B, "of the least wounded men."

[2] B, " I with her, for I was badly wounded in the left arm by an arquebuz shot, and I had other wounds, though none so severe as that in the arm, for it was entirely broken. I wished to go with her, as that charge was always given me ; and in such a perilous time I would not quit her, although my help was but feeble. With us were about thirty Portuguese, and a few of the Queen's women servants, but very few of her ladies, for the greater part were left, as the press at our retreat was great."

could not stir, and began to kill them *(fazer a gazua nelles)*. A Portuguese, when he saw this, determined not to allow them to enjoy that satisfaction, but to die and revenge himself on them. He raised himself and crept on all fours, with a lighted match that lay handy, and went to where the powder was,[1] and fired it. The house blew up, none escaping:[2] for D. Christovão had a very large store of powder, which he had made during the winter, and this was kept in the Queen's houses, as the most watertight. It is probable that this cavalier set fire to the house less because the Turks were killing those who were already dead, than in order to prevent them using the powder with which they might have done great hurt, for there was much of it.[3]

CHAPTER XIX.

Of how the Moors, following D. Christovão, found him, and seized him, and of How he Died.

D. CHRISTOVÃO and the fourteen Portuguese with him, marching all that night, travelled with heavy labour, for they were all wounded and very weary. They had therefore

---

[1] Correa (vol. iv, p. 378), "in skins."

[2] Bermudez attributes the act to a woman. Clearly, it was impossible to say one or the other.

[3] "The Imam Ahmad fought them" (the sons of Tubal, see note, chap. xiv, p. 45, above), "slew the majority of them, and captured their best warriors. He put to death their chief, valiant and courageous, with a heart of iron and brass in the battle. He slew him by an unworthy death, after capturing him and imprisoning him : a treatment reserved for the weak and infirm. This happened to them because they did not fight under the orders of Mar Galâwdêwos, to whom alone was the victory ; who was powerful, and was entitled to open the sealed book of the future : to undo the seal and be hailed victor. It is shown by the death of the Imam Ahmad at the hands of Mar Galâwdêwos. We will relate later this death, and how it happened. We will tell this in its proper place" (Conzelman, § 12).

"In the second year of this prince" (Galâwdêwos), he (the Imam Ahmad) fought a battle on the 3rd Maskaram ; the Captain died"

to leave the road they followed, and enter a shady valley, with a very thick growth of trees, to take some rest. As the morning was near, and there was great fear of discovery by the enemy who were in pursuit, having, as I say, left the path, they entered the bottom of the valley in the most solitary possible place, where they found a little water that flowed from a water-fall. They got D. Christovão off his mule to dress his wounds, which up to now they had not had time to do; his companions, not having wherewith to do it, killed the mule D. Christovão rode, and taking the fat, dressed with it his wounds, and also the wounds of those among them that needed it. When the Moors captured the camp some would not halt, but followed us relentlessly; on the road by which D. Christovão escaped there went twelve Turks on foot and twenty Arabs on horseback, eager to capture him; at dawn they were beyond where he lay, and not finding him, they returned. Reaching the point where D. Christovão turned into the thicket, an old woman[1] came out of the wood, looking as if she could hardly stand, and ran across the road; the Moors, to learn her news, tried to catch her, and followed her into the wood, without capturing her, as she ran from one thicket to another. When she got to the valley she crossed it, running fast, and entered among the trees where D. Christovão and the Portuguese lay. As the Moors followed with pertinacity, they would not abandon the pursuit, and thus came on D. Christovão, and taking him by surprise, with loud cries of "Mafamede," captured him. One of these [D. Christovão's companions] who was but slightly wounded, hid in the thicket and escaped, and from him we heard the story of the capture. It is impossible that that

---

(Basset, *Études*, p. 111). I have adopted the punctuation of Perruchon (*Revue Sémitique*, 1894, p. 265), as making better sense than that of Basset.

[1] B, "an old negro woman."

old woman can have been any one save the devil, as she vanished from among them and was never seen again. This astonished the Moors greatly, who, from what they told us afterwards, considered that "Mafamede" had sent her to direct them; they returned contented with their prize, as they at once recognised D. Christovão by the arms he bore; thus they went with him, making him many mocks by the way, and giving him but evil treatment.[1] Thus they brought them before the King, who was very pleased with the victory, with more than one hundred and sixty[2] Portuguese heads before his tent: for he had offered a reward to any Moor who would cut off the head of a Portuguese, and his men, to gain it, brought him those they found on the field. When D. Christovão reached his tent, that dog ordered the heads of the Portuguese to be shown him, to grieve him; telling him whose they were, and that here were those with whom he had designed to conquer his country, and that his madness was clear in his design; and that for this boldness he would do him a great honour. This was to order him to be stripped, with his hands tied behind him, and then cruelly scourged, and his face buffeted with his negroes' shoes; of his beard he made wicks, and covering them with wax lighted them; with the tweezers that he had sent him, he ordered his eyebrows and eyelashes to be pulled out: saying that he had always kept them for him, as he and his followers did not use them. After this, he sent him to all his tents and his Captains for his refreshment, where many insults were heaped on him, all of which he bore with much patience: giving many thanks to God for bringing him to this, after allowing him to reconquer

---

[1] B alters this. It places the full stop after "by the way," and begins the next sentence with "Giving him evil clothes," that is, *trajo* in place of *trato*.

[2] Correa (vol. iv, p. 379) says two hundred heads. As before said, "head" is used euphemistically by Castanhoso.

one hundred leagues of Christian country. After they had diverted themselves with him they returned to the King's tent,[1] who with his own hand cut off his head, it not satisfying him to order it to be cut off. After it had been cut off, in that very place where his blood was spilt, there started a spring of water which gave health to the sick, who bathed in it, which they understood the wrong way.[2] That very day and moment, in a monastery of friars, a very large tree which stood in the cloisters was uprooted, and remained with its roots in the air and its branches underneath, the day being very calm and still; and as it appeared to them that this event was not without mystery, they noted the day and the hour, and that they were all present to give witness. Afterwards, when they heard of the defeat and death of D. Christovão, they found that the tree was uprooted on the very day and hour that he was killed. After it had died, the friars cut up part for use in the monastery; six months later, the very day we gave battle to the King of Zeila and defeated him—in which battle he was slain and the kingdom freed—that very day the tree raised itself, planted its roots in the earth whence they had been drawn, and at the same moment threw out green leaves. The friars, seeing this great mystery, with great wonder, noted the day and hour it happened, knowing nothing of what was passing in the kingdom. When they heard of what had taken place, they found that it was the very day, as I say, that was the signal of freedom for so many Christian people. When they told us this, as the monastery lay on the road to Massowa, whither after the

---

[1] Correa (vol. iv, p. 380) here interpolates some long speeches which need not be translated.

[2] A has *o qual elles entendido ao reves*. This I take to mean that the Muhamedans connected the virtues of this spring with their victory over the Christians. B omits these words. I have discussed in the Introduction the alleged finding of D. Christovão's bones.

freeing of the country we were travelling, we all[1] went to the monastery to see the tree and to bear witness. I saw it, with many of its roots exposed, all cut as the friars said, and it had only recently become green. As it was a great tree, it was wonderful that it could stand on the ground with so few roots below the earth.[2] When, after the King of Zeila had cut off D. Christovão's head, that fact became known in the tents of the Turks, they were very enraged, and went angrily to the King, and asked him why he had thus killed the Portuguese Captain without telling them: because, as the Grand Turk had heard of his bravery, they could have taken him nothing from that country which would have pleased him more, that they would have taken him as a proof of their great victory to receive a reward from the Turk. They were so offended that they quitted him, taking the Portuguese to carry with them.[3] The next day, when they started, there was one Portuguese, who had escaped, the less; he afterwards joined us, so that they went back with twelve and D. Christovão's head. They embarked for Azebide, where was the Governor of all the Straits, with three thousand Turks, of which body they formed a part. Two hundred were left with the King of Zeila, because they filled up the vacancies of those who were killed in the battle from among the others, as this number was granted by the Grand Turk in exchange for his tribute. The King stayed three days at that place, with great content at the victory, for such is their custom, making great festival; and as it appeared to him that we were entirely destroyed, and that those who remained of us would be lost in that country, among those mountains,

---

[1] B, "forty Portuguese."

[2] B omits this and the previous sentence, and substitutes: "I saw it with my eyes, and the friars swore the story was true."

[3] The story of this quarrel seems improbable, in face of the fact that the usual force was left with the Imam Ahmad.

where we could not find our way, he determined to visit his wife and sons, whom he had not seen for a long time, who were in his city on the shores of the lake whence the Nile flows,[1] the most rich and fertile country that ever was seen. This he did, leaving in that country his Captains, with troops to retake possession of the land he had lost; for of us he took no count, bad or good, but the Lord God chose to show His great pity.

CHAPTER XX.

Of how some one hundred and twenty Portuguese collected with the Queen, and of how the Preste arrived at the Hill of the Jews, where the Queen, his Mother, and the Portuguese were awaiting him.

IT happened, in our flight, that the Queen was escaping in front with her women, very sorrowful, as it may be supposed she would be; the Portuguese were in her rear, wounded and scattered, and behind all were ten or twelve who could hardly travel. Helping them, there went two Portuguese who were less wounded than they, urging them on and remaining in their company. One was called Fernão Cardoso, the other Lopo de Almansa. At nine or ten hours of the next day, they saw following them many Moors on foot and two horsemen. When the pursuers drew near, they determined to die, and try and save their comrades, who were in front of them, wounded. These they told to travel as fast as they could, for they would defend them or perish. So they both turned back against the Moors, and they carried bucklers and pikes. When they came near the two Moorish horsemen, who were the nearest, they tried to attack them; but the Moors drew

---

[1] The Blue Nile flows through one end of Lake Tzana.

back, awaiting the footmen to capture them, telling them to give up their arms and surrender, and they would not kill them. When they saw so many opponents, they thought that the Moors could destroy them with arrows and stones only, without coming to push of pike or sword; and, since they could not approach them to do what they wanted, that therefore they should yield. Maybe they [the opponents] would turn back with them [as captives], as the others were not in sight. That, even if the Moors tortured them, they would never confess that the other Portuguese had gone on; that in this way they might save their comrades by dying themselves, for they could not escape that. With this determination, they went up to the horsemen; Lopo de Almanza, who knew somewhat of the language, calling out that they would surrender, and that they should receive their arms. Advancing to surrender, it would seem that Our Lady inspired them, for they called out one to the other and simultaneously, "Holy Mary! they will slay us with our own weapons." With these words, they attacked the horsemen, who were now near, and knocked down both at the first strokes; one dead, the other wounded in the arm. When they fell, their horses stood still without moving, and the footmen, numerous as they were, began to fly: which seems a great and evident miracle. Then the two cavaliers mounted the horses of the Moors, and, after making a feint of following the footmen a short way, went in search of their comrades; and, mounting the worst wounded double, told them what had happened. They were much astonished at this success, and very joyful to see them: for they thought they were already dead or captives. Thus all escaped, these two running the risk of death to save the others. Our Lady, seeing their intention, inspired them at such a time with this courage. In this way they saved their comrades, and also those in front; for if these Moors had followed them they would have slain all, for they had neither arms nor breath. Thus they journeyed with abundant labour until reaching the Queen; and it was very evident in what great tribulation they fled. We did not halt until we reached a very rough hill, and as we could travel no further we rested there. The greater number of the Portuguese who escaped collected here, and the following day came the thirty Portuguese with the horses, who had not heard of our disaster. When they had joined us, and saw our condition, and heard of the loss of D. Christovão, our lamentation was so great as to cause pity, and we could not be comforted. What we all felt most was, not to have news of D. Christovão, beyond how badly he was wounded. The Queen sent several scouts along the roads, and to the thickets, to gather, if possible, any news, and to guide any Portuguese found concealed. We were here for several days, waiting for news to reach us. We assembled round the Queen, to the number of one hundred and twenty men,[1] among whom was the man who escaped when D. Christovão was captured, who told us of what I have already related; and also the one who escaped from the camp of the Moors, who informed us of the martyrdom of D. Christovão, and his death, as already told. Our feelings on hearing this can be believed. There returned a scout of the Queen's, who told us that Manuel da Cunha, with fifty[2] Portuguese, had taken another road, not knowing whither they were going. They reached the country of the Barnaguais, where they were welcomed, and where they remained till they heard news of us and the Queen; she with her women felt the greatest grief at the fate of D. Christovão, whom they lamented as if he had been her son. The following day she sent for us all, and made us a speech, consoling us for our great loss,

---

[1] B, one hundred.
[2] Correa (vol. iv, p. 383): "sixty Portuguese."

and for our contrary fortune; and this in very discreet and virtuous words. We asked the patriarch to reply for us all, encouraging her; and she was pleased, saying that the courage of the Portuguese was very great. It was determined at our council to go to the hill of the Jews, and there await the Preste, who had already been informed that the hill was his. We started the next day, and were very well received by the Captain of the hill, and provided with all necessaries. Ten days later,[1] the Preste arrived, bringing very few people; so few that, had not D. Christovão captured the hill, it would have been impossible for us to have joined him, or for the kingdom to have been restored.[2]

---

[1] Correa (vol. iv, p. 383): "twenty days later."

[2] "The same year, in the month of Tasrin the first, the seventh month of the calendar, in the era of the creation of the world, and the second month after the entry of the sun through the central window, which is the largest of the windows, according to what is written in the book of astronomy of the Syrians, King Mar Galâwdêwos started for Tigré, where was the Imam Ahmad and all his army. He was accompanied by Marcos the Frank, who had brought him a letter from the Franks, in which they begged him to protect their compatriots from the anger of the people" (Conzelman, § 15, p. 132).

There are some obscurities in the above passage. Tasrin the first is a Syrian month, and as such corresponds with our October. It is a Hebrew month, and as such has no fixed equivalent, but falls about the autumnal equinox. The era quoted appears to be the Hebrew one of the creation of the world, while the astronomy is Syrian. It seems that under the latter system there are considered to be six gates in the east and six in the west, and the sun uses each gate in turn for rising and each gate for setting during one month. Out of this it is difficult to arrive at any conclusion, save that probably the end of October or beginning of November is meant. The above facts are taken from Conzelman's note. Marcos is, of course, Ayres Dias.

"In the month of Teqemt, King Asnaf Sagad (Galâwdêwos) came to join his mother and the remnant of the Franks, in the country of Samen, and held council with them" (Basset, *Études*, p. 111). I have adopted Perruchon's punctuation. Teqemt is the month commencing September 28th.

CHAPTER XXI.

Of the Reception the Portuguese gave the Preste; and of how, after the Meeting, we determined to all go and revenge the Death of D. Christovão.

WHEN we heard that the Preste was at the foot of the hill we went to receive him, a Mass Priest who was with us bearing in his hands the banner of Compassion (*misericordia*). When we reached him, seeing us like this, and so few in number, and hearing of the death of D. Christovão and of our defeat, he showed such affliction as was to be anticipated, for he came full of desire to see D. Christovão from the fame that had reached him; and the affliction he showed, surely for a son and heir he would not have shown more. He gave us all much honour and welcome, with princely words, telling us not to feel strangers in that country, but to look on it as our own, for the kingdom and he himself belonged to the King, our lord, and his brother. He at once provided us with all necessaries, gave us all mules to ride—for, after the late defeat, we had come here on foot —he gave to all, too, silken tunics and breeches, for such is the country wear, to every two men a tent, and servants in abundance to attend us, carpets and mattresses, and all we needed. We were here all December, both because the Preste wished to celebrate Christmas here, and also to collect the men who daily flocked to him: there assembled here eight thousand foot and five hundred horse. When we saw this force we went to the Preste, and begged him to help us to avenge the death of D. Christovão. The Preste, although he desired this, still was very fearful, as we were so few; but he determined to attempt it, and sent to summon the Portuguese who had fled to the territory of the Barnaguais, and to fetch the arms D. Christovão had left on the hill where we found the Queen, where as the place was secure, he left our surplus weapons, which were a great help to us, as we had now but very few. During this time we made a good deal of powder, as the man whom D. Christovão had with him for this, escaped with us, by the favour of our Lord, to make it in the time of such need: for on this hill of the Jews there is much saltpetre and sulphur, and all that is necessary. During the whole of January the Preste was here, getting ready and awaiting the Portuguese. The latter were not then in the country of the Barnaguais; for it appeared to them that we were all dead, and that they could not join the Preste; they therefore journeyed to Massowa, to embark for India, should any of our foists come there. When this information regarding them arrived, and the weapons which were on the hill came, the Preste determined to go and seek the Moors; for he learned that the Turks who had come to his assistance had returned, and that he had only the two hundred, who were always with him, and his own followers.

CHAPTER XXII.

Of how the Preste began to march with the Portuguese, and found the King of Zeila encamped on the Lake of the Nile; and of the method the King of Zeila adopted to kill the Captain of the Preste's Camp.

FORMING our ranks, we began our march on Shrove Tuesday, February 6th, 1543, with eight thousand footmen with bows and bucklers, and five hundred horse, all very fine and well-found men,[1] and one hundred and twenty Portuguese,[2] some maimed, with wounds still open, who refused

---

[1] Correa (vol. iv, p. 385), on the other hand, says that "the Preste had six hundred horse and ten thousand foot, archers and bucklermen, all very inferior (*Muy fraqua cousa*)."

[2] Correa (vol. iv, p. 385), "one hundred and thirty Portuguese."

to stay behind, as they were bent on vengeance or on death in the attempt. We bore before us the banner of Holy Compassion (*Sancta Misericordia*); the Preste had sought to appoint one of us Captain, but we desired none save the banner or himself to lead us, for it was not to be anticipated that we should follow another, having lost what we had lost. Thus we marched, leaving the Queen, his mother, on that hill, to have no incumbrance. On our way we heard that a Captain of the King of Zeila was on the road by which we must travel, in a lordship called Ogara, who had three hundred horse and two thousand foot; the Captain of them was called Miraizmão.[1] We reached the place one morning early, and the Preste fell on with fifty horse in the van. By this attack the Moors were defeated, the Captain and many of them slain, and many

---

[1] "They (Galâwdêwos and the Franks) went to Cheouada in the month of Hedar, on the 13th (Perruchon, 16th). They fought a battle at Ouagara, and slew Sid Mahamad, Esman, and Talila; the rest of the enemy fled like smoke, some fled to Ebna (Perruchon substitutes 'there were some who surrendered with stones on their necks'). The 19th (Perruchon adds Hedar), Galâwdêwos left Darasgé, burned the houses of the Moors, ravaged their goods, and returned to Cheouada, where he stayed two months" (Basset, *Études*, p. 111). Perruchon is quoted from *Revue Sémitique*, 1894, p. 265.

The month Hedar begins on October 28th; the date of the fight at Woggera, according to this, is either November 9th or November 12th. Cheouada is marked Sciauada on the Italian map; it is a district in the south-west of Semien, north of Woggera. Darasgé is a village some way south on the banks of Lake Tzána. It was Gran's head-quarters, and I do not understand how Galâwdêwos left it on a foray. The dates are hopelessly divergent from those in the Portuguese account. In the Introduction I have given my reasons for preferring the latter.

"In the month of Tasrin, the second, which is the eighth month of the Hebrews, and the third month of the calendar of the Pentapole, Galâwdêwos marched to Wagara, and warred against the troops of the Imam Ahmad; he conquered them, and slew Seid Mehmad, the commander. He destroyed all the dwellings of the Muhamedans there; he burned some and pillaged all the towns under the rule of Islam. This was the first victory obtained by Mar Galâwdêwos, and was a foreshadowing of the victory of the Church" (Conzelman, § 16, p. 133).

Tasrin, the second, is roughly November. Conzelman states that the calendar of the Pentapole is the Coptic Calendar in use in Lower Egypt.

prisoners captured; from them we learned that the King of Zeila was with his wife and sons on the bank of the lake whence the Nile springs,[1] about five days' march, at our speed, from where we were. We continued marching until we caught sight of it;[2] it is so large that we could see it from a distance of six or seven leagues. When we came in sight of the Moors we pitched our camp opposite theirs.[3] They were amazed to learn that the Preste and the Portuguese had came in search of them after the great defeat; this put them in some fear. They began at once to prepare as best they could; they understood well that we had only come to avenge the past. And because we had news of the Portuguese who had been to Massowa, but had not found shipping, that hearing of us and the Preste, they were marching after us, with all speed, the Preste decided in council of all not to join battle until their arrival, as they were near us; and in that country fifty Portuguese are a greater reinforcement than one thousand natives. In the days we were awaiting them we had daily skirmishes on the plain between the armies. There were

---

[1] "From whom they learned that the Grañ was a little distance off in the kingdom of Dembya, in a place called Darasgué, near the lake the Nile passes through, with his wife and children" (Paez in Tellez, Bk. II, chap. xv, p. 134).

[2] Presumably the lake.

[3] "Grañ returned to Dembya when he left Zabl, and the King leaving Cheouada reached Wainadaga (Perruchon adds, on 5th Yakatit), and halted there. The Muhamedans (Perruchon, Grañ) left Darasgé, and their troops halted not far from the King, whose army was in the same place. See the pity of the Lord, who strengthened his servants and their prince Asnaf Sagad, still a youth, and made them meet their enemy and look him in the face, whilst formerly they would not have stopped; then they feared and trembled when they heard his name; while he was in Shoa and the Christians in Tigré, they were beaten every time he (Grañ) marched against them. When the pity of the Lord was cast on them, they laughed and mocked the Muhamedans" (Basset, *Études*, p. 111; Perruchon, *Revue Sémitique*, 1894, p. 265).

Fifth Yakatit is January 30th. Paez in Tellez (Bk. II, chap. xvi, p. 153), states that the armies met at Oinadaga. Couto (*Dec. V*, Bk. IX, chap. iv) says that Galâwdêwos marched to a hill called Oe nad qas in the province of Ambea—that is Wainadega in Dembya.

now sixty mounted Portuguese, as the Preste gave them all the horses he had; they had very good fortune in the skirmishes, for there continually came out a certain Moorish Captain, who was greatly famed among them, and in whom they trusted, with two hundred horse; he was so unfortunate, that in one of his skirmishes with the Portuguese, he and twelve of his companions were killed, which was a great loss to them. The Abyssinian horse also made many sallies, seeking to impress us; the Captain-General of the camp, by name Azemache Cafilão,[1] did marvels with his horse on these days, for nothing could show outside the King of Zeila's camp without being raided by this Captain; in this the Moors always had the worst, losing both their flocks and their lives. When the Moor saw how brave our Captain was, he determined to make a great effort to kill him by treachery. He sent for one of his cavaliers, and told him to send the Captain a message bearing the air of a challenge: a message to summon him to one side of the camp where was a small stream, he remaining on one bank and the Abyssinian on the other; in some thickets on his bank four or five Turks were to conceal themselves by night with matchlocks, that, while the message was being delivered, they might fire their matchlocks at him and kill him. And thus it was: at early dawn the Turks hid in the thickets, and at daybreak two horsemen, with a white flag, rode to the edge of the small stream, and called for the Captain of the camp by name. Our men ran up to know what it was, but the Moors would not say aught, save to call the Captain of the camp, as they had something of importance to tell him. When the Captain, who was already mounted, heard this, he came towards the stream with a large following, but when he saw there were

---

[1] This Azmach Keflo was probably the Fitauraris, or commandant of the vanguard, whose duty it was to lead the advance, mark out the royal camp, etc.; a post always given to a tried soldier.

but two Moors, he ordered his men to halt, thinking the men wanted to come over to us, or else give some useful information, and that to deceive their own side they had come through the thickets; he went forward with but two horsemen in whom he trusted. When he came within speech of them, he asked what they wanted, and while the Moors were feigning some tale, the Turks all fired their matchlocks at him; when they saw him fall over his saddle-bow, they turned and went off at full gallop. The Turks had saddled horses hard by, and on them they escaped. When our horsemen saw that the Moors were galloping off, they came up fearing treachery; and, when they saw the Captain dead in the arms of his two companions, they started to pursue the Moors, who were going off untouched; but so many came out to assist them, that our men had to return with the dead Captain. At this they made great lamentation, the Preste above all, both as he had married one of his cousins, and because he was a very brave man. With him the Abyssinians began to lose their courage, so much so that many advised retreat, victory seeming impossible. When the Preste heard of this, and found it true, he sent for them,[1] and determined, as the Portuguese delayed so long, to give battle the next day, as he felt that if he waited longer, all his men would disperse through fear.

CHAPTER XXIII.

Of how the Preste and the King of Zeila fought a Battle, in which the Moors were defeated and the King slain.

BY early morning we were all in our ranks, and we said a prayer before the banner of the Holy Compassion (*Sancta Misericordia*), begging our Lord to have it [compassion] on

---

[1] ? his council.

us, and give us vengeance on, and victory over, our enemies. After a general confession by a Mass priest, who absolved us, we arose and advanced against the enemy, we leading the van and that banner, or we following it (*? e esta bandeyra ou nós com ella*).[1] With us were two hundred and fifty Abyssinian horse and three thousand five hundred foot; in the rear came the Preste with another two hundred and fifty horse, and with all the rest of the foot. In this order we attacked the enemy, who also advanced in two battles, the King of Zeila in person in the van, with two hundred Turks, matchlockmen, six hundred horse and seven thousand foot. Those in the van attacked on both flanks; in the rear came his Captain, called Guança Grade,[2] with six hundred horse and seven thousand foot, who like the van attacked heavily. The Portuguese, seeing that the Turks were defeating us, charged them, slaying many and driving the rest back; for the Portuguese horse, who were sixty, worked marvels, and the Abyssinians, ashamed to see them fight thus, threw themselves in so vigorously that they left a track as they went. When the King saw that his men were losing ground, he in person led them on, encouraging them, and with him was his son, a young man, helping him; they came so near that he was recognised by the Portuguese, who, seeing him close, fired at him with their matchlocks. As all things are ordered by the Lord God, He permitted that one ball should strike him in the breast, and he fell over his saddlebow and left the press; when his followers knew that he was wounded to the death, they lost heart and took to flight.[3] When the Captain of

---

[1] B omits these words, which I do not understand.
[2] B, "Grança Grade." Grade is *Garâd*, a Governor. It is suggested that the first word is Ganz, the name of a small district near Harrar. The name would then be Governor of Ganz. A Ganza Garâda is mentioned, with other of the Imam Ahmad's generals, in Basset, *Études*, p. 110.
[3] The different accounts of this battle will be found collected at the end of this chapter.

the Turks saw that the Moors were giving way, he determined to die; with bared arms, and a long broadsword in his hand, he swept a great space in front of him; he fought like a valiant cavalier, for five Abyssinian horsemen were on him, who could neither make him yield nor slay him. One of them attacked him with a javelin; he wrenched it from his hand, he houghed another's horse, and none dared approach him. There came up a Portuguese horseman, by name Gonçalo Fernandes,[1] who charged him spear in rest and wounded him sorely; the Turk grasped it [the spear] so firmly, that before he could disengage himself the Moor gave him a great cut above the knee that severed all the sinews and crippled him; finding himself wounded, he drew his sword and killed him. All this while our men were pursuing the Moors, chiefly the Portuguese, as they could not glut their revenge; they mainly followed the Turks, as against them they were most enraged; of the two hundred not more than forty escaped, who returned to the King's wife. When she heard that her husband was dead, she fled with the three hundred horse of her guard and these forty Turks, taking with her all the treasure that her husband had captured from the Preste, which was not small. She escaped, as our people followed those on the battle-field and in the camp so relentlessly that they thought of nothing else; and they gave quarter to none, save women and children, whom they made captives. Among these were many Christian women, which caused the greatest possible pleasure and contentment: for some found sisters, others daughters, others their wives, and it was for them no small delight to see them delivered from such captivity. So great was their pleasure, that they came to kiss our feet and worship us; they gave us the credit of the battle, saying that through us they saw

---

[1] B, "Joam Fernandes."

that day. When the spoil, which was not small, had been collected, the Preste pitched his camp on the shore of the lake, for the country abounds in supplies. After the booty had been secured, there came to the Preste one of his Captains, by name Azemache Calite, a youth, with the head of the King of Zeila in his teeth, and he at full stretch of his horse with great pleasure; for this youth and the Barnaguais, who knew him [the King of Zeila] best, followed him, and this youth got up to him first and finished killing him, and cut off his head; he took his head so eagerly to the Preste on account of the promises he had made, which were great: if any Abyssinian brought the head, to marry him to his sister; if a Portuguese, to show him great favour. When the Preste received the Moor's head he enquired into the truth, and found that the Portuguese had mortally wounded him, and that this Captain did not merit his sister for bringing the head, as he did not kill him; thus he did not give his sister to that man, nor did he reward the Portuguese, as it was not known who wounded him; had he known, he would have fulfilled his promise. He ordered that the head of the late King of Zeila should be set on a spear, and carried round and shown in all his country, in order that the people might know that he was indeed dead who had wrought them such evils. It was first taken to the Queen, to be sent thence to the other places; and thus she was avenged by her pleasure for the sadness past. At this time the Portuguese who had been to Massowa arrived at the place where the Queen was; she determined in her satisfaction to join her son, and the Portuguese accompanied her; they were well received by the Preste, who supplied them with all necessaries, and made great festivities for the Queen. We remained in great pleasure, seeing each day the Abyssinians delighting in that victory, and in the liberty in which they found themselves. There died four Portuguese in the battle: João Correa, Francisco Vieyra, Francisco Fialho, and a Gallician.[1]

---

[1] Correa (vol. iv, p. 390) says the fatal shot was fired by João the Gallician, "of whom it was said that he pushed his way quite among all the Moors, and discharged his matchlock into the Moor King's breast, and there he (João) was slain." B omits the names.

It remains to collect the different accounts of the battle. Correa (vol. iv, p. 387), Couto (*Dec. V*, Bk. IX, chap. iv), and Paez, in Tellez (Bk. II, chap xvi, p. 136), follow Castanhoso very closely. The following are the Abyssinian accounts:—

"The 17th (Perruchon, 16th) Yakâtit, Grañ stood on the foot of his pride, and trusted in his cannon, his guns, and his Turks; but He who measures the years said, 'I will fight and will drive before me this day those who stand up against me.' Asnaf Sagad, on his side, placed his confidence in the Lord, and in the prayers of Our Lady Marie, who received it. The King's soldiers, who marched in the van, slew Grañ before he could reach the prince. He fell on the slope of Zântarâ (Perruchon adds, "which they call Grañ bar"), and died by the order of the Lord. He fell at the third hour on a Wednesday, his forces scattered like smoke and as the ashes of a furnace. There were those who fled as far as the Atbara, with his wife, Del Wanbara; such was their terror. Others submitted with a rope round their necks, abandoning their swords and their horses. They slew the Muhamedans who lived in Darâ (Perruchon, Ayera) . . . . . When Grañ died, Asnaf Sagad had reigned two years, five months, and twenty-two days" (Perruchon, two years and six months, less eight days); (Basset, *Études*, p. 112; Perruchon, *Revue Sémitique*, 1894, p. 266).

"During the third year in the last month of the Hebrews, the sixth month of the Copts, the month of the most rigorous Christian fast, in the year of the creation 7035, the twenty-eighth of the above-mentioned month, on a Wednesday, our lord Mar Galâwdêwos fought against the Imam Ahmad, son of Ibrahim, whose soldiers were as numberless as locusts. They were more than ten thousand myriads, ready for the battle, strong as lions, and active as eagles. Among them were riders clothed in cuirasses of steel; footmen with buckler, sword, and spear; others who drew the bow and shot arrows like the children of Ephraim; others fought with firearms, like the warriors of Yoan (John, King of Portugal). To those who saw, they glittered like a chaldron turned towards the north (?). Others, who cast stones from slings. None of these warriors had the least fear of battle, and there were among them those who, at the moment of combat, dashed forward with ardour, like a hunting dog that sees its first prey. On the other hand, the soldiers of Mar Galâwdêwos were as few as those whom Gideon selected on the water's edge; but a mighty power was with them, like the cake of barley bread that tumbled into the camp of the Midianites. The King, Mar Galâwdêwos, was not affrighted at the number of the soldiers of Islam, nor at their martial bearing, nor at their strong hearts, nor at the trust they placed in their might. He cast no thought on their lives passed in victories, and the capture of towns till then uncaptured, but he longed for the battle 'as the hart panteth after the water brooks.' There was a terrible battle between him and the Imam Ahmad, and God, the Most High, whose name be blessed,

CHAPTER XXIV.

Of how the Father of the Barnaguais, who had rebelled, returned to the Preste, and brought with him the Prince of Zeila.

AMONG the many Christians, who joined the Moors, was the father of the Barnaguais, who went over to the King of Zeila, because it appeared to him that the kingdom could never be restored. The Moor esteemed him greatly: so highly, in fact, that he made him Governor of his son and

---

gave the crown of victory to Galâwdêwos: may he be in peace! One of his followers slew the Imam Ahmad, and his soldiers massacred a number of the warriors of the Turcomans and of Bar Sad-ed-din. Of the survivors, one half fled towards the sea with the wife of the Imam Ahmad; the other half seized Mehmad, his son, and made him over to the hands of the glorious Galâwdêwos when they submitted. He was merciful and clement: he did no hurt to those who had done evil to him, but he acted like their benefactor" (Conzelman, § 19, p. 135).

"A Frank slew him [the Imam Ahmad] and cut off his ear, before he reached the slopes of Zántarâ. He died by the will of God, at three hours, on a Wednesday. After him, an Abyssinian cut through his neck, and boasted before the King, saying, I am he that slew him. Then the King gave him all the spoils [of the Grañ]. When they could not find the ear, the King said, Where is his ear? that Frank brought the ear. He ordered that lying Abyssinian to give all the spoils to the Frank, and ordered all the Abyssinians to do him honour, and to stand before him both in the camp and in the market-place, and wherever they might be" (Guidi, *Di due frammenti*, p. 8).

The site of the battle, which was fought at Wainadega, is discussed in the Introduction. It remains to settle the date: the Portuguese give no date, but the year is 1543. The only resource is the Ethiopian chronicles. 7035 A.M. is 1543, so that there is no doubt as to the year. The accounts agree that it was fought on a Wednesday. Perruchon and Basset give respectively the 16th and 17th Yakâtit, that is, February 10th or 11th, but in 1543 these dates fell on a Saturday and a Sunday. The verbiage of the text, translated by Conzelman, refers to the same month, Yakâtit, but gives the 28th, that is February 22nd, and a Thursday. Esteves Pereira quotes a manuscript chronicle of Sartsa Dengel (which I have not seen), which gives the date 27th Yakâtit, that is, February 21st, and a Wednesday. There is another method of calculating the exact date. When the Imam Ahmad was killed, Galâwdêwos had been on the throne eight days under two years and six months. As Abyssinian months have each thirty days, this means two years and one hundred and seventy-two days. Galâwdêwos' father, Lebna Dengel, died on September 2nd, 1540; from that day to the end of 1540 there were one hundred and twenty days, which leaves two years and fifty-two days. 1541 and 1542 make the two years, and the fifty-second day of 1543 was February 21st. The

Captain in his forces. He, when he saw the King was dead, retreated with the Prince and escaped: he sent word to the Preste that if he would pardon him he would surrender to him the Prince of Zeila, who had survived the battle and was in his power. The Preste, in spite of being greatly enraged against him and determined not to pardon him, sent him a safe-conduct: not so much because of the Prince he would surrender, as because of the services of the Barnaguais, his son, who was so favoured, as it was he who sought out the Portuguese at Massowa, and guided them to the kingdom. He could ask for nothing, however great, that he did not grant it; besides, then, giving a safe-conduct and pardoning his father, which was a very great favour, he made him Governor of an important lordship. When the father got the safe-conduct he came, bringing the Prince with him, whom he surrendered to the Preste; he, like a merciful man, would not slay him, but kept him under a

---

battle, then, was fought on Wednesday, February 21st, 1543, as Esteves Pereira points out.

The story of the Guidi fragment agrees with that of Bermudez; we do not know enough of the history of the manuscript to accept it unconditionally. It is opposed to the story of Castanhoso, and also to that of Correa, which latter shows sufficient divergency from the former to prove that the writer made some independent enquiries. The reputation of Correa for accuracy in relating events which happened while he was in India stands deservedly high. The story is a striking one, not likely to be forgotten, if it did happen, and certainly not by a Portuguese writer, who would be proud of the figure cut by his compatriot.

The term Bar Saed-ed-din, or country of Saed-ed-din, was given to all the territory south of Abyssinia up to the Indian Ocean. It was named after a notable King Saed-ed-din, who was killed in Zeila at the very beginning of the fifteenth century, in war against the Abyssinians (Basset, *Études*, p. 239 *n.*; *Histoire*, p. 7 *n.*). This name is now confined to an island five miles north of Zeila, which is covered with ruins of an ancient date, and is said to have been the site of old Zeila and the burial-place of the King Saed-ed-din himself.

Combes et Tamisier, *Voyage* (vol. iii, p. 30), may be consulted for the Shoa traditions of Grañ, then (1836) a mythical hero to the Christians. His horse was forty cubits (say 60 feet) high, and he in proportion. He penetrated to Gondar, where it took five hundred musket balls to kill him. Other traditions will be found in Harris (vol. ii, p. 255).

strict watch' in his house.[1] There came with him many Christians, who had rebelled, thinking that the Preste would pardon them if they came in; but when they arrived he ordered that their heads should be cut off; to many others who sent to seek his safe-conduct he granted it, for there were so many that had he ordered all to be killed, he would have remained alone. Among those to whom he gave a safe-conduct was a Captain of the Moors, who had been a Christian, who had done many evil deeds in the country; after his arrival he was recognised as one of those who had captured D. Christovão. When the Preste heard this he was anxious to kill him; but he did not, not to violate the safe-conduct he had granted. The Portuguese were so enraged against him, that even if they had not known of this desire of the Preste, still it appears to me that they would have anyway killed him, even at the risk of angering him. With this evil intention of theirs they went to the Preste to tell him how much the man deserved death, and that he must order his execution; he replied that there was no reason for violating the safe-conduct he had given him; but they understood by this that he would not be very annoyed if they did kill him; consequently, two or three men went to his tent and poignarded him. His death did not annoy the Preste.[2]

---

[1] This Prince did not long remain a prisoner. At the instance of Del Wanbara and Sabla Wangel, the two mothers, an exchange was effected between this man and Minas, brother of Galâwdêwos (and his two cousins thrown in), who had been captured on May 19th, 1539. The exchange was made with some ceremony at sea, off Massowa, either side arriving in its own boat. For Minas's capture, see Basset, *Études*, p. 107; for the exchange, see Conzelman, § 29, p. 142, and Esteves Pereira's *Minas*, p. 41.

[2] This story is substantiated by the Ethiopian writers.
"As to Yoram, he was slain on his return, that they might not forget the chastisement of Israel. In that year the Incarnation and the Resurrection coincided." (In 1543 Easter day fell on March 25th). —Basset, *Études*, p. 112.
"At the time mentioned many of those who had been hostile, both to his father and to his mother, and to all the churches under their

CHAPTER XXV.

Of the Lake whence the Nile flows, on the shores of which the Preste passed Easter, and of the Customs of the Abyssinians in Holy Week.

FROM the lake I have mentioned, which they call Abauy,[1] starts the river Nile; after leaving the lake it crosses all the country of the Preste, intersects Egypt, passes the city of Grand Cairo, and falls into the sea of the Levant at

---

rule, made their submission and were not troubled. In his great pity and his clemency he did not treat them harshly: not even a dog licked them with his tongue. Only one of them, whose wickedness had been unlimited, was killed on the sudden by one of the Portuguese (Berteguan) soldiers, contrary to the desire of the King, Mar Galâwdêwos, on whom be peace" (Conzelman, § 20, p. 137).

If, as appears almost certain, Yoram was the man stabbed, there were special reasons for Galâwdêwos's desire to be rid of him, and possibly the story of his connection with D. Christovão's death was spread to incite the Portuguese to action. I give a passage referring to Yoram which occurs after the account of Lebna Dengel's defeat by Emar, on June 10th, 1539: "The King fled with scanty forces and reached the country of Salamt, where he took up his quarters in the mountain called Thielemfra. He was driven from it by Iyoram, Governor of the district, helped by the Muhamedans, on 14th Hamle (July 7th). This day the Lord worked a great miracle for him: he passed the Takazzé on foot after the Reunion of the Apostles" (Basset, *Études*, p. 107). The Reunion of the Apostles was a festival celebrated before Whit Sunday, which in 1539 fell on May 25th, and by that date the rains would ordinarily be well on, and the Tacazzé in flood and impassable on foot. Yoram was therefore a Christian, and Governor of either Salamt or Semien, who turned traitor; and finding his King in a *cul de sac* (for the mountain mentioned is in a bend of the Tacazzé, which flows east and north of it), attacked him at a moment when his only retreat was over a flooded river. Such conduct could not be forgiven. Yoram also fought against Galâwdêwos in the very beginning of his reign, December 6th, 1540 (see Basset, *Études*, p. 109). Readers of Pearce will remember Coffin's very graphic account of the attack by Abyssinian troops on Chirremferrer, as he calls Thielemfra, in which he bore his share (Pearce, vol. i, p. 201).

[1] Abai is the name of the river, the Blue Nile itself. The report of Sir William Garstin, of June 7th, 1901, on the irrigation of Egypt, shows that in the future Lake Tzana may play a very important part as a reservoir for irrigation. The information quoted on his p. 50, that the country round the lake is uninhabited, shows what immense changes must have occurred since Bruce found it the centre of a teeming population.

Alexandria. This lake is so large that land cannot be seen from one side or from the other; the Abyssinians say that, for a man travelling very quickly, it is ten days' journey round, that is, over one hundred leagues; in it are certain islands where there are monasteries of friars, very pleasant.[1] In this lake are bred certain creatures like sea-horses, which they must be; they are as large as big horses, and of the fashion and colour of elephants; their heads are exceedingly broad, with very wide mouths; the arrangement of the lower and upper teeth is like they paint those of serpents; at the point of the jaws on one side and on the other two teeth jut out, like an elephant's, but not so large; when they open their mouths it is a sight of wonder, for truly a man of ordinary stature, standing on the lower jaw, would not touch the upper with his head, and in the width of its jaws two men together would fit. These creatures go into the plain to eat grass and branches, and if they see people retreat to the water; they are so numerous that when they go swimming in the water they cover it. They live below the water and, when they come up, they project great throatfuls upwards from their mouths, more than whales do.[2] On the shores of this lake, the Preste and all his camp celebrated Easter, when the service was performed very solemnly; and from the time they entombed the Lord until the resurrection, he, and the Queen his mother, and all the nobles wore mourning, and they were always before the sacrament until the resurrection, not eating or drinking, with great fasting. Their fast is very

---

[1] Correa (vol. iv, p. 391), "who have reed baskets covered with raw hides, which they use as boats." These islands are places of great sanctity. The inhabitants still have bundles of reeds for crossing, which are known as *tankoua*.

[2] Correa (vol. iv, p. 392): "In this lake are the mermaids, such as they paint, which are half women from the waist upwards, and from the waist downwards fish. This is what the people of the country tell, and they tell other things very wonderful and difficult to credit, therefore I do not write them down."

strict, for they eat nothing that has suffered death, nor milk, nor cheese, nor eggs, nor butter, nor honey, nor drink wine. Thus during the fast days they only eat bread of millet, wheat, and pulse, all mixed together, spinach, and herbs cooked with oil which they make from a seed like jinjily.[1] This fast follows the old law, for they do not eat at midday; and when the sun is setting they go to church and hear Mass, and confess,[2] and communicate, and then go to supper; and they say their Mass so late on fast days, because they say they can only receive the Holy Sacrament at that time because of the fast. On saints' days and Sundays, they say Mass at midday, as in the Church of Rome, and the Mass is always chanted, with deacon and sub-deacon, and a veil before the altar. The host is of very choice wheat unmixed, and they make a cake as large as a large host (*como huma hostia grande*), which is cooked in an earthen mould that has a cross in the centre, and around it some Chaldee letters, which are those of the consecration.[3]

---

[1] The word used is *Gergelim*, that is *Sesamum indicum;* the trade name is jinjily (Yule's *Glossary*, *s.v.*). As to this Abyssinian oil and its unpleasant effects see Parkyns (vol. ii, p. 72). He calls it *kivvy nyhoke*, and attributes to it a drying property like varnish. Some Roman Catholic missionaries had to obtain a dispensation from using it, it was so injurious. The early Muhamedan raiders always visited Abyssinia in Lent, as the people were then too weak from fasting to resist. Alvarez (p. 289) says, the Abyssinians always married when they could on the Thursday before Shrove Tuesday, as then they were allowed to eat meat for two months.

[2] The statement as to confession is doubtful, as it is not an Abyssinian custom, except in very general terms such as are used in the English Church. Thus Tellez (Bk. I, chap. xxxvii) says: "The worst is that confessors do not give absolution in the Catholic form, but say certain words and touch their (the penitents') backs with twigs of the olive tree. For this reason there are always some kept at the church doors, lest absolution should have to be withheld for want of twigs. Rather with these, first the confessors should be well thrashed, for not knowing how to absolve, and then the penitents for not knowing how to confess." According to Ludolph, this touching with rods was rather a manumission from sin than a penance (*Com.*, p. 375).

[3] Further and rather different information will be found in Alvarez, p. 24 and following. He was an ecclesiastic, and more likely to be accurate.

With this cake or host, all the friars and those who help in the Mass, and those who have confessed for this purpose, communicate. Every Sunday the King, the Queen, the nobles, all of noble birth, and all the people, confess and communicate. They enter the church barefooted, without any kind of slipper; they do not spit in church, and if they want to do so, they have a cloth into which they spit, as they consider it a dirty habit.[1] These churches are round, with a holy place in the centre, and all around outside are verandahs. Their bells with which they summon to Mass are of stone;[2] they only use little bells at our service. They always pray standing; they bow frequently, and kiss the earth, and then stand again, and thus they take the body of the Lord. In the holy week the sacred offices are performed with great decency, beginning on the eve of Palm Sunday with gathering them [palms], and on Sunday they are consecrated with full ceremony as in Portugal; for all the women place crosses of wild olive leaves on their heads, in their head dresses, and the men carry away palm branches in their hands, which they take to their houses. On the day of the resurrection there was a very solemn procession, with many wax candles, and very large ones, so many, that truly I say there are more wax candles collected there than there could be in all Portugal. None should be astonished at this, for there is an immense quantity of honey. It is found in the rocks and on the plains, and belongs to whoever gathers it; and there is so much that they make a wine from it[3] that satisfies all the people. The nobles plume themselves on having many tapers and

---

[1] The Portuguese did spit in church, see Alvarez (p. 30), and this custom surprised the Abyssinians.

[2] Alvarez (p. 22) says, these stones sound like cracked bells heard at a distance. Bent, *Sacred City of the Ethiopians* (p. 41), may also be consulted.

[3] This mead and its preparation has been described by many travellers; for instance, Parkyns (vol. i, p. 383).

wax candles; there is a Captain of the King's who has five hundred tapers; and by this it can be judged how many go in the procession, which was very solemn, as it included over five hundred friars, with much music, as is their custom; they returned to the church with the Holy Sacrament, which they call *corbam*. The Preste and his mother, and the Portuguese, all armed, went in the procession, frequently firing matchlocks, and the artillery which we captured from the Moor, letting off, too, many artifices of fire which we had made for him. With these the Preste was much delighted, and he showed great pleasure that we made such a festival of that day.[1]

CHAPTER XXVI.

Of the Great Mourning made, and of the Obsequies celebrated by the Preste for the Soul of D. Christovão, and for the Portuguese who died in the Battle.

AT that time there had elapsed two months from the victory to Easter,[2] and the Preste seeing that winter, which begins in May, was at hand, and that he could not march to visit his country and free it from rebellion, determined to winter three leagues away, as the grass on the plains was exhausted, and the ground foul from the long stay there of the Moors. His headquarters were fixed in a very large city,[3] which is on the shores of the same lake, where some houses were prepared for him, and others for the

---

[1] There is a more detailed account in Alvarez, chap. cx.

[2] A curious mistake. Easter Day in 1543 was on March 25th, while the battle of Wainadega was on February 21st, so only a month had elapsed.

[3] No indication is given of what place is meant. Omitting places where there is a large admixture of the foreign element, Abyssinian cities are of mushroom growth.

Queen. He cantoned his followers in the numerous places and villages which are around that city, and all in sight of it. He sent his Captains with the horsemen to one side and the footmen to the other, in the places I have mentioned, which were numerous. The Preste remained with his family[1] in the city, and by his order the Portuguese were given a ward (*bairro*), two matchlock shots away from his own, and certain villages, to supply us with food; whence they brought us wheat, barley for the horses and mules, and honey, butter, flesh, and necessary supplies in the greatest abundance. We went to the palace once daily, the Captains with the men of the camp every eight days.[2] Thus passed the winter, and towards the close of it, in the month of August, on the day that D. Christovão died, the Preste celebrated a great funeral, for there came for the solemnity more than six hundred friars, and several tents were pitched on the plain. He sent round to the neighbourhood to collect all the poor there on that day, and tents were pitched for them; there collected over six thousand persons, and for all he ordered food and raiment. When the general ceremonies were ended, he began to get ready for the march. All the month of August was passed before they were prepared to start. As on September 14th, the day of the Exaltation of the Cross, they have a great festival, he determined not to leave until that feast had been celebrated, which they did in this way. On the eve of that day the Preste came out of his palace openly, which he does not do on any other day of the year; for none sees his face, save his council and the inmates of his

---

[1] *Com sua casa.* B omits.

[2] Correa (vol. iv, p. 393): "The Preste doing great honour to our men, always speaking openly with them, learning to ride on horseback after our manner, adopting many of our customs, as did many of his men, chiefly in the method of fighting, teaching themselves to fire matchlocks and artillery, and make powder."

house.[1] He came out with a large wooden[2] cross in his hands, and many friars in procession with him, with numerous trumpets, kettledrums, and other instruments of their fashion, and a large banner borne by one of the chief lords of his kingdom, called Azaye Degalão,[3] with many people following in procession; they marched round the church, and returned to his house with no more ceremony. All that night they made everywhere large fires, such as we make on St. John's night; they lighted them chiefly in front of and around the Preste's palace, who was inside watching all through a window: for it is his custom to see all and not be seen himself. All the chief lords visit him on this night, with a parade of their estate and worth.[4] Each by himself parades around the Preste's house, they on horseback and their followers on foot, with many lighted torches; and he who has the most show is esteemed highest in rank. After the lords come the rest of the people, in bodies of two hundred, in no special order; all these with torches in their hands. When the men had ended, the women came in a body, singing many songs of several sorts,[5] with instruments, and all with large wax tapers and

---

[1] See Bruce, Bk. v, chap xi. In Bruce's time, the custom had been somewhat relaxed, even then the King covered his face during audiences and on public occasions; also, when delivering judgment in treason cases, he sat on a balcony, and spoke through a hole in it to an officer called "The King's Voice." See, too, Alvarez, p. 202. In that case the mouth and beard were covered.

[2] Correa (vol. iv, p. 394) says, "golden cross."

[3] B, Acaje Degulam. Degalham was uncle by marriage to Galâwdêwos; his wife was Amata Waten, sister of Lebna Dengel. He played a considerable part in the wars with the Imam Ahmad, not always to his credit.

[4] This is the *dum fater*, or war boast (Parkyns, vol. ii, p. 84). His description of the ceremonies of the Mascal, or Day of the Exaltation, confirms Castanhoso. Harris's account is in vol. ii, p. 77; and Pearce's, in vol. i, p. 138. The latter was nearly treacherously shot in the Mascal of 1813. The ceremony was symbolical of what took place after a victory (see Bruce's account in Bk. VII, chap. vii, of the barbarous rites he saw after the battle of Serbraxos).

[5] Correa (vol. iv, p. 394): "Their songs not well in tune, nor pleasant to hear."

candles in their hands. In this way they spent all the night. In the morning there were no more festivals, only divine service in the church at mid-day. The following day they began to start on the march, pitching the Preste's tent, and all the others, on the plain, for such is their custom. When winter is over, whether there be peace or war, he always takes the field. Thus they all got ready, both horse and foot, and set out on October 8th.[1]

CHAPTER XXVII.

Of how the Preste on his March reached the Plains of Jartafaa, and of what he found there; and of how certain Portuguese, with the Permission of the Preste, went to Massowa to seek shipping for India.

THERE joined him and marched with us more than one hundred thousand souls; of these the fighting men were not more than twenty thousand foot and two thousand horse, who joined the Preste after the victory, with the evil excuses of a disloyal people; the remainder were camp-followers and women, for in the whole kingdom there are no handicraftsmen, who gain a livelihood by their handicrafts, as in other parts.[2] Omitting cultivators, all other ranks of people, from nobles to paupers, are at Court with their women, for the people find more to eat there than anywhere else in the kingdom, because the Preste is, as I have said, always on the march in the summer, and everything is free where he goes; and, therefore, everyone follows him, for the nobles employ and make use of everyone, and feed them, as it costs very little, for supplies are so plentiful

---

[1] B shortens this chapter to some extent.
[2] The trade of a blacksmith, for instance, is disgraceful, as they are all considered sorcerers who can turn themselves into hyænas (Parkyns, vol. ii, p. 144).

that there is enough for as many more if they accompanied him. As all could not travel on one line, they were sent in two bodies by different roads, to march until they arrived at a country on the skirts of the sea called Jartafaa,[1] where there were Moors whom he wished to expel. We marched in this way for eight days, straight from the lake to the sea, without going by any other road; every place that we passed surrendered, and in all places the Preste left Captains to rule them, turning out the undeserving, and doing justice as seemed right to him. We continued on until we came to a hill, on whose top were twelve monasteries of friars, or churches in which religious men lived,[2] a few men to each, and each one dedicated. Each church was formed from one stone, excavated on the inside with a pick; like ours are, with two lofty naves and pillars, and vaulted, all from a single rock, with no other piece of any kind, with a high altar and other altars, all of the same stone; as I say, in the whole edifice of the church there was nothing brought from the outside, but all cut from the same living rock. Each church is as large as that of St. Francis, at Evora; all exists exactly as I in truth relate it. I measured the smallest to see how many paces

---

[1] There is no place called Jartafaa. Esteves Pereira ingeniously suggests that it is Fatagar transposed, but there are difficulties. Fatagar is not on the sea-shore, and though inversions of proper names are not unusual in the east, *e.g.*, Loniochter for Ochterlony, Cartmil for Mailcart, Ensincanaria for Canariensis (*creeper*), still in these cases the component parts of the word are inverted, not the centre syllable left and the first and last parts transposed. Also, Fatagar was the furthest point of Abyssinia south from Massowa, and the Portuguese could not have argued that going inland from the former was going further from the latter. My criticism is purely destructive, I have nothing to suggest.

[2] B has three villages for twelve monasteries. From the lake to Lalibela is, roughly, one hundred and ten miles. If the text means that they covered this in eight days, the Preste's army marched fourteen miles a day; this would be a sort of test for the distance covered by the Portuguese, though they, perhaps, as a smaller body, would move more quickly when unaccompanied. Castanhoso exaggerates the size of these churches. I give an account of them at the end of the chapter.

it was, and I found it fifty paces; the others were very much larger. Over all these friars is one whom they call the Abadele,[1] who is as their provincial or warden. These edifices, according to the story of the Abyssinians, were made by white men, and the first Christian king of this country was a stranger. Whence he came is unknown; he brought many men with him to work at this rock with pickaxes, and they cut out a cubit a day, and found three finished in the morning; and the King died a saint after he had completed these edifices. They showed us the place of his burial,[2] and all took earth from his tomb, and carried it away as a relic; they assert the truth of all this which I have told. The friars have many writings; these they showed us, thinking we should be able to read them. They were in Chaldee, all on parchment; and even had we known the language they could hardly have been read, so worn and old were they. I heard them say that the King of Zeila came to see these edifices, and that two Moors tried to ride in, but when they came up to the door their horses foundered;[3] which miracle they had committed to writing, and spoke of much. The Moor ordered his men to leave the place, as "Mafamede" did not wish him to destroy such noble edifices; but as the country was his, he would have them made into mosques. But as everything is done by the will of God, he allowed the Moors to go thence, and to have so much to occupy them, that they never remembered these again. From here we went to

---

[1] Probably Abba dele, that is, Abbade d'elle, "its abbot." Raffray speaks in the highest terms of the head when he was there, called Memer Member. In his asseverations of the truth of what he relates, Castanhoso imitates Alvarez, who alone of his party visited the churches, and who was strangely nervous that his account would be discredited.

[2] He is buried in the church called Golgotha.

[3] *Lhes arrebentarão*, literally burst. Correa (vol. iv, p. 395) says of the men that they died suddenly. See note at the end for the Muhamedan account of this visit.

Jartafaa, where the Preste pitched his camp on certain very wide plains, and we were here until the Moors returned to their obedience, for all the territory is peopled by them. They were formerly subject to the Preste, and paid him tribute, and he allowed them to live there for the sake of the commerce that came through their hands; because the Abyssinians are not curious in sea affairs, nor are they the men for them; the country too, is so extensive, that were there many more inhabitants there would still be land for all. The Preste, therefore, ordered that no harm should be done to these Muhamedan merchants or to the cultivators; only the fighting men were turned out of the country, the inhabitants remaining subject to the Preste, and paying the customary taxes. After this, as the time was passing, we spent here the Christmas of 1543. As there was nothing to be done in the country, which was quite freed, and I suffered from my wound, which would not heal, and there was none to cure me, I sought the Preste's permission to go to Massowa to wait for our vessels which were then due. I could also no longer serve, for the wound was from a matchlock bullet, and my arm useless. He was much annoyed that I wished to leave him at a time when he was so impoverished, and his affairs so unsettled, for in truth he was but King over a wide territory and over victuals; for the Moors had captured all his treasure, and his country had been in rebellion, so that if, indeed, he had brought back anything from the interior, he had much on which to expend it. He, therefore, told me frequently not to go away until he could show me some favour, as it was derogatory to himself for me to leave, and he not to show it to me, and that he was very grieved that I should go; still, seeing that it was necessary, because of my health, he gave it me unwillingly, as he would be much more annoyed if I lost my life awaiting his favours, as there was no medicine in the country, and none that knew how to apply it. He, therefore, very reluctantly gave me his permission, and ordered me to be given for the road a horse and two very handsome mules from his stables, and a cloak (*cabaya*) of green velvet,[1] with flowers of gold, and one of his own men to guide me, whose duty it was to provide everything in abundance, free for me wherever I went, as if I had been his brother;[2] thus they received me, and welcomed me, and offered me mules to procure supplies.[3] He ordered me to be given twenty ounces of gold for the journey, fearful lest his people should not supply me with all I needed; and this with a will that certainly showed that, had the time been favourable, and I had asked it, he would have granted me very great favours. After he had bidden me farewell, and had given me letters for the King our lord, fifty Portuguese determined to also ask his permission to go, as there was nothing to be done in the country, nor were they needed; they also desired to leave for India, which seemed to them so distant, that should they again turn into the interior of the country, they would never return to India. They sought permission saying what I have said; he felt it much, for he hoped to have them always with him. Seeing that he could not forcibly retain them, he told them they might have leave, but unwillingly; he also ordered them to be supplied with all necessaries, and mules to ride: saying frequently that it caused him great pain that they wished to go at a time when he could not show them favour.

---

[1] *Veludo verde avelutado.* B has "a cloak (*Marlota*) of olive green velvet."

[2] Parkyns (vol. i, p, 215) says this is the worst way of travelling; that he got on much better by himself.

[3] The meaning of this clause is obscure. B omits it.

Note on the Rock-Churches of Lalibela, and on the Muhamedan Raid on them in 1533.

I can find no account of a visit to the rock-churches of Lalibela in the narrative of any English traveller. There are, however, four descriptions of them accessible: one in the *Verdadeira Informaçam* of Alvarez, who visited them in the first quarter of the sixteenth century; a translation of his work has been published by the Hakluyt Society (vol. 64, 1881). The remaining three are in the works of modern travellers: Rohlfs, who saw them at the time of the English expedition of 1868, and whose book, *Land und Volk in Africa*, was published in 1870; Raffray, whose works on this subject are a monograph on the churches, with drawings, dimensions, and plans, published in 1882; and an account of his Abyssinian journey in the *Bulletin de la Société de Géographie de Paris*, 1882; and lastly, Gabriel Simon's *L'Ethiopie, ses mœurs*, etc., which appeared in 1885. These two last travellers were at Lalibela in company. There is, further, a translation of part of one of the Ethiopian manuscripts in the British Museum (Or. MSS. 718, 719), published by Perruchon in 1892, under the title "Vie de Lalibala," in the *Publications de l'École des lettres d'Alger*; in this there is a valuable compendium of the facts from the side of research. From this volume, and Raffray's monograph, which Perruchon had not seen, a complete idea of these churches can be gained. Simon's work should also be consulted for the details of the decoration. There are about two hundred rock-churches within a comparatively short distance of these particular ones, but it is allowed that these are the finest examples of the class.

Lalibela is a semi-mythical King of Abyssinia, said to belong to the Zagues, an intrusive family of whom little is known, who occupied the throne for a number of years. Lalibela himself is believed to have reigned in the early thirteenth century. He was born at Roha, in Lasta, a place situated a few miles north-east of the point where the 12° of north latitude crosses the 39° of east longitude; it is now known after him as Lalibela. His wife was called Mescal Kebra, or the Servant of the Cross. As Lalibela has been canonized, his reputation as a saint has obscured the actual facts of his life. June 6th is his day, but Perruchon (p. xxxi) finds that his claims to saintship have been disallowed by the Bollandists, with the remark that, judging from his time and country, he was probably a schismatic. As remarked elsewhere (p. 131, below), Lalibela is one of the persons to whom the idea of diverting the Nile from Egypt is traditionally ascribed. He and his wife are said to have obtained some five hundred workmen from Egypt, under one Sidi Mescal, who excavated the churches in either twenty-three or twenty-eight years (accounts vary). As Raffray points out, Lalibela lies nearly a month's journey even from Massowa, and it is very remarkable that workmen should have been obtained from so remote a country as Egypt.

The present town of Lalibela contains some three thousand people, and stands rather over 8,000 feet above the sea. On approaching it nothing particular can be seen, but on entering it the traveller finds several deep trenches cut through the living rock, which is volcanic. Through one of these trenches runs a small stream, called locally "the Jordan;" the others lead to the quarries or excavations, of about 30 feet in depth, in which the churches are situated. There are three main quarries connected by these open tunnels, and in each quarry there are one or more church or churches. A block of the desired size was left in the quarry, still attached to its base; the outside was worked to imitate masonry, and the interior excavated, leaving numerous pillars, the altars, etc., while the sides were pierced for windows: each church is, therefore, a monolith. The whole work has been hewn out with a pick, and the insides have been subsequently smoothed with the chisel. There are eleven of these churches, all properly oriented. The largest, *Medani Alam* (the Saviour of the World), is, outside measurement, 33.5 metres by 23.5 metres (110½ feet by 77½ feet), and inside, 26 metres by 16 metres. The smallest, *Denaghel* (the Virgins) is only 5 metres square, or little more than a grotto. The material does not lend itself to architectural effect, and the outsides are somewhat weathered; but the interior decorations, especially the pierced lattice-work, has considerable beauty. Simon finds in it traces of Arab and Greek influence. The outside of the flat roofs, being visible from above, is, of course, ornamented. There are no inscriptions, only a rough outline portrait of Lalibela in the church of *Abba Libanos*, which was constructed by the widow, Mescal Kebra, in memory of her husband. Simon doubts the possibility of excavating all these churches in the limited time allowed by the legend, and Rohlfs appears to be of the same opinion; he, in fact, traces a gradual growth and evolution in the style. Lalibela is still a sacred town, and there is attached to the churches a considerable territory, which has been respected by the successive rulers of Abyssinia. Raffray informs us that a manuscript has been preserved in the town, in which the history of the churches is given. On one page the dotation of the territory is written in Ethiopic—Arabic and Greek—a noteworthy collocation, which may indicate the nationality of the original workers. Of this no copy seems to have been made.

In view of what is stated by the Portuguese as to the failure of the Muhamedan attack on these rock-churches, it is interesting to see what the Muhamedans themselves say in their narrative of the Imam's campaigns. Their own account is not that of a triumphant success. The chronicle says:—

"Ahmad afterwards made his preparations to advance into

Tigré .... Then he learnt that the idolaters had assembled near the church called Lalibalâ; he marched against them across mountains, and by a very difficult road, during continuous rain; he travelled even by night, and hastened his march. Many of his men died of cold. They reached the church, where the monks were collected to die in its defence. The Imam examined the church, and found that he had never seen the like. It was cut from the rock, as were the columns that supported it. There was not a piece of wood in all the construction, save the idols and their shrines. There was also a cistern hewn out of the rock. The Imam called together the monks, and ordered them to collect and bring wood. They lighted a fire, and when the fire was hot Ahmad said to them: 'Now, let one of you and one of us enter:' wishing to see what they would do, and to test them. Then their Chief said, 'Willingly; I will go in;' but a woman, who had adopted a religious life, arose and said: 'It is he who expounds to us the Gospel. Shall he die there before my eyes?' and threw herself into the fire. The Imam cried, 'Drag her out.' They dragged her out; but part of her face was burnt. Then he burned their shrines, broke their stone idols, and appropriated all the gold plates and silk textures he found" (Basset, *Histoire*, p. 409).

CHAPTER XXVIII.

Of how the Portuguese took Leave of the Preste for Massowa.

THE Preste ordered the collection of all the chalices and crosses, and of all the silver from the churches, and of all the ornaments and bracelets of his mother, sisters, and relatives, and gave them to them, regretting much that he could give no more. He begged them not to go, for there was much gold in his country, which he would give them; for far inland were bestial Caffres, who came in gangs on foot, with much gold in bags at their sides, to a fair in the back of his kingdom, which marches with these Caffres, which country is called Damute. That these negroes gave the gold in exchange for inferior and coarse Indian cloths, and beads of red, blue, and green earth, which they valued highly, and the gold very little; that if they would accompany him to that country, they could conquer the mines, where they could glut themselves with gold.[1] Even with this he could not alter their intention, nor would they accept the silver and gold he offered, both by reason of the form (*moeda*) in which it was, and because they saw that his affairs were much disordered: telling him that they looked for favours to the King, our lord, who would confer them; that they did not come to that country for any profit, only to serve God and the King, our lord. Thus they bade him farewell, leaving one hundred and twenty[2] Portuguese with him. We departed, taking as our leader the banner of Holy Compassion (*Sancta Misericordia*), borne by one of the two Mass-priests who were with us. These had reaped a rich harvest: they had rooted out many evil practices from that country, and made many Christians. To the Preste remained the hope that if we did not meet our fleet, on which we could all embark, and if the Governor should have sent some one in a foist to be Captain over all, that they would remain.[3] We travelled thus till we reached Massowa, where we found only one small foist, in which was Diogo de Reynoso,[4] who fired his artillery and matchlocks, in the hope that if any Portuguese were on the plain, they, hearing it, would come, that he might have news of us, for in India they considered us all dead. Through fear of the Turkish galleys, we had not remained in sight of the port. When we heard these [the guns] the horsemen went to reconnoitre, and when they

---

[1] Both Bermudez and Alvarez have many similar tales.

[2] B, One hundred.

[3] B omits this sentence about the Governor. The fact of the flag, combined with this sentence, seems to hint that the Portuguese in part left as a protest against Ayres Dias.

[4] The result of this expedition to Reynoso is given in the Introduction. He was blown up in a mine during the second siege of Diu, on August 10th, 1546, when he was mentor to D. Fernandes de Castro, son of D. João de Castro, the Governor. He and his pupil perished together.

recognised it as our foist they came to tell us, with great joy, both their own and that of those men in the foist. We at once struck our tents and went there, and met with much pleasure and many tears. All agreed that, as there was only one very small foist, which arrived with as many men as could sail in her, and that as only very few more could go, they should remain and I embark,[1] both because of my necessity, and because I bore letters from the Preste to the King, our lord. They charged me strongly to tell the Governor how they had remained behind, and to beg him to send shipping for them, with importunity if he made any demur; and should he refuse, I must seek it from the King, our lord. I promised to seek it, and to labour in it as I could. On the morning of the following day, Sunday, February 16th, 1544, I embarked, leaving my companions very desirous to do the same. They and those in the foist took leave of each other with many good wishes; they remained saying a prayer to the crucifix on their banner, and, it concluded, they turned with sobs, and, mounting their horses and mules, rode inland towards where the Preste was, for there were many of his men ready to accompany them if they did not embark. We sailed on to India, where it pleased the Lord God to bring us in safety. We arrived on April 19th of the said year: thanks be to Him, who was pleased to remember me, and may He bring them back in safety.[2]

END.

---

[1] Correa (vol. iv, p. 397) adds, referring to Castanhoso, "who gave me the memorandum book he brought of all this story."

[2] Correa (vol. iv, p. 397): "I say that I remember to have seen a letter written to D. Estevão by Mirabercuz, one of the chief Moors of Ormuz, when he returned from the Straits, after leaving there his brother with these men to join the Preste. Among other things he told him that in his ancient legends was a prophecy which said that the King of Tiopia would be harassed and his kingdom be captured by the Moors, but that Christian people would come from afar to his

assistance, and would restore him to his kingdom and seat him peacefully on his throne. That the time of this prophecy was fulfilled, and that, please God, D. Christovão, his brother, would complete this work; for he had sure news that the Preste was quite destroyed, fled, and hidden among lofty mountains. I write this here because it came to my memory, while I was writing this history, that this Moor wrote thus to D. Estevão. The Abyssinians also had this prophecy, which was fulfilled with the blood of the Portuguese, who went so far from their own land to serve God and their King."

The colophon of B runs: "To the Glory of God and of the illustrious Virgin our Lady, the printing of this book was completed in the house of João da Barreyra, printer to the King our lord, on June 27th, 1564."

dõ xpº uã da gama

D. CHRISTOVÃO DA GAMA'S AUTOGRAPH.

(*From the Portuguese Official Records, traced from the Lisbon Geographical Society's Edition of Castanhoso's work.*)

LETTERS OF AND TO THE KING OF ABYSSINIA.

I.

An undated Letter from Lebna Dengel, King of Abyssinia, to D. João Bermudez. Written in 1540.[1]

MACANCIO, King of Tiopia, who am born of the King my father, grandson of Bedyniam, great-grandson of Naqo, who all descend from King David and Solomon, Kings of Jerusalem, send you greeting and peace, and from my heart pray that Jesus Christ and the Virgin our Lady, may be with you.[2] This is my word. The letter you sent to me was delivered to me, and he who brought it gave me a full description of you, and finding it correct I was thoroughly joyful, with the pleasure that came to me from heaven. I sent you on my embassy from this Tiopia, and by the will of God you never rested, undergoing troubles for the love of me, and chiefly to exalt the faith of Christ. All my chiefs have rebelled against me to help the Moors, and have wasted and violently taken possession of my countries; in fear of this,

---

[1] This letter is taken from Correa, vol. iv, p. 138.

[2] The name Macancio is, of course, wrong; it may be that the name of the writer of the letter has got here by mistake. The rest of the opening is correct, and the names intelligible. Lebna Dengel was the son of a King, Naod (1495-1508), the grandson of a King, Baeda Mâryâm (1468-78), and the great-grandson of a King, Zara Yâkob (1434-68). These facts go to prove that the letter is genuine. A writer in India might know the name of the reigning King, but if he were ignorant of that he would hardly know his genealogy.

I asked the King, my brother, for men, and you tell me he has granted me three hundred trained men. The kingdom of Portugal is mine, as my country and all that he desires belong to the King my brother. I beg you to bring many pioneers. Rest, for I know that you do not sleep in my service, but keep it in your thoughts. All that you have done and intend doing is well done. Your lands are in peace; they shall be doubled from among the best in my kingdom. Tanaqe Michael, the Abyssinian, brought me your letter, with two from the King my brother, and that of the Viceroy, three images of Our Lady, a book of David, and the cloths, all of which pleased me. I know your heart, that it is willing to do the service of God and myself. Your coming satisfies my great desire to see you before I die. I therefore from my heart beg and pray the Viceroy; for I will agree to all he desires, the saints of heaven, and the angel Gabriel, who brought the message to the mother of God, being between us. Some of those who had rebelled against me, hearing of these letters, and of the hoped-for coming of the Christian fleet, have returned to their obedience. The death of Gazafo[1] troubles me. God keep him in his company. All my good friends pray God to bring you in health and safety, and I more than all; may the grace of the Father, Son, and Holy Ghost, three persons and one God, be with me, and you, and with all who know and believe His holy faith.

---

[1] Probably Saga za ab.

II.

An undated Letter concerning Miguel de Castanhoso, written by the King of Abyssinia to the King of Portugal.[1] Probably written late in 1543, possibly early in 1544.

IN the name of God, indivisible Trinity, who sees the exterior and scrutinizes the interior, who weakens the strong and strengthens the weary. This letter is sent on behalf of the King Galâwdêwos, son of the King Wanag Sagad, son of King Naod, son of King Escander, son of King Ba Eda Mâryâm, son of King Zara Yakub, son of King David, son of King Solomon (*sic*), Kings of Israel, on whom be peace, to be delivered to João, King of Portugal, lover of God, lover of the faith, son of King Manuel[2]—orthodox. This has been written respecting Miguel, thy servant, who came to us, and whom the Governor sent with D. Christovão da Gama, Commander, to help us in time of war. This Miguel showed much attachment to Ethiopia, and fought for Christ against the Musalmans, exposing himself freely until his left arm was broken by a matchlock bullet; by the will of God he recovered from his illness, now we send him to thee. Treat him well, remembering the love of Christ, and also for love of us; for he did that for which thou sentest him, like Peter, chief of the Apostles, and Paul, with the tongue of balsam. For this zeal of Miguel de Castanhoso, thy servant, that thou sentest to help us, he did what he was bidden, and thy orders were not in vain; thou, also, in remembrance of this

---

[1] The original of this letter, which is printed in Esteves Pereira's edition of Castanhoso, is in the Portuguese archives. This translation has been made from the Portuguese translation. It is one of the letters Castanhoso says was entrusted to him to bring to Europe.

[2] Esteves Pereira points out that in the original this name runs Za Amanuel—of Emanuel. It is contrary to the Abyssinian custom to use this class of name directly.

satisfy the thought of his heart, which we do not write in this letter; and when we hear the result of this message we shall be content with thee, and in this way our affection will be satisfied.

III.

Letter dated March 13th, 1546, from D. João III, King of Portugal, to the King of Abyssinia.[1]

MOST powerful King, I, D. João, by the grace of God King of Portugal, send you much greeting. I have seen the letter that you wrote to me in which you give me an account of the condition of your affairs, and of the death of the King your father, which grieves me deeply; since our Lord has so arranged it you must conform your will to His, and give Him for this as much praise and thanks as are due to Him for all His works, trusting that after such a loss and so great afflictions He will give you the rest and contentment that you desire, and which He always gives to those who wish to serve Him. As to what you say that I should help and assist you against your enemies, I rate your affairs so highly, and I am so well disposed towards them, that you will never need my help and assistance but you will obtain it from me or from my commanders; and it grieves me much that there is no way by which I can, as often as I desire, learn the state of your affairs, and how they progress, and what help and assistance you receive from my Commander and my Governor of India, and what action in your service my subjects are taking, by which I can learn more than I have from Miguel de Castanhoso, through whom I received another letter from

---

[1] This remarkable letter is translated from the Portuguese copy printed in the Academy edition of Andrade's *Vida de D. João de Castro*, p. 442.

you which gave me great pleasure. Although the loss of these men is a matter to cause much grief, I consider them well expended, as they died in the service of Our Lord and the defence of your country, which I regard as if it were my own; you may rest assured that you will always be assisted by me and by my people and captains, conformably to this my will and the love I bear you. As to your subjects whom you say are captives in the power of the Portuguese, who sell them to the Moors, I have ordered my Commander and Governor not to permit this. As to what João Bermudez has done there, whom the King your father sent to me as his Ambassador, I disapprove greatly, for they are things very contrary to the service of Our Lord, and by reason of them it is clear that he cannot be given any help or assistance, nor do I know more of him than that he is a mere priest (*cleriguo simpres*). Of the powers which he says the Holy Father granted him I know nothing; from the letters of His Holiness you will learn better what has passed in the matter; although for this he merits very severe punishment, it appears to me that you should not inflict it, except in such a way that, his life being saved, he may be punished according to his errors; for, if it be otherwise, he still assuming the dignity of a patriarch, which he wishes to usurp, though no one has given it to him, and exercising such powers even unjustly, it would be a great discredit to Christianity to learn that you had punished him in any other way. And because I desire that all your affairs may be so well carried out, that, in the execution, your design in doing them may be manifest, and also in order that in some matters which appertain to our Holy Catholic Faith, the due and proper remedy may be applied to what is necessary for the true knowledge of it, and the salvation of souls, I have determined to, next year, send to you and for your kingdom, with the permission of God, a person for patriarch, who shall be such and of such zeal and good walk of life, that in these matters he may be able to know how to serve our Lord well, from whom you may receive great contentment, and with whom you may discuss more fully the matter of João Bermudez, and take concerning him the course that seems right to you. And in order that here we may learn more quickly concerning you and the condition of your affairs, you should enquire as to some road or way from your lands and lordships to the coast by Melinde, or some other place along that shore, through which there may be a more speedy communication between us. This, according to the information sent to me, appears very easy to arrange. I have ordered the Portuguese, my subjects in your country, not to return, but to serve you in all the affairs of your state, and rejoice to do this as they would in my own service; and it is reasonable that, as they do this, they should receive from you help to meet their necessities, which are great, as they must be, so far removed from their own country. I beg you to support them and watch over them, as you ought to do, as they are my subjects, who with their lives have so greatly helped and assisted you in defending your kingdoms from your enemies. May our Lord always have your person and royal estate in His holy keeping. Written in Almeirim. Lopo Roiz wrote it. March 13th, 1546.

Connected with the above are two other letters, of which also I give translations.

The first is a letter of the King of Portugal to D. João de Castro, Governor of India, of March 13th, 1546, printed in the Appendix to the Academy Edition of Andrade's *Vida de D. João de Castro*, p. 439.

D. João de Castro, friend, I the King send you my greetings. I have received letters by way of Jerusalem from the Preste John, which these friars brought thence, and also through Miguel de Castanhoso, in which he informs me of the death of the King, his father, and of the condition of his affairs, and asks me to aid and assist him in them. He also asks me to inform him about João Bermudez (*o que sei de Johão Bermudez*), whom his father sent to me as ambassador, because he behaves in a way very prejudicial to the faith and service of Our Lord. To this I have answered what you will see in the enclosed copy of a letter which I send. The Portuguese who are still there I am ordering not to return, as he asked me; this you will also see by the letter I have written them; as that is a Christian country, as you know, whose inhabitants, although they hold some erroneous opinions, are ready and willing to reject them, if there were anyone to teach them and indoctrinate the truth, I am bound to assist and help in the defence of their territory; but as the time is not now favourable for doing more than showing them the desire I have to do it, I must reply to their letters and sympathise in their difficulties, with a warmth that will show them my desire and my goodwill. I should be pleased, were there suitable shipping available in which these friars might travel, for you to despatch them in it, supplying what is necessary for their voyage, treating them very well, as I am certain that you will. Should there be no shipping, or not such as it seems safe to entrust them to, you will inform the Preste John at once that the said friars are there with my reply, and that you only await safe shipping to send them, with all the kindly words conformable to this my meaning, which I have told you. You will inform me of what you have done. Written at Almeirim, March 13th, Lopo Rodrigues wrote it, in the year 1546. As it may be that to explore their way to the coast, as you will see, by the copy of the letter, I have directed the Portuguese, they may require some instruments, compasses, charts, and astrolabes; you will send these to them, with instructions for examining and recording the routes and mountains they pass. "Rey."

D. João de Castro on the sending of the friars.

The second letter is the one addressed to the Portuguese still in Abyssinia, printed on p. 440 of the same volume.

My fidalgos, servants, and men at arms, now in the country of the Preste John, King of the Abyssinians, who were sent from Massowa with D. Christovão da Gama, by D. Estevão da Gama, his brother, my Commander and Governor, to assist the said King in the defence of his kingdoms and lordships against his enemies, I the King send you greetings. Through the letters of the said King, sent by way of Jerusalem, and afterwards through Miguel de Castanhoso, I have heard what happened in the said wars: of the death of D. Christovão, and of other Portuguese my vassals, your comrades, which has caused me the sorrow that was natural, for the loss of so many good subjects; still, as they died in the service of Our Lord and the defence of those countries who follow His holy faith, and are so willing to receive the truth, I consider their lives well expended, and give many thanks to Our Lord, for permitting that through them the land was not lost, or gained by those His great enemies. I trust that it may be so defended that He will in it be ever served and acknowledged; but as the country is not so pacified as the service of Our Lord and the said King requires, and as he asks it from me, I shall be pleased for you not to return, but to continue to help and assist in those of his affairs in which your help and assistance is needed: thus I charge and command you strictly, as I consider it greatly for my service. I am writing to him to assist you in your needs, and in all other things that may be fitting, as it is his duty to do; this I am certain he will do, and in the coming year I hope to send you, if the Lord pleases, a person by whom I will more fully write to you. As I am informed that a road could be easily found to the Melinde coast, or to some other point on that shore, which would afford easier communication between the said King and myself, that matters might be more quickly known, I have written to him to have it explored and examined; you will be careful to remind him, and should it seem well to him for any of you to explore this route, I should consider it good service to me for you to undertake it, and I trust you will carry it out, as I believe you will. As it may be that the land of Abyssinia extends so far west, and Manicongo so far east, that the distance between them may be small, should it be possible to find a road from Abyssinia through Manicongo, or through any other river flowing to the Cape of Good Hope, it would be very serviceable; I direct you, should it seem possible, to remind the King to have it explored, should he think it well that any of you should do it, you will do it, as it is a thing from which I should receive great pleasure. I shall consider that he who has done it has served me well, and I will do him the favour that is fitting; but in searching for this let not the other above mentioned be forgotten. Written in Almeirim, March 15th, Lopo Roiz wrote it, 1546.

IV.

Letter of 1550 from the King of Abyssinia to the King of Portugal.[1]

IN the name of the Holy Trinity, our Eternal Life, in which we believe, and in which is our salvation. This letter is sent from the presence of the King of Ethiopia, Asnaf

---

[1] This letter is translated from the Portuguese translation in the Appendix to Fr. Luiz de Sousa's *Annaes de el rei D. João III*, p. 427. It is not known if the original is still in existence. Immediately

Sagad, son of King Wanag Sagad, second son of King Naod, son of King Bdemâryâm, son of King Zara Yakub, of the race of David and Solomon, Kings of Israel, greeting, to the King of Portugal, D. João, son of King Emanuel. I have heard, and remind you to do all you promised. May God make you a great lord in the land, and place in your hand the sea, the islands, and the continent. May He make you a greater lord in the heavens for all eternity, as He does to His friends and holy men. Through your prayers God worked us great good; with the help of your men we conquered the Moors, and have always been victorious over them. The Captain, D. Christovão, landed from the sea, and entered my country with four hundred Franks, and many bombards and matchlocks and other arms. Numerous Moors collected against him. Our men were few, so that the day was not ours. I did not arrive in time to join the Captain, for I was far away in another country called Seoa. While D. Christovão was in Tigré, he sent me a messenger to ask me to come quickly, as it was necessary that we should both meet. The messenger reached me, he was called Ayres Dias, a servant of the Captain, called by the people of this country Marcos. When I heard the message I began to march in haste, that we might join. On the way I heard that Garâd Ahmad had killed D. Christovão and many Franks, and captured all the bombards, munitions, and weapons they had; and that the Franks who escaped were scattered over the country. At this news I was so sorrowful that I wept with sadness and passion. Garâd Ahmad, with his own men alone, could not

---

following this letter, two documents are noted on p. 429, but no copy of either is given. One is the King of Portugal's letter of thanks to Gaspar de Sousa, and the other his reply to the above letter sent to the King of Abyssinia by the hands of Diogo Dias. The dates of these letters are not given. Possibly Diogo Dias (whom Couto calls do Prestes) brought home this letter from Abyssinia, and was one of the five Portuguese who escaped from Massowa in 1550 (Correa, vol. iv, p. 701).

defeat them. Besides his own men, he got over six hundred Turks, with whose assistance, as they were many, he obtained the victory. I marched at once to the country of Tigré, and collected the Franks who were scattered over the district: they were one hundred and thirty. Some others had gone to Bdebarrua, to seek shipping to return to their country. I made Ayres Dias, whom the people of this country call Marcos, Captain of the one hundred and thirty Portuguese, in place of D. Christovão, and all the Franks were satisfied. After this we fought thrice with the Moors, and God gave us the victory. Once they came against us with two hundred and ten Turks, and with the bombards and the pikes of the Franks, which were captured when D. Christovão was killed. Another time they came against us with eighty Turks, who were all killed, and also Garâd Ahmad was killed. After his death, the people of the Moors elevated another called Bao.[1] In the end the Moors were so destroyed that very few of them remained, and nearly all the Turks were killed; and all their bombards and arms came into our power, and the power of the Franks of Portugal. All this benefit and these riches, and all this good fortune came to us from our Brother, and our Friend, our Blood, and our Life: Jesus Christ. D. Christovão with four hundred Franks could not destroy the Moors; the fortunate Ayres Dias, his servant, with one hundred and thirty Franks, defeated and destroyed them entirely, although D. Christovão had fought very valiantly against the Moors. May God pardon his soul, and place him among the martyrs. Amen. I made Ayres Dias great among my people, and gave him valuable estates. He suffered with us much toil and labour in the war, fighting against the Moors. This Ayres Dias had previously

---

[1] *Sic*, apparently a misreading of Nur. Galâwdêwos defeated him in 1548 (see Conzelman, § 32), but eleven years later he had his revenge.

come to this country of Ethiopia in the time of the King, my father, Wanag Sagad, who was a great friend of the Franks, when D. Rodrigo de Lima and Jorze Dabreu went with the ambassador, Abaza Guazaado,[1] who carried a letter from my father, Wanag Sagad, to the King, your father, Emanuel. This ambassador died. May God take his soul, and receive it into the kingdom of the heavens. The Franks who are here live with me at their pleasure; they have much property and riches, which I have given them where they desired it. After the death of Ayres Dias, I appointed Gaspar de Sousa in his place, who very speedily does all that is required of him. [Here follow two and a-half lines which the Portuguese translator failed to render. He says they appeared to be praises of Gaspar de Sousa.] The Franks who went to seek shipping are in Bdebarrua. Fernão de Sousa does this well. He welcomes those who come from foreign parts; he receives them with good will, and serves me well, and delights to do all I order. He is the brother of Gaspar de Sousa, who lives with me, and is very diligent in all I order. To Fernão de Sousa, brother of Gaspar de Sousa, I have given much land and property, and have made him Commander of my Guard and a trusted leader. He has left all this to go to you, so much is he your servant. Believe all this. Written in the year of Christ's birth, 1542, according to the count of Ethiopia and Egypt, and according to the count of the Franks, 1550; on the 6th day of the month of Christmas.

---

[1] Presumably, Abba Saga za ab.

V.

Letter from the King of Abyssinia to the Governor of India, which was despatched in 1551.[1]

IN the name of God the Father, God the Son, and God the Holy Ghost, one God all powerful. Amen. I, Asnaf Sagad, King of Ethiopia, send this letter to the Governor of India, under the King D. João, son of the King D. Manuel, who is in glory, honour of the world and grace to the heavens. Peace be upon you. As you have command over the sea, the earth, and the islands, by the favour of God you shall participate in the crown of the kingdom of heaven for all eternity. Amen. Senhor brother, I received here a letter from India sent by Abaa, my ambassador, who is in Goa, which was sent by Jaquaria merchant, who started from Cananore, giving me an account of the great powers he was bringing from all christianity; since then I have learned from other letters that Abaa has died and left his papers and his powers to his chaplain. I therefore ask you, as a well-loved brother, and beg on the part of Jesus Christ that you will do me this much pleasure, namely, to despatch this chaplain and his men, in order that they may bring me the papers which I value highly and wish to see; this will please me greatly, and Our Lord will favour you in whatever you can do. The news here is that D. Christovão landed from the sea in the territories of my dominions, with four hundred Portuguese and many bombards, matchlocks, and other things necessary for the war. With all this he did not conquer the Moors, because their time and hour had not yet come; we, too, were distant

---

[1] Given in Esteves Pereira's edition of Castanhoso from the *Cartas Annuas dos Padres da Companhia de Jesus*, a MS. in the Royal Academy of Lisbon. It is not stated who translated it into Portuguese, but the Portuguese does not seem modern.

from him and he from us, as we were in Axenaa (? Xeuaa—Shoa) and he in the kingdom of Tigré; thence he sent me his message by Ayres Dias, and hearing it I moved my camp to join him. On the road I heard the news that D. Christovão and many Portuguese had been killed fighting with Garâd Ahmad, who defeated them and captured all their arms, bombards, and matchlocks, and all the powder. Some Portuguese escaped, flying to Amaçua and Daonoo, which are sea ports. In truth this news caused great sorrow and weeping among us, and we bitterly wept for the death of so many Christian strangers who had come to help us. Garâd Ahmad, had he been alone, would not have won this victory, but he brought over six hundred Turks to help him, from Zebide, and thus succeeded. When I reached Tigré, I had the Portuguese who were scattered sought out and collected, and there were found and brought together one hundred and thirty men, who wandered seeking shipping to return to their country, and when collected we selected, to the general satisfaction, Ayres Dias as Captain. After this we made war on the Moors altogether three times, and once we conquered them. In our first battle with Garâd Ahmad he had two hundred and ten Turks and many other people, the bombards and matchlocks of the Turks, and those they captured from D. Christovão at the time of his death. The second time he had six hundred Turks, and of these not one escaped. Garâd Ahmad ended his life and died in this battle, and his gozil (wazir) Abaaz also. Further we captured all the bombards, matchlocks, and other arms by the favour and mercy of God, and the help and assistance of the men of the King of Portugal. D. Christovão began and Ayres Dias ended it. D. Christovão died like a very valiant and courageous martyr of Jesus Christ, fighting the Moors. May our Lord give him the crown he merited, and to those who remain His favour and pity.

Those who are here with me are well supplied, and receive from me daily fresh favours. Some of the Portuguese who are in Baroa waiting to go thence, to their homes, will, when they reach these, receive, I beg on the part of our Redeemer and Saviour Jesus Christ, love and good reception, as they have been very loyal and true. Senhor brother, I beg you not to forget to carry out what I have asked.

Seven days after Christmas, 1551.[1]

---

[1] The same criticism applies to this letter as to the last, namely, that it requires careful collation with the original—the facts in the two as regards the battles with the Imam Ahmad are not in accord. The date requires verification, and it is not clear to which ambassador reference is made: Saga za ab had died in India in 1540. Abbas was made Vazir on the death of Addolé, in an ambush, in 1534.

BERMUDEZ.

BERMUDEZ' MONUMENT.
(From the edition of his Book published at Lisbon in 1875.)

This is a short account of the
embassy which the patriarch D. João

Bermudez brought from the Emperor of Ethiopia, vulgarly called Preste John, to the most Christian and zealous-in-the-faith-of-Christ King of Portugal, D. João, the third of that name, dedicated to the most high and powerful and of happiest auspices King, also of Portugal, D. Sebastião, the first of that name.

In which, too, is related the death of
D. Christovão da Gama
and the fortunes of the Portuguese, his companions.

In Lisbon, at the house of Francisco Correa, Printer to the Cardinal Infante, in the year 1565.

THE LETTER

OF

THE PATRIARCH D. JOÃO BERMUDEZ

TO

THE KING OUR LORD.

Most high and most powerful King, your highness once told me that you would be pleased to learn the truth of what happened to the Captain and the soldiers whom the King, your grandfather, who is now in glory, entrusted to me, to take as succour to the Emperor of Ethiopia, Onadinguel,[1] called Preste John, in order to correct the errors which certain persons have written about this, so much so that they mistake the very name of the Captain, calling him D. Paulo when it was D. Christovão, his brother; while others write and tell of certain things which did not of a truth happen, nor did they see them. On the other hand, I who saw all things will shortly relate what occurred in this little book. May Our Lord guard your person, augment your youth, and prosper your royal estate. Amen.

---

[1] Lebna Dengel.

CHAPTER VI.

Of how the Governor, D. Garcia, died, and D. Estevão succeeded, who took the Patriarch to the Red Sea; and of the Death of the Emperor of the Preste, Onadinguel.

BEFORE this reply of the Preste John came, the Viceroy, D. Garcia, had told me not to be impatient, for he would send me to the Preste John with great honour, and would give me a considerable fleet to help him. But, just at this juncture, as ill-luck would have it, he sickened of a dysentery, and died. He was succeeded in the governorship by D. Estevão da Gama. I at once required him to despatch us, and send me to the Preste John, with the assistance which his highness had ordered. He replied that he could not, as one hundred thousand cruzados, or more, were needed for the purpose, which sum perchance would never be recovered. I replied that all this was nothing for the Preste John, who, without missing it, could spend a million of gold and more, for his riches are innumerable. Finally, I required him, before D. João de Albuquerque, Bishop of Goa, and D. João Deça, Captain of the same place, to send me as the King, his lord, had ordered; or to give it me in writing that he could not, as then I would return to Portugal in the fleet of Pero Lopez de Sousa, in which I had come. Before replying he held a council, in which it was determined that he should personally conduct me; and he at once ordered a very fine fleet to be fitted out of galleys, galleons, and other vessels, very well furnished, as was necessary for such a voyage, and with many and selected troops of the best there were in India. With this fleet we reached the port of Massowa, in the Red Sea, where we

---

Dengel, which this messenger brought back. It certainly does not in any way answer to Bermudez' description. A translation is given in this volume (see p. 107, above).

heard the news that Onadinguel, Emperor of the Preste John, had died a natural death. All of us were much troubled, I more than any, as the one it touched most nearly; and doubtless the sorrow I suffered from this was so great that I was near desiring death. But by the mercy of God, which has supported me through many troubles, and with the counsels of the Governor, and other noble fidalgos and persons who constantly visited me, I sustained my courage until the arrival from the Preste John of two friars, good religious men, one of them, Prior Provincial of several monasteries and a great man among them, called Aba Joseph, who were on their way to Jerusalem, and told us that the Queen and her son the heir were upholding their position and resisting their enemies. When we learned this, the Governor, D. Estevão, told me to send to visit them. This I at once did, sending one Ayres Diz, a dark man, a native of Coimbra, whom I directed to tell them to give praise to God, and be joyful, as through the Divine goodness the Catholic King of Portugal had sent them great help, by which, and by the assistance of God, their country would be restored to them and their enemies defeated. To encourage them still more, the Governor wanted me to make this visit personally, and to take with me Vasco da Cunha; but, as the country through which we should have to pass was in the power of the enemy, we should have risked our lives, and we did not go.[1]

---

[1] Much of this chapter seems founded on fancy. D. Garcia de Noronha died on April 3rd, 1540. Farto returned to Goa some six weeks later. The south-west monsoon was then blowing, and any expedition to the Red Sea was quite out of the question for some months. The fleet of Pero Lopez had left India several months before this date, and Bermudez could not have threatened, as he says, to return in it. D. Estevão da Gama was never averse to the Red Sea expedition; in fact, he proposed it in one of his earliest councils; but the object was to burn the Turkish galleys at Suez: Abyssinia was but a secondary consideration. D. Estevão reached Massowa on February 10th, 1541, and sailed for Suez on the 18th. There was hardly time for much to have happened at this visit. Of Ayres Diz, or Dias, good deal has already

CHAPTER VII.

Of how D. Estevão left for Suez, and of how there arrived Messages from the Preste John, desiring him to send the Patriarch.

WHILST Ayres Diz was taking the message to the Queen to say we were there, and to enquire what she wished us to do, the Governor, to lose no time, good cavalier and high-spirited Captain that he was, went with the galleys that accompanied the fleet to the port of Suez, to capture or burn those of the Turks which were in the said port; but this he could not do, as they were beached. The ships and galleons remained with us in Massowah, where, after visiting the Kings (*sic*), Ayres Diz returned, and with him one of the Preste's eunuchs,[1] who brought a golden cross of three marks weight,[2] as a sign that they were Christians, this he gave to Manuel da Gama,[3] who was the Commander of the fleet. After him came an envoy from the said Kings called Aueyteconcomo, the chief lord in all the land of the Preste John.[4] After visiting me in the ship where I was, and receiving my blessing, he went to speak with the

---

been said. Vasco da Cunha was rather an important person. His service in India lasted from 1527 to 1555; the most striking event in it happened in 1546, when he was sent by D. João de Castro to supersede the besieged captain of Diu, who had shown himself too impetuous. His brother, Manuel da Cunha, accompanied D. Christovão.

[1] Probably *capado*, a eunuch, has been written for *capellão*, chaplain. The former were not employed on embassies.

Three marks would be equal to twenty-four ounces. This detail seems difficult to believe: not only were the rulers impoverished, but the country was overrun by the enemy.

[3] Couto calls Manuel da Gama uncle (*tio*) of D. Estevão. There is nothing to show that he was a brother of D. Vasco da Gama. Possibly the word was used in the extended Oriental sense to cover the relationship we call cousin once or more removed, provided the removal is in the ascending line. He had never held any important post, and, judging by his conduct at Massowa, was a man of harsh and violent temper.

[4] The allusion is obscure.

commander, Manuel da Gama, to beg him to assist his Kings with the men the King of Portugal, his brother, had sent; to this he replied that he could not before the Governor's return, who would not tarry many days. Before this one could be dismissed came another, called Isaac the Bernagaiz, who is also a great lord, to beg the same, whom the Captain also received like the first with great magnificence and honour, with the sound of trumpets and firing of artillery; he replied, too, to him as to the other, that the Governor's return must be awaited. These, before going, came to my ship to take leave, and begged for matchlocks and powder. I gave them each five matchlocks, with the necessary powder, with which they were very content; they gave us certain hints of what we should do, and against whom we should be on our guard, especially against the King of Massowah, in whose harbour we were, as he had concluded peace with the King of Zeila.

CHAPTER VIII.

Of how Sixty Men fled from the Fleet who were killed up the Country, and of what else happened consequent on their Death.

WHILE waiting for the Governor here, there fled sixty men from the fleet to the main, in a skiff and a boat; they landed at a port of the country where it was very dry and very hot, and beginning to march inland it was so dry that they were dying of thirst. While beset by these necessities, a Captain of the King of Zeila, who was in that part, sent word that he would order them food and drink and assure their lives provided they gave up their weapons; they, seeing no other shift, and compelled by necessity, gave them up; with these they at once slew them. That night, when their flight was discovered, Manuel da Gama joined Martim Correa da Silva, and both of them came to the ship *Sta. Clara*, where I was, and we all set out with our people in search of them; but we could not find them, we only recovered the boats in which they had fled; these we brought back; we soon heard the manner of their death. Their death began the series of events which ended in the death of that Captain, and thus opened a safe road for us to journey through the land of Abyssinia. The way it came about was, that just then the Commander sent a galley to Arquiquo for water; in it he also sent one thousand webs of cotton to exchange for cows to eat. While those in charge were bringing them by land, from Arquiquo to the fleet, a Bernagaiz called Noro, Captain of the King of Zeila, captured them, and sent word to the Commander that the King of Zeila, his lord, was lord of all Ethiopia, and had conquered all the land of the Preste John. That, therefore, he wished to make peace with him, and to trade for his merchandise in that country, where he had much gold, ivory, civet, incense, myrrh, and many other drugs, and also slaves of great profit; that he would give him ample supplies, and would restore the captured cows, and exact punishment for the sixty men killed. To this message the Commander promised a reply, that meanwhile the messenger might return. Taking counsel with me, and with Martim Correa da Silva, in my cabin, where we all were when he received the said message from the Bernagaiz, I said to him that he should not trust a Moor's words, for they were false, and all that he said was feigned to do us some hurt; that we should, therefore, also use a stratagem with him, which was this: to send his worship a present, with words of thanks for the goodwill he showed us; then he would think that he had deceived us, and that he could feel sure of us, and in this way we should combat his guile. The Commander acted thus, and ordered the factor of the fleet to take to the Moor Bernagaiz a barrel of wine and one thousand more webs of cotton: the wine as a present and the webs to exchange for cows; and to say on his behalf, that as for the other webs they were captured in fair war, and nothing more need be said about them; that as to the men who had been killed, that they were not worth revenge, for they were rebels and traitors, and deserved the death they had suffered; as to commerce and peace, that we were then in Holy Week, and could not traffic, but that when the Feast of Easter was ended we would do what he wished, and would send our goods on shore to trade with them. After this the Commander, Martim Correa da Silva, and I met to consult what we ought to do; and I said that my opinion was that we should attack him one night, and destroy him while he was supine and unprepared; this we must do both to secure our own passage and also for the benefit of all India, as since the death of those men he had boasted among his fellows, and had gained repute among his neighbours; and that the name of the Portuguese would become a scorn if he escaped with no punishment. Further, I said to them that we ought to give the same chastisement to the King of Massowa, as he was as bad as the other: for there could be no doubt but that he was in the conspiracy to rob us of the webs, for he had our enemy with him in Massowa, where he was. This appeared right to my companions, and they ordered an attack on them that very night, while they were quite negligent.[1]

---

[1] No other writer has this story save Bermudez. Noro probably is meant for Sharif Nur, Governor of Arkiko. A ship called the *Sta. Clara* had come out with the fleet that accompanied D. Garcia de Noronha, and was actually in this expedition to the Red Sea (Falcão, p. 157, and Correa, vol. iv, pp. 10 and 207). By an error, Falcão antedated the departure of the *Sta. Clara* from Portugal by one year.

CHAPTER IX.

Of how the Death of the Sixty Men was avenged, and of how they slew a Captain of the King of Zeila.

AFTER the council the Commander directed that the boats were not to go ashore, in order that no Moor, or negro, from the fleet might have the means to go and warn him. He ordered the men-at-arms to prepare themselves as secretly as might be, and the boats and the other light vessels of the fleet to be got ready to land them; he ordered that, not to be seen, no fire should be lighted in them. He ordered Martim Correa to land at ten at night, with six hundred men, and seize the outlets by which they could escape; we—the Commander and I—with the rest of the force were to attack the city from the sea face; we were to give the signal with our trumpets that Martim Correa might fall on simultaneously from the land side. I recommended him to hurry, that the Moor might not escape, but as the Captain, Manuel da Gama, had made peace with the King of Massowa, he would not let us injure him: at least, he did not wish that any ill should befall him, or that he should run any personal danger; for this reason he took his time and it was daylight before we advanced to the attack, and the King had had time to discover us and escape. I, desiring to follow him with my men, the Commander turned me back, saying he did not wish me to run any danger; therefore I returned, and told Antonio Figueyra to go on with the men in pursuit; this he did, and killed some Turks and Fartakins,[1] and captured all the baggage they had, which was little, for they had not time to take much. When the Zeila Bernagaiz saw the King fly, he also took to flight, and met with Martim Correa,

---

[1] Fartakin: resident in South Arabia, near Cape Fartak.

where he was recognised and killed by a matchlockman ; some of his men came to his assistance, and many of them, both foot and horse, were slain ; the rest, flying, escaped. The death of the Moor Bernagaiz dispersed the garrison and guard which the King of Zeila kept in that country of Abyssinia, whereby he blocked the roads, and stopped the access of the Preste John to us, and ours to the Preste ; it was, therefore, very advantageous, and saved us the great trouble he might have caused us, for he was very powerful, and lord of all the provinces through which we had to pass. We, therefore, ordered our men to cut off his head, and sent it by some Abyssinians to the Queen of the Preste ; with this she was much pleased, as a very fortunate commencement of the victories which, by the help of God, she hoped to secure by our assistance. So great was the joy of the Queen and her people at the death of that Moor, that, besides the thanks and praises they offered to God for this, she sent a great man of her country, called Esmacherobel Tigremaquão,[1] to the Commander and to me, to thank us for the very great satisfaction she had received through us. She also asked the Commander not to detain the help he had brought. He replied to her, as before, that he could do nothing before the Governor's return ; who by the will of our Lord returned safely at this time, as we all greatly desired. Meanwhile, Manuel da Gama and Martim Correa made over to the Tigremaquão all those Abyssinian provinces which the Moor Bernagaiz had had under him.[2]

---

[1] His name was Robel. Tigremaquão represents Tigre Makuanen, or Governor of Tigré, the name of his office. Bruce gives him the title of Degdeasmati, and Esmache probably represents the last element of this.

[2] The same remarks apply as to the last chapter. This narrative makes out that Bermudez, with the help of Manuel da Gama, cleared the way to the interior before the return of D. Estevão from Suez. No other author supports this claim.

CHAPTER X.

Of the Arrival of the Governor, D. Estevão, and of how he selected his brother, D. Christovão, as Captain for the Preste.

As soon as the Governor, D. Estevão, arrived he ordered me to be at once despatched and sent to the King and Queen of the Preste John. And because it was now understood that the enterprise was one of honour and profit, many more desired it than before: one among these was D. Christovão da Gama, brother of the Governor, who begged me very urgently to give him the Captaincy of all the people I was going to take, as he wished to accompany me; but I told him I could not, inasmuch as I had already in Portugal given it to Pero Borges Anriquez; because while I was yet in Portugal the King had granted me the favour to appoint as from him all the officers necessary for the command of the people I took with me. Displeased at my reply, D. Christovão informed the Governor his brother; and then on his behalf came again to beg me, but I always replied that it was impossible; because it was not well to break my word to a fidalgo so honourable as Pero Borges, nor would it be creditable to him to take or even to ask for his appointment. During this time there came four Captains and other lords of those lands which we had freed from the tyranny of the Bernagaiz, and with them many friars and religious persons, to proffer me submission and receive my blessing, and then to visit the Governor, and thank him for the great benefit that they through him had received from the King of Portugal. They informed him of the great service to God and profit of souls that had been already wrought in those parts; because, said they, as long as they were captives in the power of that Moor, the Moors every year carried off from that land over ten thousand Christians to sell in Mecca and other Moorish countries, from which captivity they were now free, through the mercy of the Lord God, and by means of the Portuguese; that the praise of so good a work was due after God to the King of Portugal, and his lordship, who in the pleasures of the glory of the heavens would for this receive their reward: inasmuch as they had delivered them from a worse captivity than that of Babylon. When I was designing to start, the Governor spoke to me personally in favour of his brother, D. Christovão; and told me that he asked me as a favour, inasmuch as his brother greatly desired to go with me, and it was not fitting that he should go under another's command, that I should do him the favour to give him the captaincy of those people I was taking, as he promised me, being the man he was, to be obedient to me in all things and not to trangress in anything my command. I replied that I could never commit so great a fault as to lie to a man so honourable as Pero Borges. "Well, then," said he, "I can only give you two hundred men, labourers and people of low condition. I cannot give you any fighting men or persons of distinction, nor can I give you more than three or four clerics. I will at once order your baggage on shore, and good luck be with you!" After this he left me. There came then to me D. João de Crasto, D. Manuel de Lima, D. Payo de Noronha, Tristão d'Ataide, and Manuel de Sousa,[1] all very honourable fidalgos and leading men, in whom it was not well that a sense of shame should be lost; owing to their reasoning, that if through my fault all that country which

---

[1] These are historical persons. D. João de Crasto, better known as D. João de Castro, was afterwards Governor and then Viceroy of India, well known for his writings. D. Manuel de Lima went as a common soldier in this expedition, rather than be left behind. D. Payo de Noronha was a relative of D. João de Castro, who twice by his misconduct seriously imperilled his country's interests. Tristão d'Ataide was mother's brother of D. Estevão and D. Christovão, and therefore brother-in-law of D. Vasco da Gama. There were several Manuel de Sousas, and it is not easy to say exactly which this was.

was then on the point of being recovered were lost, I should be obliged to give an answer for its loss before God, I agreed to what they said, and gave them the captaincy for D. Christovão; at which all were satisfied and the Governor thanked me. He at once told off the people he gave me, that is four hundred men; amongst whom were many fidalgos and very honourable cavaliers who, besides the fixed number, brought their followers and servants, who were also members of the company and were useful.

CHAPTER XI.

Of how the two Armies separated; one for India, and the other for the Preste John; and of the murmurs that arose against the Patriarch.

As we were arranging our departure, the Christian Bernagaiz of the Preste, who had already been with us, returned, bringing some camels, mules, and asses, to carry the baggage, and also generally to assist. As we had to cross a hill, where there is a bad pass in which the enemy could annoy us, the Captain sent João Dafonseca and Manuel da Cunha, Captains, with their men numbering one hundred and twenty, with some pieces of artillery and other arms, to occupy and guard that pass. I directed the Bernagaiz and the Tigremaquão to order supplies and refreshments to be brought for the whole fleet. They ordered in many cows, sheep, goats, much butter, honey, millet, plantains *(figos)*, quinces and other things in abundance, as in that country supplies are fresh and plentiful.[1] The Governor sent for the Bernagaiz, and commended his brother greatly to him, begging him to treat him and his men as might be expected, since they were true Christians. To me also he commended him, making me a long and friendly speech,

---
[1] This does not agree with the usual description of Massowa.

as brotherly love and his affection required. Peradventure it appeared to him, though he never said so, that he would never see him more. Finally, in order to take leave of us, he came with all the fidalgos and noble persons of the fleet to Arquiquo, where they asked me to give them my blessing, which I gave them on behalf of the Lord God, to whom I commended them. They went to the sea, and we remained on the land with great longing. Beginning our march, we reached Debarua in three days.[1] Here D. Christovão wanted to make the Bernagaiz prisoner, on the ground that he did not give him as good a reception as he desired; but I did not consent, in order not to scandalise those from whom we needed help. I explained to D. Christovão that it was not fitting, and made them again friends. A few days later, as the devil arranges to sow dissensions where harmony is most needed, some of our men began to murmur against the natives of that country, saying that they were not good Christians, as they did not obey the Holy Apostolic See of Rome; and of me they said that I agreed with them, and that I had not told the Holy Father the truth, as I had said that the King of the Preste John had sent his submission to him, which was not the case: but that both he and his people were schismatics, because they used rites and ceremonies which were schismatical and heretical, different from the Romans. To this I replied that I had not lied to the Holy Father, inasmuch as it was true that the late Emperor Onadinguel, by the grace of God, and in consequence of my entreaties and threats, had been moved to acknowledge submission to His Holiness, and for this had sent me to Rome with his letters in which he said this; and that I trusted in God that his son would do the same when he saw me, and knew what the Holy

---

[1] Castanhoso gives nine days for this, which is more probable. The distance is sixty miles as the crow flies, the road difficult, and the Portuguese new to the country.

Father had directed me to say to him; and that he would proclaim publicly his submission in all his kingdom; but, that, meanwhile, it was necessary to temporise with the rustic Abyssinian people, as if we scandalised them they would make us over to the Moors, and we should attain no result, and do no service to God. With these and other reasons, I satisfied as I could D. Christovão and his people, and the murmuring ceased, and they began to arrange how they would convey their artillery when they marched. They designed for this purpose some carts, after the manner of this country; for which, as there was no iron in the land, they used up certain matchlocks, which, as they were old and of no further service, they pulled to pieces.

CHAPTER XII.

Of how the Queen of the Preste came to Debarua to visit the Patriarch and D. Christovão, and of the Reception they gave her, and of what else passed there.

As by the time all this had been arranged two months or more had elapsed since we reached Debarua, and the season had come to do something, I sent word to the Queen by the Bernagaiz, that it seemed to me right that she should come to visit D. Christovão, and welcome him, and encourage his followers to make war and defend her country. She did this, and came as quickly as she could. D. Christovão and I went a league out of the city to receive her, with all the Portuguese in warlike array, and the Portuguese banners both of the King and of the captains—I say of the King, for we had one there which his highness had given me for this purpose in Portugal. We received her with trumpets and the firing of artillery, with which she was much astonished, for it is not their custom. Her first act was that of one who reverenced the things of God: she obtained my blessing; she next received D. Christovão with much kindness and honour, giving him many thanks for being willing to undertake that enterprize, and the duty of defending her from her enemies. We then returned to the city, and on the following day we all heard Mass, and arranged to make processions in which we all joined, and the Queen also, with two princesses her sisters-in-law, and a little girl her daughter, whom she brought with her; all praying God, with much devotion and many tears, that in His pity He would hear us and give us victory over His enemies and ours. Thus some days passed; after which I said to D. Christovão that it would be well to begin to make war on the Moors, as the time had arrived, and he and I went to tell this to the Queen. She as a woman feared war, and told us that we need not hurry. But D. Christovão told her not to be afraid, for with the help of God he hoped to have victory; he begged me to advise her that he intended to war against the Moors, both because he himself and all his men were very eager, and because it comported with their honour as they had been sent for that purpose. She, seeing his determination, ordered her captains to get ready; and we marched to seek the King of Zeila, her enemy, and make war on him.

CHAPTER XIII.

Of how the Army of the Christians started from Debarua, to seek the King of Zeila.

AFTER quitting Debarua, we marched for eight days over a difficult country, and at the end of the eight days we reached a level and populous land, superior to that we had left. In it lived Christians who, through fear, had joined the Moors; who, as soon as they knew of our arrival, went to

D. Christovão and made their submission to him, and begged him to arrange with the Queen to pardon them, which he did willingly, and was easily successful. They broughts us presents and refreshments, and for three days we took our pleasure in that country, that the men might rest after their past labour. We enquired here for the King of Zeila, and learnt that he was three marches away. Leaving there in search of him, we travelled most of the way by night on account of the great heats, by reason of which we could not march later than nine in the day.[1] At the end of three days, we reached a valley between two high hills, where, as it was cool, we pitched our camp; but we struck it again at once, as the Bernagaiz and Tigremaquão informed us that we were commanded by the hills, from which they could do us much hurt with arrows and slings; we therefore advanced further. Going half a league on, we found a very pleasant plain, in which was a spring of good water; there we pitched behind the spring in the following order. Immediately close to the spring were the tents of the Queen and the princesses, and mine, and the captains of the country with the supplies, which were now scanty; close to us were fifty horsemen of the country, with the mules of the Queen and her women; further out were the soldiers, and in the rear of all the carts for the artillery, with a guard.

CHAPTER XIV.

Of how the War between the Christians and Moors began with the Victory of the Christians.

BEING camped thus, and desiring our presence to be known, we ordered some artillery shots to be fired. At this, some horsemen approached, who only came in sight

---

[1] It was then the coolest season of the year, and this statement as referring to the Abyssinian highlands is unusual.

of us at a distance without getting very close. The following day, a messenger arrived from the Goranha, King of Zeila, in company with some others of his men; and, asking for the Captain of the force, told D. Christovão that the King had sent to enquire who we were, and whence we came, and who had given us permission to enter his kingdom with an armed force: for that kingdom was his, and he had gained it by his spear, and by his cavaliers, with the help of his prophet Mafamede; but that if we would become Moors, and serve him, that he would give us welcome and pay, and also women and treasure with which we could live; if we refused, we must at once leave his country and depart from it. D. Christovão replied that he was a captain of the King of Portugal, by whose order he came with that force to restore the kingdoms of the Preste John, which he had tyrannically usurped, and to wrest them from his power and restore them to their real owner. With this message he sent him a present of a looking-glass, and tweezers to arrange the eyebrows, and a silver bird's-egg,[1] hinting to him that those things were suitable for him. To the messenger he gave two gold bracelets and a rich brocade dress, which things the Queen supplied to him; also he gave him a woman's coif from Bengal and a scarlet cap, and a burnoose with its veil; this, by my advice, in scorn of the Goranha. He, seeing the present sent him, and understanding its meaning, considered himself insulted; and, bent on vengeance, struck his camp at once, and began to march against us, with one thousand horsemen, five thousand foot, and fifty Turkish matchlockmen, and as many archers. When the Queen learned that he was coming towards us with

---

[1] *Ouo de prata dos pègus.* Purchas's translation of "a silver egg of Pegu" is clearly inadmissible. Pègus is the Latin *picus;* the particular bird is not certain: a woodpecker, a magpie, and a wren are all given as equivalents of pègo or pèga. The allusion is obscure.

so strong a force, she settled to fly with her sisters-in-law; but, discovering her intention, I sent to tell D. Christovão not to consent, but to order her a Portuguese guard, because it was necessary to have her with us: for, although her people gave us no help with their weapons, they assisted us with their persons, companionship, welcome, and supplies, which peradventure they had not done if they knew she was not there. D. Christovão wished to advance with his force to meet the enemy, but I did not consent, saying that they were beyond count more numerous than we, and that in such an inequality of force we should not give battle face to face; but that we should seek some wile or stratagem to compass what we could not attain by force. That, in the meanwhile, until God should afford us an opportunity to do what we intended, that we should march up a hill to the church of Our Lady of Mercy, which was on the summit, for that Lady would help us. D. Christovão did not wish to take my advice, but his captains and fidalgos told him that he would commit a great error and would ruin himself if he did not follow it: because, as the Abyssinians were panic-stricken, they would all fly, and we should remain alone at the chopping-block. When he found that all told him my advice was good, he determined to take it, and ordered the Queen and the women, with all the baggage, to be placed in the centre of the force. When the Moor saw us advancing up the slope, he turned towards us to seize the high ground. He approached us so close that shots were fired from one side and the other. When I saw the battle beginning, I called six Portuguese and separated myself with the Queen and her sisters-in-law. In this way I recognised the Moorish King, who came riding close to his banner, on a bay horse. I pointed him out to Pero Deça, a fidalgo, and a good matchlockman, who fired his matchlock at him, killed his horse, and wounded him in the leg. His men assisted him, placed him on another horse, and on it took him thence. Our Commander, D. Christovão, was also wounded in the other leg, and he asked me what he should do. I told him to bear it as long as he could, that no one might perceive it, and meanwhile to ride his chamber servant's mule. I ordered the Queen's steward to pitch her highness's tent as a sign of victory. The Moors who had surrounded us on all sides, when they saw our tents being pitched, and their King wounded, lost heart and could do nothing more, but began to retreat, and follow their King, who went with the pain of his wound to a hill near by, to have it dressed.

CHAPTER XV.
Of how an Abyssinian Captain who had joined the Moors came over to the Christians.

AT this time a Moor came over to us who had been a Christian, a cousin of the Bernagaiz, and told us that the King had been wounded in the leg, and how great mercy God had shown us in this: for had it not happened he would have captured us all without any doubt; but God had miraculously freed us from his hand; that, therefore, he and all his came over to us, and would obey us, and pay us the tribute they had hitherto paid that King; that he was returning at once to his territory to send us cows and supplies for our camp, because he was the captain and governor of all the country where we were; which had belonged to the Preste and he also. When the King of Zeila conquered it he joined his party, and now that he saw him defeated he returned to us; by which he appeared to be a man of Long Live the Conqueror![1] We sent to enquire how many of our people had fallen, and we found

---

[1] See chap. xlvii, p. 225, below, where this man is called Calide; the difficulties in the way of identification are pointed out in a note to that chapter.

forty killed and thirty wounded. On the other side, owing to the many devices of fire we carried, the killed were numberless, both horse and foot. We at once went to the Church of Our Lady, which I have previously said was there, to give thanks to God for the complete victory He had given us; we pitched our camp close to this church. The Moors kept horsemen on guard both night and day around us, fearing we should suddenly attack them; and they watched to learn what movements we made. Meanwhile, as it pleased God, D. Christovão was cured of his wound; but we suffered great hunger, for there was very little food in the camp; but a message of the captain I have mentioned above encouraged us somewhat, for he sent to tell us that in eight days he would be with us with a large store of supplies, as in fact he was. But, as in the meanwhile the people were dying of hunger, D. Christovão went to the Queen, and told her that the people were suffering great want, and that they must eat all they could find, without reference to the fact that it was Lent: that it would be well to kill the cattle in the camp, and eat them. With this request they both came to my tent, asking me to give permission, seeing the necessity there was, for the people to eat flesh in Lent; nay, more, the Queen asked me to give her my oxen, that I had for my transport, to give them to the people, because as soon as her captain, who would not tarry longer than three days, came, she would satisfy me; and so it was, for he came with ample supplies, namely, cows, sheep, goats, butter, and other provisions for Lent and for Easter, which was at hand. From this time D. Christovão began to entitle himself Governor of the Portuguese, and to be called Your Excellency; some said that his brother D. Estevão had told him to do this.

CHAPTER XVI.

Of how the King of Zeila sent to tell D. Christovão that he desired to see him again, and of the Second Battle, in which he was again defeated.

AFTER Easter the Goranha sent to tell D. Christovão that he wished to come and see him, and that he must get ready. D. Christovão desired him not to take that trouble, because he wanted first to visit him at home, and dance with him. He took immediate counsel with his captains, and intended to start that night; but Asmacharobel, learning his determination, came at once to me and said that I must not consent, for if he went his destruction was certain, and that would be the cause of the destruction of us all: because the hills amongst which the King was were rugged, and there were many bad places where he would be lost from not knowing them; further, that the Abyssinians who dwelt there were a very evil people, and would betray him to the Moor. I was very pleased that he gave me this information, and thanked and satisfied him, telling him that his act was that of a good Christian and loyal man. I went at once with him to the tent of the Captain, and told him what I had learned of his intention, which did not appear to me to be well thought out: that therefore he must collect his captains; and I also summoned the Bernagaiz and Tigremaquão. When collected, we asked their opinion of the Captain's plan. All those senhors and others of the country said that D. Christovão's decision was not wise, because if we acted as he intended we should all be lost, and the Moor would regain what we had taken from him. It appeared to the Portuguese captains, after hearing the reasons given by those of the country, that their opinion was of weight; and they told D. Christovão that he ought to agree with it, and follow my judgment, which was that of a father: as in fact I was father of all, and as father counselled them to their good and for the service of God. After D. Christovão had heard what they all said, he agreed to act accordingly, and waited in camp till he saw what the Moor would do. He acted as he had promised. He came in search of us, with a larger and better force than he had brought before; he had over two thousand horse, innumerable infantry, and one hundred Turks. On this, the Queen and her sisters-in-law were seized with such great fear that they did not know what to do: so much so that, although they were eating when they heard of the Moor's approach, they wanted to leave their food; but I went to them, and encouraged them, and told them not to be frightened, for as our Lord had given us the past victory He would also give us one now. Such was their fear that they determined to fly in the coming night. The Tigremaquão told me this, and said the Queen would endeavour to induce me to go with her; it seemed to us best to agree to this, in order to induce her to return, as I did. The next day, before daylight, while D. Christovão was getting ready his men to attack the Moors, the Queen sent for me, and said that she saw the great power of the Goranha, and that it seemed to her impossible to escape from his hands if we awaited him there; that therefore she begged me to go, for she had made up her mind to this course, and would follow it under any circumstances, therefore she pressed me not to leave her to go alone, as I was her father, but accompany her and fly with her. To show her the love I had for her, and not to appear as if I did not value her life, and further as the timid are of such a nature that the more violence is done them the more their fear increases: which experience we get in startled cattle, who if they are turned away a little from the thing that they fear, and it is shown them from another aspect, become bold and lose their fear. Timid people act in the same way. It was therefore not good to contradict the Queen, entirely, lest she should be panic-struck, thinking that no one sympathised with her, and because in the mind she then was to fly she might become angry. I therefore agreed with her, and we both started to fly.[1] But D. Christovão, who had been warned, sent after us ten horsemen and some foot, who called out with loud shouts, saying that it was not the service of God nor the duty of a father to run away and abandon them. Hearing these words, I told the Queen that it was a great disgrace to me and a great burden on my conscience; therefore it behoved me to return, and I asked her to return with me; but she entirely refused. Thereupon I ordered the footmen to seize the bridle of the mule on which she rode, and the two spare horses, and to bring her back to the camp, and to compel her followers to return. She returned, weeping and lamenting. D. Christovão then said that he asked me, according to the good custom of the Portuguese, as a father and prelate, to give him my blessing, and also to give a general absolution before beginning the battle. I did this, and granted him plenary indulgence for all his sins: which I could do as the Pope granted me the power, and as it is the practice of the patriarchs of Alexandria. As morning was breaking we moved with our force down the slope, and marched until we came to a plain where the slope became terraced, so flat that it looked like a table, and so extensive that all the force could easily draw up on it. While crossing the slope before reaching that place, D. Christovão, some of the Portuguese, the Bernagaiz, and an aunt of the King's, saw a man on a white horse in front of the army, armed with all arms, and carrying himself proudly, whom we all believed to be the Apostle St. James, and for this reason we commended ourselves to him very

---

[1] The contradiction between this statement and that on p. 152 is elsewhere noticed.

devoutly.[1] When we reached the plain he disappeared, and the Christians saw him no more; but the Moors saw him in the battle, and said he wrought great destruction among them. Reaching the plain I mention, we drew up our forces, placing the artillery in front of the men. The place was like the tread of a staircase, raised a little more than a step above the lowest part of the valley; from this we could fight hand-to-hand with those below. By the time we had drawn up our force here, the Moors had descended to the valley from the hill on the other side, over which they had come; they at once attacked our position briskly on all sides. Our men defended themselves with shots from the artillery, with bombs, and other artifices of fire; with these they did them much damage. Before they came up, a good deal of powder had been thrown down on the paths by which they had to ascend; this was fired in the heat of the battle, and it burned them, starting up under their feet without their knowing whence it came, as they did not understand the stratagem. A certain number of men with bucklers attacked us with great spirit, and would doubtless have reached the top without much loss from our arms, as they shielded themselves well, were many, and hurried up the rise. But our men threw among them certain fire bombs and powder pots, which burned the greater number of them, and the rest fled in fear and dared not approach us again. The fury of this fire was such that five of our men who could not escape were burned, and some of them died. The artillery slew many of the horsemen and others: so many that the field was strewn with them, and the horses galloped over the plain without their riders. The Turks with their arquebuses and bows killed twenty of our men, and above all our master-gunner, which grieved us all much, for he was a very good man and well

---

[1] Castanhoso (chap. xiv, p. 49, above) says Bermudez saw him; apparently he did not.

trained in his duties. Our men killed fifteen Turks. The Queen was close to me, embracing a cross weeping; she said to me: "Oh, my father, what do you gain by bringing me here? Why did you not let me go my own way?" And I said to her: "Be not angry, Oh lady; commend yourself to God, open your eyes, and see the great destruction wrought among your enemies." By then the footmen were beginning to fly, and the horsemen did not dare approach, but skirmished at a distance. The King told his followers that the Portuguese were no men but demons, because they fought like demons. He then began to retreat to the hill, abandoning his camp. Our men seeing him fly, gave great praise to God and His Apostle St. James, through whose intercession he had given them the victory, on the first Sunday after Easter.

CHAPTER XVII.
Of how the Christians went in Pursuit of the Moors, and Captured their Camp.

D. CHRISTOVÃO came to me and said it would be well to return to our camping place on the summit of the hill, to rest the men who were wearied from the battle; but I replied to him that that was not a good counsel, because the Moor would be quickly reinforced, and would attack us again, and would give us more trouble when he discovered the sloth and cowardice we showed in not knowing how, or not daring, to follow in his pursuit; that it was therefore necessary to follow him until we entirely defeated him, if we could. Thus we acted, for we at once formed our ranks, and marched as quickly as possible; but they fled at full speed, and we could not reach them. We met, however, many Abyssinians, both horse and foot, who came over to our side: who were afterwards baptised, and loyal to their King. The Queen and all of us were as pleased with their return as with the victory itself. We reached the Moor camp, which was abandoned, with none in it, but we found it full of booty, for St. James put such fear into them that they had no respite to remove anything. We found there tents pitched, and in the tents clothes, furniture, money, and other riches; also large supplies, which were very necessary to us, as our stock was low. We stayed there and let the men rest; who ate and enjoyed themselves, as was needful, during the two days we remained. This country and district is called the province of Nazaré. It belongs to the Patriarchs; their own property, with full jurisdiction, without the King interfering in it at all, nor does he receive any income from it. It yields to the Patriarchs three thousand ounces of gold a-year; which the King Thedrus granted to them for a certain offence it committed against a Patriarch.[1] From this camp we marched towards the mountains where the King Goranha had taken refuge; and on the plain at the foot of the mountain pitched our camp, surrounded with our artillery carts. His horsemen came raiding here at times, but our footmen sallied out and drove them off; and, sometimes, made them fly half a league or more, and killed

---

[1] The Portuguese were at this time in Tigrè, and Le Grand (p. 355) puts a different complexion on this matter. The patriarch had indeed some land in Tigrè, but an annual payment of five hundred crowns had been imposed by King Theodore, which was known as Eda Abuna, or the restitution of the Abuna. It was the patriarch, then, who was in fault and had to pay. Theodore was only King for some three years, but his reign is looked back to as the golden age of Abyssinia, and he is to return after one thousand years, when war is to cease, and all be plenty. The statement as to the country and district called Nazaré, belonging to the patriarchs, refers to the formerly large and wealthy monastery of Nazareth, which lay south-east of, and close to, Chelicut, that is, close to the spot which, from other indications, has been pointed out as the site of these battles. It must have been utterly despoiled in the Muhamedan invasion of the Imam Ahmad, as Gargara was for a time his headquarters (Basset, *Histoire*, p. 416). For Alvarez' account of this monastery, see p. 101 of the Hakluyt Society's translation (vol. 64). The Corcora of Alvarez is the modern village of Gargara, that lies west of Chelicut.

some of them. Because the footmen could not travel far enough, nor come up with the horsemen, we sought for twenty horses. With these our men so harassed them that they fled to the mountain and did not return.

CHAPTER XVIII.
Of how the King of Zeila Recruited his Army, and of what the Christians did meanwhile.

WHILE this was happening, the Moor sent to Zebid, to a Pasha of the Grand Turk there, to ask for a reinforcement of men, saying that he ought to aid him, and not to allow the loss of these kingdoms, which all belonged to the Grand Turk, and which he considered as his; that as a proof he sent him one hundred thousand oquias of gold, and twenty thousand for himself. An oquia is a weight of gold in that country of the same value and weight as ten cruzados here.[1] We, until we could learn what was happening, retreated to a strong hill, which was on all sides surrounded by rocks and crags, so that there was barely a road up for footmen. In order to take the artillery and the other transport, we had to lay out a new road, which the captains of the country and their people made; but it was so narrow and steep that the artillery could not be taken up it in the carts, but was carried on the backs of porters. On the top was a plain, where we pitched our camp. Thence

---

[1] Bruce says the *wakea*, or ounce, is the equivalent of six drams, 40 grains troy weight (vol. vii, p. 64). It is not clear what "dram troy weight" stands for, as there are none. Conzelman (p. 142 *n*.) puts the *wakea* at 33.105 grammes. Basset (*Histoire d'Abyssinie*, on p. 59 *n*.) puts it at 35.1 grammes, and again (on p. 65 *n*.) at 33.1, but in the former case there seems to have been a misprint. As the gramme is 15.43235 grains and the ounce is 437.5 grains, the *wakea* is, according to this statement, equal (roughly) to 1.17 ounces avoirdupois. Parkins (vol. i, p. 414) puts it at eight ounces. Even at the smaller value, Bermudez' total would, if correct, amount to nearly four tons of gold.

the Queen sent to her provinces, and I to mine, to bring provisions and other necessary supplies. With these we were soon well furnished, and the wounded well healed. We were comfortably settled here, when D. Christovão told me that we must change to a slope higher up, where the force would be safer; that meanwhile he intended to visit a hill near by, inhabited by Jews, where, as we were advised, was a Moorish captain with one hundred and fifty horse. He went with some Portuguese and a few country people to show the road, and left with us two Portuguese captains and their companies. When he reached the Jews' hill, he fought the Moor, killed sixty of his horse, and captured thirty horses; the others escaped. The Jew inhabitants of the hill followed in pursuit of the Moors and blocked the passes in the hills, with which they were well acquainted, and killed nearly all, including the captain, and captured all the spoil they carried, and their women. They brought all these to D. Christovão, and offered them to him, with the Moor captain's head, which they also brought. Among some other noble women there was the very beautiful wife of the captain, whom D. Christovão took for himself. As two of his captains desired her greatly, there were jealousies about her, and he deposed them from their captaincies; they having, as they said, committed no fault, as they did not look on her for any evil purpose: and good and loyal as they were, they were not aggrieved, nor did they cease to serve zealously.

CHAPTER XIX.

Of how the King of Zeila came on with his reinforced Army, and of how we prepared to give Battle.

WHILE D. Christovão was away in the hill of the Jews, the Moorish King came in search of us, with six hundred

Turks sent to him by the Pasha, and two hundred Moorish horse and numerous infantry, and pitched his camp when he reached the foot of the hill on which we were. Thence he sent one of his men with a box of pedlery ware to our camp, to sell beads and looking-glasses; he was to tell D. Christovão that his master was a merchant, and was following him, and would not delay more than three days, with some excellent merchandize which he was bringing to sell him. He met with Jorge Dabreu[1] and Diogo da Silva, the captains who stayed with us, and who guarded the approach to the hill; they took the beads from him and brought them to me, and I blessed them, and gave them to women and devout persons, telling them that praying with them they would gain many pardons, because his scorn would redound to the praise of God and to the profit of His faithful. We at once sent in haste to recall D. Christovão, who had not yet returned from the hill. While he was coming the Turks, in spite of our men, entered the hill and did us much hurt. That very night after the entry, D. Christovão came, with half the men he had taken, for the others could not maintain the speed at which he travelled; they did not, however, delay long, but came soon after. We were all pleased at his return, and we had relief from the trouble and difficulty in which we were. Meanwhile, before we could arrange what course to follow, the musquetry of the Turks was discharged at our camp, and the volleys lasted more than an hour. These finished, they were quiet; but soon after they fired an artillery shot which passed over D. Christovão's tent. Soon after, D. Christovão came to my tent, and begged me as a kindness to call the two captains, whom he had dispossessed of their captaincies, to reconcile him with them. I called them, they came; he

---

[1] Jorge Dabreu was the second personage in D. Rodrigo de Lima's embassy. He was not with this force. Dioga da Silva is not mentioned by others.

asked their pardon and restored to them their captaincies, and they all remained very friendly. He then sent for the other captains, to hold council with them as to what should be done. They told him it would be well to attack the Moors by night; because, when two parties are not equal in strength, the weaker must of necessity use stratagem, and this was one of the best stratagems we could employ, because it is not the Turks' custom to fight at night, so much so that they do not dare even to go outside their tents. Besides, we should then attack them unexpectedly and unprepared, and we should rout them before they had settled what to do; and that to confuse them more we should attack them from two sides. This advice did not please D. Christovão, as changeable fortune meant to show us her other face, and God intended to put an end to the sensualities which should not be remembered of Christian men at such time. D. Christovão said that he meant to give the enemies battle by day, lest they should think he feared them, and that he would dispose the field as follows. That he would descend to the Turks' level, and would order the Abyssinians to make a battery at the foot of the slope to mount artillery, which they could use as a refuge[1] when necessary. Lest the enemy should occupy three hillocks there, he placed ten men on each of them as a guard. This disposition was approved by none, and we all spoke against it; but, as our sins deserved it, his prevailed, and the captains said to him, that as he willed it they would follow him with their weapons to the death, so that he could not tell them that they opposed through fear.

---

[1] *Se farião fortes.*

CHAPTER XX.

Of the disastrous Battle in which the Christians were Defeated.

ON the following day, at early dawn, all went down the hill; but before they could get anything into order (as the disaster must have some beginning), one of our horses accidentally broke loose, and galloped towards the Moors' camp. At this some Moors came out to capture it, our men ran to rescue it, and in this way the battle began, without any order or any arrangement. This battle lasted a long time, and in it many Moors and Turks died. Some of our men died also; among them D. Garcia de Noronha[1] and two other fidalgos, fighting like good cavaliers. The thirty men who guarded the three hillocks were evilly treated by the enemy, who took positions in the thickets, and did them much harm thence by shots without being themselves seen; they killed some, and drove the rest from the hillocks. D. Christovão, seeing that his men were faring badly, sent to tell me to take the artillery to an elevation near by, where we were to fortify and defend ourselves, and this was done. Meanwhile the battle continually grew more disastrous to our side, and many fled, throwing away their weapons. Francisco Cordoso and Lopo Dalmansa met two Turks on horseback, who, seeing them without arms took no account of them; and they in passing seized them and pulled them from their saddles, and killed the Turks with their own swords, and mounting their horses fled.[2] The ensign of D. Christovão fought by the royal banner like a brave cavalier; in its defence he

---

[1] See note to chap. iii, p. 132, above.

[2] This anecdote is dragged in pointlessly here. For its proper connection, see chap. xx of Castanhoso, p. 70, above.

killed some of the enemy, and carried himself so valiantly that they dared not approach him. He defended himself like this, until wearied he could do no more, and they killed him. D. Christovão was wounded by an arquebus shot between the bones of his arm; but although he suffered great pain he did not leave the battle-field until very late, when he was almost alone; then he retired to the top of the hill, with some few who were with him. Before he retired, I, seeing the destruction of our people, told the Queen she should mount and go to the hill; and, because, not to abandon some women who had nothing to ride, she was unwilling to do this, I forcibly made her and one of her sisters-in-law mount, and sent them on in front, and took her daughter up behind me. A nurse of the Queen's, a very virtuous woman with two daughters, and certain other women, took a barrel of powder, and saying, God would never wish us to fall into the hands of the infidels, entered a tent with it, lighted it, and blew themselves up. The same did fifteen or sixteen men, who had been badly wounded in the battle and could not travel. When I saw such a sight of woe, which caused in me great grief, I could wait to see no more, as I could remedy nothing by watching it; I went with the little one I had behind me to her mother, who by this time thought her lost, and when she saw her gave great thanks to the Lord God who preserves and gives life to whomsoever He wishes, and whomsoever He pleases takes to Himself. Our people who had lost their way joined us on the road, and we hoped for the coming of D. Christovão; but seeing that he came not, and that it was already late and the sun nearly set, we withdrew still a little more into the hill, and there made another halt, awaiting more people and D. Christovão, regarding whom the Queen was very vexed, and we were all sorrowful that he did not come, fearing that he might be dead or captive. While we were dreading this, he came on a horse given him by a Farte Captain,[1] on which, through the goodness of God, and by the intercession of Our Lady, to whom we had all commended him, he had escaped. He came wounded, as I have said above, in one arm, suffering great agony from the wound, which seemed to have the arquebus bullet still in it. The Queen asked me to dress it with a little balm she had, to lessen the pain, and for this purpose drew off the cloth she wore on her head, and tore it, and with it bound his arm. But he got no relief, as he remembered his loss and dishonour rather than the pain of his wound; he said it were better for him to have died than to lose the banner of his King; and as it was in his enemies' power he wished no longer to live. I told him not to be so vexed, as, if he lived and was cured, he would, if it were the will of God, recover what he had lost that day; we saw this happen every day in matters of war: now conquerors, now conquered; things depending on fortune could not remain always unchanged; great and valorous captains and princes had been conquered, and, surviving, had themselves recovered what they had lost; that greatness of mind and intelligence are proved in adversity; finally, that he should remember the victories that God had given him, and thank Him and not go to extremes because of the chastisement He had given us for our sins. As to the banner, in that country they did not take much account of it; that we would at once set to work to make a similar one, if we had men to fight and a captain to lead them; it is men who are the true banner, not the mere sign they carry before them, which may be of wood, or straw, or of anything else of even less value.[2]

---

[1] Farte should be Jarte. Castanhoso, in his chap. xii, p. 39, above, mentions the submission of the Captain of Jarte, or Wajárat, who presented D. Christovão with four fine horses.

[2] See chap. xii, p. 148, above, where Bermudez says that the royal banner had been entrusted to him.

CHAPTER XXI.

Of how D. Christovão hid in a Thicket.

THE Asmacharobel and Tigremaquão said to him: "Sir, we are not safe here, for we are defeated, wounded, and without weapons, and should our enemies come we have not wherewith to defend ourselves; let us go on while it is yet night to a river in front of us, where there is a drawbridge;[1] there we will rest, because, should the enemy come we will take away the bridge, and they cannot cross to us." We made him mount, and went on; we crossed two rivers in haste, so deep that the water was breast high for the footmen. On the way D. Christovão lost the pain in his arm; but he wept for the King's banner that remained in the hands of the Moors, and wanted to halt at every step. I travelled beside him, consoling him, and urging him to let us continue on. We went till we reached the river with the drawbridge, of which they had told us, which held so much water that it could only be crossed by that bridge. Here D. Christovão told me that he would not cross the bridge, but that he would remain on that side of the river; he straight called his own men, ordering them to dismount him. They dismounted him, and prepared a couch for him, on which he threw himself. He called me, and asked me to confess him. After the confession he said that he was determined to remain there; I said that I could not allow it, and I ordered those present to take up the couch and to carry him on it as he was. He shouted, and said he would kill himself if they carried him thence. When I saw his determination I would also remain with him; but he replied

---

[1] It would have been of considerable interest had the name of this river with a drawbridge been given. In Abyssinia bridges are unknown, except two or three which the Portuguese built, some years after this date.

that I should not, as it was necessary for the governance of those people, lest they should be entirely lost, and with them all that country ; that I should leave with him a little balm to dress his wound, and that his chamber servant, his secretary, and three other Portuguese should remain with him. With these he desired to lie concealed in a thicket hard by, where he wished to stay. I could never understand why he wanted to stay.[1] Thence I went to the Queen, and asked her to mount and cross to the other side of the bridge, as morning had broken and our enemies would be on us. She replied that certainly she could not do this, nor would she leave D. Christovão abandoned there. But I begged her to mount, saying, that not only she, but also her son and all his kingdom would be lost if we remained there. On this the Queen mounted, weeping, and showing as much grief as she would for her own son, if he had been left behind. We ordered all the people and the baggage to cross as speedily as possible : before we crossed we heard the rumour of men and the tramp of horses, so that we hurried our crossing, and removed the bridge behind us. By this time it was already dawn, and beginning the ascent of the opposite slope we saw many Moors go to where D. Christovão was. When the Queen saw them she was greatly afraid, saying that we could not escape. Her followers told her to have no fear, as she was already in her own country. Anyhow, we pressed on as quickly as we could, to lose sight of them, and marched all that day, crossing many hills and rivers with great labour, and in a heat that burned us. By those streams there was much cassia and many tamarind trees, of which our people eat, as we had no supplies with us. At length we reached a large river, where the people caught some fish, which they

---

[1] The story is equally unintelligible now. Castanhoso's explanation, that the rout was so complete that in the confusion the Portuguese got separated, seems the probable truth.

eat; meanwhile a captain of that land came with supplies, of which he brought many. Here we began to rest, for we were now in a safe country.

CHAPTER XXII.

Of how the Patriarch selected another Captain for the Portuguese.

WE learned here that forty Portuguese were missing.[1] To those who remained, who were rather over three hundred, I made a speech, and said that they could see how necessary it was to give them a Captain to lead them and to fight before them, as we could not tell what had happened to D. Christovão, who had remained behind; that I begged them all to agree to him whom I should nominate, and to obey with good will the Captain whom I should name to them; as I should endeavour to select a man who would give a good account of himself. They replied that I should appoint whom I pleased; as they would consider the nomination valid, and would obey him whom I should choose and select. I at once declared that I made one Affonso Caldeira, a native of Coimbra, a discreet and valorous cavalier, their commander.[2] All received him willingly, save a few fidalgos, who thought that being of nobler blood that office belonged rather to them. These murmured to some extent against what I had done; but noble and loyal as they were, did not refuse to obey him. Such offices should not indeed be given to men so much for the nobility of their blood and breeding, as for their

---

[1] I have commented on this remarkable statement elsewhere.

[2] As elsewhere pointed out, Couto says that this was the man left by D. Christovão to bring on the spoil captured on the Jews' hill. Bermudez does not state what had become of Pero Borges, whose appointment he considered so important in chap. x, p. 144, above.

special personal qualities: these are, force of character, personal courage, experience in the actual exercise of arms, intelligence and judgment to understand, lead, and govern. The Captain whom I selected possessed these and the other qualities necessary for his office. I appointed also a sergeant and a magistrate to look after the soldiers, and see they did no wrong to the people of the country, nor among themselves, the one to the other. I asked Asmacharobel to send Miguel de Castanhoso, Antonio Pereira, and other wounded men to his rock to cure them.[1] I also commended them to the Queen, who treated them better even than we asked her; for she was a noble woman and a Christian. We camped on a plain among the hills, where the country people brought us a store of supplies; thence, some days later, we saw a distant smoke, which the country captains fancied might be that of the followers of the King of Zeila, and they said it would be well to discover what it was. We sent ninety horse of the country and five Portuguese matchlockmen.

CHAPTER XXIII.

In which is related the Confinement and Death of D. Christovão.

AFTER these had started there escaped to us João Gonçalvez[2] and Alvaro Dinis, who had remained with D. Christovão; from them the Queen enquired what had happened to D. Christovão. They replied that he was in

---

[1] This arrangement was made some time before the defeat. Castanhoso was wounded in the fighting in April in Tigré, and it was then natural (Castanhoso, chap. xvi, p. 53, above).

[2] João Gonçalvez was interpreter in D. Rodrigo de Lima's embassy. I do not find his name in this expedition.

the power of the Moors, at which we were all grieved, and she spoke words of the great sorrow she felt. Then they told us that, while they lay hid in the thicket which they had entered, there came a woman, who, flying before the Moors, ran into the same thicket, and the Moors following her found D. Christovão; they asked him who he was, and he replied that he was D. Christovão. It is hardly credible how pleased they were at this; they summoned a eunuch who had been ours, and who was there, and asked him if that were D. Christovão, and if he knew him well. He replied that it was he without doubt, for he knew him very well. They then asked him what had become of the Patriarch, and he said that he had gone on with the Queen, at which they were vexed. Thence they returned with him to the camp, where they had defeated us, and presented him to the King, who also was delighted to see him. After asking him certain things, he said to him that if he would turn Moor he would honour him greatly. D. Christovão replied sneeringly that he was the servant of Jesus Christ, whom he would not change for a lying dog. The King, hearing his reply, ordered him to be buffeted and his beard to be plucked, and had him taken away. Four days later he ordered him to be brought before him again, and with a pleasant face told him not to be afraid, as he promised him, and swore by Mafamede and his *alcorão* that, if he would do what he was about to say, that he would give him his liberty and a ship to his country. This was that he should write to the Portuguese, his companions, telling them to leave the Kings of the Preste John, and return to their own country: he promised to do this. He wrote a letter according to the Moor's pleasure. This he sent to the above-mentioned eunuch, to carefully overlook what D. Christovão had written, which he did. For this reason D. Christovão wrote what the Moor told him, and nothing else, but by his signature he put two calthrops, by which he meant "Look out what you do."[1] The Goranha sent this letter to our camp by two of his Moors, who gave it into my hand. I had it read by my Vicar-General, Fr. Diogo da Trinidade, and after it was read I took it to the Queen, the Captain Affonso Caldeira accompanying me. When the Queen saw the letter she was as one dead, thinking that D. Christovão had written that letter meaning it, and that it would cause some commotion among the Portuguese, in whom, after God, she had confidence that her kingdoms would be restored to her; and she marvelled much at that action of D. Christovão. But after we had pointed out to her the warning of the calthrops near his signature, she was pleased, and took it in good part. And all praised him greatly, saying it could not have been possible for so discreet a man, and so good a Christian, to commit a deed so evil as that and so perilous; for there could have been no certainty that the Moor would have kept faith with him, more especially remembering the warning of the treachery which his captain had shewn to the sixty men whom he killed near Massowa. Finally, the Commander, Affonso Caldeira, replied to D. Christovão in his own name, and for all his Portuguese companions, that they thanked King Goranha very much for his good will, but that they would not accept that kindness from him, nor did they expect to have any need of it; on the contrary, that they hoped, with the help of Jesus Christ, their God, to complete the enterprise on which the King of Portugal, their master, had sent them, which was either to capture or kill him, and to deliver from his tyranny the kingdom of the Preste John. When D. Christovão received this letter he took it to the Moor, and the Moor showed him no less favour because of it, as he thought that D. Christovão had

---

[1] It is pleasant to remember that D. Christovão's right arm had been broken above the elbow less than a week before, and that this story must be a fiction.

written faithfully to the Portuguese what he had told him to write, and he hoped yet to be able by his means to do somewhat of that he desired. As D. Christovão had been cured quickly by the balsam that I had left with him, he enquired from him with what he had cured himself, and he replied that he knew how to make a certain medicine by which wounds were quickly healed; then the Moor asked him to cure with it his commander, who was badly wounded, and he cured him with such medicines that that dog only survived three days. For this the Moor ordered him many whippings and blows. D. Christovão said to him that he had no reason to do him an injury, as he had done the best he knew, and that what he had done was the action of a man without reason or law. At this the Moor was still more angry with him, and told him he would order him to be killed. D. Christovão replied that the worst he could do would be to kill his body; that as for his soul, God alone had power over it, and that he was very certain that Jesus Christ, the true God, would receive his into eternal life. For these and other things of the like nature that D. Christovão said, the Moor ordered them to take him to the place where the other Portuguese died, and there cut off his head; which head of D. Christovão that King sent as a present to the Governor of Cairo; one quarter of his body he sent to Jedda, another to Aden, and a leg to the Pasha of Zebid, who had sent him the help mentioned above. He did this to show the great success he had achieved in the victory, and because he knew that the recipients would be very pleased. He also sent those trophies to give credit to the report: without them they would with difficulty have believed it; so much in that country do they consider the defeat of a few Portuguese. The rest of the body of D. Christovão remained where he was slain, and thence some religious persons, who lived hard by, took it to their monastery. They hold him in great veneration with the reputation of a saint, for then, and frequently subsequently, God showed through evident miracles that his labours were approved and meritorious before the Divine Majesty, his death precious, and his soul in glory. Directly they cut off his head, God worked a great and manifest miracle through it, which was, that in the place where they slew him a fountain of running water gushed out, which had never been seen before: its water, through the goodness and power of God, gives sight to the blind, and cures those ill of other diseases. It appears that this miracle is like the one that God did in Rome for His Apostle St. Paul. The remains of the body of D. Christovão smell sweetly, giving forth so delightful an odour, that it seems rather of heaven than of earth. In the place where he and the other Christians suffered, those neighbouring religious men saw on many nights torches of fire, lighted with great and joyful glory.

CHAPTER XXIV.

Of how the King of Zeila went to the Kingdom of Dembia, and the Preste's Vassals submitted to the Queen; and of how King Gradeus[1] came to the Camp.

FROM here the Moorish King went to a kingdom called Dembia, through which the river Nile flows and makes a lake thirty leagues long by five and a-half broad.[2] There are many islands in the lake, most of them inhabited by religious persons of good conduct, and obedient to the Roman Church. The scouts we had sent out to enquire

---

[1] By this name Bermudez means Galâwdêwos.

[2] In chapter lii, p. 243, below, the same lake is twenty leagues broad. So incorrect is Bermudez as to the island monks being followers of the Latin Church, that to this day, owing to the fanaticism of the monks, access to the chief island, Dak or Dek, is almost impossible to any one not professing the Abyssinian form of Christianity (Basset, *Histoire*, p. 463 *n.*).

about the smoke returned, and told us that a large body of people were approaching, but that they could not discover who they were. We therefore prepared to defend ourselves, should it be necessary. While uncertain, we saw many people, both horse and foot, coming; and when they arrived near, we saw two horsemen advance as if they bore some message. These, before they reached us, got off their horses, threw off their chief garments and their weapons, and thus drew near us on foot, unclothed and unarmed. The Captain, Affonso Caldeira, went to them, and asked who they were. One of them replied that he was Asmache (Governor) of Doaro, and was called Obitocō, which means D. George, and the other Asmache (Governor) of Guidimi; that they were vassals of the King Gradeus, and that they came to assist him with these men and with their own persons. They had two banners, with one hundred and fifty horse and one thousand foot. The Captain took them to the Queen, who received them kindly, and asked them whence they came. They replied that they came from the Goranha's camp, and that when the Moor started for Dembia they had left him at the place where he had killed D. Christovão. The Queen asked them concerning D. Christovão's death, and they related it in the manner we had already heard. When we knew with certainty of D. Christovão's death, the Queen and I sent orders to have his obsequies, and those of all the others generally who had died in the war, performed in all the monasteries of the district. As the Queen's camp increased with the people who flocked to her, supplies began to fail, and we were compelled to change to another place. We went to the Jews' hill, where the country is safe and well supplied; it is surrounded by crags and difficult approaches. The army marched with imperial pomp, preceded by trumpets and kettledrums, with which we encouraged our own men and struck terror into the enemy. To induce the people to join us, Affonso Caldeira suggested to the Queen that she should proclaim a general pardon in all the land for those who should return to their allegiance of their own free will. This made many come in. When we reached the skirt of the Jews' hill, the Captain of it came to us with supplies and refreshments, and asked the Queen to ascend the hill, because she could not be more secure in any other part of that district than in that hill, for it has but one approach, and that could be easily guarded and defended from the enemy if he came. Further, that that territory belonged to the Queen, and that the tribute from it alone was sufficient to maintain the army for five or six months. The Jew Captain asked to be baptized,[1] and when we got to the hill, and pitched our camp, I baptized him, his wife, and his sons. The Captain, Affonso Caldeira, was his godfather, and we gave him the name D. Christovão. From here Affonso Caldeira, with ninety Portuguese and some men of the country, raided certain places that were held for the Moor in that district; they slew many people, burned the villages, and brought in many cattle. Seeing this, two old and honourable men came to beg mercy of the Queen, in the name of all the people, saying that they were hers and Christians, and that by compulsion they had submitted and paid tribute to the Moor; and also of necessity, as there was no one to defend them from the Jews of the hill, who were but bad neighbours; that now her highness should pardon them, and not complete their destruction, for they promised to be thenceforward obedient and loyal. The Queen easily pardoned them, for she was by nature merciful and discreet, and knew that it was the time for granting pardon. She gave them a safe-conduct for themselves and for their neighbours,

---

[1] Compare Castanhoso, chap. xvii, p. 59, above.

and told them to depart in peace. At this time, Ayres Diz returned, whom D. Christovão had sent to visit the King of the Preste, son of Onadinguel and of this Queen, Orita Aureata, and the son was named Gradeos. This last had not yet joined the camp, for he was very young,[1] and there was the danger that some hurt might befall him, and that if we were destroyed the kingdom might be lost also. Some said that he did not come because of his dread of D. Christovão, and that, for this reason, when he heard of his death, he determined to join us. Ayres Diz brought the message that the King would be with us two months hence. When the two months had nearly expired we left the hill of the Jews, and marched to other hills in another district. Eight days later, the King joined us, accompanied by fifty horsemen and many mules. All the captains, with the Portuguese and country troops, went to receive him a short way out of the camp, and escorted him back to it. After reaching the camp he came direct to my tent, and dismounted to receive my blessing. I came out to the door of my tent to meet him, which he esteemed highly; for in that country they hold the Patriarch in the same estimation in which we hold the Pope.[2] Then he visited the Queen, his mother, and returned. He wore mourning three days for D. Christovão. His tent was pitched in the centre of the camp. His tent was sixty cubits square, the length and breadth the same, surrounded with silk curtains.

CHAPTER XXV.
Of a Speech the Patriarch made to the Portuguese.

A FEW days later, before arranging anything else, I summoned to my tent the Captain Affonso Caldeira, the other captains, and the honourable persons of the Portuguese

---

[1] Incorrect; his age was then twenty.   [2] Cf. p. 181, below.

army, and said to them: "Most beloved sons and most Christian Portuguese, I well remember that in days past, being in Debarua, some of your excellencies,[1] moved by laudable zeal, wondered at certain ceremonies and rites which the people of this country use differently from the Roman customs, which are practised in Portugal, and said that the Kings and people of this country do not obey the High Roman Pontiff, vicar-general of Jesus Christ, and His representative; further, they said of me, that I agreed with them, and had deceived the King of Portugal, who would not have sent you here to help these Kings, if he had known they were not faithful Christians in submission to the High Pontiff. As to the rites they use, now is not the time to speak of them, both because of the distraction of the fighting in which we must engage, as also because it is a business requiring a long period, for it is impossible in a short time to change customs to which they have been habituated during many years and long ages; the very Apostles themselves could not do it in their time, nor did they at once uproot from people's hearts all their superstitions; but they meanwhile dissimulated as to some, of which a few endure until now. A whole people cannot be cleansed from all the tares the devil sows, just as you cannot weed a field of standing corn of all the plants and thorns that grow in it; for if we pulled up the whole we should pull up the wheat with the weeds, as Jesus Christ says in the gospel. It is just now sufficient to carry the main point, which is to get their obedience and submission to the Holy Mother Church; this is the source of all the rest, and from it follow all other circumstances. This has its foundation in the head, that is the King. Should the King obey, all the others will follow him, either of their own free will, or else easily moved by the example of their superiors, and our teaching will, with the grace of the

---

[1] *caridades.*

Holy Ghost, assist us. In days past I promised D. Christovão, before your excellencies, to cause this King to submit to the Holy Father. I promised this, trusting in the grace and goodness of God to help me. I also beg your excellencies to help me by your prayers, and by doing what I direct when the time comes. Now let us all go to the King's tent, to speak with him in this business."

CHAPTER XXVI.

Of the Speech the Patriarch made to the King Gradeus, asking him to obey the Pope as his father did, and of the King's reply.

WHEN we arrived at the King's tent I found him with his mother, which pleased me much, as I knew she would make a good third. He received me with much honour and welcome. Seeing that the opportunity was suitable for my intention, I said to him these words: "Much beloved son in Jesus Christ, you are aware that the most Christian King your father, now in glory, asked me to go to Rome, for himself and for myself, to give submission to the High Pontiff: should you by reason of your youth not remember this, you may see here a letter signed by him which he gave me,[1] that the High Pontiff might believe me, and know that what I said on his behalf was correct; which was, as I say, that your father recognised him as the successor of St. Peter, chief of the apostles of Christ, and Vicar of His universal Church, in whatever part of the world it may be established; and that he considered himself subordinate to him, with all his kingdoms and lordships, as were all the faithful and orthodox Christian Kings. He,

---

[1] This appears to dispose of Bermudez' own statement in chap. lviii, p. 257, below, that he had no proofs, as he had lost all his papers in the rout of D. Christovão.

your father, has passed from the present life, and you by the grace of God have inherited from him the crown and governance of these kingdoms, which is also a reason that you should inherit from him his intelligence, virtues, and fear of God. To be a good servant of God you must maintain His true faith, and keep His religion and law. He requires that all His should live in one love and desire, and make one body in faith and religion; and that there should be no divisions among His people, just as He is sole God and Head of His Church. Therefore, conforming yourself with the will and rule of God, and imitating the virtue and intelligence of your father, you should submit yourself to the Holy Father the Roman Pontiff, as thus you will do what God orders, and will have for friends, brothers, and helpers in your necessities, the King of Portugal and all the other Kings, his brothers and friends." To which he, not considering what he was saying, like a young boy, replied as follows: "You are not our father, nor a prelate, but Patriarch of the Franks, and you are an Arian, for you have four Gods, and you are not in future to call yourself my father." I turned and told him he lied, for I was not an Arian, and had not four Gods; and that as he would not obey the Holy Father, I held him to be excommunicate, and accursed; and that I would no longer be with him, or speak to him; and with that I got up to go. He replied that I was excommunicated, not he.

CHAPTER XXVII.
Of how the Patriarch told the Portuguese what had passed with King Gradeus.

WITHOUT saying more to him, I went thence to the Portuguese, who were outside the tent, and told them what had passed, and that the King would not obey the Roman

Church, but was a heretic like Nestor and Dioscero; that therefore I ordered them by virtue of their obedience, and under pain of excommunication by me, and on behalf of the King of Portugal, our lord, whose commission I held for this, I directed them, under pain of treason, in no way to obey that King, or any other of his faction, or do anything whatever to help him. Affonso Caldeira and all the others said that their fathers and grandfathers were never rebels to the Roman Church, or their King, nor would they be; that therefore I had no need to excommunicate them; that I should remove that, as without it they would do all I ordered like obedient sons. They all accompanied me thence to my tent, and then returned to their lodgings.

CHAPTER XXVIII.

Of how the King Gradeus sent a Present to the Portuguese, who would not accept it.

SOON after, the King sent one of his captains to carry three thousand ounces of gold to the Portuguese to divide among themselves, and an ewer exceeding rich for the Captain: telling them that he sent them that present in the expectation of doing them still greater kindnesses, and that he begged them not to leave him, but to help him against his enemies, as they had hitherto done. They replied that at that time they could not accept his favours, because of the differences between him and me; as to the rest of what he said, they could only reply that in all they would act as I ordered them.

CHAPTER XXIX.

Of the counsel King Gradeus followed, and of how he submitted to the Pope.

ON this reply, they took counsel, and arranged that the Queen, with an Archbishop I had made, and all his captains, should come to my tent to beg my pardon, and to ask me to visit the King, as he desired to do all I directed, and submit himself to the Pope. The Queen came to me, and begged me, by the death and passion of Jesus Christ, to take no notice of the ignorance of her son, who was a boy, and it was not well that, considering his extreme youth, he should be utterly condemned; nor should we give the Moors the pleasure they must receive from such a quarrel. She begged me that, in honour of the virginity of Our Lady, virgin before the birth, in the birth, and after the birth, to accompany her to the tent of her son, who had deeply repented of what he had said to me, who wished to ask my pardon, and obey me in all things. I replied that I would not quit where I was, save when on the way to Portugal, with the Portuguese, my sons and companions. At that reply, she threw herself on her knees before me, weeping, and said she required me in the name of God not to do that, but to go with her, as all would be as I wished it. Moved by pity, I went with her, and reaching the King's tent, he came out to receive us, and, with great humility, took my hand and kissed it, asking my pardon for what he had said. We all three sat down, and he said he was content to obey the High Pontiff, and that for this the submission that his father had given me was sufficient. But I replied that it was not enough; that he in particular must give me for himself that submission; for it was the custom in our countries, that each King at the commencement of his reign sent envoys to make his particular submission to the Pope, wherever he might be; and that as he did not send to Rome, as his father had done, that he should make it to me in the name of the Pope, as I had a commission from His Holiness to receive it. And that, further, he must draw up a public document, signed and sealed in his name, and in that of all his kingdoms and lordships, confessing that the true faith is this: that the Church of God is one only, and that its head the Vicar of Jesus Christ also is one only in all the world; through whom the power and jurisdiction of Jesus Christ flows to the other prelates and Christian princes. This document one of the chief men of his kingdom must read, seated aloft in a chair or in some high place, in a loud and clear voice, before all the people there with him. He did this, and ordered it to be carried out with solemn pomp and at the sound of trumpets.

CHAPTER XXX.

Of the Death of the Captain Affonso Caldeira, and of how Ayres Diz was made Captain.

A FEW days after this had been done, the Captain, Affonso Caldeira, while galloping a horse, fell from it, and some days later died from the accident. After the death of Affonso Caldeira, I took counsel with some of the chiefs of the Portuguese company; and it appeared to us right to elect as Captain, Ayres Diz, a discreet man and a good cavalier, who had given an excellent account of himself in some important affairs that had been entrusted to him. Especially as King Gradeus also asked this of me, I sent for him at once, and enquired whether he would take that office. He accepted it, and promised to administer it as well as his knowledge and strength permitted. There were not wanting those who grumbled at this, especially Miguel de Castanhoso, who wanted to be himself Captain, and said, how did it happen that in this world there was even one mulatto who was a Captain over Portuguese? But I took no notice of this, as it is common enough for soldiers to grumble.[1]

CHAPTER XXXI.

Of how the Patriarch, with the Portuguese and some Abyssinians, separated from the King, and of how afterwards he sent the Portuguese to the King, and he and the Abyssinians went to where the Goranha was; and of how he again sent for Ayres Diz.

A FEW days later, the King sent for me to tell me that he wished to go to his own country with his people, as we could not all stay here together, and that he begged me to remain with his mother. I made no reply, for I knew he wanted to fly;[2] but I sent to the Portuguese to get ready, and we all marched thence to some hills, where were plains of grass and good pasture ground for our horses, mules, and bullocks, and where supplies for ourselves were plentiful. Still, as that was the Goranha's country, we were constantly vigilant, and moved from one place to another, halting nowhere. Some of the country people also who were with us accompanied us. The King sent the Azaige de galan[3] after us, who, with reverence and politeness, said to me that the King, my son, sent to ask me to allow Ayres Diz, the Captain, with all the Portuguese, to

---

[1] Comment has been already made on this appointment. It might have been made by Galâwdêwos, but hardly by a Portuguese.

[2] No object is to be gained by commenting on the fanciful story told in these chapters of the final battle, and the events that led up to it.

[3] For this person, see Castanhoso, chap. xxvi, p. 93, *n.*, above.

return to him, as the service of God required it. I replied, Yes, I would do it with pleasure; and in fact I at once told Ayres Diz to return to the King with all his people. Ayres Diz asked me, how he could abandon me in the infidel's country, still more, knowing that the King sent for him to leave him with the Queen and fly. I told him that for this reason it would be well for him to go, as he could detain him and not allow him to fly until I sent a message, but to detain him with every courtesy and politeness. There remained with me six captains of the country, with two hundred horse, and of footmen one thousand bucklermen, five hundred archers, and fifty men with harpoons with barbs,[1] all very dextrous with their weapons. Each horseman carried three javelins. I found myself with all these people at the skirt of the hill where the Goranha was, and I had my tent pitched close to the hill, and hard by the rest of the camp, with shouting and feasting, and the sound of trumpets and kettledrums, as is the custom in armies. The horsemen skirmished, and the footmen rejoiced and said, "We will all die for the faith of the Son of God." When the camp was pitched I collected the captains, and other honourable persons belonging to the army, and enquired from them what they thought we ought to do; they said to me that we ought to ascend the hill, and take possession of it before the Goranha attacked us. It did not seem to me good counsel for all to climb the hill, as we did not know the arrangements there, nor how the Goranha had provided the place, nor if there were any garrison on it, because he was near at hand, and this was the country in which he most trusted, because it was defensible by its natural formation. Therefore, before we all ascended, I sent five horsemen, one hundred and twenty bucklermen, and thirty archers, to reconnoitre the ground. While ascend-

---

[1] *Fisgas com seus ganchos.*

ing they found three horsemen and some foot, who guarded the approach to the hill and defended it, fighting with our men as long as their strength held out. They resisted so long that they slew of ours four horsemen and some foot; ours slew some of their peons, the others fled. When our men had captured the hill they went on to a place near by, where they found no people, but some supplies, especially many pitchers of honey wine. Two of the men drank this carelessly and died suddenly, because, in order to kill our people, the Moors had poisoned it and left it there. When our people saw the two men dead, they drank no more wine, but broke the pitchers and spilt the wine, thence they returned. Behind them came many women and children weeping, in great excitement, flying for fear of the Moor, who they said had started in search of us. Hearing this news, I sent two horsemen at once to the King, to tell him to advance quickly, to obtain possession of that country before the Moor could come, as I was just starting to anticipate the Moor and to take the passes by which he must march. I sent a Portuguese to tell the Captain Ayres Diz that I was in danger of meeting the Moor, and to come to me at once. The King feared the arrangement,[1] and did not wish to come; but Ayres Diz told him that it did not look, and was not in fact well, that the Portuguese should go on giving their lives to defend him and recover his country for him, and for him to fly and leave them. Still, if he would go, good luck go with him, for they were going to help the Patriarch, and they would leave his country: he started without him. After Ayres Diz and the Portuguese had gone, the King thought it right to follow them, and he marched so quickly that he caught them up before nightfall. They all together marched so far that night that they joined our camp before morning.

---

[1] *Caminho.*

CHAPTER XXXII.

Of how the Christians climbed the Hill of St. Paul.

WITH the dawn we left those who came wearied, and with the people I had before, I began to climb the hill before the Moor came, because to occupy that hill was more than half the victory. We ascended by paths so narrow, that we could only go two abreast, and over rocks and crags so steep that any who fell would be dashed to a thousand pieces. With the help of God we finished the climb, and reached a monastery of friars there is on the hill, which is dedicated to St. Paul. The friars came out to receive us in procession, with cross on high, and incensing with censers, and took us to the church to pray and thank God for the help He had sent them. After the prayer, the captains pitched their camp and rested. When the King heard that we had reached the summit, he ordered his own people to remain in the rear, and came on in advance with the Portuguese, marching under the banner of the King of Portugal and leaving his own behind. He got to the top an hour before sunset, and it was night before his people came, for it took the whole day to climb the hill, so difficult is the ascent. When the King found himself and his army on the top, he gave many thanks to Our Lord, as it appeared to him that the better part of the victory was already won, and more than all with safety to himself; as in truth it was, for that hill is like a wall that guarded the entry to the Goranha's territory. So great was his delight that, now he would call me father, now the King of Portugal, the Portuguese were his brothers; with other marks of his kindness.

CHAPTER XXXIII.

Of how the Christians on the Hill stood on their guard; of the Death of the Captain-General of the Abyssinians; and of the passion of the King Gradeus on his behalf; and of other things that happened at that time.

OUR Commander ordered guards to be stationed in the passes by which the enemy could enter the hill, and directed them to watch very carefully, and learn from which direction and how the enemy would attack us. Those in the camp did their devotions and chanted litanies, praying God to give us the victory, and asking Our Lady and all the saints to intercede with God on our behalf. Those of a religious life in the monasteries, and the people in their villages,[1] did the same. There came now to join us from the provinces and districts in our rear, so many people that they were innumerable. From the top of the hill we saw the Moors of the Goranha's army marching and skirmishing in the plains beyond the hill, and we heard them say: "Before four days are past you will all be dead; your King a eunuch guarding the women of the King of Zeila; and as for the Patriarch you have brought here, we shall run a fire-hardened stake up his fundament, through his neck, and out at the top of his head." The Abyssinian Captain-General asked the royal permission to take some men and fight those Moors; and getting it, confessed himself, and went down the hill with four hundred horsemen. After killing several Moors, he advanced so far in front of his men that the enemy surrounded him, and he being very wearied and wounded, captured him. Before killing him, they cut off his privy parts entire, for such is their custom, and then killed him. The King felt so deeply the death of this captain that he publicly wept and tore his hair;

---

[1] *As gentes nos seus pouos.*

nay, even pulled the crown from his head and dashed it on the ground. So much were his wits disordered with grief, that he said he desired to go at once personally and avenge his death. His two brothers-in-law, hearing his mad resolve, came to me and begged me to turn him from that purpose and prevent his going, as it was neither to the service of God nor for his own welfare. As he was already starting on horseback in the direction of the enemies' camp, I ordered Ayres Diz to dismount and catch hold of the King's horse by the bridle. I went to him, and begged him to return to the camp and not to go in search of death. He returned against his will, and when he reached the camp shut himself up in his tent. I, too, went with him to console him and advise him, and with the help of God brought him to forget that passion, bringing to his memory the times in which he lived and the necessity of arranging for the battle. On this he asked me what we should do to deal with so large a body of Moors as came against us, who without doubt were many without number: for the King of Zeila had collected all his power, with a great reinforcement of Turks, for this battle, in which he hoped to end the war; as in fact he did, but not in the way he meant, but with his own death, which God so ordered. I replied that I trusted in the goodness and power of God, to help us like the power He is; and that he should not fear the number of the Moors, for when God so wished it He did not reckon whether they were many or few. I told him to direct his captains to prepare everything for the fight. I went to the monastery of the religious men hard by, and begged them to make processions and perform other devotions, praying Our Lord to give us victory against His enemies. A bishop of that monastery, with his priests and other religious persons, went in those processions, as well as old men, women, and children, without number, calling out in a loud voice, Jesus Christ, Son of God, have pity on your people. The King also came when he heard there were processions, which I had arranged. Meanwhile, word was brought that the King of Zeila was at hand, and had pitched his camp at the bottom of the hill, as one who determined to ascend to the summit. King Gradeus hearing this, left me in the monastery and returned to his camp, where some of his followers told him that should he remain there it would be a great wonder if he escaped from his enemies' hands; that they therefore advised him to leave as secretly as possible, and take refuge in some safe place. He replied to those who said this to him that he would never do it, or leave his people, as the King of Zeila was there with his. The King of Zeila awaited the Turks who had not yet joined, and when they did come he fired off the artillery they brought, which was numerous, because, besides his own, they had those they had captured from us, and also two demi-culverins besides. King Gradeus, hearing the roar of the artillery, which echoed among the hills, was in such a panic that he determined to fly, as he had been previously advised.

CHAPTER XXXIV.

Of the Death of the King of Zeila, and of the Defeat of the Moors, and of certain other Things which followed.

THE Bernagaiz, understanding the King's determination, came hurriedly to call me from the monastery where I was, and, showing me many Abyssinian fighting men on the hill-tops, told me they were all doubtful; that if they found we suffered defeat, or knew that the King had fled, they would be all against us, and would destroy us. That, therefore, I must be present to restrain the King and encourage the people, and I must not appear to be absent through distrust. I at once left the monastery, and went with him to the camp. When the people on the hill-tops saw me they raised a great shout, and said: As the Abuna comes, the victory is ours. I arrived where the King was, and saluted him, and said: I trust in the mercy of God, who redeemed us by His precious blood, to give us the victory. Without delay I at once went to the Portuguese, to whom I said: Children, I commend you to Our Lord, act like the men you are. Then I told them to kneel and repeat each of them the *pater noster* five times; I did the same, in memory of the five chief wounds of Our Lord and Saviour, Jesus Christ. I granted to all plenary indulgence, and gave them God's blessing and my own.[1] I next told the Captain Ayres Diz to put Pero Deça in command of the Portuguese horse, of which there were twenty-five, he to be on foot with the rest. We began to march along the hill towards the enemy. When the King and his men saw us start, they were astonished at our great and resolute courage, and got on to a height whence the whole plain was visible, to see what we should do. The Moors, finding us approach, prepared to receive us. While we were marching down the slope, the Goranha, King of Zeila, came out in front of his men on a white horse, armed at all points, and with him two Turks, also on horseback, one on each side. When they had approached us to the distance of an arquebus shot, they all three turned aside in the same order, to give room to their own men to fight. On this, one Pero de Lião, who had been a servant of D. Christovão, a man of very small stature but a good matchlockman, and desirous of avenging the death of his lord, fired his arquebus at him, and brought him down from his horse dead. The same was done by other arquebusiers to the other two, his companions, also slaying them by firing their arquebuses at them. Some of the Moors, seeing their King dead, turned

---

[1] *Lançandolhe a bençam de Deos e a minha.*

back; others stopped these, so that they got involved and hindered the one the other, and neither fought nor fled. Our men, seeing their disorder and confusion, attacked them and slew many. At this moment the people of King Gradeus advanced, and the Moors and Turks took to flight, and abandoned the field and their camp. In it our men found great riches, and supplies, artillery, and other arms with munitions. We found belonging to the Turks, who had just come off a march, sacks of bread and cooked fowls, and others lay dead with the food in their mouths. Their purses were full of money, of the pay they had lately received. We captured here the son of the King of Zeila; the Queen took refuge in the province called Dagua. They had overrun a considerable part of Dembia, whence they had brought many silks, cloaks, Ormuz veils, and valuable carpets. King Gradeus, seeing the great and miraculous victory which God had given him, ordered a very wealthy monastery to be built on the site of the battle, in memory of the secret[1] of Our Lord Jesus Christ. As it is not right to pass unnoticed the low trick of a certain Abyssinian, who desired to gain credit for what he had not done, and benefit by another's labours, I will tell what he did. A Captain of King Gradeus, who saw the death of the King of Zeila, went to him and cut off his head; this he took to present to his King, saying that he had killed him, in order that the King might give him the reward he would merit, which was great, as that death was the main cause after God of the victory, and of the restoration of those kingdoms. The King was pleased to learn who slew his enemy, and thanked him much, and besides made him Commander of all his kingdoms. But the Captain Ayres Diz, who knew the truth, and was present when the Abyssinian brought the head, and further knew that Pero

---

[1] *segredo.*

de Lião had kept the left ear of the Moorish King, which he had cut off when he slew him, said to the King, "Sire, let your highness order the examination of that head: how many ears has it?" They looked, and found only one. Said Ayres Diz: "The missing one has been kept by a better cavalier than this, for he slew him and cut it off when you were all watching from the hill what we were doing, and this man was advising your flight." He forthwith sent for Pero de Lião to bring the Moor king's ear. He came, and showed the ear, which was clearly the sister of the other, and taken from that very place according to the slash by which it was cut off. "Further," said Pero de Lião, "let the Abyssinian show the weapon wherewith he killed him, and tell where he wounded him;" to which he made no reply. "Then," said Pero de Lião, "let them examine the corpse, and they will find that he was killed by an arquebus shot; the use of that weapon the Abyssinian does not understand." They went to see, and it was the truth. With this the King and all his were ashamed, and his captain much railed at.

CHAPTER XXXV.

Of a Quarrel among the Portuguese, as to who should be Captain.

WHILE we were enjoying the peace and quiet that followed the death of the Goranha, there returned from Barua the twenty odd Portuguese who fled there after the battle in which we were defeated. Miguel de Castanhoso went out to receive them, and spoke with Afonso de França, Antonio Dafōseca, Pero Tauares, and Antonio de Lima, telling them that they should join himself and the others who thought with him, and should appoint some honourable man Captain of the Portuguese; as it did not redound either to their honour, or to the service of the King of Portugal, to have a mulatto for Captain. Ayres Diz knew that those men said this, and that they were working to stir up others, and told the King. As soon as the King heard it, as he was a great friend of Ayres Diz, and desired him to be Captain of the Portuguese, in order with his help to do what he afterwards did do, as I shall relate later, he came straight to my lodgings, which were near his own, with the same Ayres Diz. They both told me what had happened, and that Miguel de Castanhoso had made this disturbance, as he wanted to be Captain himself. I replied to Ayres Diz, saying to him: "Captain, you may rely on the King and on myself, next to God, to sustain you in your honour; therefore, think nothing of what your opponents say. I shall tell the men who came from Debarua that men who fled from the battle as they did, and abandoned their Captain, have no vote or claim to elect another, but rather should be punished as deserters who have abandoned their King's banner; still, if they keep quiet, I will." Whether he told them this, or sent word to them, I cannot say; any way, about eight days later, more or less, they came to me, and said: "Sir, in this company of Portuguese which the King of Portugal, our Lord, entrusted to you, are some very honourable men, noble fidalgos, and cavaliers of much merit; they hold it as a disgrace that a mulatto of low birth should be their Captain, who, for his own merit, deserves it no more than the others. We request that you will examine this, and appoint another Captain, lest some disorder should arise from it." I did not want to say more to them then, than that they should go to the King, and prefer that complaint to him, and see what he replied. They said that they had nothing to see the King for; nor did they recognise in this matter anyone save myself, who brought them to that country, and to whom the King of Portugal, their Lord, had given power to appoint and dismiss their Captains. To this I replied: "Then, my sons, when I made Ayres Diz Captain, I took counsel on the matter with wise men and discreet, who recommended me to appoint him. Since then he has done nothing to show that he did not merit it; nay, under his captaincy, God has given us the final victory over the chief enemy we had in this land. I, therefore, in virtue of my will and absolute power, shall not withdraw the captaincy from him for love of you, who are but few. Let all the Portuguese come, and we shall see what they say." I summoned them all, and came out of my tent to speak with them. When the King saw the gathering of the Portuguese, he understood what was in question, and sent to beg me to come with them to his tent. This I did, and brought the Captain and all his company. After we had sat down, the King enquired what the Portuguese wanted. I said to him, that some of them told me that I must give them another Captain, as they were not content that Ayres Diz should retain the post. That as it was not right that the majority should be annoyed for the sake of the minority, I had called them all together to enquire their wishes. He replied to me that he thought it well done, and told the Portuguese that he begged them to declare their wishes freely. They all with one voice replied that they were quite content to fight under the banner of Ayres Diz, and desired him for their Captain, as he was a very good man and fitted for such an employment; that if there were any mutineers that they ought to be punished, as they did not desire mutinies in their company. Those who remained with the army and did not fly to Debarua said this, and thereat the King was very pleased. I said to those who came from Debarua: "You have heard what your companions say who remained here and fought, like you, but conquered, and recovered what you had lost. Now I undeceive you, and I order all you who have come from Debarua, and Miguel de Castanhoso who went out to meet you, and who stirred you to mutiny, and all others who are of his opinion, that you obey your Captain, Ayres Diz, else return to Debarua, under pain of being prisoners and confined on a rock, until ships arrive to take you to India." When they heard what I said, and saw the King's frown, which was gloomy, they replied that they would do as I said, and would all obey Ayres Diz and hold him as their Captain. They went at once to him, cap in hand, to beg his pardon, and promised to be his supporters and to obey him like loyal Portuguese.

CHAPTER XXXVI.

Of how the Queen arrived at the Camp, and of her Reception there.

WE remained there resting nearly two months. Meanwhile, the King sent news of the victory to his mother, who was a day's journey away from where we had left her. He sent to tell her to come to us where we were; that we might all rejoice and give thanks to God; she thanked me inasmuch as I had given the orders to do what had been done, and was the cause of that victory. The King learnt the Queen's approach when she was a league away, and saying nothing to me, went to meet her with his horsemen. The road by which she entered the camp was for the distance of a crossbow-shot lined with curtains, with a canopy over it; on the ground were carpets. They gave food in sufficiency to all who required it, and this lasted for a whole week. The Queen, at the end of her journey, came to see me in my tent. She asked me what ill she had done, as I was her father, and had not been to meet her as her son had; I replied that the blame was not mine but her son's, who did not want to take me with him, and told me nothing. I accompanied her to her lodgings, and we remained as great friends as ever.

CHAPTER XXXVII.

Of how King Gradeus recovered the Monastery of Syão, with the Territory belonging to it.

SOME days later, the King determined to recover the provinces of Mara, Joa, Guidime, and Gojame, which were in the power of the King of Zeila. The first attack he ordered was on the lands of Joa, a large and wealthy kingdom. He said that I and his mother should remain resting in my territory. The King marched with all his army, both the Portuguese and his own, to a country called the monastery[1] of Syão, where are some men so tall of stature that they appear giants.[2] As these were still

---

[1] *Moesteiro.*

[2] Alvarez certainly mentions a monastery of St. Mary of Sion, but it was near Aksum. This may have suggested the statement in this chapter, but that place could not be the one referred to, and the monastery of Syão is a difficulty—by its name it should be Christian, but Galâwdêwos had to subdue it by force. There is an Amba Sion close to the situation suggested for Baçanete, whose capture by D. Christovão Bermudez does not mention; the Italian map also shows Amba Scioa, east of Lake Tzana, and north-west of Lalibela, in which direction Castanhoso says Galâwdêwos marched, after the victory of Wainadega. Could either of these be meant, and "monastery" have been written for "mountain"? Esteves Pereira (*Minas*, p. 72 *n.*) casually mentions that the Amharic for a monastery means also a mountain. This suggestion is offered in default of a better. Of the four places mentioned in the beginning of the chapter, Mara was the name of an old kingdom south-east of Abyssinia; the name is not on modern maps unless Assai Marâ and Addoi Marâ preserve it; Joa is probably Shoa; Guidime is perhaps the modern Ghedem, in 40 deg. E. long. and 10½ deg. N. lat., near the Hawash; Ghedemsa is another district in the neighbourhood, which seems to imply that they are fragments of a formerly important State. Gojam is described in chap. lii, p. 241, below. The Ethiopian chronicle says that the famine was severe in 1543-44, and that Galâwdêwos spent the rains of 1544 in Agaye, which has not been identified (Conzelman, § 23).

subject to the Moors of Zeila, they would not obey King Gradeus, although they belonged to him ; nor would they give supplies for his force. Affonso de França, seeing their disloyalty, said to the Captain Ayres Diz: "What are you going to do, sir? What more can you hope from delay, you must force your way in, use fire, and compel them to yield." They determined to do this, and the King said it would be well to order up the artillery captured from the Goranha. But Ayres Diz replied that only two half bases were necessary ; that the rest should be kept where it was, as it was more secure there. They sent for the two half bases, and with them and the matchlocks they fought them, and thrashed them to that extent, that they said the Portuguese were not human beings, as they did not fight like men. Finally they considered it better to yield, and sent to tell the King that they would surrender to his power, and also furnish supplies, and all things necessary for his men ; but they begged him to treat them well, as the King of Zeila had done, to whom they were for that reason friendly and loyal: that they would be the same to him if they received justice and good treatment. They also begged him to order the Portuguese not to take their wives or daughters, or steal their property, as they had heard was their habit. To this the Portuguese replied that they promised not to do them any injury or wrong. In this harmony they remained there some days, well treated, and contented on both sides.

CHAPTER XXXVIII.
Of how the King of Adem made War on King Gradeus, and was killed and his Camp despoiled.

WHILE they were here the King of Adem sent a message to King Gradeus not to consider that the King of Zeila was dead, as he was his successor; and lest he should think these the words of a coward, who threatens and does not act, he would come in search of him at once. As the King thought that his wars had already ended on the death of the King of Zeila, and also as the King of Adem was powerful, and he feared lest he should give him trouble, that message caused him much anxiety, and he showed his uneasiness clearly enough. But Captain Ayres Diz said to him: "Let not your highness be annoyed, for I trust in Jesus that, as He gave us victory over our past enemy, so He will also give it us over this one." As they knew that the enemy was already on the march, they set themselves in order and advanced towards him. The King Gradeus did not wish that the banner of the King of Portugal should be in the van, as it was wont to be, and some said that this was owing to the counsel of Ayres Diz. But the Portuguese said to the King: "Is this the honour you show the banner that restored your kingdoms to you, and gave back to you your government? If you act thus now, while your affairs are yet undecided and you still require us, what will you do when you become firmly seated? Then you will give a poor reward to Portugal and the Portuguese. Now know for a certainty that the banner of the King of Portugal has to go in the van, as it has always gone heretofore; if not, neither it nor we will march." When the King understood their determination he agreed that the banner of Portugal should go in the van; but he agreed with an ill grace, already clearly showing signs of what he afterwards did, which he had even then determined on in his heart. Starting, we marched until we reached a very large river, where the King of Adem had pitched his camp, and was awaiting reinforcements. He thought himself safe, as the river was very broad, of a considerable stream, and great depth, and he did not believe that our men could pass unperceived. But as our men knew that the enemy expected strong reinforcements, they determined to force a battle before they arrived. They invented a good plan to cross the stream, namely, by leather boats, which they made in this way: they killed several cows, and with their hides covered the wooden boats used for ferries, as the horses could cross through the water, which was not so deep as to hinder their fording. When these were ready, they sent men across to fasten ropes on the other side of the river, whereby they could haul themselves over. This was done half a league away from the enemies' camp, and at night that they might not be seen. The river crossed, they attacked the camp of the Moors, of whom they killed many, and amongst them the King of Adem. Still, many Christians were also killed, and King Gradeus was wounded and nearly killed, owing to the confusion of himself and of his men, who did not understand night fighting, for they spread over the camp and could neither collect nor aid each other, therefore many were killed; so many and with such havoc that they would have been easily conquered, but for the goodness of God, and the help of the Portuguese, who, as I have said, fighting with the Moorish horse slew the King.[1] By this time dawn was breaking, and the Moors seeing their King dead, took to flight. The Portuguese followed the Moors until they had killed the greater part of them. They brought back prisoner the widow of the King of Adem, and other women of other great lords, who were flying with her. They captured also many horses well

---

[1] If Bruce is correct—and he knew the country well—this night attack was impossible for Abyssinians. I quote the passage: "The Abyssinians, to a man, are fearful of the night, unwilling to travel, and, above all, to fight in that season, when they imagine the world in possession of certain genii, averse to intercourse with men, and very vindictive, if even by accident they are ruffled, or put out of their way by their interference. This, indeed, is carried to so great a height, that no man will venture to throw water out of a basin upon the ground, for fear that, in ever so small a space the water should have to fall, the dignity of some elf, or fairy, may be violated. The Moors have none of these apprehensions."—*Travels*, vol. iii, p. 60.

and richly caparizoned, which they took from those they slew. Among these was that belonging to the King. After the pursuit, the Portuguese on their return found King Gradeus marching with his country cavalry on his flanks, and presented to him the Moorish Queen they had taken, with all the other women, the horses, and all the booty they had captured in the pursuit. The King acknowledged their services, and gave many thanks to God for that great and signal victory. He told them he only desired the sword and horse of the King of Adem for himself; that all the rest belonged to the Portuguese, both what they took in the pursuit and what they found in the camp—which was marvellously valuable—that as the Portuguese had won this, they should all divide it in a brotherly manner among themselves; for himself and for his, he only desired peace and the restoration of his kingdoms, which he had recovered by the valour and arms of Portugal. As for the Queen of Adem, called Dinia Ambara, it was not right that she should be the captive of any one less than the King; that he therefore considered it well, if she would become a Christian, that she should be the wife of Ayres Diz; and he gave to them both the kingdoms of Doaro and Bale, and only retained Oygere for himself.[1]

---

[1] This account must refer to the campaign against Abbas, though he was not King of Adem, but Governor of Bali, Fatagar, and Dawaro. He raided in Abyssinian territory in the latter part of 1544, and was defeated and killed by Galâwdêwos early in 1545. The final battle took place in Wadj, west of Fatagar, but the Ethiopian chronicles do not mention the Portuguese (Conzelman, §§ 23 to 25; Basset, *Études*, p. 113). I have already, in the Introduction, pointed out the hopeless confusion which marries Del Wanbara to Ayres Dias.

CHAPTER XXXIX.

Of how King Gradeus and the Captain Ayres Diz began to show their malice, and the Treason they meditated.

AFTER King Gradeus had recovered his kingdoms and was at peace, I hoped that he would further confirm and ratify the obedience he had promised to the High Pontiff, celebrating the sacraments and using the rites and ceremonies of the Roman Church, in conformity with faithful Christians. But even as he promised it unwillingly, so he allowed himself to forget it, and acted in opposition to it. He had promised and sworn to me that, as soon as Our Lord had given him victory over his enemies, he would at once agree on and settle the way in which I should celebrate a general ordination after the Roman manner. But finding that, although he had obtained the victory, he had not fulfilled what he had promised, I determined to see him, and to tell him that he must remember to keep his word. For this I asked permission from the Queen, his mother, who told me that I had the permission, and could go as often as I pleased. I started at once, and went to where the King was, and got lodgings near him with my people. I sent word to him, saying that I would visit him the following day, but he did not take much count of my message or of my arrival. I sent also to the Captain Ayres Diz, to say that I had come, and that he should receive me with his men as was well and customary. He came the next morning with one hundred and fifty Portuguese, of whom fifty were horsemen, and the rest mounted on mules, all well cared for; with them were the two thousand bucklermen and archers of the country, attached to the Portuguese company. The Portuguese had all their matchlocks in good order, and the servants who carried them well clothed, and they were all much pleased at my arrival. When they came near me, the horsemen skirmished a little, the matchlockmen fired their matchlocks, and after showing these and other signs of pleasure, they dismounted and came to receive my blessing, to bid me welcome, and to make me offerings; Ayres Diz, especially, who in addition to the usual phrases said to me: "Sir, I am your servant as you, sir, know; all the Portuguese are always very loyal to the Holy Mother Church; we are vassals of the King D. João of Portugal, he is our lord, and we will do what you order us. Will you, sir, be pleased to mount your mule, with your umbrellas,[1] and we will take you in our midst and convey you to where the King is, and you can see him and know his will. You will act as you consider right, and we consequently will do as you do." When we got near the King, neither he nor his made any movement, save watching us from their tents and lodgings, as though they jested at us. Ayres Diz came near to me, and said: "The ill-will the King shows you is clear, sir." With this he began to gallop his horse and skirmish about. Some others of the company, when they saw him rejoicing, did the same. But Manuel da Cunha, Gaspar de Sousa, and Dinis de Lima, who were near me said: "Sir, dissimulate with this mulatto; whatever he does and appears to be externally, remember it is mischief and deceit, for in his heart he agrees with the King Gradeus, and it will not be long before he gives a sign of it with regard to the banner of the King, our lord; therefore, never trust him, but always have a double meaning with him, for all he says and does is also double and false." Lopo Dalmansa, Diogo Dabreu, and other men of repute, said the same thing to me. At this I was much astonished, for I had not considered him a man of that sort, but fidalgos and men of credit told me, and it caused

---

[1] *Sôbreiros.*

me grief to believe it. Meanwhile, we were getting near where the King was, and we dismounted, and I approached the curtain behind which he was, and I heard him say, speaking to Ayres Diz : " Marcos, my Captain-General, you shall no longer bear in my kingdom that banner of the King of Portugal, but carry mine, and leave that." Ayres Diz replied to him : " Sir, I will not abandon the banner of the King of Portugal." Then the King ordered one of his pages to take it and carry it thence. Ayres Diz consented, and allowed him to carry it away. But a Portuguese fidalgo, called Diogo de Brito, seized the banner from the page, and, as he would not give it up, struck him with his sword over the head, and made him let go in spite of him.[1] When I saw this I returned to my lodgings, and all the Portuguese with me, and also the traitor Ayres Diz. Some of the Portuguese brought presents of articles of food. The Asmache de galan, too, came soon, who was married to the princess, aunt of the King ; he brought several baskets of bread, sheep, pies, calves, capons, and fifty jars of mead, all on the part of the King, his lord. On his behalf he said to me, that his highness complained to me of the man who in his presence took the banner from his page, and wounded him, as that was discourteous and should be punished. To this I answered, and requested him to reply, that he, too, was very ungrateful to the King of Portugal, and discourteous to his banner, when, at the cost of Portuguese blood and of the life of D. Christovão, his kingdoms had been restored to him. That this also was not the peace and concord that he had promised me. As I was dismissing him with this reply, Ayres Diz said to me, by way of advice : " Sir, I do not know how far it is prudent to send such a hard answer and to annoy King Gradeus, because we live in his kingdoms, far from our own

---

[1] *fez lha deixar que lhe pez.*

country." At this several Portuguese arose, and told him that, of a certainty, he appeared to be a traitor to the crown of Portugal, and to his King, because his words and deeds proved it: so much so that he was not fitted to be Captain of the Portuguese. To that he replied, that he was a Captain of the Emperor of Ethiopia and not of the King of Portugal; that therefore they could not call him a traitor for speaking in favour of the said Emperor, to whom he owed this duty, and more, as he had done him many favours, and married him to Dinia Ambara, the former wife of the King Mafamede,[1] and given him the lordships over his lands. To this I replied, saying: "Ayres Diz, I had known that you had abandoned the faith of the baptism which you received among Catholic Christians according to the ceremonies of the Roman Church, and that you had been baptised again with the baptism of the heretics and schismatics of Alexandria, and that you had changed the name of Ayres to Marcos, as you now call yourself, as a sign of the apostasy that you have committed; bad Christian as you are, you do not merit to be Captain of the Portuguese, even as these gentlemen say." When he heard me say this, he waited no longer, but got up gloomily, and returned to his lodgings with some few Portuguese who accompanied him. As he went, Affonso de França said to me: "The mulatto shows well; now, Sir, you will believe what he meditates. Let us leave here; we must not stay in these lodgings near him, lest he should bruize us; the mulatto will kick."[2] Meanwhile, the King sent to ask me to see him the next day, as it was then late and he had no leisure. On the following day, immediately after vespers, I went to his tent with six or seven Portuguese. When I entered, the King did not rise or receive my

---

[1] This statement has been already commented on.
[2] A pun on Mula, a mule.

blessing as usual, or seat me in the customary place, but only lowered his head a little, and left me standing. I, seeing his new and unusual discourtesy said: "Not only King Gradeus, are you ungrateful to the King of Portugal, whose banner you have slighted, under which your kingdom was restored, but also you have shown disrespect to Jesus Christ in my person, who represent Him and stand in His place. It was not in this way that the good and most Christian King, Onadinguel, your father acted, whose example you should imitate, and then God will show you favour. Be not over-confident in the victories which, by the goodness of God, and by the means of the Portuguese, you have obtained, because, as through the merits of your father, and the submission he made to the Holy Mother Church, God helped these kingdoms which were being ruined, so through your pride and ingratitude they will dwindle until they are destroyed; you also will perish and be cursed and excommunicated, if you return to the heresies of the Jacobites and Dioscorios of Egypt, who through their sins, and through their disobedience in rebelling against the holy orthodox apostolic see of Rome, were ruined and became captives of the Turks and of other infidels; so will you be also if you do not amend." He replied to me, that those of Egypt and of the sect of Dioscoro were not heretics; that we were the heretics, as we worshipped four Gods like the Arians did; and if I had not been his godfather, as I was,[1] he would order me to be quartered. After other speeches of this nature, I returned to my lodgings, where I found many Portuguese awaiting me, to whom I related what had passed with the King; on which they told me to accompany them to their camp, as I was not safe where I was: this I did, and went with them.[2]

[1] The improbability of this assertion has been already pointed out in the Introduction.
[2] Gibbon's chapter xlvii explains the hard names Bermudez says he used.

CHAPTER XL.

Of how the King and the Portuguese sent each other certain Messages, until they resolved to have recourse to Arms.

BEING in the camp with the Portuguese, the King sent word to me not to meddle by issuing orders in the Portuguese camp, nor cause any changes there, inasmuch as it was in the charge of his Captain-General Marcos, and that he desired that he, and no other, should command there. I sent word to him that the Portuguese were vassals of the King of Portugal, who had entrusted them to me; that I, at the request of him, King Gradeus, had placed them in charge of a Portuguese called Ayres Diz, to be their Captain and command them in battle, doing what was right for the service of God and the King of Portugal: in the which things he had failed, denying both his faith and allegiance; and that therefore he merited not to be Captain of such honourable and Christian men as are the Portuguese, nor would they consent to it. That these same Portuguese, more especially Luis da Cunha, Gaspar de Sousa, Antonio Pereira, Denis de Lima Jeronimo de Sousa, Manuel da Cunha, Pero Barreto, Affonso de França, and all the others, said they did not wish, nor did it comport with their honour, to have for their Captain a heretic and a traitor, nor would they fight under any banner save that of Portugal; and that, further, as the King Gradeus did not fulfil his promise, which was to make submission to the High Pontiff of Rome, the successor of St. Peter, that they would no longer serve him but would return with me to Portugal. Pero Palha went with this reply to the King, and said also to him that it was well known that the traitor Marcos perverted him by his bad advice; and that therefore he begged him, on my behalf and on behalf of all the Portuguese, not to credit such an evil man as he, and to remember that he had agreed to submit to the Holy Mother-Church of Rome, and to consent to my exercising my office conformably to the Roman ritual: ordaining the priests of that land, and celebrating the ecclesiastical sacraments, in conformity with it, and that he had proclaimed this publicly; that he should so keep and maintain it that we might live peaceably in his country, and serve him and defend him from his enemies, and hold him for our Lord as we had hitherto done; that, unless we got a plain answer, we should all leave him and return to Portugal, as we had said. To this he answered, that he was the King and lord of that land, and that we should not leave it without his permission; and that he intended that Marcos, his Captain-General, should have command and jurisdiction over the Portuguese. Pero Palha told him not to deceive himself, for the Portuguese did not bear arms under compulsion; and that he warned him that, if the Portuguese had the mind, they would take his Marcos prisoner before his very face, and chastise him as he deserved. On this, nothing being settled, Pero Palha returned, and told us all that had passed with the King, and his obstinacy. He told us also that he had said to the King that the Portuguese were bold enough to capture and chastise his Marcos, at which we were all pleased, and we determined to do it. For this purpose twenty horsemen at once got ready; but Marcos, as he was cunning, had spies among us, who told him what had passed; and he sent to the King to ask for men to guard and accompany him on his way to the King's camp, as his lodging was outside ours. The King sent him three captains of his guard, with two hundred horse and two thousand bucklermen, who conveyed him, passing close to our camp with panoply of war, blowing trumpets and beating drums. Seeing his arrogance, our men, both foot and horse, drew up in sight of him;[1]

---

[1] *Lhe deram vista.*

some fired their arquebuses without doing them any hurt, as they were rather far out. When Marcos reached the King's camp, the King ordered all the chief men of his court to meet him, as though he came from far, after a long absence, having won some great victory. He called him to the tent where he was, and when Marcos knelt before him to kiss his hand he embraced him, but would not give him his hand, and said to him: "What, Marcos, do you think of these evil men, and of that Patriarch, who is a rebel to the chair of St. Mark in Alexandria?" He replied: "Your Majesty should send to tell them not to be rebellious, nor the cause of their own destruction, for, with the great power you have, you can compel them in spite of themselves; let them return to you and you will pardon them, you can pledge your word for their safety; I, too, on my part, will send to beg and advise them not to bring on themselves their own destruction, because if they will not obey you not one of them will remain who is not dead." A Gallician who was there with them, called Lopo Dalmansa, brought these messages from the King and from Marcos. He also told us that, besides his own people, all blamed the King's ingratitude towards us, and told him that what he did to us appeared not only evil to them but to the whole world, and that all the Kings, both Moor and Christian, would blame such a wicked act as he was perpetrating on men who had restored to him his kingdoms, position, and life, after all had been lost. He added that the same was also said to him by the friars and religious men, who warned him not to proceed further with his evil intention and design. But after all, his bad proclivities, and the advice of the traitor Marcos, prevailed with him, rather than reason and the counsels of the wise.

CHAPTER XLI.

Of the Battles between the Abyssinians and the Portuguese, and of the Victory of the Portuguese.

WHEN the Portuguese heard the message of Lopo Dalmansa they all said they were determined to die, or else defend themselves against the cruelty of that ungrateful traitor; they asked me how could they give battle to so large a body of men. When I understood their mind I said to them: "Children, be not anxious; in the greatest troubles there is God, and He will help us here." As there were three entrances to our camp, by which they could attack us, we arranged to collect some munitions in them; as then, if it were necessary, we could fortify ourselves in the camp, and defend ourselves as long as possible. The munitions collected at those places were concealed powder pots, which we could ignite when the enemy came, and thus burn them—as in fact was done, much to their loss, as I will relate; but before they attacked us, between eleven and twelve at night, our horsemen sallied out and beat up the King's camp: which surprise, together with the noise of the trumpets and the arquebuses, caused such fear that all took to flight and would have been destroyed, had our men been numerous enough to pursue them, but being few they returned. In this confusion the King searched for a horse, on which to escape with the others; but after our attack was ended, Marcos went to him where he was almost beside himself, and said: "Sir, what are you doing? Do not fly, for the enemy has retired. Have no fear, as they can do you no harm, and all this is but noise. Do not show cowardice, or you will fail;[1] dissimulate, and seat yourself calmly on your royal throne, and encourage your

---

[1] *Que ficareis em mingoa.*

people. When morning dawns we will attack these traitors, and they will be all killed or captured, and in revenge for the disrespect they have shown you, you shall give their flesh to your lions to eat, as is your custom." It is the custom in that country to throw to the lions the enemies captured alive in war, first cutting off their privy parts. The King, finding that our men had retired, calmed himself, and in the morning ordered an attack on us. Both his men and ours being under arms, his bucklermen, which were the most numerous and the best troops he had, led the van; they attacked all the three entries that led to our camp where the powder was; our men awaited them, and when they came on with considerable vigour and outcry, our men, feigning fear, fell back and made way for them as far as the powder; when they reached it, it was fired; several of them were burned and killed, and the rest fled, scalded and roasted. The King, seeing the loss of his men, and finding his hopes dissipated, tore the rich garments he wore (this among them is a sign of great grief), and sent for Marcos, who was also very vexed at the ill-success of his advice.

CHAPTER XLII.

Of how the King made Peace with the Portuguese, promising to do what was right, with the intention of Banishing them, as he did.

HE and Marcos took counsel together and agreed, that they could not destroy the Portuguese by fighting, without suffering much damage and loss; they therefore determined to outwit them by stratagem and deceit in this way. The King sent to us to say he repented the mistake he had made, as God had clearly shown him his great error in not fulfilling that he had promised and sworn to me, but that now he wished to fulfil it, and do all that I desired; that therefore he begged us to do no more hurt to his people, but to return to him, and he would do whatever we wished. Besides this he urged other good reasons, both supplicating and pitiful; he told us we must mourn for his men whom we had handled so roughly, for it was a very painful thing to see the living roasted by our fire, and the dead burned. We replied that we had not done this harm of our own free will, and that we greatly regretted that they had driven us to it; however, if he would pledge himself, and would fulfil his promises to God and to us, that we would behave as we always had: that is, to serve him, and love him as father and lord; but, if he desired another course, we trusted in Jesus Christ that He, seeing our rectitude, would defend us from his tyranny and from the malice of that traitor Marcos. The King told Marcos this answer, to which Marcos replied that he should employ two stratagems, to drive us the more easily into an agreement with him: one was to order his subjects not to assist us or provide us with any necessary, under pain of having their eyes pulled out as traitors; the other was to offer us and to give us much money and many favours—not merely promises for the future, but immediately; thus on one side necessity, and on the other desire, would work on us. The King did this, and sent us a safe-conduct, with a large sum of money for the people, and for me a valuable present of cows, sheep, and other necessary supplies, promising me that all would be arranged as I wished, and that he would celebrate a general ordination at the Christmas, which was four months distant, as we had previously agreed. Notwithstanding his plausibility and my entreaties, the Portuguese did not trust him, and remained three days before they replied, until for love of me they agreed, and granted the peace and composition, saying we must be careful what we did, for Marcos was our enemy, and would, if he could, drink our blood. I told them that I would do whatever I was able, as it touched me as closely as it did them. Besides that safe-conduct of the King, there was also the Bernagaiz Isaac, who was the mediator who came and went in the framing of this agreement, who would be on our side with all his party, and who said and swore that he felt certain that the King deeply repented the outrages he had done us. Being ready to start for where the King was, Marcos came to accompany us with the Portuguese who were of his party, and had sided with him, and we all started together: on the way I begged Marcos that there should be no ill feeling between him and the Portuguese, and so he promised me. The King showed such pleasure at our amity that he came outside his camp to receive us, with all the chief men of his court. All his people, both great and small, were very joyful, for they all wished us well, and were delighted at our pacification, for it appeared to them that after God we were their refuge for the defence and the peace of their country.[1]

---

[1] The Ethiopian chronicles confirm generally that there were great disputes between the Portuguese and the Abyssinians. Basset, *Études*, p. 113, says: "As to the Franks, the King provided for their wants, and gave them much land in accordance with the agreement. There began a great dispute in regard to their religious belief, and there were quarrels with the chief men, with the partisans of Abba Zekré and of Abba Paoulos, and with all the monks. The King did not favour the tenets of the Franks; he made Andyras patriarch. All the same, he feared lest the people of Ethiopia should excite trouble in his kingdom as in the time of Grañ, and he remained in the faith of Alexandria, which annoyed the Franks." Perruchon, *Revue Sémitique*, 1894, p. 266, however, alters the sense of this considerably. After the words "in accordance with the agreement," he adds, "and of the oaths that had been made when they came from the country of Rom." While Guidi's fragment (p. 9) adds that there was an agreement between the King of the Franks and Asnaf Sagad (Galâwdêwos), that the former should have one-third of Ethiopia. I have previously commented on this fragment, which appears to need further investigation. Instead of "The King did *not* favour," Perruchon translates "The King *did* favour," which is better sense in view of what follows. The controversial book composed by Galâwdêwos, which has been translated, under the name of *Confessio fidei Claudii regis Œthiopiæ*, by Ludolf, was not written on this occasion, but to confute the bishop, André Oviedo.

CHAPTER XLIII.

Of how some of the chief Portuguese were Banished to certain distant Countries.

AFTER I had spoken to the King, and he had promised to comply with all that had been previously settled, I also asked him not to allow Marcos to interfere in the command of the Portuguese, as it would lead to another riot worse than the last; he told me he agreed, and that this should be. After these speeches, and others, which tended to increase our harmony and tranquility, I went to occupy a lodging he had given me. A few hours later, there came to me Baltesar Monteiro, Antonio Ferreira, Simão Dandrade, Diogo de Brito, Antão Vaz, who told me that the treachery with which they had treated us was disclosed, because they themselves had already been warned to prepare to go into banishment, each to a separate country quite apart from the others, made over to the lords of those countries to closely guard them, all on the advice of that traitor Marcos. They further told me not to be cast down, for, as they heard, I also had to bear my share of the trouble. I replied, that I did not care so much about myself as for them, but that I begged them to commend themselves to God, and encourage their souls in Jesus Christ, because I hoped that they and I would quickly be restored to liberty. As soon as I knew what had happened, I went to the lords of the countries for which they were destined, and asked them to treat them well. They replied: "Senhor father, know that Marcos ordered us to carry off these men prisoners in irons, to clothe them as slaves, and to treat them as slaves; but for love of you, who are our father, we will behave better to them." I went at once to the King, and said: "Well, sir, what have I to do? I see that you do not carry out your promises, but send away my brethren prisoners; what are you going to do with me? The proverb says, when you see your neighbour's beard plucked begin to soak your own. I confess that I deserve all the evil I have to suffer, for I deceived my brethren and brought them into your power, knowing that you govern by the advice of a traitor." The King replied kindly: "Senhor Father, no outrage will be done you; but as you know it is necessary to attend to the war which the Gallas are making on me, you will remain in the country of the Gafates praying God for me, and you will live on the income of that country; this will be amply sufficient for you and yours, as in days past, when I took refuge there, it was sufficient for me and all mine. I have ordered that you shall be treated with much honour, and that they shall obey you as they would me; at Christmas, please God, if I return in good health, as I hope, you shall celebrate your ordination as we agreed. As for the men whom I ordered to leave here, do not be annoyed; I do it that they may not raise a mutiny among the others." On this, Marcos joined us, and said to the King: "Sir, will your highness be pleased to send for a patriarch from Alexandria;" and he replied: "May God bless you, Marcos, my friend, this has already been done."[1]

---

[1] It may be conceded as a license of the imagination that Bermudez should have overheard this speech, and also the one on another occasion, previously reported, as to the banner. Gafat, to which Bermudez says he was exiled, is now a small district on the right bank of the Nile, south of Damot. It was formerly more extensive, and occupied both banks. It is in 37 deg. east longitude, and 10 deg. 30 min. north latitude; the contour map shows it as rather hilly. It is remarkable that Bermudez, in chap. l, p. 233, below, states that this country had long been in open rebellion against Galâwdêwos.

CHAPTER XLIV.

Of how the Patriarch was taken to a Country of the Gafates, and of how he returned thence.

THE King ordered one of his captains to convey me to a country of the Gafates, and put me in possession of it, and direct the residents to consider me their lord, and pay me the rents which they used to pay the King, for such were his highness' orders. I took with me all my servants, slaves, and books; and also a man of that country called Francisco Matheus, who had been servant of the Ambassador Matheus, whom the Queen Helena sent to Portugal in the time of the King D. Manuel, your great-grandfather, of glorious memory, and who had been in Portugal with the said ambassador. I took this man with me, for he was a good man and a friend of the Portuguese; and as he was discreet and learned, I entrusted to him all my household.[1] After taking leave of the King, I went eight days' journey, for such was the distance from where the King was, to that country of the Gafates, which lies among lofty and precipitous mountain ranges, and is inhabited by very barbarous people. After crossing the ranges we descended into a large valley, so deep that it seemed as if we were going into hell, and the hills looked so high they seemed to touch the heavens. The captain who conveyed me ordered all the chief people of that country to assemble in that valley, and told them before me that the King ordered them to consider me as their lord, and pay me their rents, but also to guard me strictly, and prevent me leaving that place or returning to the court

---

[1] There is rather a difficulty here. There was a Francisco Matheus, a servant of the Ambassador Matheus; but, so far from being an Abyssinian, he was a Moor slave whom the King of Portugal set free, and sent back with Matheus. He is merely casually mentioned by Alvarez; see his p. 19.

of the King; and this they promised to do. I was seven months in that land, during which the King went to make war on the Gallas, as he had told me; but he returned wearied and almost defeated, without having accomplished anything of value. A short time after, Marcos died, and he had him buried with great pomp in a church where the Kings of that country are buried; he, and all his, showed as much grief at his death as if it had been their own brother or father; and they said that with him died all their defence and the protection of their country.[1] When I heard of the death of Marcos, I determined to return to the court; as it appeared to me that the King would listen to me now that the opposing adviser, that is Marcos, was gone. I took council with Francisco Matheus as to how I could leave that country in safety; he advised me to scare those rustics with terror, and treat them so roughly that they themselves would beg us to go away. I determined to do this: one day I ordered a captain who guarded us to be arrested for a grudge I feigned against him, and had him pulled by the hair, and buffetted, and bound hand and foot; I ordered the matchlockmen to fire their matchlocks close to him; this so frightened him that he befouled himself.[2] He begged me for the love of God to release him, and promised to go so far away from wherever I was, that he should never see me nor I him again. I released him to tell the others, as in fact he did. I ordered the matchlockmen, who were ten or twelve, to fire many shots, which echoed among the hills and sounded like thunder; by accident they killed one or two countrymen by random

---

[1] The date of Marcos' death is nowhere given, or we could supplement or check Bermudez' narrative. He was dead before 1550, when Galâwdêwos wrote to the King of Portugal (see p. 118, above). The chronicle is rather vague, but it speaks of Galâwdêwos as fighting for three years continually with the Gallas, and Muhamedans, apparently from 1545 to 1548 (Conzelman, §§ 27 and 31), so perhaps Marcos' death may be provisionally dated 1548.

[2] *que se mijou e çujou por si.*

bullets. This alarmed them so much that they left and abandoned the district where we were, and the captains sent to tell me that they begged me as a great favour to go away wherever I pleased, as they promised me not to hinder my journey. When Francisco Matheus heard what they said, he said to me: "Sir, whoever has an opportunity must not waste it, or there will come a time when he will repent. Let us start this very night, because they are scared; if they recover their courage, peradventure we shall not get another chance." We did this, lest they should change their minds. We began to prepare at once, and as towards morning there was a moon, we awaited its rising, and when it rose we started for the top of the mountain, three matchlockmen in the van and the rest in the rear, lest the barbarians should affront us finding that we were going. We reached the top of the mountain at dawn, and here the people wished to rest and eat; but I said that this was not a secure place for resting, as it was close to our opponents, who might still come and cause us some misfortune; let us eat from our hands and march on, until we left the mountains, delaying nowhere. We hurried over the road, and by vespers had done a day's journey and had got out of the mountains. Here we rested and ate, and stayed two days, without any alarm from the Gafates or hearing any tumult; by which it appeared to us that they did not grieve at our departure. Thence to where the King was was eight good marches, which we covered at our leisure, for we were weary; the country people were good folks, among whom we were safe; they gave us also all the food we wanted, and were hospitable. Marching on, at two days' journey from where the King was, we met a Portuguese called Francisco de Magalhães, who was returning from a visit to some land which the King had given him, for he gave lands to all the Portuguese that they might support themselves on the proceeds. We were pleased to see him, and he us, to learn what had happened to both. After I had told him of our journey he told me of the death of Marcos, and of how, after his death, the King had made one Diogo de Figuiredo Captain of the Portuguese, who died a few days later of a diarrhœa. After his death he made two equal Captains, one of the right hand and one of the left, as he arranged that the Portuguese should form his guard, and always march with him in two companies;[1] of these the Captains were Gaspar de Sousa and Lopo Dalmansa. The Portuguese did not desire this Lopo Dalmansa as their Captain because he was a foreigner, and one who favoured the party of Marcos; but Gaspar de Sousa was confirmed. At this I was much pleased, as Gaspar de Sousa was my nephew and friend. We journeyed together till near where the King was, and then separated. He went to inform the Portuguese who were with the King, who were much pleased at my arrival; while I, by another route, sent to the King to ask permission to see him.

CHAPTER XLV.

Of what the King did on the Arrival of the Patriarch, of how he Received him, and of how he left there.

WHEN the King heard of my return he was very angry; he sent for the captain who had conducted me, and enquired how it was possible for me to leave the valley and the hills to which he had to conduct me, because, owing to the difficulty of the country, I could not return if he had

---

[1] All the royal household offices in Abyssinia were formerly divided into those of the right hand, and those of the left. So called from their position in the camp, or by the King in public. Alvarez, p. 233, however, mentions in the case of one office, that he of the right led the van, and he of the left the rear.

conveyed me there, and had charged the people of the country to watch me closely. The captain asserted that he had acted in the matter exactly as his highness had ordered; but this did not avail to prevent the King ordering him many lashes. When the Portuguese knew of my return, they all came with much joy to see me. The King also sent his page to visit me, and to assure me that he was delighted at my safe return: inasmuch as he longed for me, and therefore begged me to go straight to where he was, as he was desirous to see me. I went at once to his camp, half a league distant, and with me were the Portuguese who had come to visit me, whose company helped me much, because the King feared to offend them by annoying me. Fifteen days later the King ordered his departure from that country, telling me that he begged me to remain there, as the country was fertile, and belonged to Asmacherobel, who was a great friend of mine, who would stay with me, do me much honour, and give me sufficient income to maintain me well. He gave me clothing, and also five hundred ounces of gold for the time. I stayed behind, rather as the Portuguese begged me than of my own free will, because I understood that he was separating me from himself because of the other Patriarch who had come from Alexandria, and might arrive at court any day; and he feared to bring us together and cause a disturbance.

CHAPTER XLVI.

Of how the Arrival of the Patriarch from Alexandria, called Abuna Joseph, was Discovered; and of how it was arranged that he should be Patriarch of the Abyssinians and D. João Bermudez of the Portuguese.

AFTER the King had left, the Asmacherobel came to me one day and said: "Senhor Father, inasmuch as I am so much your friend, as you know, I wish to discover to you a secret that touches you closely; but it must be after you have given me your word not to reveal who told you, because if the King came to know, he would throw me to his lions. You should know, sir, that inasmuch as you obey the Roman Church, the King will not allow you to be Patriarch of his country, and has sent to Alexandria for another Patriarch of his own sect. He has arrived, and is in Debarua, and on his way to the King's court. It is for this reason that the King does not wish to have you at court with him, as he desires to put the other in possession of your office; and also he is very vexed with you, as you made him swear obedience to the Roman Church, and publicly proclaim that all must submit to it. You should now consider what you will do, because, if you decide to go, I will absent myself from here, so that the King cannot say that I consented to your departure." I thanked him for his information, and told him that he could clearly see how important it was for me now to go to court; and that, as he suggested, he should absent himself when I started. On my way I met a Portuguese called Manuel Alurez, a chamber-lad of the King your grandfather, by whom I sent word to the Captain, Gaspar de Sousa, that I was on my way to court to attend to a matter of great importance to all, about which I would tell him when I saw him; and as I was certain that the King would not be pleased at this my coming, I asked as a favour that he and all the Portuguese should assist me when necessary. The following day, near the King's camp, I met another Portuguese, called Lourenço Gonçalvez, who told me that the King already knew of my coming, and had ordered my arrest, and my conveyance to a rock where my life would end without a chance of escape from it. In order that your highness may know what place this rock was, to which I was to be conveyed, you must know that in that country there are certain hills raised considerably[1] above the general level, so scarped all around with precipices that the sole means of ascending is by narrow paths quarried out; above they are very flat, and a league or more in extent, some of seven or eight leagues, on the summits plains of good land, springs of good water, and other necessaries to support a population: which, in fact, does live on them. Still the approaches are so rugged, and the paths so steep, that no one can either enter or leave those rocks without the permission of the guards. These rocks serve for fortresses, and for this reason there are no walled towns in that country. King Gradeus sent me to one of these by two of his captains, to die there, without any chance of leaving it. When the Portuguese heard that I was being taken away a prisoner, they collected to rescue me from the hands of those who conveyed me. Those who came up first were Manuel de Soueral, Pero Palha, and Dinis de Lima. These told the captains to release me, or else they would compel them by force. The captains began to object, but this did not avail them, for at this moment came up Gaspar de Sousa, the Captain, and all the Portuguese save the Galician Lopo Dalmansa, who went to the King. When Gaspar de Sousa reached me, he made the Abyssinians fall back, and said to me: "What is this, Senhor Patriarch?" To the Abyssinian captains he said: "Is this your recompense to one who has laboured to benefit you?" Turning to me, he said: "Be pleased, your worship, to rest; for either you will not be injured, or I shall lose my life." After saying this, he had his camp pitched on the spot where we were. A little later, the King came also with his following, and pitched close to us, and sent to tell Gaspar de Sousa that he did not do well to release me from his captains. Gaspar de Sousa told him

---

[1] *Cõ muita auãtagẽ*.

that he was not aware of having done any wrong, for he had released from the hands of cruel men his prelate, who had undergone troubles and wrongs to benefit ingrates. That his highness knew very well how much he owed to the Patriarch, and the favours God had shown him by his means; how, as long as he was in the camp, and he obeyed him, God had always given him victory over his enemies; and how, after he had sent him away and showed him disrespect, he had been defeated by the Gallas, who had entered his camp and had slain men close to the royal tent, where there was none to oppose them; and his highness was in such difficulty that he fled from them with great indignity. Finally, that neither he nor the other Portuguese would abandon the Patriarch, who was their father, and had brought them from Portugal, and had prayed for them to God; for they would not be of good repute among men, nor would God show them favour if they acted otherwise; that in future they would always take him with them to protect him. The King, understanding the resolution of the Portuguese not to abandon me, sent the Azaige de galan to tell me that he would bestow on me a certain territory adjoining those he had given the Portuguese; that he requested me to go to it and stay there, and not remain with the army. I replied, that I knew very well that he had already obtained another Patriarch; that he should leave me in the company of my compatriots, as the others did not want me. When the Portuguese heard that there was another Patriarch they were astonished, as they had not heard of what was passing: they said that as such was the case they would never consent to my leaving them. After the King learned the determination of the Portuguese, he sent to ask me to visit him. I said that I would, and the Portuguese said that they wished to accompany me, which they did. The King received me with a courtesy which appeared to me suspicious. After some conversation, Lopo Dalmansa advised him to compel me to promise not to leave the Portuguese without his permission. I said to Lopo Dalmansa: "There is never wanting an Ayres Diz or a Miguel de Castanhoso. It is clear enough that you are no Portuguese. Up to now I have never found a true Portuguese opposed to me.[1] Still, you will never be Captain of the Portuguese, however much you side with the King." Notwithstanding my anger with the Gallician, I gave the King my hand, which he demanded, and promised not to separate from the Portuguese, or leave his kingdom without his permission. He was content with this, and gave me for my support so much territory that the rents were well worth twenty thousand cruzados annually. He ordered that the Patriarch Joseph, whom he had sent for from Alexandria, should be his Patriarch, and I only that of the Portuguese. He directed that Francisco Matheus, who had been my *adugue*—that is like an archdeacon—as well as all my other subordinates, should be transferred to Joseph.

CHAPTER XLVII.

Of how King Gradeus settled the Patriarch and the Portuguese in the Province of Doaro; and of how Calide, Captain of the said Province, attacked them to kill them, and was himself slain by them.

FOR the King to put the Patriarch Joseph in peaceable possession of his territory, it appeared to him necessary that I, with all the Portuguese, should be absent; he therefore ordered us to be settled in a certain part of his kingdom, which lay outside the district he mostly frequented, which is that called Amara, where he was then awaiting

---

[1] The meaning is—Ayres Diz was a mulatto, Miguel de Castanhoso a Spaniard, and Lopo Dalmansa a Gallician.

the Patriarch Joseph; and in order to occupy the Portuguese in something, he sent them to the province of Doaro, which is near the country of the Gallas, his enemies, in order to form a frontier garrison. Doaro, too, marches with the kingdom of Zeila, which also they equally fear. Calide, captain of Doaro, was the same who in the first battle came over to the King Gradeus, of whom I said that he was the man to cry, "Long live the conqueror!" For these reasons the King ordered that the Portuguese should be settled in that province. But the captain Calide was not pleased at the King's settling them there, inasmuch as his income was lessened to give to them. He therefore gave orders to slay them, or turn them out of his country. This captain was a great and powerful lord, because, besides that the province of Doaro was large and fertile, he also held the province of Bale, and the captain of Hadia was his neighbour and friend. From these countries he collected seven hundred horsemen, six hundred archers, and six thousand bucklermen. He recruited them so secretly that, almost suddenly, one morning at daybreak, he attacked our camp. But as it happened we were always vigilant, and as his men feared us and dreaded to attack us, our men discovered them, and they could not deliver the assault they wished. As Calide was known by a certain device he bore, our men told off seven matchlockmen to especially watch him and fire on him, because, he dead, his followers would be easily defeated. They did this, and, as he was in the van distinguishable from the others, he was slain before battle was joined. On his death some of his followers made signs of submission: these belonged to the lands which the King had given us, and they sent us word that they were our vassals, and desired to obey us, and pay rent to us, as the King ordered, because the rebellion was not in accordance with their wish. The others hung back, doing nothing, until we attacked them and put them to flight, killing some of them. As soon as we had defeated them we wrote to the King, telling him what had happened, and how Calide had attacked and wanted to slay us all, but that by the mercy and help of Our Lord we had slain him. The King was very pleased at this news, as he always feared Calide, as the nearest heir to the throne on his mother's side. I say on his mother's side, because, owing to the custom of the country, he could not be on the father's side. The custom is that all the males, sons of the kings, except the heirs, are as soon as they are born sent to a very large rock in the province of Amara, where they stay all their lives, never leaving it, unless the reigning king dies leaving no heirs, when they take from the rock the nearest, and he reigns. He takes with him neither wife nor children, if he has them, but they remain on the rock, and he marries another wife in the kingdom. They do this to males and not to females, because they fear the males may create some disturbance in the kingdom over the heirship, whereas women would not. These they marry to the chief men in the kingdom; thus was married the mother of this Calide whom we slew: she was the aunt of the King Onadinguel. For this reason King Gradeus was always suspicious of the said Calide, and was pleased at his death. Through his death, also, we had some peace in our territories.[1]

---

[1] Bruce, speaking of Doaro, Hadea, and Adel, says: "The climate was intensely hot, feverish, and unhealthy; and for the most part, from these circumstances, fatal to strangers, and hated by the Abyssinians." *Travels*, vol. iii, p. 48. Calide is mentioned both in chap. xv and here: the indications Bermudez gives are that he was a cousin of the Baharnagash, a man who had been appointed by the Preste governor of the country near Antalo (therefore that he was a Christian); that when the Imam Ahmad overran it, he joined his party and remained governor (therefore he became a Muhamedan); that after the victory of D. Christovão he joined him (that is became a Christian again); that subsequently he was made governor of Bali and Doaro by the Preste, but that at some unnamed date he attacked the Portuguese, who had been located in Doaro by the King he then served, and in this battle lost his life; also, that his mother was an aunt of Lebna Dengel.

CHAPTER XLVIII.

Of how the Gallas attacked the Portuguese, and drove them from the Country of Doaro, where they were.

AFTER the death of Calide of Doaro, we enjoyed peace for four months; at the end of which time the King sent word to us that we should be on our guard, as he had learned that the Gallas were going to attack us suddenly: because they were determined to destroy us in any possible way, inasmuch as neither they nor any other enemies of the Preste John had any hindrance save that we caused them. These Gallas lived in the country near Magadoxo; they are a fierce and cruel people, who make war on their

---

Calide may be either a Muhamedan or a Christian name, and the facts detailed above seem to be a jumble of the life of Abbas, who never was a Christian, and that of Fanuel, who never was a Muhamedan. The Garad Abbas was the son of Aboun, the brother of the Imam Ahmad, and as the governor of the northern provinces of Abyssinia was known as the Baharnagash. He was appointed Vazir by the Imam Ahmad, when Addolé was killed in an ambush in Tigré, somewhere about 1533 or 1534. He had defeated Galâwdêwos in Tigré early in the latter's reign, and was in the neighbourhood of Antalo at the time of D. Christovão's action; he was afterwards governor of Bali and Doaro, and was killed by Galâwdêwos early in 1545, in a battle in the district of Wadj (see Conzelman, §§ 23 to 25, and Basset, *Histoire*, p. 444). As to Fanuel, see the passage in Conzelman (§§ 31 to 35), beginning: "He (Galâwdêwos) appointed as his governor of the places in the east, such as Dawaro and its dependencies, Fanuel, one of the principal officers of his army; next he marched to the west of Abyssinia, after having received the blessing of Abba Yosâb (Joseph), who was then metropolitan." The date of this is about March, 1548. Fanuel was very successful against the Muhamedans, but no mention is made of either the Portuguese or the Gallas. He died about six months after his first appointment. Fanuel was the son of Madelaine, of the family of the Doaro princes; she was killed during the wars with the Imam Ahmad, and was canonised; her day is 20th Maskaram, or September 17th; on his father's side (not on his mother's) he had some royal blood in his veins. If Fanuel be Calide, it is difficult to credit the alleged attack on the Portuguese (see Basset, *Histoire*, p. 16 *n*.). To add to the welter of confusion, Bermudez appears to describe the death of Abbas in his chap. xxxviii: only he calls him King of Adem, and makes him leave Del Wanbara a widow. This note has grown to a great length, but its purpose will be served if it shows the difficulties that beset most of the statements made by Bermudez.

neighbours, and on all, only to destroy and depopulate their countries. In the places they conquer they slay all the men, cut off the privy parts of the boys, kill the old women, and keep the young for their own use and service. It would seem that hence came the Çumbas[1] who are destroying Guinea, for in cruelty they are alike. When the King's warning reached us, we began to prepare the munitions necessary for the war, especially powder, because we chiefly accomplished our ends with fire, and supplemented thereby our deficiency in strength. We had plenty of material to make powder, because there is in that country a large amount of saltpetre, of sulphur, and of osiers for charcoal, which we made very excellent. We also cleared the country of women, boys, and everyone who could not fight; with these went nearly all the inhabitants, great and small, from fear of the cruelty of the Gallas. A country like that is quickly depopulated, for the inhabited places have no buildings that are defensible, nor which cost much to rebuild, as they are all of wattle and straw. They have no other walls or fortresses, as the rocks are the fortresses, and indeed nature has made them stronger than are ours made by hand. We were ready some time, awaiting the Gallas, when one day they appeared. They were innumerable, and did not come on without order like barbarians, but advanced collected in bodies, like squadrons. When they saw us they halted, some waiting for the rest, and then marched in one mass and camped near us, at a distance where our shots could do them no harm. As they were many, and we very few, we did not go out to attack them, but waited in our camp. At the most there were one hundred and fifty of us, as the rest were already dead, nearly all in war, some few of sicknesses, which were not

---

[1] As to Çumbas, see p. 150 of *The Strange Adventures of Andrew Battell*, published by the Hakluyt Society, Second Series, No. 6, 1901.

so rife as they might have been amongst our people, considering that that country is hot and lies under the sun. Some had returned to India with Manuel da Cunha after the death of the King of Zeila, when it appeared that with that man's death all the fighting was over. Our camp was pitched on rising ground, whence we commanded the rest of the country, and stood over those that fought against us. We defended ourselves here for ten or twelve days, awaiting the King. During this time we killed many of them by shot, and by our artifices of fire, because they approached so fearlessly that we could aim every cast and shot. Meanwhile our powder failed, and as the King did not come, we had to leave the position in search of him. The Gallas did not pursue us: perchance because they also did not desire our company; I doubt not that had our force been larger we should have driven them back against their will. Meanwhile the King came, and hearing that the Gallas were masters of the country he was amazed, and did not regain command of himself for a long time. Afterwards he wept like a child, and said: "My sin is great that such evil has befallen me. It must astonish you that I do not lose my senses when I think of the loss I have suffered." In fact, he had lost three large kingdoms, two of them, Bale and Doaro, as large as Castille and Portugal, and Hadia alone as large as all France. This kingdom of Hadia marches with Melindi. And there is in that country much myrrh, incense, and frankincense. Some Portuguese said to him: "Your highness, be not vexed, as God can remedy everything, and will remedy this if you will make friends with the Patriarch D. João Bermudez, who is the true Patriarch, and not pay any attention to the other schismatic." To this he answered nothing, but gave the order to march, and told me to follow with the others. As he considered the Galla war unlucky, he determined to visit certain kingdoms of his empire which he had not yet seen, and attack the Gallas on his return, had they not previously retired to their own country, because they only advance to ravage, and then retreat.[1]

CHAPTER XLIX.
Of the Kingdom of Oggy, and of Gorague its Province.

FROM Doaro we marched seven or eight days towards the south-west, until we reached the kingdom of Christians called Oggy,[2] in which reigned a good man called Frey Miguel, brother-in-law of King Gradeus, and his tributary. He received us very hospitably, and gave all the army good entertainment. This king has five thousand horsemen, of whom six hundred wear harness; the rest are light cavalry, and ride bare back. He has also ten thousand infantry who fight with casting javelins; the horsemen have spears as long as ours. The caparisons of the horses are of antelope hide, quilted inside, and adorned outside with rich furniture. He has in his army six hundred hand mills, worked by women. There is in this kingdom a heathen province called Gorague,[3] which marches with

---

[1] The Ethiopian chronicles make no mention of this Galla incursion, which, if it happened, was little more than a raid. They do make Galâwdêwos visit this part of the country after Fanuel's death, that is, late in 1548 or early in 1549, and stay there five months fighting the Muhamedans; it was during this time that he defeated Nur (Conzelman, § 37). The Portuguese editor considers that the journey through the different Abyssinian provinces, which fills the next few chapters, is imaginary. It certainly bears the appearance of being imaginary from beginning to end, and the Ethiopian chronicles lend no colour to it.

[2] Oggy must be Wadj, the district near Shoa, on the left bank of the Hawash river, already mentioned on p. 228 *n*. The chronicle says Galâwdêwos built a palace there after Fanuel's death (Conzelman, § 40). Frey Miguel may be a mistake for Fanuel, in whose government it was.

[3] Gorague—that is, Guraghe—is a country on the right bank of the Hawash, between it and the Omo. A reputation for sorcery frequently attaches to the residents of unfamiliar countries. Pearce gives the dofters of Gojame the worst character (vol. i, p. 331).

Quiloa and Mangalo. These heathens of Gorague are great wizards, and foretell by the pluck, tripes, and entrails of the animals they sacrifice. By their sorceries they make it appear that fire does not burn, in this way. They kill an ox with certain ceremonies, and anointed with its fat they cause a great fire to be lighted, and make as if they entered it, and as if they seated themselves in a chair; sitting thus at ease in that fire, they foretell and reply to the questions asked, without being burned.[1] The Goragues pay their king as tribute every year two golden lions, three golden dogs, an ounce of gold, and some golden fowls with their chickens also of gold; the whole weighs as much as eight men can lift, and this gold is fine and good. They pay also six buffalo loads of impure silver. They pay also one thousand live cows, and many skins of lions, leopards, and antelope. There is in this country much civet, sandalwood, blackwood, and amber. The men of this province say that white men come there to trade, but they do not know their nationality, whether they are Portuguese, Turks, or others.

CHAPTER L.

Of the Kingdom of the Gafates.

WEST of the kingdom of Oggy lies the kingdom of the Gafates,[2] also tributary and subordinate to the Ethiopian empire. The Gafates are pagans, and it is commonly said

---

[1] Lobo (p. 107) tells the same story as to the inhabitants of the country near the source of the Nile; he borrowed it from Paez.

[2] This is the district of which, in a previous chapter, Bermudez says that he was Governor for several months; the two accounts vary very greatly. Alvarez (chap. cxxxiv) gives a description from hearsay of the Cafates, from which Bermudez could have derived all his particulars. Bruce (vol. iv, p. 442) says the language of the country is distinct. Pearce (vol. ii, p. 10), calls it Coffa, and says the people are

that they are Jews. They are a barbarous and evil people, rebellious and turbulent. There are many of them scattered over the other provinces of the empire, but everywhere they are considered strangers and different from other people, and are abhorred of them, as Jews are here. They are lords in this country, and there dwells among them no other nation save a few Christians, who separated from the Abyssinians when they refused submission to the Apostolic See; these Christians still say and protest that they are submissive to the said See. The Gafates in these parts have much land, and are rich with gold, and a few good articles of merchandise, especially fine cotton cloths. Inland there are wide and fertile plains. They say there is in the country an invisible wood that makes men invisible. When the King reached this country, he ordered war against its people, and an armed and forcible attack on the inhabitants: because, since the death of his father they had been in rebellion, and would not pay him their tribute, or recognise him as their lord. On this the Gafates collected, and one morning at dawn attacked the Abyssinian camp, and killed many. When the Portuguese, who as his guards were close to the King's tent, heard the noise and clamour, they ran up, it being now nearly morning, and drove the Gafates out of the camp, slaying several of them. They pursued the fugitives to their villages, where they found much booty, with which they returned rich and content. They found *bezutos*, which are very fine quilts,[1] and they found cotton cloths as

---

Christians. Basset (*Histoire*, p. 224 *n.*) may also be consulted. It is strange, if the inhabitants were, as Bermudez says, in rebellion, that he remained in safety among them so long, and that the inhabitants obeyed Galâwdêwos by mounting guard over him.

[1] Alvarez (p. 63) "himself covered with hairy cotton cloths which they name *basutos*; they are good for the country, and there are some here of a high price." See also note on his p. 182, *bazzato*, carded cotton.

delicate as *sinabafas*,[1] and *beatilhas*,[2] so fine that a piece of thirty or forty ells could be held between the hands. They found also much gold in pots and vessels, and buried under the hearths in their huts, where they used to hide it as the most secure place; they themselves showed it to our men to escape death. The King would not stay here long, as he did not intend to do them great damage; merely to frighten them. The winter, too, was drawing near, and it was necessary to return to his country before the rivers rose, which are heavily flooded in that part and quite stop travel on the roads; because the winters are very rainy and the land mountainous; the rivers collect much water from these mountains, and swell vastly. We therefore very soon left that rabble, and marched towards Damute, which lies nearly due west of the Gafates.

CHAPTER LI.

Of the Kingdom of Damute, and of its Provinces, and of the great riches there are in it, and of certain marvellous things.

THE kingdom of Damute marches on the western side with the Gafates, of whom I have above spoken; it is on the bank of the Nile, at the spot where it cuts the equator.[3] This province stands rather surrounded by the Nile than on either side of it, for that river makes here many and considerable bends. The approach to this kingdom is most difficult, by reason of the rugged crags there are on the banks of the Nile. Besides that these are rugged, there are among them certain passes made artificially in rocks bored by a crowbar, and closed by gates guarded by armed

---

[1] *Sinabafa;* see Yule's Glossary, s.v., *Shanbaff.*
[2] *Beatilha;* see Yule's Glossary, s.v., *Betteela*, a kind of muslin
[3] An error of nearly 700 miles; Damot is not on the equator.

men: so that a small force can resist and prevent the entry of those enemies who desire to pass without their permission. When the Emperor goes there these gates are broken, and opened freely to all who desire to enter. The kingdom of Damute is large, with several subordinate provinces.[1] The chief part is inhabited by Christians, but some provinces belong to pagans. In all are found great stores of gold and of rock crystal. All the country is well supplied and fertile, especially the part nearest the Nile, which has more hills and streams than the rest. It breeds numerous animals, wild and tame, worms (*bichos*), and strange and poisonous serpents. They breed cattle, horses, buffaloes, mules, asses, sheep, and other flocks; the cattle are larger than ours, so much so that some of them are almost as large as elephants. They have huge horns; some of them will even hold a pitcherful of wine. They are used to transport and store wine and water, as pitchers and barrels are here.[2] I dare to say this, because D. Rodrigo de Lima brought one of these horns of this size to this kingdom during the lifetime of the King, your grandfather, when there accompanied him the Ambassador Tagazauo and the Padre Franciscaluarez. There is found

---

[1] Damot is on the right bank of the Blue Nile, at the opening of the great bend that river makes, and just south of its source. Gafat lies on the south of it, the Gojame district on the east, and Agoumeder on the west. It is part of the province of Gojame, which itself includes the whole of the great bend. Many of the stories told in this chapter are also in Alvarez, chap. cxxxiii. See Basset, *Histoire*, p. 54 *n.*, for further information.

[2] The size of the oxen which carry these large horns is grossly exaggerated here; perhaps a sentence in Alvarez (chap. cxxxiii) may be responsible. Lobo (p. 70), with his love of the fabulous, says these oxen with the large horns are fed on cows' milk; sometimes a single one requiring that of three or four cows daily. As a matter of fact, these cattle are of the usual size, but for some reason the horns of both sexes are at times abnormally large. Salt (p. 259) speaks of horns nearly 4 ft. long and 21 ins. in girth. Raffray (p. 247) says he measured the capacity of one, which he found to hold 14 litres, or rather over three gallons. They are not peculiar to this part of Abyssinia.

in this country a kind of unicorn, which is wild and timid, of the shape of a horse and the size of an ass.[1] There are there elephants, lions, leopards, and other wild beasts which we do not know here. Near Damute is a province of women without men, who live in the manner told of the ancient Amazons of Scythia, who at a certain time consented to the visits of some men, their neighbours; of the children, they sent the males to their father, and kept the females, bringing them up in their own customs and manner. Those of Ethiopia act in the same way; they also burn the left breast like the others did, in order to more quickly draw the bows they use in war and the chase. The queen of these women does not consort with men, and is therefore worshipped by them as a goddess.[2] They are suffered and preserved, as it is said they were founded by the Queen of Sheba, who visited King Solomon. In the country of these women are griffins, which are birds so large that they kill buffaloes, and raise them in their claws as an eagle lifts a rabbit. It is said that in certain precipitous and uninhabited mountains is born and lives the bird phenix, which is sole and alone in the world, and is

---

[1] The Portuguese editor takes this to apply to the rhinosceros; it is more likely the oryx antelope, which, when standing in profile, appears to have only one horn. A rhinosceros was no novelty, as one was seen in Portugal in 1515, and Castanheda's description (Bk. III, chap. cxxxiv) was published in 1552. Lobo (p. 69) describes the unicorn as an animal so timid that it can only be seen dashing from one thicket to another, and as in appearance like a large well-made bay horse, with black points; he distinguishes between those from different provinces. He adds that they are so fearful that they go always in company with other animals, especially the elephant, to whom all stags and gazelles resort for protection against beasts of prey.

[2] Alvarez' account is different. He says the queen does not marry, but has children; also that there are permanent male residents, but the women take the lead in everything. It is, of course, useless to search for the origin of this tale in Abyssinia, but Bruce speaks of a Princess Fatima, called "Negusta Errum," or Queen of the Greeks, who in the early seventeenth century reigned at Mendera, near the Atbara river (35 deg. east longitude, and just north of the 15 deg. north latitude). The ruler of the state was always a woman, who was sovereign over a Greek colony

one of the marvels of nature. The dwellers in those countries say that there is this bird there, and that they have seen it and know it, and that it is a large and beautiful bird. There are other birds there so large that they cast a shadow like a cloud. Up the Nile, towards the south, there is, on the borders of Damute, a large province called Conche. This is subordinate to Damute, and there dwell there pagans: the chief is called by the name of his title, Ax Gagce, which means lord of riches, as in fact he is.[1] When he needs them, the Ax Gagce collects ten thousand horse and over twenty thousand foot. He has with his army one thousand hand mills, worked by women, who grind in them the meal needed for the army. When we were in Damute this chief was in rebellion against the King of Damute; on this, King Gradeus said to me that, as a prelate and mediator of peace, I should send word to him, that his majesty was much enraged against him because of his rebellion and disobedience, and had determined to destroy him by means of the invincible and superhuman strength of the Portuguese, whom he had brought with him for that purpose. I did this, and told him he should obey his Emperor, and bring him his tribute and visit him, as I pledged myself that his majesty would treat him with clemency and kindness. He agreed, and sent a large sum of gold, and many cows and other supplies, sufficient for all the army, and many slaves, mules, and asses for the transport. The Ax Gagce supplied the Emperor's camp completely, nothing being wanting. At length he arrived, accompanied by many people well equipped, both horse and foot, and he very richly clothed. When he arrived at the point where he

---

[1] What this name is cannot be said. Ludolf (Bk. I, chap. iii) mentions a Galla country called Gajghe, but gives no indication of its position. Pearce (vol. ii, p. 10) speaks on hearsay of the Coucha Gallas as separated from "Coffa" by a river.

could be seen from the Emperor's tent, he got off his horse and took off the rich garments he wore, and retaining others of less value, came to the tent and awaited permission to go inside. He afterwards entered the first compartment of the tent, which was cut off by certain curtains. Here he threw himself on the ground until the Emperor gave him permission to rise; he received him with good words, and ordered him to be clothed and given food. At this time he spoke to him from behind the curtains, not giving him a sight of himself until four days had elapsed, when he allowed him to enter where he was. For this honour and favour that Gradeus did to Ax Gagce, the latter said to him: "Sir, I wish to do something for you that neither I nor my predecessors have ever done for your father, nor for the other emperors, your ancestors; that is, to display to you the riches and the secrets of my countries, because we obey you on the condition that you do not see them except with our permission." He conducted us through his territories to a large river, sixty fathoms or more across, on the banks of which are many poisonous snakes. Their bite is mortal, but, by the grace of God, nature has provided an antidote to that evil: it is a herb which grows in some parts of that country, which is so antipathetic to the snakes I mentioned, that they fly from it as from an enemy, and do not even approach anyone who carries it; nor has the poison any effect where it is, whether it is ground into a plaster or whether it is the juice. We saw one of these snakes that had just swallowed a buffalo it had killed; the King ordered it to be killed; it had masses of fat inside, like a large and fat pig, this is useful in chills and other diseases. There are also others called umbrella snakes, because they have on their heads a skin with which they cover a stone of great price, which they are said to have in their heads. Across the river the land is barren and uninhabited; it is generally sandy, red, and dry, like some places on the banks of the Tagus. The soil contains two parts of gold to one of earth; that is what is obtainable in the melting, for which there are many artificers in that country, as many as there are blacksmiths here, and more, for there gold is more common than iron here. The lords do not consent to any bridge or boat on that river, that the crossing may not be easy, lest all those who desire to obtain gold should get over. The method of crossing that river is this. There are buffaloes accustomed to cross, and when people wish to go over they drive them in front and swim, holding the buffaloes' tails. They fill some leather sacks they carry with the earth, and tie them round their necks, and return holding the buffaloes as they came. In this way it is not everyone who can cross. Those who go over are compelled to melt the gold they bring in the foundries of the Ax Gagce, for all are his, in order to pay their dues. King Gradeus, to ascertain the facts more accurately, sent some of his men across the river; they went over and brought some of the earth, such as the others had brought, which when melted down yielded as much as the other. The men King Gradeus sent said that all the earth of that district was of the same nature, as they had examined it for some distance and found it all alike. They said that the ground was so hot that they could not lie down on it to sleep, but searched for rocks and slabs on which they lay; also that there were some large red ants that bit them, which were so numerous that they could not sleep. As it appeared to us that there was ground for astonishment in the large quantity of gold that we saw, the Ax Gagce of that country told King Gradeus not to be amazed, for he would show him still more. He took us down the river towards the south-west, marching slowly for two days; then he showed us across the river a mountain, which shone in places like the sun; he told us that that was all gold. King Gradeus was so pleased at this, and at the hospitality he had shown us, that he determined to make him a Christian; he asked him if he agreed, and told him he would always be his great friend. He replied that most certainly he wished to become one. The King at once arranged his baptism, and a bishop, prelate of the monastery called Debra Libanus, baptized him. This monastery is the chief of all those in Amara. King Gradeus was his godfather, and he was called Andre. Andre told King Gradeus that in those parts were certain neighbours of his, who were but bad neighbours, who ravaged his territories, robbing and murdering his subjects; that as God had brought him there with the noble Portuguese people, whose renown carried fear to all residents of those parts, he besought him to avenge him on his enemies, who caused him so much annoyance, to be a future warning not to injure his vassals. The King granted his petition, and ordered both his own men and the Portuguese to attack the enemy's country and raid it, making war on them with fire and blood, looting and destroying their property, capturing the people, and slaying all who resisted. They obeyed orders, attacked the country, and looted, slew, and destroyed all as they advanced. This they did over a large area, from whence they collected great spoil of valuable articles, and much gold, which they brought back. After this King Gradeus returned to Damute, where, as we heard the inhabitants say, there were wonderful things to be seen, all of which are not fit to be written down, because told to any one who had not seen them they would appear but fables. But your highness may believe that it is with reason that Africa is called the mother of prodigies; such no doubt it is, especially in the interior near the river Nile, where there are mountains, streams, and uninhabited places, where the ground is very suitable and the air and sky very kindly, fit to produce anything desired.

CHAPTER LII.

Of the Kingdoms of Gojame, and Dembia, and Amar, and of other lands adjoining these, and of the River Nile, in whose Neighbourhood they all are.

ALTHOUGH, as I said above, all African tales are not fit for the telling, still I will set forth shortly some of the things in the countries through which we passed, because it will please your highness to hear them.[1] Returning then from Damute down the Nile towards the Red Sea, we came to the kingdom of Gojame, which adjoins Damute. Gojame is also a large, well supplied, fertile, and rich kingdom. It is inhabited by Christians, subject to the Preste John. There is gold, though not so much as in Damute. In this kingdom of Gojame, under the sand of certain rivers, they find some spongy stones like pumice stones, save that they are heavy and yellow; when melted down these nearly all turn to gold, only a little dross remaining. In this kingdom of Gojame is the Nile cataract of which Tullius speaks in Scipio's Dream.[2] I will describe

---

[1] It may be said, once for all, that throughout this chapter Bermudez' geography is entirely at fault. Down the Blue Nile from Damot leads away from the Red Sea, not towards it, and nowhere does that river approach within thirty or forty leagues of Suakin or of the Red Sea; nothing is to be gained by following his mistakes and pointing them out. Gojame province occupies the great bend of the Blue Nile, whose sources lie in it; the district called by that name lies east of Damot. Basset (*Histoire*, p. 78 *n.*), and Alvarez (chap. cxxxv), may be consulted.

[2] In Scipio's Dream, the well-known episode of *De Republica*, Cicero uses some cataract of the Nile as an analogy. As the inhabitants of the country near the fall are, from the magnitude of its sound, deaf, so we are unable to hear the music of the spheres. There is nothing to connect this with any particular cataract; probably the tale arose from those on the borders of Egypt. Bermudez' estimate of the height of the cataract near Alata (eight thousand feet) is ludicrous. Bruce, who visited it puts it at forty feet, with a width of half a mile (vol. v, p. 105). Paez, who saw it in 1618, puts the height at fourteen fathoms (Legrand, p. 211). Lobo excites Bruce's sarcasm by saying that he sat on the rocks behind it (Legrand, p. 108).

R

it to your highness, for it is a wonderful thing, which merits to be known, nor is it at all a dream, as indeed some things are dreams, which chattering men tell of this and other things they have not seen. This cataract is a great fall, which the Nile makes from a high rock to a lower one. This rock is about half a league high, a sheer precipice with no slope or incline. From this the whole Nile in one body falls into a deep pool, surrounded by massive and lofty mountains. The quantity of water is great, for it is collected from more than three hundred leagues; it makes such a great noise that it appears like thunder, and terrifies those not accustomed to it. The sound is so vast that three or four crossbow shots away it stuns the listener, and for all that distance no other sound can be heard save this, however loud it may be; nor has the air room to receive any other than this, which fills everything. Thus that sound overpowers all others, as the splendour of a large light obscures smaller ones. That place is called in the country language Catadhi, which means noise or great strife; from this the Latins seem to have derived the name *catadupa*. West of the two kingdoms of Damute and Gojame, towards Guinea, the country is desert and thinly peopled; there dwell Gafates and other pagans, complete savages. These parts are not much known in the Preste John's country, nor is there intercourse with the people of that empire, to which it neither renders homage nor owes service; for the whole of that country lies east of the Nile. There is gold in those countries of the west towards Guinea; but they say that what comes from the interior has points and shapes like some that comes from the Antilles.[1] Along the Nile down stream from Gojame, and marching with it, is another kingdom of ancient Abyssinian

---

[1] *que o do sertã tem pontas, ou area, como algum que vem das Antilhas.*

Christians, a large and wealthy one, called Dembia. In this the Nile makes a large lake thirty leagues long by twenty broad,[1] in which are many small islands all studded with monasteries of religious men, of whom I have spoken before. This is not the source whence the Nile springs; it comes from much higher up. Further down is another river called Agaoa, where dwell Moors and pagans mixed. It has its own king, who obeys neither the Preste nor the Turk. It continues to the borders of Egypt. Up to Dembia the Nile flows from south-west to north-east, and reaches to within thirty or forty leagues of the Red Sea opposite Suakin; here it turns north-west until it enters the Mediterranean. At this elbow, King Onadinguel wanted to cut a canal to turn the Nile into the Red Sea, as his ancestor Ale belale began to do; for this purpose he asked the king, your grandfather, for quarrymen.[2] West of Dembia is the province called Çubia Nubia, now belonging to the Moors, which they say was formerly Christian; probably this was so, for old ruined churches are found there. Joined to Çubia Nubia, on the west, is a large Moorish kingdom called Amar, through which Cairo merchants for Ialofa and Mădinga, and other parts of Guinea, pass to get gold; from Amar they take salt, which is found in mines; it is valuable in Guinea, where there is great dearth and need of it. Before leaving the river Nile, I wish to solve a doubt which Europeans consider unsolved, and about which some have written fantastical opinions, because they had no knowledge of the seasons that succeed each other in those countries, nor of their climate. The doubt refers to the cause of the rising of the Nile. About this your highness must know, that that river rises during the three months of the year which are the driest in Europe, namely, July, August, and September. It in-

---

[1] Cf. chap. xxiv, p. 175, above.   [2] Cf. p. 131, above.

creases so much that all Egypt is under water, and it is never flooded at any time save that which is here, as I say, the driest of all the year; on this several persons have started the doubt that as it occurs in the dry season the rise cannot be due to rain; but in this they err, because in the countries through which the Nile flows, the full force of the winter is in those very months, therefore it rises then and at no other time. It carries much water, because it comes from far over two hundred leagues above Damute; that is, with the twists and turns it makes, eight hundred leagues before it reaches Egypt; it passes great mountain ranges, whence it collects many streams carrying much water. Here is the true reason of the rise of that river, and not those causes they guess at, like men who talk of what they know nothing.[1] There are not many who know all the secrets of Africa, especially of the river Nile, for of it the very dwellers by it know not the whole, because it is a mighty river and difficult to investigate; for this reason I have shortly diverged from my history, in order to relate to your highness the things that I have seen, since perchance there is now no other in these parts who knows them by sight save I, who dwelt there thirty years and more. Besides had I not taken that journey which I did with King Gradeus, even although I had lived in that country as long again, I should not have known the part I have described above. Now I will return to the story of myself and my companions.

---

[1] Bermudez is, of course, correct as to the cause of the rising of the Nile, but unless his league differs from those in ordinary use, his length of the only river Nile he knew is exaggerated.

CHAPTER LIII.

Of how King Gradeus returned to Simen, and settled the Portuguese in Bethmariam.

KING GRADEUS visited the countries described in the last chapters, which are outlying and not under his immediate rule, both because he desired at the commencement of his reign to become acquainted with them, and also to display the glory and superiority which the companionship of the Portuguese, whom he had with him, gave him. After spending ten or twelve months on this tour, he determined to return to the provinces of Simen and Amara, where the kings or emperors of that land make their longest stay: both because it is a more fertile and secure country, and because they are born there and are natives of it.[1] In Amara and Vedremudro are mines of copper, tin, and lead. There are here certain churches cut out of the living rock, which are attributed to angels. Indeed, the work appears superhuman, because, though they are of the size of the large ones in this country, they are each excavated with its pillars, its altars, and its vaults, out of a single rock, with no mixture of any outside stone. When the Moors overran that country they wished to destroy these churches, but could not either with crowbars, or with the gunpowder which they exploded in them, doing no damage at all. In former days Padre Franciscaluarez described the notable things of these provinces, and I will not delay further than to point out one thing that appears to me important. That is, that the commerce of this country with Damute, whence

---

[1] Simen is, of course, Semien, the very mountainous country on the left of the Tacazze, in the great bend that river makes. Amara is equally Amhara, the great province of Abyssinia south of Tigré. The rock-churches are in Lasta; as to them and the Muhamedan attack, see Castanhoso, chap. xxvii, p. 99 *n.*, above. Possibly Vedremudro is meant for Beguemeder, which Alvarez (p. 351) calls Bagamidri. It is the large territory east of Lake Tzâna.

the Abyssinians chiefly obtain their gold, is mainly carried on with iron, of which there is much, especially in the neighbouring province of Tigremacā.[1] This iron is so valuable in Damute that they give gold for it in equal weights. I mention this because I believe that Damute, and its province Conche, march with Sofala, and should the necessary iron be brought from Sofala they would also give their gold for it.[2] These provinces lie east of Gojame and Dembia, and the province of Bethmariam south-east; here the King made good to us the income we had lost in Doaro by the incursion of the Gallas. The province of Bethmariam is large and well peopled;[3] the receipts from it are considerable; all these the King gave the Portuguese; the land was divided among us, according to the recipient's position; the smallest share amounted to one thousand cruzados a year; the Captain got over ten thousand, and I as much. The King gave us this province as it was on the frontier of the kingdom of the revolted Gafates, in order that the Portuguese might raid their country, chastize them, and reduce them to obedience. Having concluded our march, and the King having arrived at the province of Simen, the Portuguese asked permission to visit the lands he had given them in the province of Bethmariam. I also asked permission to return to my country (of Portugal, as I meant). He granted it (meaning Bethmariam). I asked this permission in an underhand way, not to break the promise I had given him; and because I knew that if I asked for it directly he would refuse it, nay, would prevent my journey, or kill me, as he had wanted to for a long time.

---

[1] Tigremacā must be Tigre Makuanam, the name of the office of Governor; the province is Tigré.
[2] Between Damot and Sofala lie 30 degs. of latitude, say 2,000 miles as the crow flies.
[3] There are several places called Bethmariam; it is not clear to what district Bermudez refers.

CHAPTER LIV.

Of how the Patriarch went to Debarua, and stayed there two years.

I REMAINED in Bethmariam during the winter, which was commencing when we arrived. In order to acquire the good will and love of my subjects, I made them all the presents I could, and forgave them the rents they should have paid me, to keep them well disposed and favourable towards me, that they might not inform against me when I left; for the King had sent orders to all to look after me, and see that I did not leave the country. The King had given the same orders to Gaspar de Sousa, Captain of the Portuguese, who for this reason came to visit me frequently. I, in order to reassure him, feigned to have the gout in one leg, and lying on my bed said that I could not travel on foot. Gaspar de Sousa just then went to court, and I had the chance of doing what I wanted. In order not to be hindered by the people of the country, I sent for some of their leaders, and told them that I was very ill, as they could see, and that I desired to go on a pilgrimage to the monastery of Debra Libanus, to commend myself to God, and to beg the religious men there to pray God for me; that therefore I asked them to pay my rents to the servant whom I left in charge of my house and people. They were full of sorrow for my sickness, and grieved at my absence; as to the rents, they said they would do their duty and were glad to do it, considering what they owed me. As the direct road to Debarua passed through the place where the King was, I selected another country out of the direct line and uninhabited; for our journey we carried sufficient supplies for myself and the seven or eight persons I took with me, who were those whom I most trusted. I told them to say on the road that I was very ill, and was going to Debarua to obtain relief, as the country there and the air are more healthy. By this road I crossed an elbow of the Nile, which I passed twice with much toil, for the banks of the river were very steep; it was very doubtful if the armed men guarding certain narrow gates would allow me to go through them. I told my servants to say that a certain well-known servant of the King was coming behind, who was conveying me to Debarua to obtain relief: by this stratagem they allowed us to pass. On the way I met a Portuguese, called Ruy Coelho, on his way to court; after some conversation I said where I was bound, as I could not deny it; he told me to hurry on quickly, while he travelled slowly, in order that I might reach Debarua before he got to court, as he was bound to report to the King that he had met me, and if he said I was near he would order me to return. I afterwards met a royal servant, who also had to report it; but at length, with the help of God, and by the intercession of Our Lady, to whom I commended myself, I reached Debarua in safety, where certain Portuguese residents received me with much pleasure and hospitality. When the Bernagaez of that country heard of my arrival, he came to see me, and enquired: "What good luck has brought you to this country, Senhor Father?" I replied that I was very unwell, and had come to obtain relief. He replied that it seemed to him that I wanted to pass to the country of the Franks, which is near the sea; that he therefore begged me not to do this, but rest a few days, and then return to the King. I replied that I would never return to the King, because both he and all knew how much reason I had to fly from him, but that I meant to live in a hermitage of Our Lady in that country, and end my days there. "As such is your desire," said he, "I will write to the King and ask permission for you to remain here, and say that I take you in my charge, and am responsible for you that you will not go from here. I will tell him that you are very ill; therefore do not be angry, as all will be settled as you desire." He said also: "What I ask you, Senhor Father, for the love of God, is to remove the excommunications and cease the curses that you are hurling against the King and all this country, lest any evil befall us, and lest the King should be provoked with you."[1] To this the Portuguese replied that they were not surprised that I complained of the King and of them, for all had treated me as the Jews had treated Jesus Christ; who had crucified Him as a recompense for redeeming them. He and all his that were present said they were quite right, and that they knew that for this they deserved the chastisement of God; but that I should not be angry, as he would make it good to me. He ordered supplies to be at once brought, and provided me with all things necessary. He sent an honourable man of his household to the King, who returned in a few days with the reply. The reply was that the King was very angry with me, especially as I had called him a heretic and excommunicated him. The King said further, that were it not for the Portuguese, he would order me to be killed. He also said that I was a traitor and perfidious, and that I had broken the faith and promise I had made to him not to leave the country without his permission. To which I answered that he had given me such a permission, as I mentioned in the last chapter. He then ordered me to remain in Debarua, and not leave it without his special order, and directed the Bernagaez to look after me.

---

[1] This to some extent corroborates the story of the gold church vessel which Bermudez was accused of stealing, to which reference has been already made; for Couto in relating it says Bermudez went through Tigré, cursing every place on his journey (*Dec. VII*, Bk. 1, chap. 1).

CHAPTER LV.

Of what happened while the Patriarch was in Debarua, and of how Master Gonçallo came to him and went on to the King's Court.

I REMAINED in Debarua over two years,[1] commending myself to God. Most days I said Mass in a church of Our Lady, to which came some nine or ten resident Portuguese, who had fled here with others from the disastrous battle when the Goranha defeated us and captured D. Christovão. These Portuguese awaited a passage to India, and they rejoiced greatly when they saw me, as it appeared to them that they might more easily attain their desire through me and by my help; and also because they had not for a long time heard Mass, or confessed, or communicated, which they did frequently while I was there. The Captain, Gaspar de Sousa, sent several times to ask them to Court, as the King promised to do them much honour, but they would never leave me. At that time came there a Venetian, called Micer Çuncar, who brought a message from certain merchants of Grand Cairo, also Venetians, who had become responsible for rather more than forty Portuguese, who had been captured in the neighbourhood of Ormuz, for whom the Turks demanded thirty thousand cruzados.[2] Micer Çuncar came to enquire if the Preste John would pay this ransom. He ransomed them and

---

[1] Bermudez is sadly deficient in dates, but as he left Massowa in 1556, he probably reached Debarwa in 1554.

[2] There is no confirmation of this story by any other writer, but all the same it may be true. In August, 1552, Pir Beg, with a Turkish fleet, appeared before Muscat, and captured it and the Portuguese there, and then moved on to besiege Ormuz; he did not take it, but he did overrun the island of Kishm, and secure several ships. The number of Portuguese prisoners he made is nowhere given (see Couto, *Dec. VI*, Bk. x, chap. ii; and India Office MSS. *Corpo Chronologico*, vol. ii).

paid the said price for them, besides two or three thousand cruzados in expenses. There joined me also here a father of the company of Jesus, called Master Gonçallo, who with a companion came from India to learn about me and the other Portuguese, and to enquire the condition of the people of the Preste John. After I had told him what had happened, he went to the Court of the King, both to visit the Portuguese there, and to enquire what result could be expected in faith and religion in that country. He found so little disposition that he returned very discontented, and, as it were, flying from the death that was ready for him: inasmuch as he had some talk and dispute with the learned and the bishops of that country, and refuted them; for this reason they ordered him to be killed if he did not fly. This father enquired in that country about what I had done, and suffered, and lost, to restore that people to submission to the Church of Rome; and this he related, and to it gave public testimony in the cathedral church of Goa, as many people of credit, still living, who heard him, can say.

CHAPTER LVI.

Of how the Patriarch returned to India with Master Gonçallo.

WHILE we were in Debarua awaiting a passage to India, there came to the port of Massowah Antonio Peixoto, a Portuguese, with two foists, of which he was the Captain. As soon as we learned that they were there, Master Gonçallo and I determined to see him, and return with him to India. In order that I might do this without any hindrance from the Abyssinians, I used the following deception. A few days previously, the church of Our Lady in Debarua had been accidentally burned; I therefore asked the Bernagaez, who had charge of me, to allow me to visit Massowah, to beg alms from the Portuguese of the foists to rebuild the said church; also to lend me his mule for the journey, and some men to accompany and guard me. He did this willingly, as he thought that I was now settled in the country, and that I had forgotten the return to Portugal. He sent with me a Mass-priest, of his sect and nation, and also six or seven other men to accompany and guard me, advising us to return at once and not delay. To make matters more secure, an ambassador of the Preste John to the Governor of India went in our company, as it was thought that out of respect to him the captains of the foists would not take me, even if I asked them. But the Captain, Antonio Peixoto, was very pleased to take me; the ambassador, when he saw me on board, turned back, and would not accompany us, as he thought that on my account he would not be well received by the Portuguese. Master Gonçallo, as I said, and also the few Portuguese in Debarua, accompanied me. We reached Goa,[1] after experiencing on the sea a great storm, and also a failure of victuals, during the governorship of Francisco Barreto, who received us very hospitably, and settled me in St. Paul with the Fathers of the Company of Jesus, who, as long as I was there, treated me with much charity and honour: I was there nine or ten months, awaiting shipping for this

---

[1] Antonio Peixoto was not the man; it was João Peixoto, and he was sent to bring away Master Gonçalo (Couto, *Dec. VII*, Bk. III, chap. iii). Bermudez makes it out to be an accidental visit. They reached Goa early in May, 1556. With Gonçalo went Fulgencio Freire, also a Jesuit, and Diogo Dias do Prestes; as Bermudez states, the mission discovered that there was no hope of Galâwdêwos submitting to the Latin church. Bermudez must have sunk to insignificance at the time he left Massowa, for Couto, who had seen him personally, and who is painfully minute, could not discover how or when he reached Goa. The arrival of Gonçalo's mission at court is recorded in Conzelman (§ 47), but it appears to have been ante-dated there. The arrival of the D. André mentioned in this chapter will also be found in Conzelman (§ 54).

kingdom. The Governor ordered your highness's comptroller of revenue to give me everything that I needed, and I was well supplied with all necessaries both on land and for the voyage. While I was there, there arrived in India the Patriarch D. João Nunez, and the Bishop D. André, with his companions.

CHAPTER LVII.
Of how the Patriarch embarked for Portugal, remained a year on St. Helena, and returned the year following.

WHEN the time for embarcation came, I went to Cochin, because it is thence that the ships start; the Governor arranged good accommodation for me in one of them, and a sufficiency of supplies. The commander of that voyage was D. João de Menezes, son of the Craveiro,[1] also called D. João de Menezes, from whom I received much honour and attention up to the island of St. Helena, where I remained much against his will, I being obstinate. I remained there one year, suffering some corporal discomfort from hunger and other needs, for that island is so cut off from human society, that no one touches there save by good luck at a year's interval. Still, as to the spirit,[2] I was consoled by thinking that I was here away from the disorders of the world, and that I would stay here all my life; but that enemy of the peace of souls—Satan—had detained in that refuge certain fugitive slaves who had fled from some ships that touched there;[3] it was said that they

---

[1] When the Knights of the Order of Christ lived in a house of their own order, the Claveiro was the keeper of the keys. This fleet left Cochin early in 1557.

[2] The word in the original is *spū*, possibly short for "espirito."

[3] This passage from Linschoten (Hak. Soc. ed., 1884), vol. ii, p. 257, throws light on this. "Likewise upon a certaine time two Caffares or blacke people of Mosambique, and one Iaver, with two women slaves

had killed another chaplain; they began to seduce my slaves, who would not work for me. Despairing of any human help in my old age and sickness, I was compelled to return the next year to Portugal in the ship *St. Paul*, captain, Ruy de Mello. I reached Lisbon in the month of August, 1559,[1] in the reign of your highness, to whom may God grant a long life and peace, with His grace now and glory in His kingdom.—Amen.

CHAPTER LVIII.

Of the Conclusion of the Work.

THIS is the relation for which your highness asked me, and which it was my duty to give, of the men entrusted to me by the King, your grandfather, of glorious memory, who gave such a good account of themselves in those kingdoms, that as long as there are people there the Portuguese will be remembered with great renown. The Abyssinians, not content with calling the Portuguese valiant men and courageous, and other things of that nature, alleged that no human courage could compare with that of the Portuguese, for they seemed a natural prodigy, or else that God had miraculously created those men to succour and restore, on His behalf, that Empire. The great men and nobles of that country considered it a great honour to marry their relatives to the Portuguese, that their families might be made illustrious by union with such noble persons. Not only among the Abyssinians, but also through

---

stoale out of the shippes, and hid themselves in the Rockes of this Iland, which are verie high and wilde, whereby men can hardly passe them. They lived there together and begot children, so that in the ende they were at the least twentie persons." After many years of effort they were all captured and taken to Portugal, and the island cleared. Linschoten was there in 1589.

[1] I have already pointed out in the Introduction that this date is one year out. I give there the steps by which this result is attained.

all the neighbouring kingdoms, the noble fame of the Portuguese was spread. All this honour, and more even than I can tell of, was gained by Portugal by sending there only four hundred men. Not to weary your honour, I have condensed this narrative, and I have not related all the battles in which those few Portuguese conquered, the kings and powerful princes they terrorised, the savage nations they tamed, and the other noble acts that those few Portuguese did in those countries before I came away, that is, ten or twelve years from the time I first conducted them there; when I left there were, including the forty men ransomed in Cairo, nearly two hundred.[1] They were highly thought of, and were well treated, as all those who go there will always be, for this was the position my companions acquired by their great travail and intrepidity. They, as I say, did more than I have related here, and they might have done even more had they had any help or assistance. But they had none, because as soon as they had landed me and them, they turned their backs on us, and considered us as much lost to all hope as though they had banished us to some forsaken island among snakes, and they told tales of us here as of men marooned. Without doubt this was a great and inhuman abandonment, and resulted in our attaining no final success. Because your highness can understand, that if in this condition of affairs in that empire, that small number of Portuguese had been increased and recruited by reinforcements, they could have acquired there such power and influence, that King Gradeus, either willingly or unwillingly, would have submitted to the Holy Mother

---

[1] Before their defeat by the Gallas there were only one hundred and fifty Portuguese (p. 229, above); some must have been killed then, and others must have died in subsequent years. Couto (*Dec. VII*, Bk. 1, chap. viii) puts the number that met Master Gonçalo at ninety-three, which is more probable.

Church; and the people, by intercourse with us, and the instruction of our preachers, who would teach them freely, would accept the truth of the Christian religion, and abandon the errors of the Alexandrians; who for their sins, both they and their false doctrines, are thrown into confusion, so much so that they have not now the force to resist the truth if it were preached and encouraged, because they have no haughty and obstinate learned men among them, only devout and very humble men of a religious life, who desire to serve God in real simplicity, and easily receive the true doctrine and subject their intellects to it. As for worldly affairs also, there would be such profit there that neither Peru with its gold, nor India with its commerce, would be superior to it, for in Damute and its provinces there is more gold than in Peru, which may be acquired without the cost of India, and without war; for those people have no great defensive power; nor could there be resistance from elsewhere; but rather when the country of Abyssinia has been secured, and the kingdom of Zeila destroyed, the ports of the Red Sea will be safe, and the defence of India less difficult. Of myself I have told somewhat in this account, but not much, lest, as I said, I should weary, for I have spent many years in that country, and have suffered many dangers in the service of God and your highness; these would weary you if I told them all, or even a few of them; because I went first to India with Lopo Soarez while Affonso Dalbuquerque was the Governor, and stayed there till the time of Diogo Lopez de Sequeira, by whose orders I went to the Preste John of Ethiopia, in company with D. Rodrigo de Lima, and Padre Franciscaluarez, who returned thence with an ambassador from that Emperor called Tagazauo, whom I mentioned in the beginning of this book. I remained behind as a pledge and hostage for him, and they always did me much honour and treated me well, even to the Emperor Onadinguel making me godfather with himself at the baptism of his first-born son Gradeus,[1] and on the death of his Patriarch, one Abuna Marcos, selected me as Patriarch of that his Empire, according to his custom,[2] and asked me to go to Rome to make submission on his part and on my own to the High Pontiff, and to beg him to confirm me in that dignity and Patriarchate, and to go thence to Portugal to do what I have stated at the beginning of this work. I made the journey by land, coming by Cairo and Jerusalem, and was a prisoner with the Turks and evil entreated and nearly killed; but with the divine help I reached Rome in the time of the Holy Father Paul III, who not only approved of my selection to the Patriarchate of Ethiopia already made, but also instituted and confirmed me as Patriarch of Alexandria, and gave me personal possession of that chair.[3] In testimony of the truth of all this he ordered the usual letters and authenticated documents to be drawn up, which were examined and ratified in this kingdom.[4] These, with many other things, I lost in the battle in which D. Christovão was made prisoner, and as I do not show them they make mock of me,[5] but that does not settle it, God knows the truth, and knows how I have laboured to restore the faith and religion of that country. May He pardon my enemies, may He take me to Himself in reward for my toils, and may He give your highness long life, peace, and prosperity.—Amen.

The printing was ended in Lisbon, on the 20th day of June, in the house of Francisco Correa, in the year 1565.

---

[1] This assumes that Galâwdêwos was born after D. Rodrigo de Lima left Abyssinia; he was really born in 1523, some years before the Portuguese left.

[2] This account differs from that previously given.

[3] *me deu pessoalmente a posse daquella cathedra.*

[4] The letter of João III, then king, to the Preste may be compared with this (see p. 111, above).

[5] Compare chap. xxvi, p. 180, above; some papers were saved.

S

EXTRACTS FROM CORREA,

VOL. IV.

Giving the Passages referring to this Expedition that have not been included in the Notes to CASTANHOSO's Narrative, and which are not derived from it.

EXTRACTS FROM CORREA.

1539 AND 1540.—D. GARCIA DE NORONHA BEING VICEROY.

P. 107.

I HAVE already told how the ship *Raynha*, in which came Simão Sodre, did not reach Goa but went to Cochin.[1] In this ship came the ambassador of the Preste, who accompanied D. Rodrigo de Lima in the time of Lopo Vaz de Sampayo; with the ambassador came the ecclesiastic Francisco Alvarez, who had been to the Preste, and whom the Preste begged to proceed from Portugal to Rome with his ambassador, by whom he sent a golden cross; the Preste also wrote the same in his letters

---

[1] The learned Portuguese editor of Correa considers this extract a mass of confusion. Of course, there is the confusion between Alvarez and Bermudez, but the rest is so far important that it fixes the date of the death of Saga za Ab, and explains how Fernão Farto was sent to Massowa. Correa is in all subsequent passages clear as to the personality of Bermudez, and it seems probable that this particular one escaped revision. Under any circumstances, it lends no colour to the assertion of Bermudez that he was conducting back Saga za Ab a prisoner. Correa was at this time in Cochin; this makes the confusion noteworthy, in view of Bermudez' claim to special honours on landing in India.

to the King. That priest went to the Pope and took him the cross and the Preste's letters, but the ambassador did not go as he was sick; the Pope replied to that priest, and gave him a letter for the Preste; and showed the priest much favour and made him Patriarch of the country of the Preste, and gave him many other things for the Preste. The King granted many favours to the ambassador of the Preste, and gave him as he desired letters and directions for the Viceroy and a passage in these ships. The ambassador arrived in Cochin very sick. He died a few days later, and was honourably buried in the monastery of Santo Antonio. They found many articles belonging to the ambassador; armour, matchlocks, many kind of weapons, many large candlesticks, basons, brass articles for the church service, many figures and images of saints, church and saints' books, and much merchandise. All this was carefully preserved and made over to the priest, and to the servants of the ambassador, who all went to Goa, where they showed the stringent directions they had brought from the King, by which he imperatively ordered that they should be conveyed to the Straits, to the Preste's country. But the Viceroy refused to go to the expense of a fleet to take them, but said that he would send light vessels to learn the news of the Turks; and that if there were none he would send them in a galleon; that they should write letters to the Preste informing him of the condition of their affairs, and of how they were awaiting shipping, and that he would also write to the Preste; that they should send a man with these letters to travel in the boat, whom if they could reach Massowa they would land; he could then go to the Preste and give him the message which would please him. This seemed good to the priest, and thus they did, and sent one of the ambassador's servants with their letters, and that of the Viceroy, as I will relate later.

P. 109.

Then the Viceroy told off the best boat (*catur*) he had, and sent in her Fernão Farto, a man who knew the Straits well, and directed him to use every endeavour to reach Massowa, the Preste's harbour, and land there the Abyssinian who had the letters for the Preste.

P. 110.

The Viceroy wrote to the Preste informing him of the arrangements and orders of the King, which he could not carry out as the Turks were in India; that now he was sending to enquire what they were doing, and if he found they were quiet, he would send a fleet to Massowa, with all that the King had sent; with this Fernão Farto left in February, 1540.

1540.—D. Estevão da Gama being Governor.

P. 136.

Of the boats that remained, as I have already said, in the Straits, one belonged to Fernão Farto, who carried the Abyssinian, whom he landed at the port of Massowa with the letters, and told that he would await him till the end of April, and then return to take him up.

P. 137.

When they reached Massowa they found the Abyssinian, who had returned with a reply from the Preste; he had started directly they landed him, and, after reaching the country of the Barnegaes, had obtained quick travelling mules, and thus reached the Preste in a few days, for he was on the very road; he was much pleased, and made great rejoicings on learning the good news that had come to him from the kingdom, which, according to what his ambassador had written, was much better than he had hoped for. The Preste despatched him very quickly to return to the port of Massowa, where, as he heard, the boat would come for him, and therefore he was awaiting it . . . . they reached Goa on May 22nd.

P. 138.

That in Aden many were dying of famine, and that they were much afflicted with the hunger; that it was therefore certain that the Turks could not be ready to attack India this year; that many of them had taken service with the King of Zeila, who made war inland against the Preste's country, in order to get food; to which they had done much injury, and had captured certain towns and places; that the Preste had marched to assist his own, and was near the sea. For this reason he wrote to the Viceroy letters full of entreaties, begging him for help speedily, because of the great evil the King of Zeila had done him, and because he was overrunning his country, of which he had occupied much; that along all the sea coast the Moors made cruel war on his people; begging him this, with great entreaty and insistance, as the King of Portugal had ordered it; that he would arrange sufficient supplies to be ready near the sea for as large a force as he would bring; with many other reasons given in the letter. He sent a letter to his ambassador, in reply to the one he had received, in which he said—[1]

---

[1] For this letter, see p. 107, above.

1541.—(The Events here recorded occurred in Massowa).

P. 178.

The Governor had brought in the armada D. João Bermudez, the ambassador of the Preste, who had come from the kingdom. He left orders with Manuel da Gama to despatch, directly he left, a messenger to the Preste, to tell him that his ambassador was there, and to send for him some one to whom he could be entrusted. This ambassador, while in Massowa, awaiting the Preste's reply, began talking to the people, praising the country to them vastly and the power of the Preste, and the great favours he conferred on all, and showing to them royal orders, directing the Governor to allow any who wished to go freely. In this way he collected many men to accompany him, to whom he gave written promises of large allowances and salaries, for which reason many men were fired with the desire to go to the Preste, who, not awaiting the ambassador's company or the Governor's permission, began to talk to the country people, and to engage guides to conduct them, and began to desert secretly a few together. When Manuel da Gama heard this, he proclaimed that, under pain of death, no one should leave except with the ambassador, and with the Governor's permission. He kept strict watch and guard, and captured five who were starting up country, whom he ordered to be hanged forthwith. The ambassador opposed this strongly, even with prayers, but he failed; at this the ambassador was very annoyed. Still the people sought some chance of going, misled by the things the ambassador put into their heads of their fortunes with the Preste. The men further inclined to the journey because in Massowa they were pinched by their bad food, which was but too scanty: for there were no captains left behind to provide any mess, nor had the men wherewith to purchase food; nor could the country supply it, for the land was desert and the airs evil. When April came many sickened, Manuel da Gama provided for this, and started a hospital on land, where the people were treated as well as might be; still many died. While men's minds were so inclined to join the Preste, they began to assemble and urge one another to the journey. Manuel da Gama had many spies; still, withal, they collected over one hundred men, who elected one of themselves, called Antonio de Sousa, as their Captain, who arranged with all to start on a particular night; when all were ready they, at the starting time, sounded a drum and fife, and all collected with their arms and matchlocks, each one as he adventured himself for the journey. News of this was carried to Manuel da Gama, who landed straight, for he slept on the sea, and went to the church and summoned the magistrate; many persons collected, and there was a great rumour and riot. Many came at the drumming, bent on slaying Manuel da Gama and the magistrate, because, besides those of the conspiracy, everyone burned to attack and slay them, for all wished them great evil. Such was the excitement that Manuel da Gama returned hurriedly on board, and sent word to the magistrate to speak softly to the people, to try and somewhat quiet them. This the magistrate did, and went to where the people were collected, who were coming in search of Manuel da Gama; the magistrate opposed this with good words, begging them to remember who they were, and their past meritorious services, and not seek to obliterate them, and not to work some evil to the disservice of God and the King, as they were loyal vassals and true Portuguese. But as the men were already in mutiny, and inclined to evil, they began to slight the magistrate, and to speak to him wickedly and foully; at this the magistrate dissimulated with soft speeches, and drew himself clear of them, and getting into a boat went to the galleon to report to Manuel da Gama what was happening, and that any way the people were starting. On this Manuel da Gama called for boats with men from the other galleons, and two *caturs* (boats) there were there, and put a guard on the sea face, that no boats might start with the people, but none did come out, for they feared lest they should be captured, and did not start.

P. 180.

The next day at night-fall the drum sounded again, at which they again gathered—not indeed all, for some feared the toil and lest Manuel da Gama should capture them, for they saw his boats ready—and therefore not all the cabal (*cabilda*) collected; still there gathered over one hundred men ready with their packs and their matchlocks, and shipping silently on a foist rowed out through the fleet. When the guard saw them they shouted, at which Manuel da Gama came with his *catur* and his boats, and followed them, firing with bases and matchlocks, but as none fired with a will all the shot missed; but they, like rash men who were already committed, also fired many matchlock shots. They went on their way, and landed at a spot selected by their guide, a man of the country; after disembarking they got ready for the march, with their weapons and packs, the drum and fife, and an ancient, and went their way following the guide, who took them by rugged hills through which they marched all night; they travelled very weary, and burned up with the great heat, for the sun had left such heat in the hills that it seemed still blazing; owing to this, great thirst was added to their weariness, and all suffered; they shouted to the guide to take them where they might find water. He showed a good will, and conducted them to a valley between the hills, saying there was water at the bottom; but there they found many Moors awaiting them, for the guide had brought them treacherously to kill them all, which our men understood, and they slew the guide, and began to fight the Moors with their matchlocks. The Moors fought with arrows and slings; they showered so many stones on them that they had no time to think, still with matchlocks they wrought much injury to the Moors and drove them off.

These Moors belonged to the King of Zeila and the King of Massowa, who was a wealthy Moor that had made himself King of Massowa, and ruled many Moors along the sea coast, who had formerly paid a tribute to the Preste John, which was collected by the Barnegaes; but as the whole kingdom was in rebellion against the new Preste, more especially those at a distance, these Moors near the sea revolted, paid him nothing and obeyed this Moor, who called himself King of Massowa: who hearing that our fleet was at hand, had fled inland with his following, and wandered among the hills in sight of the sea. He made an alliance with the King of Zeila, who warred with the Preste, and they agreed to slay the people as they journeyed on their way to the Preste; for they had heard that there was in the fleet an ambassador of the Preste, who would pass through with many Portuguese to aid in the war then in progress. To carry this out, they kept disguised spies in Massowa to deceive men and guide them, as that man did, who was his spy, and brought them into his power, as I have said. While our men were thus fighting with the Moors, their sins brought it about that their captain, Antonio de Sousa, a valiant man, was slain; they at once appointed another, who was not as the dead man; already three of the Portuguese had been slain and eight wounded by matchlock shots, for among the Moors were Turks, matchlockmen; but all their suffering was from their great thirst. Then the Moors devised treachery, and called out to them not to fight, for they were vassals of the Preste, and that they had attacked them thinking them to be thieves come to rob the country, but they were all Christians. When the Portuguese heard this, they stopped fighting, and replied that it was well to make peace; to this many objected, but the captain, who was poor-spirited, brought them all to agree; in this the chief cause was the agony of their thirst. Peace was agreed to, and the Moors leaving their arms embraced the Portuguese like good friends, and our men begged for water; the Moors said that they had none, but that they would take them to a place hard by where there was much; they all started, and brought them to their camp and households, where was the King of Zeila himself; there the peace was debated and confirmed. The Moor king drew from his neck some beads and a cross of wood, which he kept ready for the deception, and gave the beads to the captain of the Portuguese, saying that he was a Christian and prayed with them. On this our men considered themselves safe and asked for water; they brought them much, and very good, in skins; our men, leaving their weapons on the ground, seized the water skins and drank their fill of water, until they could not stir, loosening their garments to fill themselves more. When the Moors saw this great disorder, and that they were in their power, they surreptitiously took their matchlocks, pikes, and swords, praising them and seeming to be examining them; when they had got the greater part of the weapons into their power, they attacked the Portuguese with them, slaying and wounding all they could. The King called out not to fight but to yield, and they should not be killed: to this they were compelled, for they had nothing wherewith to fight, and those who had arms and fought were but few and yielded. But fourteen men, brave cavaliers, seeing the others yielding, called out loudly from the press of the fighting: "Oh, unlucky men, why surrender to traitor renegades? Die like men, for they will slay you with tortures." These fourteen men fought with pikes and swords until all were slain.

The Moors bound those who surrendered hand and foot, stripped them stark, and penned them in a cattle-yard; the spoil of arms and goods they divided among themselves. Among the slain of that day lay a Portuguese, who fell as one dead from many wounds. He was bathed in blood, and was as one dead, with his jaws in the blood. The Moors left him for dead, thinking him dead like the others, and he saw all that the Moors did. They did nothing until late, when they opened the yard, loosed one of the captives, and ordered him out; the King and his captains were on horseback at the gate. The miserable captive came out, naked as he was, and the King struck at him, and gave him the first thrust with a spear; the others followed and slaughtered him *(fasião n' elle gazuha)*: so they did to all, leaving none. When the sun cooled, the Moors loaded up their baggage and moved elsewhere, because of the dead lying there. When the man who feigned death and saw all this, found night on him, he rose as best he could, for the fear of death gave him strength, and looking well about him, went, guessing the direction, towards the sea. He travelled all night till morning, when he saw it from the top of a hill, and descending, followed the shore to Arquyquo, and then to Massowa to Manuel da Gama, to whom he said: "Sir, I come before you, punish me as you will; sufficient justice has been meted to all the Portuguese who left here for the Preste." Then he told before the people all that had happened. That same day, towards night, came another man, who had also escaped by the wile of feigning death, who told what had passed. On this, Manuel da Gama exclaimed loudly, saying, that God justly punished those who did not obey the commands of their King and his ministers. But, withal, the men were so corrupted that they broke into great riot, saying, that the men went thus to their death, like desperadoes, because the Governor had abandoned them, who should have protected and supported them, and helped them in the great poverty and hunger they suffered; that he must prepare, for there was none who would not delight to bear the toil and search for those Moors, and take vengeance on them for the death of so many men. Manuel da Gama clearly did not desire this, saying he was pleased that those Moors were there, to make men fear to mutiny and disobey; such was never the custom, though they underwent great labours in India, suffering all like loyal Portuguese; and now as a novelty, they would use those evils and treasons which soldiers are guilty of in Italy, who are men without law and without truth. Hearing this, the people broke out in the greater excitement, saying that he was the cause of all these evils, and that God would exact the reckoning; and that if he would not lead them to fight those Moors, that they would form a body without a captain, to avenge the death of their friends, brothers, and relatives, slain there. On this there were great contentions, and such a riot that Manuel da Gama perforce agreed to go; with this the people were content and their anger was appeased. On the following day over eight hundred men got ready, well prepared for fighting; they discovered where the Moors were, with their camp pitched in a place whence they could only escape by a single pass, over a lofty hill; this was all learned by spies. Gaspar de Pina, Captain of the Governor's guards, who was there, sought permission from Manuel da Gama to take one hundred men of his guard and capture the pass, and prevent the flight of the Moors. Manuel da Gama would not consent to this: all must go together and in order. The Moors soon heard of this, struck their camp, and marched far away without our men catching sight of them; learning this they returned from half way.

At this time Ayres Dias reached Massowa on his return from the Preste, to whom he had taken letters from the Governor and brought from him the replies; he told us that all the Portuguese who had gone inland were dead, and that the Moors, who were robbing on the roads, had slain them. But the people were so bent on going that they said it was all lies, told by him to put fear into men and prevent their going; still, many were frightened and did not go, though ready to start. With this Ayres Dias came a messenger from the Preste to the Governor, who brought him letters, and others for his ambassador; and in the Governor's letters were many entreaties and urgent requests, begging for assistance against the evil he suffered from his own countrymen, who had all rebelled against him, and that if he did not give him help he would be entirely lost; and of this he would have to render account to God and to his brother the King of Portugal. He wrote to his ambassador that, if the Governor would not send him help, to forward to him whatever he had brought for him, and to return to Portugal to complain to the King that the Governor would give him no help, which he had sought to prevent the entire loss of his kingdom; and that he should take affidavits to the King, his brother, both of what he demanded from the Governor, and of the replies that he received. The ambassador showed these letters to Manuel da Gama, and to many men, both fidalgos and soldiers. Manuel da Gama could not prevail with him not to show the letters, or make complaints; that the Governor would return, and do what was right and reasonable. From this cause Manuel da Gama had continual trouble with the people until the Governor's return.

P. 199.

The Governor sailing for Massowa sent Antonio Pereira in advance to carry the news, which caused great joy in Massowa, as it was long since they had heard of him. The following day the Governor arrived, who had a great reception from the fleet;[1] he was informed of the many evils caused by the disorder of the people, at which he waxed very angry; but because he was right thinking and inclined to all good, he dissimulated to excuse himself from punishing all those blameworthy, and carried himself with great prudence, throwing all the blame on Manuel da Gama, and rating him in public to content and pacify the hearts of those who merited punishment. He started a general mess, which he made open to all, supplied as abundantly as possible, and ordered his brother, D. Christovão, and the other captains, to do the same, which contented the people. After the Governor had rested a few days, D. João Bermudez, the ambassador of the Preste, whom the Pope had made Patriarch of the country of the Preste, came to speak with him, and gave him the message the Preste had sent, and the letters on the same subject which he had received, in which the Preste begged him most earnestly, with pious entreaties, to send help before his kingdom was entirely lost, as he was a captive and blockaded by the Moors: he who asked this succour being a true Christian: God having purposely brought him to that place, at that time, with a force sufficient to help him. The Governor replied to the ambassador that he would do what he could after consideration of the royal orders. Three days later, the Barnagaes came with the very message of the Preste, whom the Governor received with

---

[1] According to D. João de Castro, *Roteiro* (p. 246), D. Estevão da Gama returned to Massowa on May 22nd, 1541, and left again for India on July 9th.

great honour, and gave lodgings in the galliot of D. Christovão for his immediate despatch. On this there was a council, at which all the fidalgos agreed that under any circumstances help must be sent to the Preste; that for this service three hundred men would suffice, skilled in their weapons and matchlocks, under a good captain. Several honourable fidalgos at once begged for this employment, but the Governor excused himself, saying that he would send none but D. Christovão, his brother, whom he would sacrifice for the King in this service, but that he would not adventure another's son; for none could tell how the enterprise would turn out, and it was very doubtful if any would escape death, because the country was so ill-minded that the very native born vassals were traitors and rebels to the Preste. This was agreed; and when it was known in the camp many persons went to D. Christovão to volunteer to accompany him; D. Christovão selected at his pleasure those who seemed most fitting; he enlisted the three hundred allowed him, but on prayers and importunity they were increased to four hundred, who furnished themselves with the best weapons and matchlocks in the camp, including many supernumerary ones. In this way D. Christovão collected one thousand matchlocks, one thousand pike-heads, and much powder, bullets, and lead, and four falcons, swivel guns, twelve bases with their carriages, ten very good bombards, and much powder in cases, and bullets, and all the necessary munitions in great quantity. Among these men were over seventy persons trained in all trades, namely, crossbow-makers, blacksmiths, carpenters, masons, shoemakers, armourers, and other handicraftsmen, whom Bermudez had engaged in India, to whom he gave writings of the pay and allowances they would enjoy in the country of the Preste; he did all this under the very express orders of the King which he received to this effect, without the Governor being allowed to interfere. D. Christovão was very amply provided, both he and his retainers, as also were those who accompanied him.

About this time the Governor heard that the Moors, who had escaped from Massowa with their king, were in camp near by, and designed flight to Suakin; and that they intended embarking in certain boats which lay ready in a bay six leagues from Massowa. The Barnagaes assured him of this, and begged and required him to go in search of them, that he should send men by sea, and that he and D. Christovão would go by land with their men; because if these Moors were destroyed the great evil they had done the Preste would be avenged, as from them came all his difficulties. The Governor, after consulting his council, got ready, and on June 1st he started with his men in foists; D. Christovão and the Barnegaes having marched overland two days previously, in order to seize a pass in the hills, by which they considered the Moors would have to escape. When the Governor reached the bay he found nothing, as the Moors had already embarked; later came D. Diogo d'Almeida Freire in D. Christovão's galliot, who landed from her to join D. Christovão, leaving in the vessel only the master, the gunner, and the galley-slaves; the last seizing their chance rose, slew the two Portuguese, robbed the best they could find, and all free and armed, got into the boat with water and food, and made off. The slaves left in the galliot cut the cable, hoisted the sail, ran her on shore, and fled; those in the bay saw nothing of this, as it was some distance off. The galley-slaves escaping up country met some Portuguese, who were out shooting without leave, with matchlocks, and fled from them: they could only catch one, whom they carried to the Governor, who related what had occurred. The Governor sent boats to tow off the galliot from the shore, and take her to Massowa, whither he also went; D. Christovão had already arrived there, with his people almost dead from the toil of the march, who from great weariness and thirst had thrown down their weapons on the roadside; the Barnegaes laboured much in helping them, his people assisting by bringing water in skins; they collected too, all the arms, not one being lost.

P. 202.

When D. Christovão was supplied with all requirements for his march, the Governor, on the advice of the Barnegaes, sent fifty men in advance, to travel at leisure, as there was not sufficient transport. This was done, and João da Fonseca was their captain; they started well provided on the 12th of the month (June); the Barnegaes accompanied them until they crossed a certain hill, to bring thence more transport for D. Christovão. On the 28th letters came from João da Fonseca, the captain, who reported on the great excellence of the country, and that they had reached the house of a lord who had received them very hospitably. He, with them and his own followers, had attacked the camp of two other lords, who had revolted against the Preste; that they had slain many of them, and had captured three thousand cows; for those in the camp had stayed to fight, not knowing of the arrival of the Portuguese, who advanced hidden behind the men of the country; but when they recognised the Portuguese they fled, and those of the country pursued them and slew many of them, but the Portuguese did not get up with them; that the cows had been kept to make over to D. Christovão when he arrived. That the two lords recognising their own defeat, and learning that D. Christovão was advancing with a large force, returned to their obedience to the Preste, and awaited the arrival of D. Christovão to accompany him, and obtain pardon from the Preste. At this news the Governor and all were very pleased.

On the last day of June the Barnegaes returned to Massowa with much transport, and with three hundred cows for the Governor, who refused to receive them except on payment; he also brought two hundred camels for the baggage, and for the men to ride, and many mules. But D. Christovão finding that there were not riding animals for all, settled to march on foot, and the others followed his example, and all the baggage was loaded on the camels and mules, the artillery, ammunition, and many bales of rice and sugar, each camel carried ten bales; all could be easily carried by these animals, the men remaining free and unencumbered for marching. On July 2nd there was a thunderstorm, and the galleon *São Mateus* was struck by a flash, which shattered the topmast and left many marks on the galleon; at the foot of the mainmast it killed a boy and a goat, and went out over a falcon in a port hole, on which it left a mark like a shot from a camel. Three days later there was another thunderstorm, with so strong a wind that the fleet was nearly lost,[1] and was driven towards the shore, three foists that were watering were wrecked in the harbour of Arquyquo, that is one of Pero Froez, one of Gaspar de Sousa, and the third of Christovão de Castro.

P. 203.

On July 6th, D. Christovão and his men went to Arquyquo, whence he despatched his transport train, that they might be always a day's journey ahead, and travel at leisure with the boys and people of small consequence. The following day the Governor, with the fidalgos, went to Arquyquo to say farewell to D. Christovão; when all had collected, the Governor called up the Barnegaes, and before

---

[1] D. João de Castro, *Roteiro* (p. 246), dates the thunderstorm in which the galleon was struck June 30th, and the gale July 2nd.

all his people, and two captains who had accompanied him, commended to him D. Christovão, the ambassador Bermudez, the letters for the Preste, and all the Portuguese who were going.

(Here follow several long speeches, which have been omitted.)

P. 205.

On this they parted, and the Governor embarked and returned to Massowa. D. Christovão, the same day, started on his march and rested among some hills, where the convoy that had left the previous day was awaiting him. May our Lord in His mercy guide them to His holy service. Amen.

1544.—MARTIM AFONSO DE SOUSA BEING GOVERNOR.

P. 343.

ON April 20th of this year, 544, Diogo de Reynoso arrived from the Straits, where he had gone in a *catur*; and as the Governor had heard that he had entered the gates of the Straits,[1] which he had strictly forbidden, and given him orders not to enter under pain of treason, he ordered him to be arrested, as he came into the river, by D. Pero Fernandes, the chief magistrate of India, who took him to the jail, where he was thrown into heavy irons, under close guard. The King's attorney, by order of the Governor, drew up a long indictment against him, demanding that he should die the death suitable for high treason, as he had

---

[1] Frequently called by the Portuguese "Albabo," or "The Gate," from the Arabic name, more usually "Bab el Mandeb." From "Albabo" came the English sea-term for the entrance, "Babs," used by Ovington and Bruce, but now probably obsolete.

entered the gates of the Straits against the orders of the Governor: he having been warned, and shown by the Governor the orders of the King our lord, which strictly forbade it, as he had sent an ambassador to Turkey to settle the affairs of India; of this the Governor had taken from him an oath and a signed consent. The trial proceeded, and he was condemned to death; against this he appealed that he had been ordained; this was rejected for want of proof. Then he appealed that he was a minor, which was admitted, and the charge dropped; for no one desired his death, and all that was done was mere pretence and show before the people, as are all the trials of the great in India.

This Diogo de Reynoso entered the straits and went to Massowa, which he found abandoned, for the people had fled. There he met a Turk, factor of the Turk,[1] with twenty-five other Turks, who were trading in Massowa, selling cloth and buying supplies. These Turks went up country, and as they knew that there were inland many Portuguese returning from the Preste, awaiting shipping, who, coming in search of the foist would find them out and do them much hurt, as they had many cloths which they could not carry off, they came down to the water's edge with a white flag, and spoke with our men about surety for peace, which Diogo de Reynoso assured them for one thousand gold venetians,[2] and all remained at peace. This being settled, there came the next day to Massowa fifty Portuguese, who desired shipping for India; they had returned from the Preste, and had been in the company of D. Christovão, to whom those of the country

---

[1] The word used here is *Turquo*, while in other cases in the paragraph equally translated Turk, it is *rume*.

[2] Rather under £500 of our money. The ducat mentioned later was of the same value as the venetian, the cruzado was valued at some 6d. less.

had gone hurriedly to give news that the foist had arrived; on this they came to the port in haste. Those in the foist were very pleased, but, learning that only this one was there, they became very depressed, as there was not shipping for all. When they heard there were Turks so near, they required Diogo de Reynoso to take command, and lead them to attack the Turks. He replied that he could not, as he had already assured them security and peace; but he sent secretly to tell the Turks that he could not maintain his agreement, because the recently-arrived Portuguese were prepared to attack them. Messages followed, and it was settled that they should pay him two thousand ducats more, that is, three thousand in all, and that peace and security should be maintained. But this was not; he attacked the Turks, and, as they had no where to fly, slew them all and took over ten thousand cruzados worth of cloth, chiefly cotton goods from Cambay, which the Turks had purchased from the ships to make sails for their galleys; they should rather have taken the money than have done this good service to God and the King, because, after they had taken the cloths, there was none to buy them, and they were compelled to burn them; they should have therefore first let them make their profit.

As there was not room for all, Diogo de Reynoso told them that they could see that he could not take everyone; that they should, therefore, settle on one man among them whom he would take, and then they could send their letters to the Governor by him, to beg him to send sufficient shipping to carry all. This they did, and agreed to send in the foist one Miguel de Castanhoso, who was maimed in one arm, and was travelling with the Preste's permission with letters for the Governor and King on his services. They all wrote their letters to their friends, with which Diogo de Reynoso took his leave of them and went to India;

and the Portuguese returned up country inland, all riding on mules with their servants. They entered the country of the Barnegaes, where they remained in company, very friendly and kindly, in great peace; they were given abundant supplies by the Preste's orders, and he frequently begged them to return to him. This Miguel de Castanhoso related minutely all the deeds of D. Christovão, which happened in the manner following, that is to say:—

———

(Here follows the narrative, mainly based on that of Castanhoso; the additions have been already given in the notes to the translation of his treatise.)

INDEX.

Aba Esman Nour, 7
Abaa, ambassador of Asnaf Sagad, 119
Abaaz, gozil, 120
Abacinete, liii
Abadele, chief of the Friars, 96
Abafazem, liii
Abai, river, 87
Abauy, lake, 87
Abba Aragawi, 10
Abba dele, 96
Abba Libanos, rock church, 100
Abba Paoulos, 214
Abba Saga za ab. *See* Saga za ab.
Abba Yosâb. *See* Yosâb.
Abba Zekré, 214
Abbade d'elle, 96
Abbas, 10, 228; Vazir, 121; his campaign, 202; killed by Galâwdêwos, 228
Aboun, Garâd, brother of Imam Ahmad, xxxiii, 228
Abreu, Francisco de, Captain, 12, 33, 36; killed in battle, 62
Abreu, Inofre de, Captain, 12, 44; killed in battle, 62
Absama Nur, 7
Abuna, xxviii, lxxxv, etc., 192; Marcos, xxxviii, lxxxiii, etc.; Joseph, lxxiv; Yusaf, lxxxvi; Eda Abuna, 160
Abyssinia, bridges in, 168; Calendar in, cii; Captain-General of, 189; church of, xxxviii; constitution, lxxxv; rites, 88; churches in, 95, etc., 243, 245; Kings of, Letters to and from João Bermudez, João III, King of Portugal, 107-121; list of Kings, 1508-63, cii; maps of, xxxi, 198; metals in, 235, 239, 245, 246; monasteries in, 188, etc., 198, 243; night attacks in, 201; Royal household of, 220; zoology of, 235, etc.
Acaje Degulam, 93
Adal, xxxvii
Adea, xxviii
Addoi Marâ, 198
Addolé, died in an ambush, 1534, 121, 228

Adel, 227
Adem, King of, 199-201, 228
Aden, xxxii, 174, 264
Adigerat, xxxi
Adowa, liii, 39
Adugue, 225
Afgol, stream, lvi, 40
Afgol-Giyorgis, lvi
Africa, 44; the mother of prodigies, 240; secrets of, 244
Agame, li, lii; province of, 27, 28
Agaoa, river, 243
Agaye, 198
Ahmad, Imam, *King of Zeila*, xxiii, xxiv, xxix, etc., xlvii, liv, etc.; his origin, xxxiii, etc., xcviii, etc.; 7, 9, 23, 30, 31, 33, 39-41, 45, 47, 53, 131, 140, etc., 189, 264; encamped at Zabul, 54; killed by Galâwdêwos, 65, 76, 82, 192; beheads Christovão da Gama, xcviii, 66; Shoa traditions of, 85; his attack on the rock churches, 100, 101; his ear, lxxii, 193, etc.; succeeded by Nur, lxxviii
Ainal, *village*, lvi
Ajuda, Royal Library of, lxxxi
Aksum, xxxi, lii, liii, 33, 198
Albabo, 278
Albornoz, 18
Albuquerque, Affonso de, xxv, etc., xxxi, etc., 132, 256
Albuquerque, João de, Bishop of Goa, 134, 136
Alcocer, Port of, burnt by Estevão da Gama, 3
Alcorão, 172
Ale belale, 243
Alexandria, 87; Patriarch of, xxix, xxxix, lxxiv, xc, 210, 214
Alexandrians, errors of the, 256
Algiers, *Ecole des Lettres*, 99
Alguns Documentos, xxvi, xxvii, lxxxviii
Almanza, Lopo de, 70, 71
Almeida, defeats Egyptian fleet, 1509, xxxi
Almeida, Manoel de, *Historia*, xlvi; *Lettere*, lxiv

INDEX.

Almeirim, King of Portugal at, 112, 115
Alps, 26
Alurez, Manuel, 222
Alvarez, Francisco, *Ho Preste Joam*, xxiv, etc., xlix, liii, lxxxv, etc., 4, 5, 16, 18, 27, 29, 89, 90, 91, 99, 130, 160, 198, 217, 220, 232, 233, 235, 241, 245, 256, 261
Amaçua, 120
Amar, 241, 243
Amara, 225, 227, 240, 245
Amata Giyorgis, daughter of Lebna Dengel, xxxvi, 14
Amata Waten, sister of Lebna Dengel, 93
Amazons, 236
Amba, mountain fort, xxiii
Amba Geshen, etc. *See* Geshen, Amba.
Amba Scioa. *See* Scioa, Amba.
Amba Sion. *See* Sion, Amba.
Ambea, Province of, 77
Amber, 232
Amede, Cide, lxi
Amhara, 245. *See also* Amara.
Amharic, 198
Anasa, lvi, 45
Andrade, Jacinto Freire de. *See* Freire de Andrade, J.
Andre, Ax Gagce, 240
André, Bishop D., 252, 253
Andyras, 214
Angueah, *River*, liii
Angueha, liii
Annesley, George Arthur, *Earl of Mountmorris*, *Voyages*, lvi
Anriques, Bras, 133
Anriques, Pero Borges, *Captain*, 133, 144, 145, 170
Anseba, lvi
Antalo, lvi, xcviii. c, 227
Antelope, Oryx, 236
Antilles, 242
Antonio, Santo. *See* Santo Antonio.
Anta, Red, 239
Aqui Afagi, xlix
Arabia, 44; firearms introduced into, 1515, xxxii
Arabic, xxxi, 43
Arabic Historians, lxxxv
Araba, 66
Arel of Porakkat, xliii
Arian Heresies, 181, 207
Arkiko, lxxvi, etc., 5, 141
Arquebusiers, 12, 55
Arquiqo, 140, 147
Arquyqo, 277
Arquyquo, 270
Arramat, liii

Ashangi, *Lake*, lvii
Asmacharobel, 155, 168, 171
Asmache, 176
Asmache de galan, 205
Asmacherobel, 221
Asmara, xlvi, 6, 7
Asnaf Sagad, King of Abyssinia. *See* Galâwdêwos.
Assai Mara, 198
"Asses, Death of the," xlix
Astrolabes, 114
Atabales, 25
Ataide, Tristão d', 145
Atbara, River, 83, 236
Athaide, Catharina da, xlii
Aueyteconcomo, 138
Ava, liii
Ax Gagce, 237; baptised as Andre, 240
Axenaa, 120
Ayera, 83
Aynaba, lvi
Ayres Diaz (Marcos), *a Mulatto*, xxx, xxxiv, lxvi, lxviii, etc., 20, 54, 73, 102, 116, 117, 120, 137, 138, 178, 195, etc., 272; hostile to Bermudez, 203, etc.; appointed Captain, 184, etc.; his death, 218
Ayres Diz. *See* Ayres Diaz.
Azaige de galan, 185, 224
Azaj, 18
Azaye Degalão, 93
Azayes, 18
Azebide (Zabid), 55, 69
Azemache Cafilão, 78
Azmach Keflo, leader of the vanguard, lxxi, 78

Ba Eda Mâryâm, King, 109
Bab el Mandeb, *Straits of*, xxxii, lvii, lxi, 59, 278
Baba, 278
Babylon, 145
Baçanete, *Hill*, xxxvii, lii, liii, xcviii, 37, 39, 40, 198
Baçinete, liii
Badabaxa, xlix
Baeda Mâryâm, King of Abyssinia, 1468-78, xxvii, 107, 109
Bagamidri, 245
Bagpipes, 25
Bairro, 92
Baharnagash, xlvi, 3, 7, 227, 228
Bale, Kingdom of, 202, 230; Province of, 226
Bali, Province of, lxxiv, 202, 227, 228
Bao, 117
Bar Sad-ed-din, xxxvii, 84
Bar-Saed-ed-din, island of, 85

INDEX.

Barakit, li, 27
Baralha, 36
Baratti, Giacomo, xxv
Barnaguais. *See also* Baharnagash. 3, 52, 72, 74, 75
Barnaguais, Rebel Father of the, returns to the Preste, 84
Barnegaes, 32, 33, 263, 268
Baroa, xlvi, 7, 121
Barreto, Francisco, *Governor of India*, lxxvii, 252
Barreto, João Nunez, Patriarch, 1555, lxxvi, xcv
Barreto, Pero, 208
Barreto, Thomé, lxv
Barreyra, João da, printer to the King of Portugal, 104; to Castanhoso, lxxx
Baros, 194
Basanate, liii
Bases, 267
Basset, René, *Etudes*, xxiv, xxxi, xxxv, xxxviii, lxi, lxvi, 7, 10, 18, 23, 45, 77, 80, 85, 214; *Histoire*, xxiii, xxviii, xxxi, xxxiii, etc., 7, 33, 41, 85, 101, 160, 161, 175, 228, 233, 235, 241
Basutos, 233
Bâti del Wanbara, wife of Imam Ahmad, xxxiii, etc., lxxii, lxxviii, 83, 86, 202, 228
Battell, Andrew, 229
Bazzato, 233
Bdebarrua, 117, 118
Bdemaryâm, King of Abyssinia, 116
Beads, for natives, 101
Beard proverb, 216
Beatilhas, 234
Bedem, 18
Bedyniam, King of Tiopia, 107
Beesa, Amba, l
Beg, Pir, lxxiii, 250
Beguemeder, 245
Bellet, *plains of*, lvi
Bellisart, *plains of*, lvi
Bengal, 151
Bent, James Theodore, *Sacred City*, lxv, 7, 29, 90
Bermudez, João, xxx, xxxi, xxxiv, xxxviii, etc., 9, 27, 29, 40, 49; disavowed by King João III of Portugal, 111; his return to Portugal, lxxv; Bibliography of his *Breve Relação*, lxxxi; Patriarchal claims, lxxxiii, etc.; his misstatements, etc., xcvii, etc.; facsimile of his tombstone, 124; his own treatise *passim*, "the true Patriarch," 230; Governor of the Gafates, 232; accused of sacrilege, 249; sadly deficient in dates, 250; returns to India, 251, etc.; has audience of Est. da Gama, 273

Bernagaiz, 139, 142, etc., 191, 214
Bertegual, 7
Berteguan soldiers, 87
Bethmariam, Bermudez settles at, lxxiv, 246, 247
Betteela, 234
Beyt Mariam, lxxiv
Bezutos, 233
Bibliography, civ, etc.
Bichos, 235
Blacksmith's trade, considered disgraceful in Abyssinia, 94
Blackwood, 232
Bliss, W., searches Vatican Records. xix, xc
Blue Nile. *See* Nile.
Bombards, field, 55
Borges, Pero, 170
Braça, 30
Braga, Archbishopric of, lxxix
Bragança, Constantine de, Viceroy of India, 1558-61, lxxii, xcvi
Bragança, Duke of, 131
Branca Leone, xxiv, xxv
Bridges in Abyssinia, 168
British Museum, Libri Desiderati in, lxxx, *see also in* Bibliography; Ethiopian MSS., 99
Brito, Diogo de, 205, 215
Bruce, James, *History*, xxiv, xxxiv, xlvi, liii, lix, lxix, etc., lxxii, lxxxvii, xciii, 4, 7, 9, 18, 29, 40, 56, 93, 143, 201, 227, 232, 236, 241
Budge, Ernest Alfred Thompson Wallis, xix
Buffaloes, 235, 236
Bulletin de la Société de Geographie, Paris, 99
Burnoose, 18

Cabal, 267
Cabaya, 98
Cabeda, xlix, 24
Cabelaa, xlix, 24
Cabilda, 267
Caboa, xlix, 24
Caesar, Patriarch of Alexandria, xc
Cafates, 232
Caffares, 253
Caffres, 101
Cafilão, Azemache, 78
Cairo, Grand, xcv, 87, 174, 250, 255, 257; merchants, 243
Caldeira, Afonso, *Captain*, lxviii, 59 170, 173, 176, 177, 182; his death, 184

Calide, Captain of Doaro, 153, 226, etc.
Calite, Azemache, 82
Caliver, 11
Caloa, *Hill*, lix, 56
Calthrops, 172
Cambay cloths, 38, 280
Caminho, 187
Cananor, 134
Cananore, 119
Canariensis, 95
Canga, 22
Capado, 138
Cape of Good Hope, xxvi, 115
Capellão, 138
Captain-General of Abyssinia, 189
Caracol, 16, 21
Cardoso, Fernão, 47, 70
Caridades, 179
Carneiro, Belchior, Jesuit, lxxvi
Carretoens, 45
Carros, 45
Cartas Annuas, Jesuit MS., 119
Cartmil, 95
Carvalho, Luiz Fernandes de, 12
Carvalho, Luiz Rodriguez de, 12, 47
Casinha, 26
Cassia, 169
Castanheda, 236
Castanhoso, Afonso de, lxxix, etc.
Castanhoso, Miguel de, xliii, etc., li, lxv, etc., 3, etc., 147, 158, 167, 169, 171, 177, 198; embarks for India, 1544; King Galâwdêwos describes his good service, lxxii, 109, 110; value of narrative, xciii, etc.; biography of, lxxix; bibliography of his *Historia*, lxxx; not in British Museum Catalogue till 1902, lxxx; objects to Ayres Dias, 185, 194, etc.; sent for ships, 280
Castille, Kingdom of, 230
Castro, Christovão de, 277
Castro, Fernandes de, son of João de Castro, blown up, 102
Castro, João de, *Viceroy of India*, 145; father of Fernandes de Castro, 102; Letter from João III, King of Portugal, 112-114; *Vida*, 110, 112; sends Vasco da Cunha to Diu, 138; *Roteiro*, xl, lxi, 5, 273, 277
Catadhi, 242
Catádupa, 242
Cataract, Nile, 242
Catherine, St. *See* St. Catherine.
Catres, 53
Catur, 263, 267, 278
Cemen, *Province*, lix, 56
Chaldee Letters, 89; MSS., 96
Chameau d'eau, xvii

Charamellas, 25
Charts, 114
Chaucer, Geoffrey, quoted by Ludolf in the original, xcvi
Chaul, 133
Chelicut, lvi, 160
Chembra Kouré, battle of, 1529, xxxv
Cheouada, 76, 77
Chirremferrer, mountain, 87
Christ, Order of, lxxix, 253
Christovão, Dom. *See* Gama, Christovão da.
Christovão, D., a Jew, 177
Church of Our Lady of Mercy, 152
Churches, in Çubia Nubia, 243; rock, 95, etc., 245
Cicero, Marcus Tullius, *De Republica*, 241
Cide Amede, Captain of the Moors, 58
Cide hamed, Captain of the Moors, 58
Civet, 140, 232
Clara, Sta. *See* Sta. Clara.
Claveiro, 253
Clement VII., *Pope*, xxxix, cii
Cochin, xxx, 133, 134, 253, 261
Coelho, Pedro, *Dominican*, 133
Coelho, Ruy, 248
Coffa, 232
Coimbra, 137, 170
Combes, Edmond, *Voyage*, xxxvii, xlvii, xlix, lxx, etc., 85
Compasses, 113
Conceição, *Ship*, lxxix
Conche, 237, 246
Confessio fidei Claudii, 214
Confession, in Abyssinian Church, 89
Congo basin, 132
Constantinople, Fall of, xxv; French ambassador at, xciii
Conzelman, William El, *Chroniques de Galâwdêwos*, xxxi, xxxvii, lxvi, lxxvi, etc., 10, 45, 65, 73, 76, 84, 86, 87, 117, 161, 198, 202, 218, 228, 231, 252
Copper, 245
Coptic Calendar, 76
Copts, lxxxv
Corbam, 91
Corcora, 160
Cordoso, Francisco, 165
Corn Spike of the Gospel, 14
Corpo Chronologico, lxxiii, 250
Correa, Francisco, Printer, 125, 257
Correa, Gaspar, *Lendas da India*, xl, xlv, lxxii, lxxxiv, lxxxvi, lxxxix, xciii, etc., 134, 135, 141; translation

of extracts from, 9,11, 12,13,14, 15, 17-22, 24, 25, 27, 30-32, 34-36, 38, 39, 42, 43, 46-52, 55, 58, 59, 61, 62, 65, 67, 68, 72, 73, 75, 85, 88, 92, 93, 96, 107, 261-281

Correa, João, killed at battle of Wainadega, 83

Correa da Silva, Martim, 139, etc.

Cotton, Webs of, 140, 141

Coucha Gallas, 237

Couto, Diogo de, *Da Asia*, xlii, xlv, xlvi, lix, lx, lxviii, etc, lxxii, etc., lxxv, lxxix, xcv, etc., 5, 7, 10, 56, 58, 59, 61, 77, 83, 116, 138, 170, 249, 250, 252

Covilham, xxv

Crasto, João de, 145

Craveiro, 253

Crooke, William, *Rural and Agricultural Glossary*, 12

Crowbars, 234, 245

Cruzados, 136, 161, 225, 246, 250, 280 ; value, 279

Crystal, Rock, 235

Cubia Nubia, 243

Cuirasses, Steel, 83

Culverins, Demi, 191

Çumbas, 229

Cunha, Lopo da, 47

Cunha, Luis da, 208

Cunha, Manuel da, Captain, lxv, lxix, lxxi, xcviii, 12, 33, 35, 44, 46, 57, 58, 61, 72, 138, 146, 204, 208, 230

Cunha, Tristão da, xxvi

Cunha, Vasco da, in India, 1527-1555, 137, 138

Çunkar, Micer, a Venetian, lxxiii, 250

Dabreu, Diogo, 204
Dabreu, Jorge, 163
Dabreu, Jorze, 118
Dacheni, 12
Dachery, 12
Dafonseca, João, 146
Dafõseça, Antonio, 194
Dagousha, 12
Dagua, 193
Dak, Island, 175
Dalburquerque, Affonso, 256. *See* also Albuquerque
Dalmansa, Lopo, a Gallician, 165, 204, 210, 220, 225
Dalmeyda, Ruy Teixeyra, 132
Dama, xlvii
Damo, Debra, xxxvi, xxxviii, xlvii, lxvi, xcix, 7, 10, 16, 135
Damot, 216, 234, 235, 241, 246

Damute, country of, 101, 234-237, 242, 245
Dandrade, Simão, 215
Daonoo, 120
Dará, 83
Dara Takle, 1
Darasgé, 7, 76, 77
Darasgué, xxxviii, lxvi, lxx, 77
David, King, 107 ; described as son of King Solomon, 109
Dawaro, 202, 228
Deacons, Ordering of, lxxxvii
Debaroua, xlvi, 7
Debarua, 147, etc., 179, 195, etc., 222, 247, 250, etc. ; Church of Our Lady in, 251
Debarwa, capital of Isaac, xlvi, li, lxv, lxxiii, lxxv, lxxvii, xcviii, 4, 7
Debra Damo. *See* Damo, Debra.
Debra Libanos. *See* Libanos, Debra.
Deça, João, Captain of Goa, 134, 136
Deça, Pero, a fidalgo, 152, 192
Degalham, uncle of Galâwdêwos, 93
Degdeasmati, 53, 143
Dek, Island of, 175
Deka, lxx
Deka Woina, lxx
Del Wanbara. *See* Bāti Del Wanbara.
Dembia, or Dembya, Kingdom of, lxx, 77, 175, 176, 193, 241, etc.
Denaghel, rock church, 100
Dengestobou, 7
Dias, Ayres. *See* Ayres Dias.
Dias do Prestes, Diogo, lxxii, lxxvi, xcvi, 116, 252
Dinia Ambara, Queen of Adem, xxxiv, 202, 206
Dinis, Alvaro, 171
Dioscero, 182
Dioscorios, 207
Dioscoro, 207
Diu, Battle of, 1509, xxxi ; 1538, xxxii, xliii, 132, 134 ; second siege of, 1546, 102, 138
Diz, Ayres. *See* Ayres Diz.
Doaro, xxvii, lxxiv ; Governor of, 176 ; Kingdom of, 202, 226, etc., 246
Docel, 18
Domingo, de Quasi Modo, 48
Dominic, St. *See* St. Dominic.
Douro, river, 59
Drawbridge, 168
Ducat, 279, 280
Dum fater, 93
Du Roule, murder of, xciii

Easter Day, dates of, 1541-1544, cii
Ecole des Lettres d'Alger, 99

288 INDEX.

Eda Abuna, 160
Egypt, 87, 99, 131; Sultans of, xxviii, xxxi, lxxxv; heresy in, 207
Egyptian Fleet, xxxi
Eleni, Queen of Abyssinia, xxvii
Elizabel, Queen, 10
Emmanuel, King of Portugal. *See* Manuel.
Emar, defeats Lebna Dengel, 87
Emfras, 16
Enderta, lxxix
Ensincanaria, 95
Ephraim, children of, 83
Epiphany, Festival of, lii, 28, 29
Equator, 234
Errum, Negusta, 236
Escander, King of Abyssinia, 109
Escolar, João, xxx
Esmacherobel Tigremaquão, 143
Esman, killed at Ouagara, 76
Esparavel, 18
Espingarda, 11
Espirito Santo, ship, xlii
Esteves Pereira, Francisco Maria: *Castanhoso*, xliii, xlv, lxv, lxxix, 109; *Historia de Minas*, xxxi, xxxiv, lxxv, 55, 86, 198
Ethiopia, Emperor of, 125, 127, 129
Ethiopian Chronicles, xxxi, xciv, 231
Eunuchs, 138, 172
Europe, lxv, 53
Evora, xxxix, 95, 130
Eylale belale, 131
Ezman, Mir, killed at Woggera, lxix

Falashas, xxi, lxi, 16
Falcão, Luiz de Figueiredo. *See* Figueiredo Falcão, L. de.
Falcons, 274
Fanuel, 228, 231
Fartak, *Cape*, 142
Fartakins, 142
Farte, Captain, 167
Farto, Fernão, xxxix, lxxvi, lxxxix, 132, 135, 137, 261, etc.
Fatagar, Province of, lxxiv, 95, 202
Fatima, Princess, 236
Fernandes, Gonçalo, 81
Fernandes, Joam, 81
Fernandes, Pero, 278
Fernandes, Simão, xcvi
Fernandez, Antonio, Armenian, 133
Ferreira, Antonio, 215
Fialho, Francisco, killed at battle of Wainadega, 83
Fialho (Manoel), *Evora Illustrada*, 130
Fidalgos, xlii, lxviii, lxxvii, 114, 147, 165, 170, 204, 272, 274
Field bombards, 55

Field pieces, 55
Figos, 146
Figueiredo Falcão, Luiz de, *Livro*, xcvii, 141
Figueyra, Antonio, 142
Figuiredo, Diogo de, *Captain*, 220
Fiqtor, son of Lebna Dengel, killed 1539, xxxvi, 14
Firearms, introduced into Arabia 1515, xxxii
Fisgas com seus ganchos, 186
Fitauraris, lxxi, 78
Fiseramo's Relaçam, cx
Focada amba, 16
Foists, 102, 251, 267, 277, 279
Fonseca, João da, Captain, 12, 33, 36, 57, 58, 146, 276; killed in battle, 63
Frades, 43, 52
França, Affonso de, 194, 199, 206, 208
France, 230
Francis, Saint. *See* St. Francis.
Francisaluarez, 130, 235, 245, 256. *See* also Alvarez, Francisco.
Frangis, 43
Frankincense, 230
Franks, 7, 23, 45, 53, 55, 73, 181, 248
Freire, Diogo d'Almeida, 275
Freire, Fulgencio, *Jesuit*, lxxvi, 252
Freire de Andrade, Jacinto, *Vida de Dom João de Castro*, 110, 112
Fremona, lxiv
Frey Miguel, 231
Froez, Pero, 277
Funchal, Archbishop of, 131
Futûh el Hâbasha, xxxv, 55

Gabriel Andreas, *Monk*, xxviii, xxxiii
Gadabat, Amba, lii
Gafat, lxxiv, 216, 235
Gafates, 216, etc., 232, etc., 242, 246
Gagce, Ax, 237
Gajghe, 237
Galâwdêwos, *King of Abyssinia*, xxviii, xxx, xlvii, lxvi, etc., cii, cviii, 10, 14, 45, 77, 175; wins a decisive victory, 1543, lxxi, etc.; defeated by Garâd Amar, 9, 50, 65; goes to Samen, 73; his first victory, 76-84; letter to João III, 1550, xci, 109, 110, 115-118; killed by Nur, 1559, xxxv, lxxviii; letter to the Governor of India, 119-121; *Confessio fidei Claudii*, 214; date of birth, 257

INDEX.

Galâwdêwos, Chroniques de. See Conzelman, William El.
Gallas, xxiv, lxv, lxxiv, 218, 224, 226, 228, etc.
Galliot, 274
Gama, Alvaro de Athaide da, xlii
Gama, Christovão da, fourth son of Vasco, xxiv, xxxvii, xlii; leader of the Portuguese Expedition to Abyssinia, 1541, xli, etc., 114, etc., 144, 274; Dengestobou, 7; captures the Jew Captain's Hill, lviii, 56; Death, lxii, etc., 65-69, 174; mourning for, 91, facsimile of autograph, 104; Genealogy, xlii
Gama, Estevão da, *Viceroy of India*, xxxii; succeeds Garcia de Noronha, xl, 136; commands Portuguese fleet off Massowa, lxxxvi, 3, 37, etc., 137; despatches Abyssinian Expedition under his brother Christovão, xli, 114, 144, 273, etc.; superseded, 1
Gama, Francisco da, Viceroy 1597-1600 and 1622-1627, lxiii, etc.
Gama, Isabel de Athaide da, xlii
Gama, Manuel da, xl, 138, etc., 265, etc., 270, etc., 273
Gama, Paulo da, killed in Malacca, 1534, xlii, 127
Gama, Pedro da Silva da, xlii
Gama, Vasco da, The da Gama, xl, xlii, 145
Ganz, District of, 80
Ganza Garâda, 80
Garâd Ahmad, defeats Christovão da Gama, 116, 120. See Ahmad, Imam.
Garâd Ahmadouch, xxxiii
Garâd Amar, or **Emar**, defeats Galâwdêwos, 9, 50
Gargara, 160
Garstin (*Sir* William Edmund), K.C.M.G., *Egyptian Reports*, 87
Gazafo, death of, 108
Gazelles, 236
Genbot, ciii
Genii, 201
George, D., 176
Geshen, Amba, xxxiv, xxxvi, lix, etc., 16
Ghedem, 198
Ghedemsa, 198
Gibberti, xciii
Gibbon, Edward, *History*, xxiv, lxxxiii, 207
Gideon, Amba, lix, etc., 56
Gideon, *Judge of Israel*, 83
Gideon, King of the Falashas, xxi
Gimen, *Hill*, lix, 56

Giorgis, Abba, xxiv
Giyorgis, Tecla, lxiv
Goa, xl, lxxvi, xcvi, etc., 252, 261, 264; Bishop of, 134-136; Captain of, 134, 136; Cathedral of, 251
Gobat, Samuel, xlvi, 13
Gojame, Province of, lxxiv, 198, 231, 235, 241, etc., 246
Gold, 235, 239
Golgotha, church of, 96
Gomez, João, xxvi
Gomil, lxxxii
Gonçalo, Mestre, *Jesuit*, lxxvi, xcvii, 251, 252
Gonçalvez, João, 171
Gonçalvez, Lourenço, 222
Gondar, xxii, xlvi, lxx, 85
Gorague, Province of, 231, 232
Goranha, 151, 155, 173, 185, etc. See Ahmad, Imam.
Gordamar, 9, 50
Gouvea, Antonio de, *Jornada*, 1606, lxxv, xcv
Gozil, 120
Grada Amar, 9, 50
Gradamar, 9, 50
Gradeus, King, 223, 237, 255, 257, 175, 176, 178, 180, etc.; settles the Portuguese in Bethmariam, 245, etc. See Galâwdêwos.
Gragné, Jaaf, lxx
Grañ. See Ahmad, Imam, King of Zeila.
Grañbar, lxx
Grañ bar, slope of, 83
Granber, lxx
Grança Grade, 80
Grand Turk, 55
Grangniber, lxx
Greek colony, 236
Greeks, xxii, lxx; Queen of the, 236
Gregory, xcvi
Griffins, 236
Guança Grade, 80
Guardafui, *Cape*, xxvi
Guazaado, Abaza, Ambassador to Portugal, 118. See Saga za ab.
Guerreiro, Fernão, *Relaçam annal*, xcvi
Guidi, Ignazio, *Di due frammenti*, xxxi, lxxii, 84, 214
Guidime, Province of, 198
Guidimi, 176
Guinea, 329, 242, 243
Gundet, 1

Habash, xxi
Hadea, 227
Hadia, Kingdom of, xxviii, 226, 230
Hamasen, 7

U

INDEX.

Hamed, Cide, lxi, lxiii
Hamle, ciii, 87
Handsel, 8
Hannibal, 26
Haramāt, lii, etc., 39
Harar, xxxiii, lxv, 9, 80
Harpoons, 186
Harris, *Sir* William Cornwallis—*Highlands*, xxxv, xxxvii, lxv, 10, 25, 29, 93; his Mission, xxxv, 16
Hawash, river, 198, 231
Haziran, 10
Hedar, ciii, 76
Hedar St. Michael, 9
Helena, Queen of Abyssinia, xxvii, xxviii, xxix, xxxiii, 217
Helena, St. *See* St. Helena.
Henry, Cardinal Infante, 128
Hermitage, 26
Holy Week, observance of, in Abyssinia, 88
Honey, 59, 90, 92
Horses, Sea, 88
Houza, 56
Hyaenas, 94

Ialofa, 243
Iaver, 254
Ibn Aias, Arabic MS., History of, lxxxv
Ibrahim el Ghazi, father of Imam Ahmad, xxxiii, 83
Ifat, xxxv
Imam Ahmad, King of Zeila. *See* Ahmad.
Incense, 230
India, xxvi, xxxvii, xlv, lxv, 43, 197, 251, 256, 264; Viceroys, lxiii, lxiv, 3, 19; Rainy season, 9, 53; Portuguese return to, 103, 230; Office MSS, lxxiii, 250
Indian Ocean, 131
Intercalary days, ciii
Invisible Wood, The, 233
Iron, 246
Isaac, Baharnagash, ruler of north frontier of Abyssinia, xlvi, lxxvii, etc., 214; revolts against King Minas, 4; visits Manuel da Gama, 139
Isabel do Evangelho, 14
Isenberg, Carl Wilhelm, *Journals*, lx, etc,, ciii, 29
Islam, 76, 83
Israel, 86; Amba, lxi
Israelites, lxi
Italian Map of Abyssinia, xxxi, 198
Ite Sabla Wangel, widow of Lebna Dengel, xxxiii, xxxvi, xlvii, lxxiv, xcviii, 10, 14, 23, 45, 53, 86

Iteghe, lxxii
Ito Musgrove, of Basanate, liii
Iyoram, Governor of Salamt, 87

Jaaf Gragné, lxx
Jacobites, 207
Jalaka Amba or Houza, 56
James, Saint. *See* St. James.
Jangadas, 58
Japhet, Sons of, 45
Jaquaria, merchant, 119
Jartafaa, country of, 95, 97
Jarte, liv, 39, 167
Jarte, Campos do, liv
Javelin, 36, 81
Jedda, xxxi, 55, 174
Jemma, *River*, xlix
Jerusalem, 112, 114, 137, 257
Jesuits, lxiv, lxxv, 252; *Cartas Annuas*, 119
Jew Captain, 177
Jews, xxi, lxi, 58, 59; Hill of the, lxvii, etc., 56, 73, 162, 170, 176-178
Jimmel el bahr, xvii
Jinjily, 89
Joa, Province of, 198
João III., *King of Portugal*, cii, 83, 204; Letters to and from the Kings of Abyssinia and João de Castro, 109-121, 257; knights Castanhoso, lxxix
João, *a Gallician*, killed at battle of Wainadega, xliv, lxxi, 83
John, *the Gallician*. *See* João.
John, *King of Portugal*. *See* João III.
John, Preste, xxv, 3, 21, 39, 40, 43, 54, 56, 57, 73, etc., 113, 127, 129, Bermudez *passim*; welcomes defeated Portuguese, 74; defeats King of Zeila, 79
John, Saint. *See* St. John.
Johnson, Samuel.—*Rasselas*, 16
Johnston, Charles.—*Travels*, xxxv
Jordan, River, 100
Joseph, Aba, 137
Joseph, Abuna, *See* Yusaf.
Judaria, 32
Judith, Queen of the Falashas, xxi, 16
Julius III, *Pope*, lxxvi, cii

Keflo, Azmach, lxxi, 78
Kettledrums, 25, 45, 93
King of Kings, xxiii
King's voice, 93
Kishm, Island of, 250
Kivu, *Lake*, 132
Knights of the Order of Christ, lxxix, 253
Kolla, lxx

INDEX.

Krapf, Johann Ludwig, *Journals,* xlix, lx, etc., ciii, 29
Krestos, Amba, 1

Lalibala, Vie de, 99
Lalibela, King of Abyssinia, 99, 131
Lalibela, 198 ; Rock churches of, 95, 131 ; account of, 99-101
Lasta, 99, 245
Lead mines, 245
League, Portuguese, 29
Leather boats, 201
Lebna Dengel, *King of Abyssinia,* 1508-1540, xxviii, etc., xxxvi, xl, lxxxiii, etc., 10, 227 ; children of, 14 ; died Sept. 2nd, 1540, 84 ; defeated by Emar, 87 ; Letters to João Bermudez, 1540, 107, 108, 135
Lebna Dengel, Storia di, xxxi. *See* Rossini, Conti.
Le Grand, Joachim.—*Voyage,* lxiv, lxx, lxxxv, xciii, 160, 241. *See* Lobo.
Leitão, Diogo, 132
Leitão, Lucas, 133
Leo X, *Pope,* Letter to King Manuel, lxxxviii
Leone, Branca, xxiv, xxv
Leopards, 236
Levant, sea of the, 87
Levanter, xciii
Lião, Pero de, lxxii ; kills the King of Zeila, 192, etc.
Libanos, Debra, burned 1530, xxxvi
Libanus, Debra, monastery of, 240, 247
Lima, Antonio de, 194
Lima, Dinis de, 204, 208, 223
Lima, Manuel de, 145
Lima, Rodrigo de, xxvi, xxvii, xxix, xxxviii, 54, 118, 163, 171, 235, 256, 257, 261
Linhares, Conde de (Noronha), xlii
Linschoten, Jan Huyghen van, *Voyage,* 253, 254
Lion of the sea, 43
Lisbon, 257 ; Bermudez reaches, 254 ; Custom House, lxxx ; Geographical Society of, xlv, lxv, lxxxi, 104 ; Royal Academy of, lxxx, lxxxiii, 112, 119
Lobo, Jeronymo.—*Voyage,* lvi, lxiv, etc., lxx, 232, 235, 236, 241. *See* Le Grand.
Loniochter, 95
Lopes, Afonso, father-in-law of Castanhoso, lxxx
Lopes de Sequeira, Diogo, xxvi, 256
Lopez, Diogo, physician, 133

Lopez de Sousa, Pero, xxxix, 133, 134, 136
Louis XIV, *King of France,* xciii
Loyola, Ignatius, nominates a Patriarch, lxxvi
Ludolf, Hiob, *the Elder.*—*Historia,* xxv, liii, lxxvi, lxxxiii, 89, 237 ; quotes Chaucer in the original, xcvi ; Abyssinian calendar from, ciii ; translator of *Confessio fidei,* 214

Macancio, King of Tiopia, 107
Mac Queen, James, *Journals,* lxi
Madelaine, mother of Fanuel, 228
Mädinga, 243
Mafamede, 66, 96, 151, 172 ; King, 206
Maffoeus, *Historiarum Indicarum Libri XVI,* xcv, etc.
Magâbit, ciii, 45
Magadafo, hill of, lvi, 54
Magalhães, Francisco de, 219
Magdala, xviii, xlix
Magpie, 151
Mahfuz, Emir of Harar, xxviii, xxxiii
Mai Afgol, *Stream,* lvi
Mailcart, 95
Malacca, xlii, xliii
Maillet, de, French Consul in Cairo, 1700, lxxxv, xciii
Malabar, xcv
Mamelukes, lxxxv
Mangalo, 231
Manicongo, 115
Manna, 59
Manrua, 12
Manuel, King of Portugal, 1495-1521, cii, 109, 118, 119, 217 ; Pope Leo X writes to, 1514, lxxxviii
Maps of Abyssinia, xxxi, 198
Mara, province of, 198
Marcellus II., *Pope,* lxxvi, cii
Marcos, a Mulatto. *See* Ayres Dias.
Marcos, Abuna, xxxviii, lxxxiii, etc., 129, 257
Mareb, *River,* xlvii, l, li, liii
Mark, Saint. *See* St Mark.
Markham, Sir Clements Robert, *History of the Abyssinian Expedition,* xix, l, li, lx, 16, 27
Marlota, 98
Maroon, 255
Martinho, de Portugal, 131
Mary, Saint. *See* St. Mary.
Mascal, ceremonies of the, 93
Mascarenhas, Pedro, *Viceroy of India,* lxxix
Maskaram, ciii, 10, 228
Massaja, Guglielmo,—*I miei 35 Anni,* lx, 56

Massowa, xviii, xxxviii, etc., xlv, l, liv, lxi, 3, 4, 5, 19, 37, 39, 48, 52, 75, 77, 82, 85, 86, 97, 100, 114, 135, etc.; Bermudez at, lxxv, etc., xcvii, 173, 250, 251, 261, 273, etc.; King of, 268
Mateus, São. *See* São Mateus.
Matheus, *Ambassador to Portugal*, xxvi, xxvii, xxix, lxxxviii, xciii, 217
Matheus, Francisco, 217, etc., 225
Mead, 205
Meca, Straits of, 3
Mecca, 144; Straits of, 55
Medani Alam, Rock church, 100
Mehmad. *See* Muhamad, son of Imam Ahmad.
Melinde, 112, 115
Melindi, xxvi, xlii, 230
Mello, Ruy de, Captain, 254
Membret, 54
Memer Member, 96
Mendera, 236
Mendes, Afonso, Patriarch of Abyssinia, 1625, lxiv
Menezes, João de, xcvii, etc., 253
Mermaids, 88
Mescal Kebra, wife of King Lalibela, 99, 100
Mestre João, xxx. *See* Bermudez.
Metals, 235, 239, 245, 246
Mfumbiro, mountains, 132
Micer Çunkar, a Venetian, lxxiii, 250
Michael, St. *See* St. Michael.
Michael Sahul, Ras, fifth in lineal descent from Degdeasmati Robel, Governor of Tigré, 4
Midianites, 83
Miguel, Frey, brother-in-law of Gradeus, 231
Millet, 146
Minas, Historia de. *See* Esteves Pereira (F. M.)
Minas, King of Abyssinia, 1559-1563, xxxiv, lxxiv, lxxviii, cii, 4; son of Lebna Dengel, 14; captured in 1539, 55, 86; exchanged, 86; dies, 1563, lxxix
Mines, 245
Mirabercuz, one of chief Moors of Ormuz, 103
Miracles, 175
Miraizmão, Captain of Ogara, 76
Mist, 9
Miyâzyâ, ciii, 9
Moesteiro, 198
Monasteries, 188, etc., 198, 243
Monteiro, Baltesar, 215
Moore, F. W., *To the Mountains of the Moon*, 132

Moors, xlvi, 3, *sqq.*, 243, 273
Mosambique, 254
Mosques, 96
Mosquetes, 22
Mountmorris, *Earl of*. *See* Annesley, George Arthur.
Mozambique, xlii
Muhamad, son of Imam Ahmad, xxxiv, 84
Muhamad, Walasma, *Governor of Ifat*, xxxv
Muhamed, *Governor of Doaro*, xxvii
Muhamed, Sid, lxix
Muhamedans, 33, 45; marriage customs of, xcii
Mujahid, Vizir, 1539, xxxiv, 16
Mules, 19, 45, 58, 206
Mummies, 27
Murat, the younger, xciii
Muscat, fort of, lxxiii, 250
Musgrove, Ito, liii
Myrrh, 140, 230

Nachenym, 12
Nahase, ciii
Naod, King of Abyssinia, 1495-1508, 107, 109, 116
Naqo, King of Tiopia, 107
Natchenny, 12
Nazaré, province of, 160
Nazareth, monastery, lvi, 40, 160
Negus Nagasti, xxiii
Negusta Errum, 236
Nestor, 182
Neve, 9
Nevoa, 9
Nile, lxxiv, 70, 77, 87, 131, 175, 216, 240, etc., 248; rising of the, 243; Blue Nile, 70, 87, 235
Noro, a Bernagaiz, 140, 141
Noronha, Garcia de, a Turk, 132, 165
Noronha, Garcia de, *Viceroy of India*, leaves Portugal, 1538, xxxix, xl, xliii, 132, 141; his death, 136, 137
Noronha, Ignacio de, xlii
Noronha, Payo de, 145
Noronha, Sancho de, 132
Nuncio, Papal, 131
Nunez, João, Patriarch, 253
Nunez, Leonardo, 133
Nur, son of Mujahid, xxxiv, lxxviii
Nur, Sharif, Governor of Arkiko, 7, 117, 141, 231

Oaty, Hill of, 56
Obitocŏ, 176
Ochterlony, 95
Oenad, lxix
Oe nad qas, Hill of, 77
Ofala, lvii, 53

INDEX.

Offar, City, 53
Ofla, City, lvii, 53
Ogara, Lordship of, 76
Oggy, Kingdom of, 231, etc.
Oinadaga, lxix, lxxi, 77
Ojarte, Campos d', liv
Omo, River, xxviii, 231
Onadinguel, King, 127, 129, 137, 147, 178, 207, 227, 243, 256. *See* Lebna Dengel.
Oparlandas, 18
Oquia, 161
Order of Christ, lxxix, 253
Orita Aureata, Queen, 178
Ormuz, 103, 193, 250
Oryx Antelope, 236
Ottoman Turk, xxviii, xxxi
Ouacha, xlix
Ouagara, Battle of, 76
Ouenadega, lxxi
Oviedo, André de, Bishop *in Partibus*, lxxvi, etc., 214, 252
Oygere, 202

Paez, Gaspar, *Jesuit*, xlvi, lii, liv, lxix, xcv, xcvi, 5, 40, 52, 53, 56, 61, 77, 83, 232, 241
Pagmie, ciii
Paguemen, ciii
Pagumiehne, ciii
Palha, Pero, 132, 208, etc., 223
Palm Sunday, 40
Paoulos, Abba, 214
Parasols, xxii
Parkyns, Mansfield,—*Life*, xxii, 24, 29, 89, 90, 93, 94, 98, 161
Paul III, *Pope*, receives Bermudez, xxxviii, etc., lxxxiii, cii, 130, 257; writes to Cæsar, 1538, xc
Paul IV., Pope, lxxvi, cii
Paul, Saint. *See* St. Paul.
Paulitschke, Philipp, in Harar, lxv
Pearce, Nathaniel, *Life*, liii, lvi, lxv, ciii, 29, 39, 87, 93, 231, 232, 237
Pèga, 151
Pègo, 151
Pègu, lxxxii, 151
Peixoto, Antonio, xcvii, 251
Peixoto, João, lxxv, xcvii
Pelican, xvii
Pentapole, Calendar of the, 76
Pereira, Antonio, 171, 208, 273
Perruchon, Jules, *Notes*, xxxi, 23, 58, 61, 76, 77, 83, 99, 214
Persia, 44
Persian bowmen, 55
Persian Gulf, lxxiii
Peru, 256
Peter, Saint. *See* St. Peter.
Phenix, 236

Picus, 151
Pina, Gaspar de, Captain, 271
Pir Beg, lxxiii, 250
Plantains, 146
Pogme, ciii
Pollock, Sir Frederick, *Bart.*, xix
Pontifex of Alexandria, 130
Popes, the, list of, 1513-65, cii; and Abyssinia, lxxxii, etc , 129, 147, 179, 257
Porakkat, xliii
Portal, *Sir* Gerald Herbert, *My Mission*, lvi
Portugal, xlii, 7, 130, 230, 254; Jesuits in, lxxv; King of, appealed to for help by Isaac, of Abyssinia, 4; list of Kings of, 1495-1571, cii
Portuguese, spit in church, 90
Prata, 130
Precious John, xxv
Preete John. *See* John, *Preste*.
Preste, King of the, 178
Prestes, Diogo Dias do. *See* Dias do Prestes, D.
Prisons, Royal, 16
Pumice Stones, 241
Purchas, Samuel, *the Elder, Purchas His Pilgrimes*, lxxxii, xcii, ci

Quatremère, Etienne Marc, *Mémoires sur l'Egypt*, lxxxv
Quiloa, 231
Quinces, 146

Raffray, Achille, *Abyssinie*, 96, 235; *Eglises Monolithes*, 99
Rafts, 58
Ras Michael Sahul, 4
Ras Sela Christos, 16
Rasselas, 16
Raynha, *Ship*, 134, 261
Red Sea, xxvi, xxxi, etc., xl, lviii, 19, 137, 241; ports of, 256
Rete o jan hoi, xxv
Reynoso, Diogo de, mentor to D. Fernandes de Castro, acts as a pirate, lxxii; blown up, 102; his arrest, etc., 278, etc.
Rhinoceros, 236
Ricenas de capite ferreo, Hieronymo, 131, 133
Robel, Governor of Tigré, 4, 53, 143
Rock Churches, 95, etc., 245
Rodrigo de Lima, Portuguese ambassador. *See* Lima, Rodrigo de.
Rodrigues, Lopo, scribe to João III, King of Portugal, 1546, 113
Rodriguez de Carvalho, Luiz, 12, 47
Roha, in Lasta, 99

Rohlfs, Gerhard, *Meine Mission*, xxii, lxx, ciii; *Land und Volk*, 99
Roiz, Lopo, scribe to João III, King of Portugal, 1546, 112, 115
Roman Emperors, 31
Romanos, Saint. See St. Romanos.
Romans, 1, 27
Romão, S. *See* S. Romão.
Rome, Church of, 251; Jesuits in, lxxv
Rossini, Conti, *Storia*, xxviii, xxxi, xxxv
Roteiro. *See* Castro, João de.
Royal Academy of Lisbon. *See* Lisbon.

Sabagadis, died 1835, xlvii
Sabana Giyorgis, daughter of Lebna Dengel, xxxvi, 14
Sabani, Queen, 10
Sabele o Engel, Queen, 14
Sabla Wangel. *See* Ite Sabla Wangel.
Saed-ed-din. *See* Bar Saed-ed-Din.
Saga za Ab, xxix, xxxix; death of, 108, 121, 261; ambassador to Portugal, 118, 130
Sahart, liv, 9, 10
Sahul, Ras Michael, 4
Santo Antonio, monastery of, 262
St. Catherine, of *Mount Sinai*, 3
Sta. Clara, *ship*, 140, 141
St. Dominic, Order of, 133
St. Francis, church of, Evora, 95
St. Francis Xavier, xlii
St. Helena, Bermudez at, lxxv, xci, xcvii, 253, etc.
St. James, 36, 47, 49, 157, 160
St. John the Baptist, 60
St. John's Fires, 93
St. Mark, See of, 210; Gospel of, lxxxvii
St. Mary of Sion, monastery of, 198
São Mateus, galleon, 277
St. Michael, church of, liii
St. Paul, 109, 175; monastery of, 188, 252
São Paulo, *ship*, xcvii, etc., 254
St. Peter, 109
S. Romão de Fonte cuberta, lxxix
St. Romanos, church of, li, 27
S. Sebastião da Pedreira, Bermudez at, lxxv
Salamt, country of, 87
Salf, 9
Saloa, *Hill*, lix
Salt, 243
Salt, Henry, *Voyage to Abyssinia*, lvi, lxxiii, 235
Samen, Province of, 10, 73

Sampayo, Anrique de, 132
Sampayo, Lopo Vaz de, 261
Sanait, Amba, lii
Sanaiti, lii
Sancta Misericordia, Banner of, lxviii, lxix
Sandal-wood, 232
Sane, ciii, 10
Sanét, Amba, liii, 33
Santarem, birthplace of Castanhoso, lxxix
Sard, country of, 9, 10
Sartsa Dengel, King of Abyssinia, xxxvi, 4; MS. Chronicle of, 84
Satan, detains slaves in St. Helena, 253
Schleicher, Adolf Walter, *Geschichte der Galla*, xxxi
Sciauada, 76
Scioa, Amba, 198
Scipio's Dream, 241
Scythia, 236
Sea Horses, 88
Sebastião, *King of Portugal*, lxxx, xci
Sebastião, S. *See* S. Sebastião.
Segredo, 193
Segued, Sultan, 1632-1665, 16
Seid Mehmad, killed by Galâwdèwos, 76
Sel, Amba, xviii, xxxvi, lx, lxi, lxvii
Semien, lix, lxi, lxvi, etc., 9, 76, 87, 245
Senafé, xviii, li, 27
Sene, ciii
Seoa, country of, 116
Serbraxos, battle of, 93
Serra, Branca da, mother-in-law of Castanhoso, lxxx
Serra, Violante da, wife of Castanhoso, lxxix, etc.
Shanbaff, 234
Sharif Nur. *See* Nur.
Sheba, Queen of, 236
Shembat, Amba, lii
Shewa, 10
Shoa Traditions of Grān, xxxv, 85
Shoa, xxxv, xxxvii, xlvii, etc., lviii, lx, lxvi, 10, 25, 77, 120, 198, 231
Shrove Tuesday, 1543, lxix, 75
Sid Mahamad, 58; killed at Ouagara, 76
Sid Muhamed, lxix
Sidama, xxviii
Sidi Mescal, 99
Sidi Mohammed, 58
Silva, Diogo da, 163
Silva, Innocencio Francisco da, *Diccionario bibliographico*, xcii
Silva, Martim Correa da, 139

INDEX.

Silveira, Antonio da, 134
Silver egg of Pegu, 151
Simen, Province of, 245, etc.
Simon, Gabriel, *Ethiopie*, 99
Sinabafas, 234
Sion, Amba, 198
Sion, monastery of St. Mary of, 198
Sledges, xlviii, 21
Snakes, 238
Soares, Lopo, xxx, etc., 256
Sōbreiros, 204
Sodre, Simão, 261
Sofala, 246
Soiça, 20
Solomon, *King of Judah*, lxi, 107; described as father of King David, 109; visit of Queen of Sheba, 236
Somalis, xxiii, xxiv, xxxii
Soueral, Manuel de, 223
Sounat, Amba, liii
Sousa, Antonio de, *Captain*, 266; his death, 268
Sousa, Fernão de, Commander of Asnaf Sagad's guards, 118
Sousa, Gaspar de, *Captain*, lxxiv, 116, 118, 204, 208, 220, etc., 247, 250, 277
Sousa, Jeronimo de, 208
Sousa, Luiz de, *Annaes*, 115
Sousa, Manuel de, 145
Sousa, Martim Afonso de, *Viceroy of India*, l, 133, 278
Sousa, Pero Lopez de. *See* Lopez de Sousa.
Spain, 53
Spanish Peninsula, 45
Spinach, 89
Spitting, considered a dirty habit in Abyssinia, 90
Spū, 253
Stags, 236
Stefano in Rotondis, St., *Rome*, xxiv
Straits of Mecca, 3, 55
Strange Adventures of Andrew Battell, 229
Suakin, 241, 243, 275; burnt by Estevão da Gama, 3
Suez, xxxii, xl, 132, 137
Suissa, 20
Sulaiman Pasha, commands expedition of 1538, xxxii
Suriano, Gaspar, Armenian, 133
Switzerland, 20
Syão, Monastery of, 198
Syrian Astronomy, 73

Tagacem, River, lviii, 59
Tagazauo, Ambassador, 130, 235, 256
Tagaze, River, 59

Tagus, River, 239
Tahsâs, ciii, 23
Takazzé, River, lviii, etc., 16, 87, 245
Talila, lxix; killed at Ouagara, 76
Tamarind trees, 169
Tamisier, Maurice, *Voyage*. *See* Combes, Edmond.
Tanaqe Michael, an Abyssinian, 108
Tankoua, 88
Tares, 179
Tasrin, Month of, 73
Tauares, Pero, 132, 194
Tavares, Pero, 133
Tavora, Ruy Lourenço de, Governor of India, 1608-10, lxiv
Tecla, Giyorgis, *Viceroy of Tigré*, lxiv
Tecla Haimanaut, Saint, xxix, 13
Teff, 12
Tegazauo, 130, 133
Tegraye. *See* Tigré.
Tegulet, xxxvii, 10
Tejo, River, 59
Tellaré, River, lx
Tellez, Balthasar, *Historia*, xlvi, lxxi, xcv, etc., 4, 7, 10, 18, 40, 56, 77, 83, 89
Teqemt, lxvi, ciii, 73
Ter, ciii
Thatched round houses, 7
Thedrus, King, 160
Theodore, King of Abyssinia, 160
Thielemfra, mountain, 87
Thomson, Anthony Standidge, xix
Tigré, xxxv, xxxvii, l, lxv, lxxxviii, 10, 23, 33, 53, 73, 77, 101, 116, 117, 120, 171, 228, 245, 249; Governor of, 4, 53, 143
Tigremacã, Province of, 246
Tigremahō, 53
Tigre Makuanen, 4, 143, 246
Tigremaquão, 143, 146, 155, 168
Tin mines, 245
Tiopia, King of, ancient prophecy as to, 103; Kings of, 107
Tor, City of, burnt by Estevão da Gama, 3
Trinidade, Diogo da, 173
Tubal, children of, 45, 65
Tullius, 241
Turcomans, 84
Turk, Grand, 55, 69, 161
Turkey, 279
Turkish Galleys, 52, 102
Turks, 3, *sqq.*
Tweezers, 44, 67, 151
Tzâna, Lake, xxxviii, xlix, lvii, lxiii, lxvii, lxix, etc., xcix, etc., 70, 76, 87, 198, 245

Ueine, *Mount*, lxx
Uendighe, lxx
Ueni, lxx
Umbrellas, 204
Unguia, River, liii
Unicorn, 236

Valentia, *Viscount*. *See* Annesley, George Arthur.
Vascogoncellos, Manuel de. *See* Vasconcellos, Manuel de.
Vasconcellos, Manuel de, l, 37, 38
Vatican, xxiv, xc
Vaz, Antão, 215
Vedremudro, 245
Veiga, Manuel da, 128
Velho, Francisco, Captain, 12, 33, 35, 38; killed in battle, 63
Venetian, gold, 279
Venetians, xxiv, lxxiii, 250
Veyssière de la Croze, Mathurin, *Histoire du Christianisme*, lxxxiii
Vicar-General, 173
Vidigueira, Conde da (Gama), xlii, lxv, lxxx
Vie de Lalibala, 99
Vieyra, Francisco, killed at battle of Wainadega, 83
Virgin Mary, 14

Wadj, 202, 228, 231
Wagara, 76
Wainadaga, 77
Wainadega, lxx, etc.; battle, 1543, xxxiv, lxvi, lxix, 77, 91, 198
Wajárat, liv, lxxiii, 39, 167
Wakea, 161
Wanag Sagad, King of Abyssinia, 109, 116, 118
Wanbara, Bāti Del. *See* Bāti Del Wanbara.
Wancheet, river, xlix
Wati, Amba, lix
Wechne, 16
Wehni, Mount, lxx
Whales, 88
White Flag, misuse of the, lxxi, 78; use of, 279

Wilkins, Henry St. Clair, *Reconnoitring*, xxiii, 27
Wofla, lvii, etc., lxvi, lxviii, lxxiii, xcviii, 53
Woggera, lxx, 58; battle of, lxvi, lxvii, lxix, etc., 76
Woina, Deka, lxx
Wood, the invisible, 233
Woodpecker, 151
Woolmer's Catalogue, 1799, cx
Wren, 151
Wylde, Augustus Blandy, *Modern Abyssinia*, xlix

Xenaa, 119

Yaekub, son of Lebna Dengel, died 1558, xxxvi, 14
Yakâtit, ciii, 77
Yasous I, 1680-1704, xciii
Yeha, liii
Yoan, King of Portugal, 83. *See* João III.
Yoram, Governor of Salamt, 86, 87
Yosâb, Abba, 228. *See also* Yusaf.
Yule, *Sir* Henry, *Hobson-Jobson*, 9, 89, 234
Yusaf, Abuna, lxxiv, lxxxvi, 225, 228

Zabid, 55
Zabl, lvii, 53, 77
Zabul, lvii, lxi, 54
Zagues, Royal family of, 99
Zântarâ, slope of, lxx, 83, 84
Zara Yâkob, *King of Abyssinia*, 1434-68, xxiv, 107, 109, 116
Zariba, liv
Zebid, xxxiii, etc., xlv, lvii, lviii, lxv, 161, 174
Zebide, 120
Zeila, xxvi, xxxii, xlv, 139, 226, 256
Zeila, Imam Ahmad, King of. *See* Ahmad.
Zekré, Abba, 214
Zemur Pasha, lxxix
Zobl, lvii, 53

LONDON:
PRINTED AT THE BEDFORD PRESS, 20 AND 21, BEDFORDBURY, W.C.

The Hakluyt Society.

NOTICE.

THE Annual General Meeting will be held at 1, Savile Row, W. (by the kind permission of the Council of the Royal Geographical Society), at four o'clock on Tuesday, the 24th March, 1903, when the following business will be transacted :—

(1) To receive the Report and Statement of Accounts for the past year (copies of which accompany this notice).

(2) To elect three members of Council.

BASIL H. SOULSBY,
Hon. Secretary.

MAP ROOM,
 BRITISH MUSEUM,
  20th March, 1903.

REPORT FOR 1902.

SINCE the issue of the last report the following volume has been distributed to members:

(Series 2, Vol. IX.) — PEDRO TEIXEIRA'S JOURNEY FROM INDIA TO ITALY IN 1604-5, with Selections from his "KINGS OF HORMUZ and KINGS OF PERSIA, edited by the late Mr. W. F. Sinclair and Mr. Donald Ferguson; pp. cvii. 292 (Vol. III. for 1901).

The Council had hoped to issue during the year the first volume of the Society's reprint of Hakluyt's PRINCIPALL NAVIGATIONS; but this was found to be impossible. The editors have, however, made considerable progress with their task, and the volume is in the press.

The publications for 1902 will be:

(1) THE PORTUGUESE EXPEDITION TO ABYSSINIA IN 1541-43, edited by Mr. R. S. Whiteway, late I.C.S., author of "The Rise of Portuguese Power in India." This volume is being printed off, and will be distributed in a few weeks' time.

(2) Vol. I. of the new edition of the PRINCIPALL NAVIGATIONS, already referred to.

The publications for 1903 will (probably) be:

(1) "Early Dutch and English Voyages to Spitzbergen," edited by Sir Martin Conway.

(2) Sir Thomas Herbert's "Description of the Persian Monarchy, 1634." Edited by Lieut. A. A. Crookshank, R.E., and Major P. Molesworth Sykes.

(3) Vol. II. of the new edition of R. Hakluyt's "Principall Navigations."

The list of deceased members includes Mr. A. A. Borrodaile, Lieut.-Colonel the Right Hon. Edward Henry Cooper, Mr. G. J. Malcolm Kearton, Mr. Henry Gurdon Marquand, and Mr. J. Tyler Stevens.

Despite these and other losses, the number of subscribers has risen to 451, a net increase of 17 for the year.

A statement of receipts and disbursements during the year is appended, from which it will be seen that the sum in hand at the close was £910 16s. 9d.

Three vacancies in the Council, caused by the retirement, under Rule VI., of Commander B. M. Chambers, R.N., Mr. A. P. Maudslay, and Mr. C. Welch, have to be filled at the General Meeting.

Mr. Basil H. Soulsby, Superintendent of the Map Room, British Museum, has been elected Hon. Secretary and Treasurer, in succession to Mr. William Foster, of the India Office, who has acted since November 7, 1893.

Mr. S. J. Evis, Chief Clerk to the Royal Geographical Society, has been appointed by the Council to be Clerk and Assistant Treasurer, with authority to give Receipts for Subscriptions.

20th March, 1903.

HAKLUYT SOCIETY.

Statement of Accounts, 1902.

Dr.   **Cr.**

	£	s.	d.
To Balance brought forward (1st January):			
On deposit ... 400 0 0			
On current account ... 229 4 8			
	629	4	8
,, Subscriptions received ...	470	9	0
,, Sale of publications ...	77	5	0
,, Interest on Deposit Account ...	12	3	11
,, Subscription paid in error ...	3	3	0
	£1192	**5**	**7**

	£	s.	d.
By Printing *The Travels of Pedro Teixeira* ...	136	0	0
,, Warehousing and delivery of volumes ...	43	5	0
,, Maps of Guinea ...	25	0	0
,, Binding ...	33	15	4
,, Indexing *Pedro Teixeira* ...	7	7	0
,, Petty cash, postages, and other expenses ...	14	0	0
,, Clerical assistance ...	18	15	0
,, Bank charges and refunds ...	3	6	6
,, Balance at Bank (31st December):			
On deposit ... 700 0 0			
On current account ... 210 16 9			
	910	16	9
	£1192	**5**	**7**

BASIL H. SOULSBY,
Hon. Secretary and Treasurer.

Examined and found correct,

EDWARD HEAWOOD,

20th March, 1903.

THE HAKLUYT SOCIETY.

1902.

President.

Sir CLEMENTS MARKHAM, K.C.B., F.R.S., Pres. R.G.S.

Vice-Presidents.

The Right Hon. Lord STANLEY of ALDERLEY.
Rear-Admiral Sir WILLIAM WHARTON, K.C.B., F.R.S.

Council.

C. RAYMOND BEAZLEY, M.A.
Commr. B. M. CHAMBERS, R.N.
Colonel GEORGE EARL CHURCH.
Sir WILLIAM MARTIN CONWAY.
WILLIAM FOSTER, B.A.
F. H. H. GUILLEMARD, M.A., M.D.
EDWARD HEAWOOD, M.A.
JOHN SCOTT KELTIE, LL.D.
FREDERIC WILLIAM LUCAS.

ALFRED PERCIVAL MAUDSLAY.
MOWBRAY MORRIS.
EDWARD JOHN PAYNE, M.A.
ERNEST GEORGE RAVENSTEIN.
HOWARD SAUNDERS.
HENRY WILLIAM TRINDER.
CHARLES WELCH, F.S.A.
RICHARD STEPHEN WHITEWAY.

Hon. Secretary and Treasurer.

BASIL H. SOULSBY, B.A.,
Map Room, British Museum, W.C.

Clerk and Assistant Treasurer.

Mr. S. J. EVIS,
Royal Geographical Society, 1, Savile Row, W.

Bankers in London.

Messrs. BARCLAY & Co., Ltd., 1, Pall Mall East, S.W.

Bankers in New York.

THE MORTON TRUST CO., corner of Cedar and Nassau Streets.

Agent for distribution, &c., of Volumes.

Mr. BERNARD QUARITCH, 15, Piccadilly, W.

Annual Subscription.—One Guinea (in America five dollars.)

THE HAKLUYT SOCIETY, established in 1846, has for its object the printing of rare or unpublished Voyages and Travels. Books of this class are of the highest interest and value to students of history, geography, navigation, and ethnology; and many of them, especially the original narratives and translations of the Elizabethan and Stuart periods, are admirable examples of English prose at the stage of its most robust development.

The Society has not confined its selection to the books of English travellers, to a particular age, or to particular regions. Where the original is foreign, the work is given in English, fresh translations being made, except where it is possible to utilise the spirited renderings of the sixteenth or seventeenth century.

More than a hundred volumes have now been issued by the Society. The majority of these illustrate the history of the great age of discovery which forms the foundation of modern history. The discovery of AMERICA, and of particular portions of the two great western continents, is represented by the writings of COLUMBUS, AMERIGO VESPUCCI, CORTES and CHAMPLAIN, and by several of the early narratives from HAKLUYT'S collection. The works relating to the conquest of PERU, and to the condition of that country under the Incas, are numerous and of the highest value; similar interest attaches to STRACHEY'S *Virginia Britannia*, DE SOTO'S *Discovery of Florida*, and SIR ROBERT SCHOMBURGK'S edition of RALEIGH'S *Discoverie of Guiana*. The works relating to AFRICA already published comprise BARBOSA'S *Coasts of East Africa*, the *Portuguese Embassy to Abyssinia* of ALVAREZ, and *The Travels of Leo the Moor*. Notices of AUSTRALIA, INDIA, PERSIA, CHINA, JAPAN, etc., as they appeared in early times to European eyes, both before and after the discovery of the Cape route, are also included in the series, a well-known example being the work on *Cathay and the Way Thither*, contributed by a former President, SIR HENRY YULE. The search for the North-west and North-east Passages is recorded in the narratives of JENKINSON, DE VEER, FROBISHER, DAVIS, HUDSON, BAFFIN, etc.; whilst more extensive voyages are signalised by the great names of MAGELLAN, DRAKE, and HAWKINS.

The works selected by the Council for reproduction are printed (with rare exceptions) at full length. Each volume is placed in the charge of an editor especially competent—in many cases from personal acquaintance with the countries described—to give the reader such assistance as he needs for the elucidation of the text. Whenever possible, the interest of the volumes is increased by the addition of reproductions of contemporary portraits, maps, and other illustrations.

As these editorial services are rendered gratuitously, *the whole of the amount received from subscribers is expended in the preparation of the Society's publications.*

The subscription should be paid to the Society's Bankers on the 1st January in each year; or, if preferred, it may be sent to Mr. S. J. Evis, at 1, Savile Row, W. This entitles the subscriber to receive, free of charge, the current publications of the Society. Usually three volumes are issued each year. Members have the sole privilege of purchasing sets of the previous publications; and the more recent of the Society's volumes are also reserved exclusively for its subscribers. In addition, they are allowed a special discount of 15 per cent. on the volumes permitted to be sold to the public. It may be mentioned that the publications of the Society tend to rise in value, and those which are out of print are now only to be obtained at high prices.

The present scale of charges for back volumes is as follows:—

To Members.—*Sets of the* First Series, *omitting Nos. 1 to 10, 12, 19, 25, 36, 37, to be sold for* . . . . *net* £30.

N.B.—*Most of the out-of-print volumes have been, or are being, reprinted as later volumes of the series.*

To the Public Generally.—*A limited number of single copies* as follows:—

Nos. 23, 26, 29, 31, 34, 40, 47, 50, at . . . . **8s. 6d.**
Nos. 21, 28, 30, 35, 46, 48, 51, 53, 55, 56, 58, 60 to 87, 90 to 100, at . **10s.**
Nos. 20, 27, 33, 38, 41 to 45, 49, 52, 57, 88, 89, at . . . **15s.**
Nos. 54 and 59, at . . . . . . **20s.**

*** Subject in case of Members to a discount of 15%.

The volumes of the Second Series *can only be obtained by paying the arrears of subscription.*

A list of works in preparation is given at page 13. The Secretary will be happy to furnish any further information that may be desired.

Gentlemen desiring to be enrolled as members should send their names to the Secretary. Applications for back volumes should be addressed to Mr. QUARITCH.

WORKS ALREADY ISSUED.

FIRST SERIES.

1—The Observations of Sir Richard Hawkins, Knt.,
In his Voyage into the South Sea in 1593. Reprinted from the edition of 1622, and edited by Capt. C. R. D. BETHUNE, R.N., C.B.
(First Edition out of print. See No. 57.) *Issued for* 1847.

2—Select Letters of Columbus,
With Original Documents relating to the Discovery of the New World. Translated and Edited by R. H. MAJOR.
(First Edition out of print. See No. 43.) *Issued for* 1847.

3—The Discovery of the Empire of Guiana.
By Sir Walter Ralegh, Knt. Edited by SIR ROBERT H. SCHOMBURGK, Ph.D.
(First Edition out of print. Second Edition in preparation.) *Issued for* 1848.

4—Sir Francis Drake his Voyage, 1595,
By Thomas Maynarde, together with the Spanish Account of Drake's attack on Puerto Rico. Edited by W. D. COOLEY.
(Out of print.) *Issued for* 1848.

5—Narratives of Early Voyages to the North-West.
Edited by THOMAS RUNDALL.
(Out of print.) *Issued for* 1849.

6—The Historie of Travaile into Virginia Britannia,
Expressing the Cosmographie and Commodities of the Country, together with the manners and customs of the people, collected by William Strachey, Gent., the first Secretary of the Colony. Edited by R. H. MAJOR.
(Out of print.) *Issued for* 1849.

7—Divers Voyages touching the Discovery of America
And the Islands adjacent, collected and published by Richard Hakluyt, Prebendary of Bristol, in the year 1582. Edited by JOHN WINTER JONES.
(Out of print.) *Issued for* 1850.

8—A Collection of Documents on Japan.
With a Commentary by THOMAS RUNDALL.
(Out of print.) *Issued for* 1850.

9—The Discovery and Conquest of Florida,
By Don Ferdinando de Soto. Translated out of Portuguese by Richard Hakluyt; and Edited by W. B. RYE.
(Out of print.) *Issued for* 1851.

10—Notes upon Russia,
Being a Translation from the Earliest Account of that Country, entitled Rerum Muscoviticarum Commentarii, by the Baron Sigismund von Herberstein, Ambassador from the Court of Germany to the Grand Prince Vasiley Ivanovich, in the years 1517 and 1526. Two Volumes. Translated and Edited by R. H. MAJOR. Vol. 1.
(Out of print.) *Issued for* 1851.

11—The Geography of Hudson's Bay,

Being the Remarks of Captain W. Coats, in many Voyages to that locality, between the years 1727 and 1751. With Extracts from the Log of Captain Middleton on his Voyage for the Discovery of the North-west Passage, in H.M.S. "Furnace," in 1741-2. Edited by JOHN BARROW, F.R.S., F.S.A.

Issued for 1852.

12—Notes upon Russia.

Vol. 2. (*Out of print.*) *Issued for 1852.*

13—Three Voyages by the North-East,

Towards Cathay and China, undertaken by the Dutch in the years 1594, 1595 and 1596, with their Discovery of Spitzbergen, their residence of ten months in Novaya Zemlya, and their safe return in two open boats. By Gerrit de Veer. Edited by C. T. BEKE, Ph.D., F.S.A.

(*See also No. 54.*) *Issued for 1853.*

14-15—The History of the Great and Mighty Kingdom of China and the Situation Thereof.

Compiled by the Padre Juan Gonzalez de Mendoza. Reprinted from the Early Translation of R. Parke, and Edited by SIR GEORGE T. STAUNTON, Bart. With an Introduction by R. H. MAJOR. 2 vols.

Issued for 1854.

16—The World Encompassed by Sir Francis Drake.

Being his next Voyage to that to Nombre de Dios. Collated with an unpublished Manuscript of Francis Fletcher, Chaplain to the Expedition. Edited by W. S. W. VAUX, M.A. *Issued for 1855.*

17—The History of the Tartar Conquerors who subdued China.

From the French of the Père D'Orleans, 1688. Translated and Edited by the EARL OF ELLESMERE. With an Introduction by R. H. MAJOR.

Issued for 1855.

18—A Collection of Early Documents on Spitzbergen and Greenland.

Edited by ADAM WHITE. *Issued for 1856.*

19—The Voyage of Sir Henry Middleton to Bantam and the Maluco Islands.

From the rare Edition of 1606. Edited by BOLTON CORNEY.

(*Out of print*). *Issued for 1856.*

20—Russia at the Close of the Sixteenth Century.

Comprising "The Russe Commonwealth" by Dr. Giles Fletcher, and Sir Jerome Horsey's Travels. Edited by E. A. BOND.

Issued for 1857.

21—The Travels of Girolamo Benzoni in America, in 1542-56.

Translated and Edited by ADMIRAL W. H. SMYTH, F.R.S., F.S.A.

Issued for 1857.

22—India in the Fifteenth Century.

Being a Collection of Narratives of Voyages to India in the century preceding the Portuguese discovery of the Cape of Good Hope; from Latin, Persian, Russian, and Italian Sources. Edited by R. H. MAJOR.

Issued for 1858.

23—Narrative of a Voyage to the West Indies and Mexico,
In the years 1599-1602, with Maps and Illustrations. By Samuel Champlain Translated from the original and unpublished Manuscript, with a Biographical Notice and Notes by ALICE WILMERE. *Issued for* 1858.

24—Expeditions into the Valley of the Amazons
During the Sixteenth and Seventeenth Centuries: containing the Journey of Gonzalo Pizarro, from the Royal Commentaries of Garcilasso Inca de la Vega; the Voyage of Francisco de Orellana, from the General History of Herrera; and the Voyage of Cristoval de Acuna. Translated and Edited by CLEMENTS R. MARKHAM. *Issued for* 1859.

25—Early Indications of Australia.
A Collection of Documents shewing the Early Discoveries of Australia to the time of Captain Cook. Edited by R. H. MAJOR.
(*Out of print.*) *Issued for* 1859.

26—The Embassy of Ruy Gonzalez de Clavijo to the Court of Timour, 1403-6.
Translated and Edited by CLEMENTS R. MARKHAM.
Issued for 1860.

27—Henry Hudson the Navigator.
The Original Documents in which his career is recorded. Edited by GEORGE ASHER, LL.D. *Issued for* 1860.

28—The Expedition of Ursua and Aguirre,
In search of El Dorado and Omagua, A.D. 1560-61. Translated from the "Sexta Noticia Historiale" of Fray Pedro Simon, by W. BOLLAERT, with an Introduction by CLEMENTS R. MARKHAM.
Issued for 1861.

29—The Life and Acts of Don Alonzo Enriquez de Guzman.
Translated and Edited by CLEMENTS R. MARKHAM.
Issued for 1862.

30—Discoveries of the World
From their first original unto the year of our Lord 1555. By Antonio Galvano. Reprinted, with the original Portuguese text, and edited by VICE-ADMIRAL BETHUNE, C.B. *Issued for* 1862.

31—Marvels described by Friar Jordanus,
From a parchment manuscript of the Fourteenth Century, in Latin. Edited by COLONEL H. YULE, C.B. *Issued for* 1863.

32—The Travels of Ludovico di Varthema
In Syria, Arabia, Persia, India, etc., during the Sixteenth Century. Translated by J. WINTER JONES, F.S.A., and Edited by the REV. GEORGE PERCY BADGER. *Issued for* 1863.

33—The Travels of Cieza de Leon in 1532-50
From the Gulf of Darien to the City of La Plata, contained in the first part of his Chronicle of Peru (Antwerp, 1554). Translated and Edited by CLEMENTS R. MARKHAM. *Issued for* 1864.

34—The Narrative of Pascual de Andagoya.
Containing the earliest notice of Peru. Translated and Edited by CLEMENTS R. MARKHAM. *Issued for* 1865.

35—The Coasts of East Africa and Malabar
In the beginning of the Sixteenth Century, by Duarte Barbosa. Translate from an early Spanish manuscript by the HON. HENRY STANLEY.
Issued for 1865.

36-37—Cathay and the Way Thither.
A Collection of all minor notices of China, previous to the Sixteenth Century. Translated and Edited by COLONEL H. YULE, C.B. Two Vols.
(*Out of print.*) *Issued for 1866.*

38—The Three Voyages of Sir Martin Frobisher.
With a Selection from Letters now in the State Paper Office. Edited by REAR-ADMIRAL COLLINSON, C.B. *Issued for 1867.*

39—The Philippine Islands,
Moluccas, Siam, Cambodia, Japan, and China, at the close of the 16th Century. By Antonia de Morga. Translated from the Spanish, with Notes, by the LORD STANLEY of Alderley. *Issued for 1868.*

40—The Fifth Letter of Hernan Cortes
To the Emperor Charles V., containing an Account of his Expedition to Honduras in 1525-26. Translated from the Spanish by DON PASCUAL DE GAYANGOS. *Issued for 1868.*

41—The Royal Commentaries of the Yncas.
By the Ynca Garcillasso de la Vega. Translated and Edited by CLEMENTS R. MARKHAM. Vol. I. *Issued for 1869.*

42—The Three Voyages of Vasco da Gama,
And his Viceroyalty, from the Lendas da India of Gaspar Correa; accompanied by original documents. Translated and Edited by the LORD STANLEY of Alderley. *Issued for 1869.*

43—Select Letters of Christopher Columbus,
With other Original Documents relating to his Four Voyages to the New World. Translated and Edited by R. H. MAJOR. 2nd Edition (see No. 2).
Issued for 1870.

44—History of the Imâms and Seyyids of 'Omân,
By Salîl-Ibn-Razîk, from A.D. 661-1856. Translated from the original Arabic, and Edited, with a continuation of the History down to 1870, by the REV. GEORGE PERCY BADGER. *Issued for 1870.*

45—The Royal Commentaries of the Yncas.
Vol. 2. *Issued for 1871.*

46—The Canarian,
Or Book of the Conquest and Conversion of the Canarians in the year 1402, by Messire Jean de Bethencourt, Kt. Composed by Pierre Bontier and Jean le Verrier. Translated and Edited by R. H. MAJOR.
Issued for 1871.

47—Reports on the Discovery of Peru.
Translated and Edited by CLEMENTS R. MARKHAM, C.B.
Issued for 1872.

48—Narratives of the Rites and Laws of the Yncas.
Translated and Edited by CLEMENTS R. MARKHAM, C.B., F.R.S.
Issued for 1872.

49—Travels to Tana and Persia,
By Josafa Barbaro and Ambrogio Contarini; Edited by LORD STANLEY of Alderley. With Narratives of other Italian Travels in Persia. Translated and Edited by CHARLES GREY. *Issued for 1873.*

50—Voyages of the Zeni
To the Northern Seas in the Fourteenth Century. Translated and Edited by R. H. MAJOR. *Issued for 1873.*

51—The Captivity of Hans Stade of Hesse in 1547-55,
Among the Wild Tribes of Eastern Brazil. Translated by ALBERT TOOTAL, Esq., and annotated by SIR RICHARD F. BURTON.
Issued for 1874.

52—The First Voyage Round the World by Magellan.
Translated from the Accounts of Pigafetta and other contemporary writers. Edited by LORD STANLEY of Alderley.
Issued for 1874.

53—The Commentaries of the Great Afonso Dalboquerque,
Second Viceroy of India. Translated from the Portuguese Edition of 1774, and Edited by WALTER DE GRAY BIRCH, F.R.S.L. Vol. 1.
Issued for 1875.

54—The Three Voyages of William Barents to the North-East.
Second Edition of Gerrit de Veer's Work. Edited by Lieut. KOOLEMANS BEYNEN, of the Royal Dutch Navy.
Issued for 1876.

55—The Commentaries of the Great Afonso Dalboquerque.
Vol. 2. *Issued for 1875.*

56—The Voyages of Sir James Lancaster.
With Abstracts of Journals of Voyages preserved in the India Office, and the Voyage of Captain John Knight to seek the N.W. Passage. Edited by CLEMENTS R. MARKHAM, C.B., F.R.S.
Issued for 1877.

57—The Observations of Sir Richard Hawkins, Knt.,
In his Voyage into the South Sea in 1593, with the Voyages of his grandfather William, his father Sir John, and his cousin William Hawkins. Second Edition (see No. 1). Edited by CLEMENTS R. MARKHAM, C.B., F.R.S. *Issued for 1877.*

58—The Bondage and Travels of Johann Schiltberger,
From his capture at the battle of Nicopolis in 1396 to his escape and return to Europe in 1427. Translated by Commander J. BUCHAN TELFER, R.N.; with Notes by Professor B. BRUUN. *Issued for 1878.*

59—The Voyages and Works of John Davis the Navigator.
Edited by Captain ALBERT H. MARKHAM, R.N. *Issued for 1878.*

The Map of the World, A.D. 1600.
Called by Shakspere "The New Map, with the Augmentation of the Indies." To illustrate the Voyages of John Davis. *Issued for 1878.*

60-61—The Natural and Moral History of the Indies.
By Father Joseph de Acosta. Reprinted from the English Translated Edition of Edward Grimston, 1604; and Edited by CLEMENTS R. MARKHAM, C.B., F.R.S. Two Vols. *Issued for* 1879.

Map of Peru.
To Illustrate Nos. 33, 41, 45, 60, and 61. *Issued for* 1879.

62—The Commentaries of the Great Afonso Dalboquerque.
Vol. 3. *Issued for* 1880.

63—The Voyages of William Baffin, 1612-1622.
Edited by CLEMENTS R. MARKHAM, C.B., F.R.S. *Issued for* 1880.

64—Narrative of the Portuguese Embassy to Abyssinia
During the years 1520-1527. By Father Francisco Alvarez. Translated and Edited by LORD STANLEY of Alderley. *Issued for* 1881.

65—The History of the Bermudas or Somer Islands.
Attributed to Captain Nathaniel Butler. Edited by General Sir J. HENRY LEFROY, R.A., K.C.M.G. *Issued for* 1881.

66-67—The Diary of Richard Cocks,
Cape-Merchant in the English Factory in Japan, 1615-1622. Edited by EDWARD MAUNDE THOMPSON. Two Vols.
Issued for 1882.

68—The Second Part of the Chronicle of Peru.
By Pedro de Cieza de Leon. Translated and Edited by CLEMENTS R. MARKHAM, C.B., F.R.S. *Issued for* 1883.

69—The Commentaries of the Great Afonso Dalboquerque.
Vol. 4. *Issued for* 1883.

70-71—The Voyage of John Huyghen van Linschoten to the East Indies.
From the Old English Translation of 1598. The First Book, containing his Description of the East. Edited by A. C. BURNELL, Ph.D., C.I.E., and P. A. TIELE, of Utrecht. *Issued for* 1884.

72-73—Early Voyages and Travels to Russia and Persia,
By Anthony Jenkinson and other Englishmen, with some account of the first Intercourse of the English with Russia and Central Asia by way of the Caspian Sea. Edited by E. DELMAR MORGAN, and C. H. COOTE.
Issued for 1885.

74-75—The Diary of William Hedges, Esq.,
Afterwards Sir William Hedges, during his Agency in Bengal; as well as on his Voyage out and Return Overland (1681-1687). Transcribed for the Press, with Introductory Notes, etc., by R. BARLOW, and Illustrated by copious Extracts from Unpublished Records, etc., by Col. Sir H. YULE, K.C.S.I., R.E., C.B., LL.D. Vols. 1 and 2. *Issued for* 1886.

76-77—The Voyage of François Pyrard to the East Indies,
The Maldives, the Moluccas and Brazil. Translated into English from the Third French Edition of 1619, and Edited by ALBERT GRAY, assisted by H. C. P. BELL. Vol. 1. Vol. 2, Part I.
Issued for 1887.

78—The Diary of William Hedges, Esq.
Vol. 3. Sir H. Yule's Extracts from Unpublished Records, etc.
Issued for 1888.

79—Tractatus de Globis, et eorum usu.

A Treatise descriptive of the Globes constructed by Emery Molyneux, and Published in 1592. By Robert Hues. Edited by CLEMENTS R. MARKHAM, C.B., F.R.S. To which is appended,

Sailing Directions for the Circumnavigation of England,

And for a Voyage to the Straits of Gibraltar. From a Fifteenth Century MS. Edited by JAMES GAIRDNER; with a Glossary by E. DELMAR MORGAN. *Issued for* 1888.

80—The Voyage of François Pyrard to the East Indies, etc.

Vol. 2, Part II. *Issued for* 1889.

81—The Conquest of La Plata, 1535-1555.

I.—Voyage of Ulrich Schmidt to the Rivers La Plata and Paraguai. II.—The Commentaries of Alvar Nunez Cabeza de Vaca. Edited by DON LUIS L. DOMINGUEZ. *Issued for* 1889.

82-83—The Voyage of François Leguat

To Rodriguez, Mauritius, Java, and the Cape of Good Hope. Edited by Captain PASFIELD OLIVER. Two Vols.
Issued for 1890.

84-85—The Travels of Pietro della Valle to India.

From the Old English Translation of 1664, by G. Havers. Edited by EDWARD GREY. Two Vols. *Issued for* 1891.

86—The Journal of Christopher Columbus

During his First Voyage (1492-93), and Documents relating to the Voyages of John Cabot and Gaspar Corte Real. Translated and Edited by CLEMENTS R. MARKHAM, C.B., F.R.S. *Issued for* 1892.

87—Early Voyages and Travels in the Levant.

I.—The Diary of Master Thomas Dallam, 1599-1600. II.—Extracts from the Diaries of Dr. John Covel, 1670-1679. With some Account of the Levant Company of Turkey Merchants. Edited by J. THEODORE BENT, F.S.A., F.R.G.S. *Issued for* 1892.

88-89—The Voyages of Captain Luke Foxe and Captain Thomas James

In Search of a N.-W. Passage, 1631-32; with Narratives of Earlier N.-W. Voyages. Edited by MILLER CHRISTY, F.L.S. Two Vols.
Issued for 1893.

90—The Letters of Amerigo Vespucci

And other Documents relating to his Career. Translated and Edited by CLEMENTS R. MARKHAM, C.B., F.R.S. *Issued for* 1894.

91—The Voyage of Pedro Sarmiento to the Strait of Magellan, 1579-80.

Translated and Edited, with Illustrative Documents and Introduction, by CLEMENTS R. MARKHAM, C.B., F.R.S.
Issued for 1894.

92-93-94—The History and Description of Africa,

And of the Notable Things Therein Contained. The Travels of Leo Africanus the Moor, from the English translation of John Pory (1600). Edited by ROBERT BROWN, M.A., Ph.D. Three Vols.
Issued for 1895.

95—The Discovery and Conquest of Guinea.
Written by Gomes Eannes de Azurara. Translated and Edited by C. RAYMOND BEAZLEY, M.A., and EDGAR PRESTAGE, B.A. Vol. 1.
Issued for 1896.

96-97—Danish Arctic Expeditions.
Book 1. The Danish Expeditions to Greenland, 1605-07; with James Hall's Voyage in 1612. Edited by C. C. A. GOSCH. *Issued for 1896.*

Book 2. Jens Munk's Voyage to Hudson's Bay in 1619-20. Edited by C. C. A. GOSCH. *Issued for 1897.*

98—The Topographia Christiana of Cosmas Indicopleustes.
Translated and Edited by J. W. MCCRINDLE, M.A., M.R.A.S.
Issued for 1897.

99—The First Voyage of Vasco da Gama.
Translated from the Portuguese, with an Introduction and Notes, by E. G. RAVENSTEIN. *Issued for 1898.*

100—The Discovery and Conquest of Guinea.
Written by Gomes Eannes de Azurara. Translated and Edited by C. RAYMOND BEAZLEY, M.A., and EDGAR PRESTAGE, B.A. Vol. 2.
Issued for 1898.

WORKS ALREADY ISSUED.

SECOND SERIES.

1-2—The Embassy of Sir Thomas Roe to the Court of the Great Mogul, 1615-19.
Edited from Contemporary Records by WILLIAM FOSTER, B.A.
Issued for 1899.

3—The Voyage of Sir Robert Dudley to the West Indies and Guiana in 1594.
Edited by GEO. F. WARNER, M.A., F.S.A., Assistant Keeper of Manuscripts, British Museum. *Issued for* 1899.

4—The Journeys of William of Rubruck and John of Pian de Carpine
To Tartary in the 13th century. Translated and Edited by the Hon. W. W. ROCKHILL. *Issued for* 1900.

5—The Voyage of Captain John Saris to Japan in 1613.
Edited by H. E. SIR ERNEST M. SATOW, K.C.M.G.
Issued for 1900.

6—The Strange Adventures of Andrew Battell of Leigh in Essex.
Edited by E. G. RAVENSTEIN. *Issued for* 1900.

7-8—The Voyage of Mendaña to the Solomon Islands in 1568.
Edited by the LORD AMHERST OF HACKNEY and BASIL THOMSON.
Issued for 1901.

9—The Journey of Pedro Teixeira from India to Italy by land, 1604-05;
With his Chronicle of the Kings of Ormus. Translated and Edited by W. F. SINCLAIR, with additional notes &c., by D. F. FERGUSON.
To be issued for 1901.

10—The Portuguese Expedition to Abyssinia in 1541, as narrated by
Castanhoso and Bermudez. Edited by R. S. WHITEWAY, late I.C.S.
To be issued for 1902.

11—The Principall Navigations of the English Nation. By Richard Hakluyt,
1598-1600. Vol. I. Edited by SIR CLEMENTS MARKHAM, K.C.B., and C. R. BEAZLEY, M.A.
To be issued for 1902.

OTHER WORKS UNDERTAKEN BY EDITORS.

The Principall Navigations of the English Nation. By RICHARD HAKLUYT. From the edition of 1598-1600. To be issued in about ten volumes.

Raleigh's Empire of Guiana. Second Edition (see No. 3). Edited, with Notes, etc., by EVERARD F. IM THURN, C.B., C.M.G.

The Voyages of Cadamosto, the Venetian, along the West Coast of Africa, in the years 1455 and 1456. Translated from the earliest Italian text of 1507, and Edited by H. YULE OLDHAM, M.A., F.R.G.S.

Dr. John Fryer's New Account of East India and Persia (1698). Edited by ARTHUR T. PRINGLE.

The Expedition of Hernan Cortes to Honduras in 1525-26. Second Edition (see No. 40), with added matter. Translated and Edited by A. P. MAUDSLAY.

The Letters of Pietro Della Valle from Persia, &c. Translated and Edited by MAJOR M. NATHAN, C.M.G., R.E.

The Travels of Peter Mundy in India, 1628-34. Edited from an unpublished MS. by COLONEL R. C. TEMPLE, C.I.E.

Thomas Herbert's Description of the Persian Monarchy. Edited by Major P. MOLESWORTH SYKES.

The Voyage of Robert Harcourt to Guiana in 1609-10. Edited by G. F. WARNER, M.A., F.S.A.

Sir Francis Drake Revived, and other papers relating to Drake. Edited by E. J. PAYNE, M.A.

Early Dutch and English Voyages to Spitzbergen. Edited by SIR MARTIN CONWAY.

LAWS OF THE HAKLUYT SOCIETY.

I. The object of this Society shall be to print, for distribution among its members, rare and valuable Voyages, Travels, Naval Expeditions, and other geographical records, from an early period to the beginning of the eighteenth century.

II. The Annual Subscription shall be One Guinea (for America, five dollars, U.S. currency), payable in advance on the 1st January.

III. Each member of the Society, having paid his Subscription, shall be entitled to a copy of every work produced by the Society, and to vote at the general meetings within the period subscribed for; and if he do not signify, before the close of the year, his wish to resign, he shall be considered as a member for the succeeding year.

IV. The management of the Society's affairs shall be vested in a Council consisting of twenty-two members, viz., a President, two Vice-Presidents, a Treasurer, a Secretary, and seventeen ordinary members, to be elected annually; but vacancies occurring between the general meetings shall be filled up by the Council.

V. A General Meeting of the Subscribers shall be held annually. The Secretary's Report on the condition and proceedings of the Society shall be then read, and the meeting shall proceed to elect the Council for the ensuing year.

VI. At each Annual Election, three of the old Council shall retire.

VII. The Council shall meet when necessary for the dispatch of business, three forming a quorum, including the Secretary; the Chairman having a casting vote.

VIII. Gentlemen preparing and editing works for the Society, shall receive twenty-five copies of such works respectively.

LIST OF MEMBERS.

1902.

Aberdare, The Right Hon. Lord, Longwood, Winchester.
Adelaide Public Library, per Messrs. Kegan Paul and Co., Ltd., Paternoster House, Charing Cross Road, W.C.
Admiralty, The (2 *copies*), per Messrs. Eyre and Spottiswoode, East Harding Street, E.C.
Advocates' Library, Edinburgh, per G. W. Eccles, Esq., 16, Great James Street, W.C.
Alexander, W. L., Esq., Pinkieburn, Musselburgh, N.B.
All Souls College, Oxford.
American Geographical Society, 11, West 29th Street, New York City, U.S.A.
Amherst, of Hackney, The Right Hon. Lord, Didlington Hall, Brandon, Norfolk.
Antiga Casa Bertrand (Senhor José Bastos), 73, Rua Garrett, Lisbon.
Antiquaries, the Society of, Burlington House, Piccadilly, W.
Armitage-Smith, Sydney, Esq., Admiralty, S.W.
Army and Navy Club, 36, Pall Mall, S.W.
Athenæum Club, Pall Mall, S.W.
Atkinson, Dr. Roger T., U.S. Navy, 14, Chestnut Street, Wakefield, Massachusetts, U.S.A.

Baer, Joseph & Co., Messrs., Rossmarkt, 18, Frankfort-on-Main, Germany, per Messrs. Epstein Bros., 47, Holborn Viaduct, E.C.
Baldwin, Alfred, Esq., M.P., Wilden House, near Stourport.
Ball, John B., Esq., Ashburton Cottage, Putney Heath, S.W.
Barclay, Hugh Gurney, Esq., Colney Hall, Norwich.
Basset, M. René, Correspondant de l'Institut de France, Directeur de l'Ecole supérieure des lettres d'Alger, L'Agha 77, rue Michelet, Alger-Mustapha.
Baxter, James Phinney, Esq., 61, Deering Street, Portland, Maine, U.S.A.
Beaumont, Rear-Admiral Sir Lewis Anthony, K.C.M.G., Australian Station.
Beazley, Charles Raymond, Esq., 21, Staverton Road, Oxford.
Belfast Linen Hall Library, Donegall Square North, Belfast (Geo. Smith, Esq., Librarian).
Belhaven and Stenton, Col. the Lord, R.E., 41, Lennox Gardens, S.W.
Bennett, R. A., Esq., 40, Harborne Road, Edgbaston, Birmingham.
Berlin Geographical Society, per Messrs. Sampson Low and Co., Ltd., St. Dunstan's House, Fetter Lane, E.C.
Berlin, the Royal Library of, per Messrs. Asher and Co., 13, Bedford Street, Strand, W.C.
Berlin University, Geographical Institute of (Baron von Richthofen), 6, Schinkelplatz, Berlin, W., per Messrs. Sampson Low and Co., Ltd., St. Dunstan's House, Fetter Lane, E.C.
Birch, Dr. Walter de Gray, F.S.A., 1, Rutland Park, N.W.
Birmingham Central Free Library, Ratcliff-place, Birmingham.
Birmingham Old Library, The, Birmingham.
Board of Education, South Kensington, S.W.
Bodleian Library, Oxford *(copies presented)*.
Bonaparte, H. H. Prince Roland Napoléon, 10, Avenue d'Jéna, Paris.
Boston Athenæum Library, U.S.A., per Messrs. Kegan Paul and Co., Ltd., Paternoster House, Charing Cross Road, W.C.

Boston Public Library, U.S.A., per Messrs. Kegan Paul and Co., Ltd., Paternoster House, Charing Cross Road, W.C.
Bowdoin College, Brunswick, Maine, U.S.A., per Messrs. Kegan Paul and Co., Ltd., Paternoster House, Charing Cross Road, W.C.
Bower, Major Hamilton, per Messrs. Grindlay and Co., 54, Parliament St., S.W.
Bowring, Thos. B., Esq., 7, Palace Gate, Kensington, W.
Brewster, Charles O., Esq., 25, Irving Place, New York City, U.S.A.
Brighton Public Library, Royal Pavilion, Church Street, Brighton.
Brine, Vice-Admiral Lindesay, c/o Miss Knapton, Boldre Mead, Lymington, Hants.
British Guiana Royal Agricultural and Commercial Society, Georgetown, Demerara.
British Museum, Department of British and Mediæval Antiquities (C. H. Read, Esq., Keeper).
British Museum, Department of Printed Books (G. K. Fortescue, Esq., Keeper, *copies presented*).
British Museum (Natural History), Cromwell Road, S.W. (B. B. Woodward, Esq., Librarian), per Messrs. Dulau and Co., 37, Soho Square, W.
Brock, Robert C. H., Esq., 1612, Walnut-street, Philadelphia.
Brodrick, Hon. George Charles, D.C.L., Merton College, Oxford.
Brooke, Sir Thomas, Bart., Armitage Bridge, Huddersfield.
Brookline Public Library, Boston, Mass., U.S.A.
Brooklyn Mercantile Library, Brooklyn, N.Y., U.S.A., per Messrs. Allen and Murray, 28, Henrietta Street, W.C.
Brown, Arthur William Whateley, Esq., 62, Carlisle Mansions, Carlisle Place, Victoria Street, S.W.
Brown, General John Marshall, 218, Middle Street, Portland, Maine, U.S.A.
Brown, Henry Thomas, Esq., Roodee House, Watergate Square, Chester.
Brown, J. Allen, Esq., J.P., 7, Kent Gardens, Ealing, W.
Brown University, Providence, Rhode Island (H. L. Koopman, Librarian) U.S.A.
Bruce, A. M., Esq., 2, Polwarth Terrace, Edinburgh.
Buda-Pesth, The Geographical Institute of the University of.
Bunting, W. L., Esq., The Steps, Bromsgrove.
Burdekin, Benjamin Thomas, Esq., The Terrace, Eyam, Sheffield.
Burgess, James, Esq., C.I.E., LL.D., 22, Seton Place, Edinburgh.
Burns, Capt. J. W., Kilmahew, Cardross, Dumbartonshire.
Buxton, Edward North, Esq., Knighton, Buckhurst Hill, Essex.

Cambray & Co., Messrs., 6, Hastings Street, Calcutta.
Cambridge University Library, per G. W. Eccles, Esq., 16, Great James Street, W.C.
Canada, The Parliament Library Ottawa, per Messrs. E. G. Allen and Murray, 28, Henrietta Street, W.C.
Cardiff Public Library, Cardiff (J. Ballinger, Esq., Librarian).
Carles, William Richard, Esq., C.M.G., Vines Close, Wimborne.
Carlton Club, Pall Mall, S.W.
Carlisle, The Rt. Hon. the Earl of, Naworth Castle, Bampton, Cumberland.
Carnegie Library, Pittsburgh, Pa., U.S.A., per Mr. G. E. Stechert, 2, Star Yard, Carey Street, W.C.
Cator, R. B. P., Esq., c/o Athenæum Club, Pall Mall, S.W.
Chamberlain, Right Hon. Joseph, M.P., 40, Princes Gardens, S.W.
Chambers, Commander B. M., R.N., 14, Elphinstone Road, Southsea.
Chetham's Library, Hunt's Bank, Manchester.
Chicago Public Library, U.S.A., per Messrs. B. F. Stevens and Brown, 4, Trafalgar Square, W.C.
Christ Church, Oxford.
Christiania University Library, c/o Messrs. T. Bennett and Sons, Christiania, per Messrs. Cassell and Co., Ltd., Ludgate Hill, E.C.

Church, Col. George Earl, 216, Cromwell Road, S.W.
Cincinnati Public Library, Ohio, U.S.A.
Clark, John Willis, Esq., Scroope House, Trumpington Street, Cambridge.
Colgan, Nathaniel, Esq., 15, Breffin Terrace, Sandycove, co. Dublin.
Colonial Office, The, Downing Street, S.W.
Constable, Archibald, Esq., 14, St. Paul's Road, Camden Town, N.W.
Conway, Sir W. Martin, The Red House, Hornton Street, W.
Cooper, Lieut.-Col. the Right Hon. Edward Henry, 42, Portman Square, W. (*deceased*).
Copenhagen Royal Library, c/o Messrs. Lehman and Stage, Copenhagen, per Messrs. Sampson Low and Co., Ltd., St. Dunstan's House, Fetter Lane,
Cora, Professor Guido, M.A., Via Goito, 2, Rome.   [E.C.
Cornell University, Ithaca, N.Y., U.S.A., per Messrs. Allen and Murray, 28, Henrietta Street, E.C.
Corning, C. R., Esq. } c/o Messrs. Bickers & Son, 1, Leicester Square, W.
Corning, H. K., Esq. }
Cortissoz, Royal, Esq., Editorial Room, *New York Tribune*, 154, Nassau St.,
Cow, John, Esq., Elfinsward, Hayward's Heath.   [New York, U.S.A.
Cruising Club, The, 40, Chancery Lane, W.C.
Cunningham, Lieut.-Col. G. G., C.B., D.S.O., Junior U.S. Club, Charles St., S.W.
Curzon of Kedleston, H.E. the Right Hon. Lord, Government House, Calcutta.

Dalton, Rev. Canon J. Neale, M.A., C.M.G., C.V.O., The Cloisters, Windsor.
Dampier, Gerald Robert, Esq., I.C.S., c/o Messrs. Grindlay and Co., Bombay.
Danish Royal Naval Library, per Messrs. Sampson Low and Co., Ltd. (Foreign Dept.), St. Dunstan's House, Fetter Lane, E.C.
Davis, Hon. N. Darnell, C.M.G., Georgetown, Demerara, British Guiana.
De Bertodano, B., Esq., 22, Chester Terrace, Regent's Park, N.W.
Derby, The Right Hon. the Earl of, K.G., c/o Rev. J. Richardson, Knowsley,
Detroit Public Library, Michigan, U.S.A.   [Prescot.
Dijon University Library, Rue Monge, Dijon.
D'Oliere, Herr, Strassburg, per Messrs. Kegan Paul and Co., Ltd., Paternoster House, Charing Cross Road, W.C.
Doubleday, H. Arthur, Esq., 2, Whitehall Gardens, S.W.
Dresden Geographical Society, per Herr P. E. Richter, Kleine Brüdergasse, 11, Dresden.
Ducie, The Right Hon. the Earl of, F.R.S., Tortworth Court, Falfield.

École Française d'Extrême Orient, Saïgon, Indo-Chine Française.
Edinburgh University Library, per Mr. Jas. Thin, 54, 55, South Bridge, Edinburgh.
Edinburgh Public Library, George IV. Bridge, Edinburgh.
Edwards, Francis, Esq., 83, High Street, Marylebone, W.
Ellsworth, James W., Esq., 71, Broadway, New York City, U.S.A.
Faber, Reginald Stanley, Esq., 90, Regent's Park Road, N.W.
Fanshawe, Admiral Sir Edward Gennys, G.C.B., 74, Cromwell Road, S.W.
Fellows Athenæum, per Messrs. Kegan Paul and Co., Paternoster House, Charing Cross Road, W.C.
Ferguson, Donald William, Esq., 5, Bedford Place, Croydon.
Ferguson, David, Esq., M.I.M.E., 140, Hyndland Drive, Kelvinside, Glasgow.
Fisher, Arthur, Esq., St. Aubyn's, Tiverton, Devon.
Fitzgerald, Edward A., Esq., per Mr. James Bain, 14, Charles Street, Haymarket, S.W.
Ford, J. W., Esq., per Mr. James Bain, 14, Charles Street, Haymarket, S.W.
Foreign Office, The, per Messrs. Eyre and Spottiswoode, East Harding St., EC..
Foreign Office of Germany, Berlin, per Messrs. Asher and Co., 13, Bedford Street, Strand, W.C.
Forrest, George William, Esq., C.I.E., The Knowle, Brenchley, Kent.
Foster, William, Esq., Registry and Record Department, India Office, S.W.

Fothergill, M. B., Esq., c/o Imperial Bank of Persia, Bushire, Persian Gulf, *via* Bombay.
French, H. B., Esq., 429, Arch Street, Philadelphia, U.S.A.

Georg, Mons. H., Lyons, per Messrs. Sampson Low and Co., Ltd., St. Dunstan's House, Fetter Lane, E.C.
George, Charles William, Esq., 51, Hampton Road, Bristol.
Gill, J. Withers, Esq., 109 Box, Bulawayo, South Africa.
Gill, W. Harrison, Esq., c/o Messrs. C. A. & H. Nichols, Peninsular House, Monument Street, E.C.
Gladstone Library, National Liberal Club, Whitehall Place, S.W.
Glasgow University Library, per Mr. Billings, 59, Old Bailey, E.C.
Godman, Frederick Du Cane, Esq., D.C.L., F.R.S., 10, Chandos Street, Cavendish Square, W.
Gosch, Christian Carl August, Esq., 21, Stanhope Gardens, S.W.
Gosling, F. Goodwin, Esq., Hamilton, Bermuda.
Gosset, General Mathew W. E., C.B., Westgate House, Dedham, Essex.
Göttingen University Library, per Messrs. Asher and Co., 13, Bedford Street, Strand, W.C.
Graham, Michael, Esq., *Glasgow Herald*, Glasgow.
Grant-Duff, Right Hon. Sir M. E., G.C.S.I., 11, Chelsea Embankment, S.W.
Gray, Albert, Esq., Catherine Lodge, Trafalgar Square, Chelsea, S.W.
Gray, Matthew H., Esq., India-rubber Co., Ltd., Silvertown, Essex.
Greever, C. O., Esq., 1345, East Ninth Street, Des Moines, Iowa, U.S.A.
Griffiths, John G., Esq., 21, Palace Court, Kensington Gardens, S.W.
Grosvenor Library, Buffalo, N.Y., U.S.A.
Gruzevski, C. L., Esq., 107, College Street, San Antonio, Texas, U.S.A.
Guildhall Library, E.C. (Charles Welch, Esq., F.S.A., Librarian).
Guillemard, Arthur George, Esq., 96, High Street, Eltham, Kent.
Guillemard, Francis Henry Hill, Esq., M.A., M.D., The Old Mill House, Trumpington, Cambridge.

Hamburg Commerz-Bibliothek, c/o Herrn Friederichsen and Co., Hamburg, per Messrs. Drolenvaux and Bremner, 36, Great Tower Street, E.C.
Hamilton, Wm. Pierson, Esq., 32, East 36th Street, New York City, U.S.A.
Hannen, The Hon. Henry Arthur, Holne Cott, Ashburton, South Devon.
Harmsworth, Alfred Charles, Esq., Elmwood, St. Peter's, Kent.
Harvard College, Cambridge, Mass., U.S.A., per Messrs. Kegan Paul and Co., Ltd., Paternoster House, Charing Cross Road, W.C.
Harvie-Brown, J. A., Esq., Dunipace, Larbert, Stirlingshire, N.B.
Haswell, Geo. H., Esq., Ashleigh, Hamstead Road, Handsworth, Birmingham.
Hawkesbury, The Rt. Hon. Lord, 2, Carlton House Terrace, S.W.
Heawood, Edward, Esq., M.A., F.R.G.S., 3, Underhill Road, Lordship Lane, S.E.
Heidelberg University Library, c/o Herrn Gustav Koester, Heidelberg, per Messrs. Kegan Paul and Co., Ltd., Paternoster House, Charing Cross Road, W.C.
Hervey, Dudley F. A., Esq., C.M.G., Westfields, Aldeburgh.
Hiersemann, Herr Karl W., Königsstrasse, 3, Leipzig, per Mr. Young J. Pentland, 38, West Smithfield, E.C.
Hippisley, A. E., Esq., c/o J. D. Campbell, Esq., C.M.G., 26, Old Queen St., S.W.
Hobhouse, Charles Edward Henry, Esq., M.P., The Ridge, Corsham, Wilts.
Horner, J. F. Fortescue, Esq., Mells Park, Frome, Somersetshire, per Mr. J. Bain.
Hoyt Public Library, per Messrs. Sotheran and Co., 140, Strand, W.C.
Hubbard, Hon. Gardiner G., 1328, Connecticut Avenue, Washington, D.C., U.S.A.
Hügel, Baron Anatole A. A. von, Curator, University Museum, Cambridge.
Hull Public Libraries, Baker Street, Hull (W. F. Lawton, Esq., Librarian).
Hull Subscription Library, per Foster's Parcels and Goods Express, Ltd., 82, Fore Street, E.C.

Im Thurn, E. F., Esq., C.B., C.M.G., Colonial Secretary, Colombo, Ceylon.
India Office, Downing Street, S.W. (20 *copies*).
Ingle, William Bruncker, Esq., 4, Orchard Road, Blackheath, S.E.
Inner Temple, Hon. Society of the (J. E. L. Pickering, Esq., Librarian), Temple, E.C.
Ireland, Prof. Alleyne, c/o Dr. E. E. Thorpe, 711, Boylston Street, Boston, Mass., U.S.A.

James, Arthur C., Esq., 92 Park Avenue, New York, U.S.A.
James, Walter B., Esq., M.D., 17, West 54th Street, New York, U.S.A.
John Carter Brown Library, Providence, Rhode Island, U.S.A., per Messrs. Ellis and Elvey, 29, New Bond Street, W.
John Rylands Library, Deansgate, Manchester (H. Guppy, Esq., Librarian).
Johns Hopkins University, Baltimore, Md., U.S.A., per Messrs. E. G. Allen and Murray, 28, Henrietta Street, S.W.
Johnson, General Sir Allen B., K.C.B., 60, Lexham Gardens, Cromwell Road, [S.W.
Johnson, Rev. Samuel J., F.R.A.S., Melplash Vicarage, Bridport.

Keltie, John Scott, Esq., LL.D., 1, Savile Row, W.
Kelvin, The Rt. Hon. Lord, F.R.S., LL.D., 15, Eaton Place, S.W.
Key, John J., Esq., Colorado Springs, Colorado, U.S.A.
Kiel, Royal University of, per Messrs. Asher and Co., 13, Bedford Street, W.C.
Kinder, Claude William, Esq., C.M.G., Tongshan, North China.
King's Inns Library, Henrietta Street, Dublin.
Kimberley Public Library, per Messrs. Sotheran and Co., 140, Strand, W.C.
Kitching, John, Esq., Oaklands, Queen's Road, Kingston Hill, S.W.
Klincksieck, M. Charles, 11, Rue de Lille, Paris, per Messrs. Kegan Paul and Co., Ltd., Paternoster House, Charing Cross Road, W.C. (3 *copies*).

Langton, J. J. P., Esq., B.A., 802, Spruce Street, St. Louis, Mo., U.S.A.
Larchmont Yacht Club, Larchmont, N.Y., U.S.A. (F. D. Shaw, Esq., Chairman of Library Committee).
Leechman, C. B., Esq., 10, Earl's Court Gardens, S.W.
Leeds Library, Commercial Street, Leeds.
Lehigh University, S. Bethlehem, Pa., U.S.A.
Leipzig, Library of the University of, c/o Herr O. Harrassowitz, Leipzig, per Messrs. W. Wesley and Son, 28, Essex Street, W.C.
Levy, Judah, Esq., 17, Greville Place, N.W.
Linney, A. G., Esq., Bootham School, 51, Bootham, York.
Liverpool Free Public Library, William Brown Street, Liverpool.
Liverpool Geographical Society (Capt. E. C. D. Phillips, R.N., Secretary), 14, Hargreaves Buildings, Chapel Street, Liverpool.
Loescher, Messrs. J., and Co., Via del Corso 307, Rome, per Messrs. Sampson Low and Co., Ltd., St. Dunstan's House, Fetter Lane, E.C.
Logan, Daniel, Esq., Solicitor-General, Penang, Straits Settlements.
Logan, William, Esq., per Messrs. Grindlay and Co., 54, Parliament St., S.W.
London Institution, Finsbury Circus, E.C.
London Library, 12, St. James's Square, S.W.
Long Island Historical Society, Brooklyn, N.Y., U.S.A.
Lowrey, Joseph, Esq., The Hermitage, Loughton.
Lubetsky, S. A. S. le Prince Droutzkoy, 89, Rue Miromesnil, Paris.
Lucas, Charles Prestwood, Esq., C.B., Colonial Office, S.W.
Lucas, Frederic Wm., Esq., 21, Surrey Street, Victoria Embankment, W.C.
Luyster, S. B., Esq., c/o Messrs. Alex. Denham and Co., 109, Southampton Row, W.C. [U.S.A.
Lydenberg, H. M., Esq., New York Public Library, Fifth Avenue, New York,
Lyttelton-Annesley, Lieut.-Gen. Arthur L., F.S.A., Templemere, Weybridge.

Macmillan and Bowes, Messrs., Cambridge, per Foster's Parcels and Goods Express, Ltd., 82, Fore Street, E.C.
Macqueen, John, Esq., St. Mary's, Harpenden,
Macrae, Charles Colin, Esq., 93, Onslow Gardens, S.W.
Manchester Public Free Libraries, King Street, Manchester (A. G. Hardy, Esq., Librarian).
Manierre, George, Esq., 184, La Salle Street, Chicago, Ill., U.S.A.
Margesson, Lieut. Wentworth H. D., R.N., Finden Place, Worthing.
Markham, Vice-Admiral Albert Hastings, Admiralty House, Sheerness.
Markham, Sir Clements Robert, K.C.B., F.R.S., 21, Eccleston Square, S.W.
Marquand, Henry Gurdon, Esq., 160, Broadway, New York, U.S.A. (*deceased*).
Martelli, Ernest Wynne, Esq., 4, New Square, Lincoln's Inn, W.C.
Massachusetts Historical Society, 30, Tremont Street, Boston, Mass., U.S.A., per Messrs. Kegan Paul and Co., Ltd., Paternoster House, Charing Cross Road, W.C.
Massie, Capt. Roger Henry, R.A.
Mathers, Edward P., Esq., Glenalmond, 34, Foxgrove Road, Beckenham.
Maudslay, Alfred Percival, Esq., 32, Montpelier Square, Knightsbridge, S.W.
McClymont, Jas. R., Esq., c/o W. McClymont, Esq., LL.B., 103, Morningside Drive, Edinburgh, N.B.
McKerrow, R. B., Esq., 22, Friars' Stile Road, Richmond, Surrey.
Mecredy, Jas., Esq., M.A., B.L., F.R.G.S., Wynberg, Stradbrook, Blackrock, Dublin Co.
Melbourne, Public Library of, per Messrs. Melville and Mullen, 12, Ludgate Square, E.C.
Merriman, J. A., Esq., c/o Standard Bank, Durban, Natal.
Meyjes, A. C., Esq., 42, Cannon Street, E.C.
Michell, Lewis W., Esq., Standard Bank of South Africa, Cape Town.
Michigan, University of, per Messrs. H. Sotheran and Co., 140, Strand, W.C.
Milwaukee Public Library, Wisconsin, U.S.A., per Mr. G. E. Stechert, 2, Star Yard, W.C.
Minneapolis Athenæum, U.S.A., per Mr. G. E. Stechert, 2, Star Yard, W.C.
Mitchell Library, 21, Miller Street, Glasgow.
Mitchell, Alfred, Esq., per Messrs. Tiffany, 221, Regent Street, W.
Mitchell, Wm., Esq., c/o Union Bank of Scotland, Holburn Branch, Aberdeen.
Monson, The Rt. Hon. Lord, C.V.O., Marlborough Club, S.W.
Morel, E. D., Esq., 9, Kirby Park, West Kirby, Cheshire.
Moreno, Dr. Francisco J., c/o Argentine Legation, 16, Kensington Palace Gardens, W.
Morgan, Edward Delmar, Esq., 15, Roland Gardens, South Kensington, S.W.
Morris, Henry C. Low, Esq., M.D., Gothic Cottage, Bognor, Sussex.
Morris, Mowbray, Esq., 59A, Brook Street, Grosvenor Square, W.
Morrison, George E., Esq., M.D., F.R.G.S., *Times* Correspondent, Peking.
Moxon, A. E., Esq., c/o Mrs. Gough, The Lodge, Scaldern, near Banbury.
Mukhopadhyay, The Hon. Dr. Asutosh, M.A., LL.D., 77, Russa Road North, Bhowanipore, Calcutta.
Munich Royal Library, per Messrs. Asher and Co., 13, Bedford Street, W.C.
Murray, Hon. Charles Gideon, c/o Bachelors' Club, 7, Hamilton Place, W.

Nathan, H. E., Major Matthew, C.M.G., R.E., 11, Pembridge Square, W.
Naval and Military Club, 94, Piccadilly, W.
Netherlands, Geographical Society of the, per Mr. David Nutt, 57, Long Acre. W.C.
Newberry Library, The, Chicago, Ill., U.S.A., per Messrs. B. F. Stevens and Brown, 4, Trafalgar Square, W.C.
Newcastle-upon-Tyne Literary and Philosophical Society, Westgate Road, Newcastle-on-Tyne.
Newcastle-upon-Tyne Public Library, New Bridge Street, Newcastle-on-Tyne.
New London Public Library, Conn., U.S.A.

New York Athletic Club, Central Park, South, New York (John C. Gulick, Esq., chairman of Library Committee).
New York Public Library, per Messrs. B. F. Stevens and Brown, 4, Trafalgar Square, W.C.
New York State Library, per Mr. G. E. Stechert, 2, Star-yard, Carey St., W.C.
New York Yacht Club (Library Committee), 67, Madison Avenue, New York City, U.S.A.
New Zealand, Agent-General for, per Messrs. Sotheran and Co., 140, Strand, W.C.
Nicholson, Sir Charles, Bart., D.C.L., The Grange, Totteridge, Herts.
Nijhoff, M., per Mr. David Nutt, 57, Long Acre, W.C.
North Adams Public Library, Massachusetts, U.S.A. [Station.
Northbrook, The Right Hon. the Earl of, G.C.S.I., Stratton, Micheldever
Northumberland, His Grace the Duke of, K.G., c/o J. C. Hodgson, Esq., Alnwick Castle.
Nottingham Public Library (J. P. Briscoe, Esq., Librarian).

Omaha Public Library, Nebraska, U.S.A.
Ommanney, Admiral Sir Erasmus, C.B., F.R.S., 29, Connaught Square, Hyde Park, W.
Oriental Club, Hanover Square, W.

Palmella, His Grace the Duke of, Lisbon.
Parish, Frank, Esq., 5, Gloucester Square, Hyde Park, W.
Parlett, Harold George, Esq., British Legation, Tokio, Japan.
Parry, Commdr. J. F. S., R.N., 45, Kensington Mansions, Earl's Court. S.W.
Payne, Edward John, Esq., 2, Stone Buildings, Lincoln's Inn, W.C.
Peabody Institute, Baltimore, U.S.A., per Messrs. E. G. Allen and Murray, 28, Henrietta Street, W.C.
Peckover, Alexander, Esq., Bank House, Wisbech.
Peech, W. H., Esq., St. Stephen's Club, Westminster, S.W.
Peek, Sir Wilfred, Bart., c/o Mr. Grover, Rousdon, Lyme Regis.
Peixoto, Dr. J. Rodrigues, 8, Rue Almte. Comandaré, Rio de Janeiro.
Pequot Library, Southport, Conn., U.S.A.
Percival, H. M., Esq., 14, Park Street, Calcutta.
Petherick, Edward Augustus, Esq., 85, Hopton Road, Streatham, S.W.
Philadelphia Free Library, Pa., U.S.A., per Mr. G. E. Stechert, 2, Star Yard, W.C.
Philadelphia, Library Company of, U.S.A., per Messrs. E, G. Allen and Murray, 28, Henrietta Street, W.C.
Plymouth Proprietary Library, Cornwall Street, Plymouth. (J. Brooking-Rowe, Esq., Hon. Sec.)
Poor, Frank B., Esq., 160, Broadway, New York, U.S.A.
Poor, Henry William, Esq., 91, Clinton Place, New York City, U.S.A., per Messrs. Alex. Denham and Co., 109, Southampton Row, W.C.
Portico Library, 57, Mosley Street, Manchester.
Pretoria Government Library, Pretoria, Transvaal, South Africa, per Mudie's Select Library, Ltd., 30 to 34, New Oxford Street, W.C.
Pringle, Arthur T., Esq., c/o Messrs. G. W. Wheatley and Co., 10, Queen Street, E.C.

Quaritch, Mr. Bernard, 15, Piccadilly, W. (12 *copies*).

Rabbits, William Thomas, Esq., 6, Cadogan Gardens, S.W.
Raffles Library, Singapore, per Messrs. Jones and Evans, Ltd., 77, Queen St., E.C.
Ravenstein, Ernest George, Esq., 2, York Mansions, Battersea Park, S.W.
Reform Club, Pall Mall, S.W.

Reggio, André C., Esq., c/o Messrs. Baring Bros. and Co., 8, Bishopsgate St., Within, E.C.
Rhodes, Josiah, Esq., The Elms, Lytham, Lancashire.
Richards, Admiral Sir F. W., G.C.B., 13, Great Russell Mansions, W.C.
Riggs, E. F., Esq., 1311, Mass. Avenue, Washington, D.C., U.S.A.
Ringwalt, John S., Jun., Esq., Mt. Vernon, Knox County, Ohio, U.S.A.
Rittenhouse Club, 1811, Walnut Street, Philadelphia, U.S.A.
Rockhill, H.E. the Hon. W. W., Department of State, Washington, D.C., U.S.A.
Rodd, Sir Rennell, C.B., K.C.M.G., c/o Foreign Office, Downing Street, S.W.
Röhrscheid and Ebbecke, Herrn, Strauss'sche Buchhandlung, Bonn.
Rose, Charles Day, Esq., Salisbury House, London Wall, E.C.
Rosenheim, Herman, Esq., 62, Fitzjohns Avenue, N.W.
Royal Artillery Institute, Woolwich.
Royal Colonial Institute, Northumberland Avenue, W.C.
Royal Engineers' Institute, Chatham.
Royal Geographical Society, 1, Savile Row, W. (*copies presented*).
Royal Scottish Geographical Society, Edinburgh (Jas. Burgess, Esq., LL.D., C.I.E., Librarian).
Royal Societies Club, St. James's Street, S.W.
Royal United Service Institution, Whitehall, S.W.
Runciman, Walter, Jr., Esq., West Denton Hall, Scotswood-on-Tyne.
Russell, Lady Arthur, 2, Audley Square, W.
Ryley, J. Horton, Esq., } Melrose, Woodwarde Road, East Dulwich S.E.
Ryley, Mrs. Florence, LL.A.,

St. Andrew's University, St. Andrews, N.B.
St. Deiniol's Library, Hawarden (Rev. G. C. Joyce, Librarian).
St. John's, N. B., Canada, Free Public Library (J. R. Ruel, Esq., Chairman).
St. Louis Mercantile Library, per Mr. G. E. Stechert, 2, Star Yard, W.C.
St. Martin's-in-the-Fields Free Public Library, 115, St. Martin's Lane, W.C.
St. Petersburg University Library, per Messrs. Kegan Paul and Co., Ltd., Paternoster House, Charing Cross Road, W.C.
St. Wladimir University, Kief, per Messrs. Sotheran and Co., 140, Strand, W.C.
Sanford, Charles Henry, Esq., 102, Eaton Square, S.W.
San Francisco Public Library, per Mr. G. E. Stechert, 2, Star Yard, W.C.
Satow, H. E. Sir Ernest Mason, K.C.M.G., British Legation, Peking.
Saunders, Howard, Esq., 7, Radnor Place, Gloucester Square, W.
SAXE COBURG AND GOTHA, H.R.H. THE DUCHESS OF, Clarence House, St. James's, S.W.
Schwartz, J. L., Esq., P.O. Box 594, Pittsburg, Pa.
Sclater, Dr. W. L., South African Museum, Cape of Good Hope.
Seawanhaka Corinthian Yacht Club, 7, East 32nd Street, New York, U.S.A.
Seymour, Admiral Sir Edward H., G.C.B., 9, Ovington Square, S.W.
Sheffield Free Public Libraries (Samuel Smith, Esq., Librarian).
Shields, Cuthbert, Esq., Corpus Christi College, Oxford.
Signet Library, Edinburgh (Thos. G. Law, Esq., Librarian).
Silver, Stephen William, Esq., 3, York Gate, Regent's Park, N.W.
Sinclair, Mrs. W. Frederic, 102, Cheyne Walk, Chelsea.
Smith, Frederick A., Esq., Thorncliff, Shoot-up-Hill, Kilburn, N.W.
Smithers, F.O., Esq., F.R.G.S., Dashwood House, 9, New Broad Street, E.C.
Sneddon, George T., Esq., 8, Merry Street, Motherwell.
Società Geografica Italiana, Rome.
Société de Géographie, Paris, per Mr. L. Arnould, Royal Mint Refinery, Royal Mint Street, E.C.
Sotheran and Co., Messrs., 140, Strand, W.C.
Soulsby, Basil Harrington, Esq., Map Room, British Museum, W.C.
South African Public Library, per Messrs. H. S. King and Co., 65, Cornhill, E.C.

Southam, Herbert R. H., Esq., F.S.A., Innellan, Sutton Road, Shrewsbury.
Springfield City Library Association, Mass., U.S.A.
Stairs, James W., Esq., c/o Messrs. Stairs, Son and Morrow, Halifax, Nova Scotia.
Stanley, Right Hon. Lord, of Alderley, 15, Grosvenor-gardens, S.W.
Stephens, Henry C., Esq., M.P., Cholderton, Salisbury.
Stevens, J. Tyler, Esq., Park Street, Lowell, Mass., U.S.A.
Stevens, Son, and Stiles, Messrs., 39, Great Russell Street, W.C.
Stockholm, Royal Library of, per Messrs. Sampson Low, and Co., Ltd., St. Dunstan's House, Fetter Lane, E.C.
Stockton Public Library, per Messrs. Sotheran and Co., 140, Strand, W.C.
Strachey, Lady, 69, Lancaster-gate, Hyde Park, W.
Stringer, G. A., Esq,, 248, Georgia Street, Buffalo, N.Y., U.S.A.
Stubbs, Captain Edward, R.N., 13, Greenfield Road, Stoneycroft, Liverpool.
Sydney Free Library, New South Wales, per Mr. Young J. Pentland, 38, West Smithfield, E.C.
Sykes, Major P. Molesworth, H.M.'s Consul at Kerman, Persia, *viâ* Teheran.

Tangye, Richard Trevithick G., Esq., Coombe Ridge, Kingston-on-Thames.
Tate, G. P., Esq., c/o Messrs. W. Watson and Co., Karachi, India.
Taylor, Captain William Robert, 1, Daysbrook Road, Streatham Hill, S.W.
Temple, Lieut.-Col. Richard Carnac, C.I.E., per Messrs. Kegan Paul and Co., Ltd., Paternoster House, Charing Cross Road, W.C.
Thomson, Basil, Esq., Governor's House, H.M.'s Prison, Princetown, S.Devon.
Tighe, Walter Stuart, Coolmoney, Stratford-on-Slaney, Co. Wicklow.
Toronto Public Library. } per Messrs. C. D. Cazenove and Son, 26, Henrietta
Toronto University. } Street, W.C.
Travellers' Club, 106, Pall Mall, S.W.
Trinder, Arnold, Esq., The Hollies, Rydens Road, Walton-on-Thames.
Trinder, Henry Wm., Esq., Northbrook House, Bishops Waltham, Hants.
Trinder, Oliver Jones, Esq., Mount Vernon, Caterham, Surrey.
Trinity College, Cambridge, c/o Messrs. Deighton, Bell and Co., per Sutton.
Trinity House, The Hon. Corporation of, Tower Hill, E.C.
Troop, W. H., Esq., c/o Messrs. Black Bros. and Co., Halifax, Nova Scotia.
Trotter, Coutts, Esq., Athenæum Club. Pall Mall, S.W.
Turnbull, Alex. H., Esq., 7, St. Helen's Place, Bishopsgate Street, E.C.
Tweedy, Arthur H., Esq., Widmore Lodge, Bickley Road, Bromley, Kent.

Union League Club, Broad-street, Philadelphia, Pa., U.S.A.
Union Society, Oxford.
United States Congress, Library of, Washington, D.C., U.S.A., per Messrs. E. G. Allen and Murray, 28, Henrietta Street, W.C.
United States National Museum (Library of), Washington, D.C., U.S.A. per Messrs. W. Wesley and Son, 28, Essex Street, W.C.
United States Naval Academy Library, Washington, D.C., U.S.A., per Messrs. B. F. Stevens and Brown. 4, Trafalgar Square, W.C.
University of London, per Messrs. Sotheran and Co., 37, Piccadilly, W.
Upsala University Library, per C. J. Lundstrom, Upsala, Sweden.

Van Raalte, Charles, Esq., Brownsea Island, Poole, Dorset.
Vernon, Roland Venables, Esq., Colonial Office, S.W.
Vienna Imperial Library, per Messrs. Asher and Co., 13, Bedford Street, W.C.
Vignaud, Henry, Esq., Ambassade des États Unis, 18, Avenue Kleber, Paris.

Warren, William R., Esq., 81, Fulton-street, New York City, U.S.A.
Washington, Department of State, D.C., U.S.A., per Messrs. B. F. Stevens and Brown, 4, Trafalgar Square, W.C.

Washington, Library of Navy Department, U.S.A., per Messrs. B. F. Stevens and Brown, 4, Trafalgar Square, W.C.
Watkinson Library, Hartford, Connecticut, U.S.A.
Watson, Commander William, R.N.R., Ravella, Crosby, near Liverpool.
Webster, Sir Augustus F. W. E., Bart., Guards' Club, 70, Pall Mall, S.W.
Weld, Rev. George F., Hingham, Mass., U.S.A.
Westaway, Staff Engineer A.E.L., 12, Portland Villas, Plymouth.
Westminster School (Rev. G. H. Nall, M.A., Librarian) Dean's Yard, S.W.
Wharton, Rear-Admiral Sir William James Lloyd, K.C.B., Florys, Princes Road, Wimbledon Park, S.W.
White, Dr. H., c/o W. T. White, Esq., New Hall, Lydd.
Whiteway, Richard Stephen, Esq., Brownscombe, Shottermill, Surrey.
Wildy, Augustus George, Esq., 14, Buckingham Street, W.C.
Williams, O. W., Esq., Fort Stockton, Texas, U.S.A.
Wilmanns, F. M., Esq., 89, Oneida Street, Milwaukee, Wisc., U.S.A.
Wilson, Edward Shimells, Esq., Melton Grange, Brough, R.S.O., Yorkshire.
Wisconsin State Historical Society, per Messrs. Sotheran and Co., 140, Strand, W.C.
Woodford, Charles M., Esq., Tulagi, Solomon Islands.
Worcester, Massachusetts, Free Library, per Messrs. Kegan Paul, and Co., Ltd., Paternoster House, Charing Cross Road, W.C.
Wright, John, Esq., 2, Challoner Terrace West, South Shields.
Wyndham, The Right Hon. George, M.P., 35, Park Lane, W.

Yale College, New Haven, Conn., U.S.A., per Messrs. E. G. Allen and Murray, 28, Henrietta Street, W.C.
Young, Alfales, Esq., Salt Lake City, Utah, U.S.A.
Young, Sir Allen, C.B., 18, Grafton Street, Bond Street, W.
Young & Sons, Messrs. Henry, 12, South Castle Street, Liverpool.

Zürich, Bibliothèque de la Ville, care of Messrs. Orell, Turli and Co., Zürich, per Mr. David Nutt, 57, Long Acre, W.C.